WITHDRAWN

D1159733

¡Grito!

Reies Tijerina and the New Mexico
Land Grant War of 1967

CALVIN T. RYAN LIBRARY
KEARNEY STATE COLLEGE
KEARNEY, NEBRASKA

¡Grito!

Reies Tijerina and the New Mexico Land Grant War of 1967

by Richard Gardner

with photographs by
Richard Jamison and others

CALVIN T. RYAN LIBRARY
KEARNEY STATE COLLEGE
KEARNEY, NEBRASKA

HARPER COLOPHON BOOKS
Harper & Row, Publishers
New York, Evanston, San Francisco, London

This book was originally published by The Bobbs-Merrill Company, Inc. and is here reprinted by arrangement.

CALVIN T. RYAN LIBRARY
KEARNEY STATE COLLEGE

GRITO! *Reies Tijerina and the New Mexico Land Grant War of 1967.* Copyright © 1970 by Richard Gardner. All rights reserved. Printed in the United States of America. No part of this book may be used or reproduced in any manner without written permission except in the case of brief quotations embodied in critical articles and reviews. For information address Harper & Row, Publishers, Inc., 49 East 33rd Street, New York, N.Y. 10016. Published simultaneously in Canada by Fitzhenry & Whiteside Limited, Toronto.

First HARPER COLOPHON edition published 1971

STANDARD BOOK NUMBER: 06-090247-7

To Candido and Facundo, Fernanda and Juan, Pula and Lupe, Pacomio and Ute, H. H. and Arthur, and all the other people of honor and heart, from Ranchos to Antón Chico.

Acknowledgments

The author is indebted to the work and grateful for the help and advice of many scholars, public officials, social workers and private individuals; in particular: Facundo Valdez, Don Devereux, Steve Bunker, Peter Nabokov, and Frances Swadesh, Ph.D.

Contents

PHOTO SECTION APPEARS FOLLOWING PAGE   150

En país de los ciegos,
El Tuerto es rey.

In the land of the blind,
One Eye is king.

PROVERB POPULAR IN
NEW MEXICO

The Raid 1

IN mid-afternoon on June 5, 1967, 20 men in four cars and a pickup truck rolled down the roads of an all but empty land and into a dying town called Yellow Earth, outrage in their hearts and loaded guns in their hands. Nobody saw them coming.

Sheriff Benny Naranjo was in his first floor office at the front corner of the Río Arriba County courthouse building with jailer Eulogio Salazar. Naranjo happened to glance out the window and saw four men standing at the open trunk of a car in the dusty little plaza across Tierra Amarilla's main street, but somehow both he and Salazar failed to notice the three other cars and red pickup also wheeling into position before the courthouse.

In the upstairs courtroom, District Judge James M. Scarborough had just removed his robes after postponing the arraignment of eight men on charges of unlawful assembly and injury to animals, to wit: a cow, and releasing them on bond. The charged men had left the building half an hour before, and the judge was discussing the day's work with Justice of the Peace Tomás Córdova, Undersheriff Dan Rivera and Mike Rice, the court reporter. It had been a tense and uncertain Monday following a difficult weekend, and they were all grateful that it was over and not a little proud that peace had been so handily restored to northern New Mexico.

Down in the basement, County Assessor Estanislado Vigil was working at the files, while nearby Salvador Salazar and Cebelio Archuleta, both in jail for misdemeanors involving liquor, idled in their cells.

In the county commission room at the rear of the first floor, County Clerk Cipriano Padilla happened to be standing at the head of the table, addressing commissioners Abe Gallegos, Nick Salazar and Abelardo Martínez. Also present were secretary Mary García, County Manager Joe Sánchez and Deputy Sheriff Pete Jaramillo.

Most of the county's officials and lesser employes were in the building, with one notable exception. The man responsible for the charges upon which Judge Scarborough had based the day's arraignments, District Attorney Alfonso Sánchez, had not appeared in court that morning. In fact, he had been strangely absent all day.

1

Out in the front hallway of the building, State Patrolman Nick Sais stood examining the bulletin board, his back to the short flight of stairs leading up from the main entrance. Nearby, file clerk Dolores Romero made a selection from the candy machine. A few yards down at the end of the hall, E. R. Gleasner waited to use the phone. Inside the booth a reporter, Larry Calloway, was dictating his story on that morning's court proceedings to the United Press International offices in Albuquerque. Across the hall, typist Gloria Sifuentes stood behind the counter in the small anteroom to the sheriff's office. Inside the office, Benny Naranjo glanced out his window and saw the four men still at the rear of their car. But now they were removing rifles from its trunk.

Attorney Carlos Sedillo, who had represented one of the arraigned men in Judge Scarborough's court that morning, was about to climb into his car when he noticed several armed men moving past him and into the courthouse. He dropped to the ground.

The heavy plate-glass panels in the front doors rattled, and Officer Sais turned to see four men coming up the stairs. As he looked back at the bulletin board he felt the four men gather close around him. One of them demanded that Sais hand over his pistol.

"If he had known what was happening, he would have taken a couple with him," cattle inspector Julián Archuleta was later to say of Sais. "We've worked on rustling cases together, and he's tough."

Sais moved his right hand toward his holster. A bullet shattered his left arm and entered his chest. He fell to the floor.

"And that," E. R. Gleasner said later, "was when the war began."

Gleasner hit the floor and scrambled for cover behind the radiator. Ducking down inside the telephone booth, reporter Calloway did the same, hanging onto the receiver and his connection with Albuquerque.

In the third-floor courtroom, Judge Scarborough and Court Reporter Mike Rice had just turned to see blind attorney Monroe Fox entering with his wife and seeing-eye dog. At the sound of the first shot, and the three others which followed it in quick succession, the judge led the way hastily into his chambers at the rear of the courtroom. As the blind man was closing the door behind them, Judge Scarborough glimpsed Undersheriff Dan Rivera approaching hurriedly up the aisle. The judge called out through the locked door, asking the undersheriff if he wanted to come in. There was no reply.

Justice of the Peace Córdova had also remained behind in the courtroom. Now, in a seizure of paternal panic, he decided to rush to the aid of his wife and kids in town, and flung himself out the courtroom door and straight down the stairs.

In the first floor hallway, a bullet ricocheted off the radiator above E. R. Gleasner's head. Then someone came up behind him and poked him in the back with a rifle. "Don't look," said the gunman, bringing the rifle butt down on his head.

A few yards away, the fallen Sais had already been relieved of his bullets and handcuffs. He had also seen what seemed to be a white-haired old man pick up his pistol and run off with it. Now, through a haze of pain, he was sure he saw a beautiful girl in very tight pink trousers striding past.

"They're shooting hell out of the place, but I don't know why," Calloway told UPI headquarters in Albuquerque. From his concealment in the telephone booth, he raised his head briefly and saw a man wearing a green shirt and trousers in possession of the front stairs, brandishing a pistol and shouting in Spanish, "*¡Ya no están tan bravos!*"

Gunfire from outside the building shattered the windows over the heads of Sheriff Benny Naranjo and jailer Eulogio Salazar. The sheriff tore off his shoulder patch, removed his badge and threw it into a desk drawer.

In the county commission room, Clerk Cipriano Padilla thought it was firecrackers at first, then, through the partly open door, he saw Nick Sais fall. He started forward, accompanied by Deputy Sheriff Pete Jaramillo. The two men reached the door and had time to see Sais on his back and bleeding profusely, before they were forced back into the room, first by a young man aiming a .45-caliber pistol, followed by another young man, this one with an automatic rifle and a dagger and several sticks of dynamite in his belt. The occupants of the room were instructed to lie on the floor and warned not to leave or they would be shot. "You are all good people in here and we don't want any of you to get hurt," said the young man with the dynamite in his belt.

There were at least a dozen hostiles in the building by now. Through a crack in the phone booth, Calloway could see legs running in all directions. Lifting his head to risk another quick look, he saw a dark-haired man in clean khaki trousers, khaki shirt and visored forage cap striding directly toward him, an automatic rifle strapped to his shoulder. The man turned and entered the anteroom to the sheriff's office.

At the sound of the first shots, Gloria Sifuentes had taken one look down the hall and fled across to the assessor's office to hide with a fellow typist, Dolores Romero. Jailer Salazar had also stepped out for a look and swiftly retreated back into the sheriff's office. Sheriff Benny Naranjo's gun was in his hand when someone strode in, struck the gun from his hand, knocked him to the floor and pointed a rifle at Eulogio Salazar, who was trying to raise the window.

"Don't go out because I will shoot you. I will kill you," the man said.

Jailer Salazar stepped away from the window as if to obey. The moment the rifle barrel began to swing away from him, Salazar threw himself headlong at the window. A bullet smashed through the left side of his face as he toppled out.

Locked in his chambers with the court reporter and the blind lawyer, the lawyer's wife and the seeing-eye dog, Judge Scarborough heard feet race up the stairs, kick the courtroom door open and enter. But the footsteps turned aside before reaching the door to the chambers and crossed to the door of the small jury room.

Discovered in the jury room, Undersheriff Dan Rivera backed away from the unlocked door as the lock was shot to pieces. To Judge Scarborough and the others, it sounded like a machine gun. Three men pushed in, and one hit Rivera on the head with a gun.

"What did you hit me for, I didn't do anything to you," protested Rivera, who had been a law officer in Río Arriba for 18 years. For reply, he was hit on the arm, the nose and across the face. Then he was ordered to go down to the basement and unlock the cells.

In the basement, County Assessor Estanislado Vigil had heard the shots and started up the stairs, to be met at the top by a young man with a gun. "It was pointed toward me," Vigil later testified, "or I should say pointed in the direction where I was."

The young man ordered him to leave the hall and go to his office. "I told him I didn't know what his motive was, but I only worked at the courthouse. He said 'I know that. I want you to get out of there because I don't want you to get hurt.' "

Spurred on by the blood pouring down his cheek, Eulogio Salazar had scrambled to his feet below the sheriff's office window and started away, ignoring shouted orders to halt. A few yards from the building he was brought up short by a second bullet passing through his shoulder and knocking his hat off. He slumped against the fender of a car, and two armed men came up to guard him. Looking around, he noticed that not only was the courthouse in the hands of the hostiles, but apparently the entire town as well.

There seemed to be armed men everywhere. A number of people were watching them from vantage points up and down the street. Two State Police patrol cars and a Forest Service pickup stood driverless in front of the courthouse. Around the corner an abandoned patrol car stood blocking the road, the driver's door hanging open.

Three patrol cars, returning from a highway accident, had started toward the courthouse at the sound of the first shots, only to have five men step out and open fire on them. Patrolman Juan Santisteven had taken two bullets through his windshield before he could slam into reverse, then abandon his car, running toward the shelter of some adobe huts behind the courthouse, then over a fence, across the open fields and away.

Some of the onlookers seemed in a holiday mood. The bolder children edged forward, defying the protests of their mothers. An elderly woman hobbled across the street and into the post office-grocery store. Justice of the Peace Córdova had slowly made his way out into the street, only to find further progress blocked by a young man with a gun.

"Let him alone, I know him," said another man, and Córdova pushed through a small crowd of interested observers and hurried home to his family.

Still on the ground beside his car, attorney Carlos Sedillo had seen Eulogio Salazar get hit the second time and stagger out of view. Now he noticed a lull in the firing inside the building.

Sheriff Benny Naranjo lay face down on the floor of the front hall, his body across the anteroom doorway, his hands to his eyes. He had been clubbed to the floor of his office with a rifle butt, then ordered out into the hall. Someone thumped the toe of a boot into his ribs and asked him where his badge was. Had he perhaps eaten it? the assailant suggested. The sheriff only pressed his hands more tightly to his face.

"Now they're not so brave," the man in the green shirt said again in Spanish. *"Ya no están tan bravos."*

In the nearby commission room, Deputy Sheriff Pete Jaramillo had made one halfhearted move for his gun, but it had been quickly kicked out of reach. Now he was prodded to his feet and herded with the others out into the hall. A dark-haired man in khaki trousers, khaki shirt and forage cap jabbed him in the ribs with what looked like a Thompson submachine gun.

"Where is Alfonso Sánchez?" the man in khaki demanded. "Tell me, or I will kill you."

Jaramillo replied that the district attorney had not been there all day. He was directed to lie on his face behind a nearby water cooler. Others were asked the same question and gave the same reply. Moments later the deputy was prodded to his feet and herded with the others back into the commission room. When they were lying face down on the floor again, they were addressed by a white-haired old man with a pistol.

"You are a bunch of *vendidos*," the old man told them. "You are sellouts who have sold yourselves down the river for a dollar."

Up on the second floor, Judge Scarborough and Court Reporter Rice waited for the footsteps of Dan Rivera and his captors to fade away, then crept to an adjoining room where there was a telephone. They were not able to get through to the State Police, but they did get the governor's office in Santa Fe. As Rice was telling the governor's administrative assistant, Larry Prentice, that the Río Arriba County courthouse was under armed attack, another flurry of gunfire sounded outside the building. Then there was a loud crash from the hallway below and a jarring disturbance on the line.

Reporter Calloway had been discovered hiding in the first floor phone booth. The young man with the dynamite sticks in his belt ripped the phone off the wall, while Calloway noted that he looked something like Elvis Presley. Someone asked Calloway where Alfonso Sánchez was. He replied that the district attorney was probably in Santa Fe. As he was being marched into the commission room, he looked down and saw that Nick Sais' eyes were following him.

The wounded patrolman lay on his back, bleeding inside and out. Someone put the muzzle of an automatic rifle to the patrolman's head and said, "Let me kill this unfortunate."

"Don't," Sais said, "I've already had it."

"Leave him alone," said the young man, who had shot Sais a quarter of an hour before. An ambulance was coming, Sais was told, to take him to the hospital.

Deputy Sheriff Dan Rivera came down the stairs under guard, bleeding from the head and a broken nose. As Rivera passed Sais, the patrolman moaned. Rivera bent to help him up, but Sais protested that he was in too much pain. Continuing on his way, Rivera stepped over Sheriff Naranjo, took the jail keys from their accustomed place, stepped back over the sheriff and started for the basement.

When Dan Rivera opened the cell doors, prisoners Salazar and Archuleta stepped out. The freed men seemed confused by their sudden release, but wasted no time in disappearing up the stairs. They were followed more slowly by the bleeding Rivera who stepped over Sheriff Naranjo, replaced the jail keys in their accustomed place, and stepped back over the sheriff. He was ordered into the county commission room.

The dynamite-bearing young man entered the assessor's office. According to Vigil, he "took the liberty of going through all the cabinets and shelves," but did not take anything.

Thinking that perhaps the shooting was over, attorney Carlos Sedillo climbed behind the wheel of his car, only to see a man aiming what looked like a submachine gun through his windshield. Tearing out in reverse, he heard several shots behind him, and a bullet ricocheted off his bumper as he sped away.

The dynamite carrier shouted, "There's Alfonso Sánchez, I'm going to kill the son of a bitch," and aimed his rifle at County Commissioner Alvarado Martínez.

"That's not him," said the other young man, who had shot Nick Sais.

Out in front of the building, Eulogio Salazar's guards abandoned him. Bleeding from face and shoulder, he made his way to the house of a sister-in-law behind the courthouse, where bits of jawbone and broken denture were picked from his face before he was put in a pickup and rushed south to Española.

In the county commissioner's room, the young man who looked like Elvis Presley took a dynamite stick from his belt, fitted a fuse to it and held it near a burning cigarette.

"Cut that out," said the white-haired old man.

The ambulance arrived. The young man who had shot Nick Sais helped lift the wounded patrolman onto a stretcher. Ignoring a warning not to move, County Commissioner Nick Salazar left the commission room and helped carry the stretcher outside to the ambulance. A man demanded the ambulance keys from driver Angie Zamora, but she rolled up the window and drove forward, pushing through the crowd of armed men and bystanders, then sped south toward Española.

Someone inside the building shouted from the front hallway, "Take two prisoners."

In the commission room, the young man with the dynamite sticks tied Deputy Pete Jaramillo's hands behind his back with cord from a coffee percolator and prepared to do the same with Undersheriff Rivera.

"I'm wounded and I'm bleeding pretty bad," Rivera said. "Why don't you let me go to a doctor?"

Rivera was allowed to leave.

"Take that gringo over there," someone suggested. The young man tied reporter Calloway with electric cord and led the two hostages from the room.

Only the old man remained. There were scattered shots from outside. Finally the old man stood at the door and told those in the room to stay where they were, that a lot of people were around the courthouse and they would get shot if they tried to leave.

"You are a bunch of *vendidos*," the old man said again, then closed the door behind him.

Nobody moved to leave. There were scattered shots outside, then a flurry of gunfire, then a long silence.

Doyle Akers of the Santa Fe *New Mexican* was driving his pickup north toward Tierra Amarilla and recognized the patrol car of Deputy Sheriff Pete Jaramillo moving south. He waved, then realized that Jaramillo was not driving. There was a young man wearing a red beret at the wheel, and Jaramillo sat beside him. In the back seat, Larry Calloway of UPI sat beside a white-haired old man holding a rifle.

Akers turned off the highway and drove down into the town. The main street was deserted. Two State Patrol cars stood abandoned in front of the courthouse, riddled with bullet holes. Most of the first-floor windows of the courthouse had been broken or shot out. There were bullet holes in the front doors and wet blood on the stairs. The front hall was empty. There was blood on the floor under the bulletin board and near the telephone booth. Akers glanced into the sheriff's office, saw more blood and the sheriff's radio transmitter in shambles. Through the shattered window he could see the State Patrol cars pulling up out front and armed officers stepping cautiously from them. He started toward the closed door of the commission room.

The door opened and Sheriff Benny Naranjo stuck his head out. "Are they gone?" he asked.

Canjilón 2

I had come to northern New Mexico to revisit the land of my childhood and to finish a book. During the drive out from the tourist town of Taos to the little village of Ranchos, the real estate agent warned that I would be surrounded by those he referred to delicately as "our natives."

The house I rented had an earth roof and was made of raw, unplastered adobe. Touted by the owner as "very authentic," it had a sign out front that read *Casa Feliz*. This Happy House was rented furnished; but before I moved in, the owner took the precaution of removing a pewter gravy boat which she said her grandfather had brought around the Horn from New England.

The house directly across the dirt road was made of hard plastered adobe and had a television aerial on its tin roof. The language spoken in its cluttered front yard, however, was unassailably "authentic." One afternoon the neighbors' piglets took an interest in my garbage, providing an opportunity for introductions and the wary beginnings of a dialogue that remained disappointingly distant and strained. I was accustomed to talking to Spaniards in Spain, where, despite the tourist boom, the natives still outnumber the invaders.

I noticed that the supermarket in Taos featured five-gallon cans of lard and chicken heads wrapped in cellophane as well as creamery butter and tinned caviar. I noticed that most of my neighbors shopped at the Ranchos trading post, despite the fact that milk was three cents more there for a half gallon, with other items marked up accordingly. I noticed the file of dog-eared credit sheets under the trading post cash register and watched "our natives" laboriously writing their names and sometimes marking their "X's" below lists of daily purchases. Finally I stood in line in the Taos bank with the Spanish-American owner of the trading post, and saw him deposit a stack of welfare checks four inches thick.

For a time I bought my gas at a Shamrock station out on the highway. I learned that the Shamrock chain is Texas-owned and operated. The blue-eyed owner drove a new pickup equipped with a two-way radio, a shotgun and two rifles racked behind the seat and a holstered .45 strapped under the dashboard. I asked one of his employees if the boss was a law officer and was told, no. When I mentioned the heavy armament, I saw a curious mingling of laconic despair and excited envy in the black eyes. "He don' mess around. Somebody get in his way, bang."

I watched the Shamrock owner's wife riding her fat quarter horse in Frontier twill, and I watched her blue-eyed sons play at cowboy before going off to college in a red convertible.

I listened to dark-eyed Cándido, *vaquero sin vacas* (cowboy without cows), reminisce wistfully about his good times in the Army in Japan and Korea, where he had been fed well, had been treated as an equal and had lost an eye. I dutifully admired his aging pony, Dick, who wore a ragged army blanket between swayback and rotting saddle.

I stood with Abe Lujan of Taos Pueblo, looking through the fence at a herd of seven buffalo, and when I asked him why the pueblo kept the animals at such expense, he only hitched his blue-and-white-striped Sears blanket up in front of his face and went on looking, seeing a herd of thousands, dreaming of the day when good times would return and I and my kind, and the Spanish-speakers too, would all go away.

"*¿Hay cambios en el viento?*" I asked the old man scraping a sheepskin beside the Ranchos irrigation ditch. "Are there changes in the wind?"

"*Hay vueltas,*" he replied. "There are returnings."

I heard on the radio that a band of men belonging to a clandestine organization called the *Alianza* and led by someone called *El Rey Tigre* (King Tiger) had raided a courthouse in a town called Yellow Earth just 60 miles to the west. I heard trucks coming and going on the road through the nights that followed and the television going strong in the house across the way every night until after midnight.

A reporter acquaintance dropped by on assignment, and we drove down to Española and then the long way back up to Tierra Amarilla. I noted the comfortable familiarity with which my friend questioned the state patrolman in front of the courthouse. I saw the patrolman's eyes behind their sunglasses watching the town's main street as he said that, yes, he would say that 80 percent of the people here were sympathetic to the *Alianza*, maybe even more. As we left the town, I asked my friend if he was also going to talk to the people, and noted the absent irritation with which he replied, "No point. I don't speak their language."

When he phoned me from Santa Fe the next day, I asked him if he had talked to the *Alianza* leader, Reies Tijerina—King Tiger.

"The poor jerkoff thinks he's Moses come again," he said, and left the state the next day.

I put the book I was working on aside. Four questions had forced themselves on me: What had happened in northern New Mexico? Why? Who was Reies Tijerina? What did it all portend?

One thing was certain, nothing similar had happened to the Wild West in a long time. For nearly two hours, the courthouse and county seat of Río Arriba County, New Mexico, had been in the unchallenged possession of some 20 of its citizens, to the open delight or with the tacit approval of many others.

Few of the raiders spoke English well or were expert in Spanish. Most spoke a mixed jargon, while several read and wrote English and Spanish only poorly; one could write little more than his name. Some were cattle drovers and sheep herders; most had been or were migratory field workers, and most were men of the land. All were of a mixture of race and culture given to stubborn pride and quick passion. On that day their passion had been for expression and not articulation—action, not discussion. Ninety minutes of shouting and shooting, of waving dynamite sticks and joyously prodding the bureaucratic posture had helped them to reaffirm themselves and thereby renew an essential faith. They had drawn themselves up straight, thrown back their heads and given vent to their *grito*.

Grito means "shout," "outcry." But more than that, it can be a proclamation of indignation and pain which has reached the point of intolerability. It is a declaration of collective as well as individual resentment, expressed in a spirit of communal outrage and manly defiance. It springs from a cultural state of mind which sees the world as consisting of *los de arriba* and *los de abajo:* the rich and powerful and the poor and powerless, with nobody in between. It is the formalized plaint of those accustomed to being ground under, periodically inspired to revolt and momentarily given one throat, one voice, one word. *¡Tierra o muerte!*— Land or death! shouted the ragged followers of Pancho Villa 50 years before as they razed the Texas border, then fled deep into Chihuahua with Black Jack Pershing in pursuit.

¡Justicia y la tierra!—Justice and the land! was the *grito* of the courthouse raiders, as they fled south toward the little mountain town of Canjilón, where their women and children waited. And, incredibly, a general named John Pershing Jolly was among the legions soon to be in hot pursuit.

"It was a regular revolution," said Julián Archuleta, district cattle and brand inspector. "I was on my way up to Chama to take care of rustling, when I heard all the traffic over the radio. As I approached Tierra Amarilla, all the shooting was taking place. In the meantime, the people were getting ready to go to Canjilón. There were three or four vehicles loaded with people. I was in radio contact with the State Police and they told me to keep the cars under surveillance.

"I turned around and started following them. I met up with (Detective Lieutenant) Freddy Martínez and (Officer) Robert Romero, and we followed the cars to Canjilón. All of them went to the Tobías Leyba residence. There were about 50 people in there . . ."

Seventeen miles south of Tierra Amarilla on U.S. 84, State Police patrol cars began to converge on the Canjilón junction. There were already several cars in the village, three miles away through the dense pines of Carson National Forest. But a voice had broken into radio conversations earlier to say, "I don't want to see any cops; we've got the hostages," and State Police Chief Joe Black had ordered his men to move with caution.

The safety of the hostages was not the only consideration. The police knew, as did the state's politicians, most of its residents and certainly all of its 300,000 Spanish-speaking citizens, that the authorities had to deal not with some small gang of criminals, but with a scattered and elusive but very real community of people.

What nobody did know was exactly how many there were and how many might now be inspired to join the raiders.

Eighty miles to the south at the state capitol in Santa Fe, Acting Governor E. Lee Francis had managed to make telephone contact with Governor David Cargo, who was in Michigan talking politics with fellow Republican George Romney. Cargo urged caution, but directed Francis to activate the National Guard in preparation for his return. To startled newsmen, wondering if New Mexico had a runaway insurrection on its hands, he said, "I assume we can get the situation in hand. I hope we can. It's a very explosive thing; very difficult to cope with." And then he headed for home in a jet plane provided by Governor Romney.

Back in New Mexico, Acting Governor Francis went on the radio and in English and Spanish exhorted the raiders and any who might have joined them to lay down their arms and avoid further bloodshed; patrolman Nick Sais, undergoing emergency treatment in an Española clinic, told a reporter, "I did not run from no son-of-a-bitch, he just walked up and shot me when I went to give him my gun," adding, "Don't worry, I'll get him," as he was loaded back into an ambulance and rushed farther south to the hospital; word came through to the Canjilón junction that Jaramillo and Calloway had gotten away from their captors and were safe.

The patrol cars moved down the narrow highway through the trees, their red and yellow license plates bearing the Hopi symbol for the sun and the legend, Land of Enchantment.

The village lay out along a mountain ridge in the midst of the forest— a tenuous conglomeration of crumbling adobe buildings, pitched tin roofs and soft-drink signs. There were two small churches, a *Penitente* chapel, a post office, a school, two gas stations and two small general stores, one of them the only building in town with running water.

A mile back down the road was the U.S. Forest Service ranger station, a small complex of buildings set back among the trees. Here Chief Black had hastily set up his command post, and here the first reporters arrived to use the telephone.

Black's 20 additional men moved up the road and cautiously entered the village, to encounter only the usual barking dogs, staring children and obliquely watchful elders. Turning at the center of town into a deeply rutted road, they found a dozen officers already crouched behind their cars, guns pointed across the fields toward the small *rancho* belonging to Tobías Leyba, 800 yards further up the road, where the main body of the rebels was said to be waiting.

In Santa Fe, General John Pershing Jolly of the National Guard had reacted to the governor's mobilization order with unstinting zeal. Governor Cargo, landing at Albuquerque and driven the 60 miles to the state capital at top speed, arrived to find that his staff had transferred operations to the National Guard armory. He angrily directed General Jolly and Acting Governor Lee Francis to report to him at the capital building. But General Jolly and his troops were already in the field and rolling north toward Río Arriba—some 360 men with full field equipment, including two tanks.

The sky was clouding over above the clustered adobe buildings of Canjilón, the meadows, scattered farms and surrounding timbered slopes. The State Police helicopter fluttered low over the crowd of armed officers and official vehicles gathered at the head of the muddy road, then slid away to make its second pass over the Leyba *rancho*.

The raiders had fled Tierra Amarilla around 5 P.M. It was now seven and getting darker every minute. State Police Chief Black feared the hostiles might escape to the hills under cover of darkness, if they had not done so already. The helicopter reported that there was no sign of life near the Leyba residence, but that there was movement in a grove of oak and juniper across a meadow beyond the house. Black sent several men out with orders to work their way up behind the little ranch.

"There, they're sending kids out now," someone said. Small figures darted through the dusk across the fields. Black decided that he could wait no longer for the National Guard. His force now numbered more than 50 men, including sheriff's deputies, Jicarilla Apache police, Forest Rangers and members of the New Mexico Mounted Patrol, a volunteer organization patterning itself on the Texas Rangers. He led them straight down the road toward the house with its white-framed, blankly staring windows.

Seventeen miles to the south, General Jolly had paused with his small army opposite Ghost Ranch, in the northern corner of the lower Chama River valley. The general had information that the ranch, a Presbyterian establishment, was a primary target in a secret plan to take over northern New Mexico and create a new Cuba in the Southwest.

Leaving a detachment to guard the ranch, Jolly sent jeeps ahead to scout the narrow confines of Arroyo Seco. Then he led his main column northward on the last climb to the high country of Río Arriba, going where his predecessor of 120 years before, General Stephen W. Kearny, had either not deigned or not dared to venture.

Tourists, camped near the highway and passing in their cars, gaped at the impressive convoy. One man in a station wagon wanted to know if the country had gone to war.

Officers with rifles sprinted the last few yards to Tobías Leyba's house, flattened themselves beside doors and windows, then burst in and found its four rooms empty. The main body of Black's men crossed the cow pasture and skirted the pond below, cautiously approaching the grove of trees beyond. Reporter Peter Nabokov of the Santa Fe *New Mexican* was in advance and was one of the first to see the enemy through the trees— 39 of them, mostly old people, women and children, gathered about some pickup trucks, silent in the gathering twilight mist, munching picnic lunches and waiting.

"They seemed strangely calm and patient. A miniature community. Just people."

The two scouts burst through the trees from below, rifles leveled. "All right, now, hands on top of your heads, let's go."

Armed men closed in from all sides. Wearily, but without apparent fear, women gathered up babies, men lifted sleepy children from truck seats, old people gathered up their bundles, and they all filed out of the trees and up toward the house, where they were lined up against the wall and searched one by one. There were flinty-eyed old men who glared straight ahead in unflinching silence. There was a beautiful dark-haired girl in tight pink slacks who carried herself like some pagan queen. There was a tiny old lady with large and luminous eyes who scolded steadily. There were young girls in oversized cowboy hats who snickered at the officers clumsily patting them. There were teen-age boys who disdainfully ignored their searchers, speaking to one another in a brash slang of mixed Spanish and English. There was a man in a Hudson's Bay blanket coat who cursed softly as alien hands probed his trousers, and spat fulsomely as the officer moved on.

None of them was found to be armed; most looked as though they wished they were. An officer with a clipboard directed them to call out their names one by one.

Off to one side and unnoticed by the captives, a short, dapper man in a raincoat and narrow-brimmed hat stood watching. At the sound of a name he looked down at his polished shoes. "My cousin," he sighed, and then added in the same laconic, oddly muted voice, "now what do I do with these people, how do you do this and not make them bitter all their lives?"

None of the officers near him replied, but after a discreet pause, someone suggested that for his own safety he would do well to leave. It was now clear that most of the armed raiders had escaped; there was every reason to believe that at least a few of them were up there, in the trees, right now. Without looking toward the timbered slopes above, District Attorney Alfonso Sánchez nodded, sighed again and moved off into the gathering darkness.

It had begun to rain slowly. A shed beside the Leyba house was searched, two men rousted out and a carbine and double-barreled shotgun removed. The captives were herded inside: 10 men, seven women, the rest young teen-agers and children. They were in protective custody, they were told, and were promised that police wagons would arrive soon to take them away.

Chief Black sent some of his men up into the trees, directing the rest to begin a house-to-house search of the village. Doors were kicked in and weapons—antique and modern—were confiscated. The names most frequently asked after were Váldez, Martínez, Morales, Madril, Leyba, Tijerina and Tijerina again.

A mile down the highway at the Forest Service complex, the National Guard had begun to arrive. General Jolly, in duffle coat and combat boots, informed reporters that there would be twelve units comprised of some 360 men, with 200 transportation and support vehicles, including a mobile field kitchen and a medical van with two doctors. The tanks lurching down off their flatbed trucks were M-14s, he said. Each carried a crew of five men and was armed with 40-mm. cannon and .50-caliber and .30-caliber machine guns. He added that a helicopter and a spotting plane were expected in the morning and hinted that more lethal air support was available, should it be needed. He had 20,000 rounds of ammunition on hand, he said, but added that, "20,000 won't last long if we start shooting."

National Guardsmen were stationed with fixed bayonets at regular intervals around Tobías Leyba's shed. A tank clanked to a stop at the head of the road, its cannon pointing down the ruts toward the Leyba farm.

The people in the shed complained that there was not enough room and the roof leaked. They were issued olive drab cans of C-rations. One plump, pretty young woman expressed concern that her six-month-old daughter, whom she had left on a bed inside the Leyba house, might roll off and be hurt. She was allowed to go to her baby, but was detained inside the house and interrogated as to the whereabouts of her husband, Reies Tijerina.

No unauthorized persons would be allowed to go in or out of the area, Chief Black announced, and all would be subject to detainment, search and questioning. He added that his men were manning roadblocks and searching villages and homes as far south as Albuquerque and as far north as the Colorado line, while law enforcement agencies all over the state would be either working or on alert throughout the night. Martial law had not been declared, General Jolly assured reporters.

Conferring at the ranger station, police chief and general planned the redeployment of their combined forces, the rearrangement of existing roadblocks and the creation of new ones. As Black gathered his men in the dimly lit parking lot for reassignment, State Police Captain T. J. Chávez came up to say that a white '65 Ford loaded with guns and insurgents was reported headed into the area.

General Jolly radioed Fort Bliss for 20,000 more rounds of ammunition. "My men have orders to shoot to kill," he announced.

It was past midnight, and the night was wearing on more slowly now. The little old lady with the thick eyeglasses had already tried twice, unsuccessfully, to sneak through the line of guardsmen and escape into the night, insisting that she had to find her son Baltazar and persuade him to give himself up; or failing that, at least see to it that he ate well. Out-of state reporters were arriving to join the others awaiting developments at the ranger station and vying for the telephone in Baldonado's store up in the village. They were not allowed to talk to the captives being held just down the road. (Said General Jolly, "Let's don't get involved in civil liberties.")

When questioned as to the extent of local sympathy for the raiders, one resident said that only three families in the village were members of Tijerina's *Alianza*. However, another local pointed out that families were large in northern New Mexico, and besides there was a difference between membership and sympathy. He reminded his questioner of Río Arriba's long history of furtive resistance and clandestine organization. Chief Black estimated statewide *Alianza* membership at around 5,000. Reies Tijerina had previously claimed a statewide membership of 30,000, with a like number elsewhere in the Southwest and California. Sheriff Naranjo estimated the membership at only 3,000, with no more than a hundred likely to take up arms.

Certainly, the police were taking no chances. Cars and trucks and campers were being stopped and their occupants questioned along hundreds of miles of highway. State Police patrol cars and National Guard jeeps were crisscrossing an area of 500 square miles. Houses were being entered and their occupants questioned and on occasion arrested in Cuba to the west, in Chama to the north, in Taos to the east, in Antón Chico to the south.

Already in custody were white-haired, 72-year-old Baltazar Apodaca, Tobías Leyba, Victor and Esequiel Domínguez and six others, including Rose, 19-year-old daughter of Reies Tijerina. Captain T. J. Chávez told reporters that no more than 15 of the suspected raiders were still at large, but he added that there was no telling how many others might join them in the hills during the night.

Baltazar Martínez, the Baltazar of the old lady who had tried to escape, was "the most dangerous one of the bunch, a nut," according to Chief Black. The 23-year-old ex-Marine was reported to have attended the courthouse raid festooned in dynamite sticks. "Not only that," Chief Black added, "but he was raised in these mountains. That boy could live under a rock."

Nearly as dangerous and certainly as wanted, Captain Chávez told reporters, were the Tijerina brothers—Cristóbal, Anselmo, Ramón and, of course, Reies, King Tiger himself. He was behind this whole mess, and there was no doubt that he had led the raid on the courthouse personally.

"It was him," Sheriff Benny Naranjo had told reporters earlier. "It was Reies himself. I saw him. This is Tijerina. This was the head man that came over here looking for Al."

Tijerina was exploiting the people, Captain Chávez explained to the out-of-staters. It was the land grant thing. For years the people around here had believed that this land was theirs because it had belonged to their ancestors, and that they had been tricked out of it by slick Anglo lawyers. Especially the old people.

Word came through on the radio that State Police had apprehended three men on their way to Canjilón: Camilo Sánchez, Santiago Anaya, and Victorino D. Chávez, aged 51, 53 and 66, respectively.

There had always been confusion over land ownership, Captain Chávez continued. But never anything that couldn't be handled. Then along came Tijerina and his gang, telling the old people he would help them get back the land, adding this thing about the people of *la raza* being discriminated against and robbed of their language and culture. Exciting the women, invigorating the screwy old men, encouraging the wild delinquents. . . .

Word came through on the police radio that the white '65 Ford had finally been intercepted and four teen-age boys arrested in possession of four loaded rifles, a pistol, dynamite caps and fuses, a pair of wirecutters and an open bottle of wine.

Oh, there wasn't much doubt that a few ignorant people had lost their land to a few smart Yankee lawyers, Captain Chávez acknowledged. But that had been years ago, and there was certainly no legal basis for the *Alianza*'s claim to over half the land in the Southwest. Tijerina even wanted the Louisiana Purchase back. He was a nut all right, but he was something else as well. The raid on the courthouse had made that clear once and for all.

"I remember him as a fiery orator and a peaceful man," Larry Calloway was at that moment writing in his UPI story describing the courthouse raid. "That picture had changed. He looked every bit the revolutionary leader."

Reies Tijerina was a wild man, T. J. Chávez assured reporters. Probably trained in Cuba and sent up here to build a revolutionary organization. If there was any doubt about the *Alianza*'s objectives, they should get a copy of the Albuquerque *Journal* for February 21, 1967, and turn to the legal notices column, where they would find a "Manifesto" written by one of Tijerina's chief lieutenants, Jerry Noll, alias Gerald Wayne Barnes, alias Don Barne Quinto César del Castillo, alias King Emperor of the Indies. If they wanted to know what Tijerina was really up to, they should read that.

> KNOW YE that. It is no longer feasible for the officers and agents of the Government of the United States of America to use words with doctrinal serenity and feign to be ignorant of the incon-

16

testable existence and real consequences of historical fact or of legal realities, as an excuse for their illegal activities beyond the territorial jurisdiction of the United States of America—ignorantia legis et facto neminem excusat—THEREFORE KNOW YE That, We, shall commence to liberate our kingdoms, realms and dominions . . .

Reporters filled time scribbling background notes: Canjilón, population 500, residents all Spanish, claim to be descendants of Don Diego de Vargas, liberator of New Mexico in 1692. . . .

FBI agents were reportedly examining the courthouse in Tierra Amarilla, but the town was closed to all except police traffic. The Bernalillo County Sheriff's department announced that its squad cars were patrolling the perimeter of Albuquerque in case any *Tijerinistas* tried to infiltrate the city during the night. Flashing signal lights from the vicinity of Navajo canyon turned out to be tourists' automobile headlights reflecting off the surface of Abiquiu reservoir. A man identifying himself as "one of Reies Tijerina's followers" called an Albuquerque radio station and threatened to blow up the city's military bases.

The chill rain drifted down on National Guardsmen watching over Tobías Leyba's shed with loosely held bayonets. The tank rested in the ruts of the road, its double snout drooping, its driver dozing in the hatch. "Hey," a small boy shouted, "if you wanta fight, trade places with my brother Mario in Vietnam," and scuttled away into the mountain darkness.

"We'll see to it that these people are prosecuted, that's for damn sure," said Governor Cargo in Santa Fe. "Every person involved at the courthouse was committing a felony."

At Bataan Hospital in Albuquerque, the bullet remained in Nick Sais' left lung and his condition was described as still critical. In the hospital in Santa Fe, the wounds of 60-year-old Eulogio Salazar were described as only serious, but because of previous heart trouble, his condition was listed as uncertain. "If one person dies, they are all guilty," said Cargo.

The biggest similarity between this business and dealing with the Vietcong, National Guard Captain and Vietnam veteran Edward DeBaca told reporters, "is that it's hard to recognize your enemy."

A few miles north of Tierra Amarilla in Parkview, Undersheriff Dan Rivera was found by his sister-in-law, bandaged and sitting in his darkened car across the street from his house unwilling to enter and risk harm to his family, afraid to go elsewhere.

"Securing an area as large as this is a massive undertaking," said National Guard Major Tom Taylor, a veteran of guerrilla warfare in Korea. "The chances of finding these men are very remote, but we might get lucky."

In the hills far to the southwest, just north of the village of Cuba, Reies Tijerina brooded at a rickety table in an abandoned adobe hut. Somewhere else Cristóbal Tijerina peered into a fragment of mirror and decided to grow a mustache. In another place Baltazar Martínez crouched under a rock and hugged his rifle in arms scarred by fire and the tattoo needle. Still elsewhere Don Barne Quinto César, King Emperor of the Indies, frantically stuffed tortillas into a paper bag and scrambled for the hills.

The sky was just beginning to lighten to the east as the captives were released from Tobías Leyba's shed and allowed to light fires and pick their way down the cow pasture to bathe their faces in the pond. As the first color of dawn tinged the flattened cone of Pedernales Peak to the south, two helicopters could be seen coming side by side.

"You're damn right we're going to stay until we get them," Chief Black assured weary reporters.

Río Arriba 3

L ong before tattooed delinquent, imperial pretender and brooding tiger
came to be at large in the Land of Enchantment, there had been the
makings of bad trouble in Río Arriba. For that matter, in Río Abajo
as well, and if the whole truth be told, throughout the Southwest and in
California—wherever the United States' six to nine million people of
Hispanic ancestry carry on their disadvantaged and increasingly impatient existence.

But Río Arriba was and is a special place, a rare pocket of cultural and
economic retardation, with a long history of covert resistance and a folk
tradition that has always considered violence to be the manly and logical
reaction to intolerable frustration. Virtually forgotten in their northern
villages, the people of Río Arriba had clung stubbornly to their language,
culture and fierce racial pride through a century of reduction and loss.
They were an independent, homogeneous, predominantly rural people,
and they were deeply discontented. They were the ideal sympathetic
populace and would provide the perfect cadre and assault force for the
beginnings of what Reies Tijerina would call his holy crusade.

Río Arriba means High or Upper River, and describes the mountainous
country embracing three main river valleys north of Santa Fe. It is also
the name of the Connecticut-sized county of the same name, which includes the long basin of the upper Chama and the valley of Tierra Amarilla. Río Abajo means Lower River and describes the country south of
Santa Fe to some miles below Albuquerque on the Río Grande and as
far south as Santa Rosa on the Pecos. The Río Arriba and Río Abajo regions are together confined to the northern half of the state.

New Mexico can be described as a squat rectangle with a river down the
middle. The state's outline roughly encloses a vertical trough, with the
edges of two parallel shelves thrusting in from either side, and a slope of
rubble tumbling in from the top. The trough is the long valley of the
Río Grande. The rubble is the last high peaks of the Rocky Mountain
chain, spilling into the top of the state from Colorado. The two shelves
are the two major plateau systems flanking the central river basins: the
Great Plains to the east, the intermountain Colorado Plateau to the
northwest.

19

There are four major rivers. The San Juan drops a loop across the northwestern corner of the state, the Canadian a larger loop across the northeastern corner. The Pecos runs north to south, but is separated from the Río Grande valley by the tailout of the Rockies, traveling down along the eastern Interior Plain and into Texas, where it joins the Río Grande for the last muddy run to the Gulf.

The Pecos and the Río Grande form an inverted V on the map. Both are vital, but the larger one is more than that. They say that by the time it concludes its 1,885-mile journey, every drop of water has been used to human advantage eight times. Along its banks can be found the leavings of every stage of human development, from the rusty junk of the internal combustion age all the way back to the flint spear-points of prehistoric man. As a source of lifeblood and a main route of human travel, it is the long heart and history book of the territory.

The reach of remembered time is long in New Mexico, but the marks of men are few and far between. The landscape is vast, marvellous and for the most part empty. U.S. 85 parallels the Río Grande almost all the way from south to north, passing through Albuquerque somewhat northwest of the center of the state. Driving through Río Abajo country, from Albuquerque to Santa Fe, the traveler finds himself searching for reassurance of human permanence, marching in his mind with the Spanish captains-general and watching for fleeting signs of the other, first inhabitants.

By official affirmation of no less an authority than the U.S. Department of Interior, the Pueblo Indians have been resident in the Southwest "since time immemorial." They have lived up and down the Río Grande for at least 600 years. When Columbus landed in the West Indies, there were more than 200 of their adobe towns scattered up and down the Río Grande valley. Today there are 18.

U.S. 85 lays its wide four lanes out across the vast, sage-dotted Sonoran foothills for 62 miles from Albuquerque to Santa Fe, absolutely straight in places for up to 15 miles, with little to be seen beyond the distant glint of electric towers, a few crumbling roadside curio shops and now and then a fleeting glimpse of one of the pueblos—Sandia, San Felipe, Santo Domingo—half hidden amongst the cottonwoods along the river, earth colored and flat. Only northernmost Taos still has the older pyramidal communal buildings. The rest maintain a more muted existence, self-effacing almost to the point of furtiveness.

For the Spaniard came this way, and after him, the Yankee. Nine years after Cortez's conquest of Mexico, Núño de Guzmán started north from New Spain, spurred on by an Indian slave's tales of the Seven Cities of Cibola, "as big as Mexico City, and with whole streets occupied by silversmiths." Guzmán never crossed the great river, but Cabeza de Vaca did, wandering for nine years and finally stumbling home to Mexico, naked and raving with tales of many-storied cities and a land of great wealth called Gran Quivira. After him came the Franciscan,

Fra Marcos, who approached close enough to the Zuni pueblo of Hawakúh to see its adobe terraces glowing yellow in the setting sun, hastily planted a cross and fled home again to tell of houses made of gold, and Indians with emeralds hanging from their noses. Coronado came a year later, in 1540, exploring the Río Grande Pueblo country as far north as Taos, then pushing on northeastward as far as the mud-hut villages of the Quiviras or Wichita Indians in eastern Kansas.

Finally, in 1598, 70 years after Guzmán's unsuccessful search for the fabled Seven Cities, Captain-General and *Adelantado* Don Juan de Oñate arrived at the banks of the Río Grande somewhere near present-day El Paso. Wearing one of his five complete suits of armor, bareheaded and in the presence of the cross and royal standard, he read out some 3,000 words, among them:

"I take possession once, twice, thrice, and all the times I can and must, of the lands of said river, without exception whatsoever, with all its meadows and pasture lands and passes, and all other lands, pueblos, cities, villas, of whatsoever nature now founded in the kingdom and province of New Mexico."

The royal secretary read his certification of the deed, the trumpets blasted out a voluntary, the harquebusiers fired a salute. Oñate urged his horse forward, leading 400 soldiers and settlers north up the river to begin the conquest and conversion of the Indians and the colonization of New Mexico.

In that year, the Spaniards had been in the New World for more than a hundred years. The first English colony at Jamestown was still nine years in the future.

Just before U.S. 85 cuts its 10-mile swath of arrow-straight highway down into Santa Fe, there is a roadside marker incised with the red-and-yellow Hopi Sun and the inscription:

KEARNY'S ROUTE

General S. W. Kearny raised the

American flag at Santa Fe, August 18,

in a bloodless conquest of New Mexico.

In that year, Spaniards had been in the New World for 350 years, in New Mexico for 250.

The highway does not go through Santa Fe's meticulously preserved Old Spanish Town, but follows the corridor of used-car lots and drive-in movies flanking the city. A more modern nightmare of neon and plastic could not be found, but its flimsy garishness is quickly forgotten as the highway crests the red hills behind the capital and heads northward across another vast plain of juniper-dotted hills, dry arroyos and crumbling mesas. Off to the right are the timbered slopes of the Sangre de

Cristos, far ahead, the low, smoky peaks of the Colorado Rockies. Flashing by at extended intervals are the sudden color of gas station complexes, the adobe houses of small *rancheros,* a windowless *Penitente morada* or sanctuary with its man-sized cross beside the door, the dusty access-road and untended trees that mean a pueblo: Tesuque, Nambe, San Idelfonso. A huge overhead sign points the way west to Los Alamos, the highway takes a sudden turn over a sandy eminence and then swoops down into Española, last stop before the 2,000-foot climb to the high country of Río Arriba.

Despite a garish facade of modernity (23 motels, 10 hamburger joints, 12 automotive agencies), Española is still basically a frontier outpost. Three routes lead north: one northeast up the Río Grande gorge to Taos; one straight north toward El Rito and Ojo Caliente; the third northeast up the Chama River valley to Tierra Amarilla, Chama and Colorado beyond. Each tine of this three-pronged fork is over a hundred miles long. Dirt roads crossing between the three routes are difficult even for four-wheeled-drive vehicles in summer. In winter, even jeep herders and horsemen think twice before attempting the worst crossings. The traveler from one northern point to another is invariably obliged to come the long way back down to Española before heading northward again.

Española is not only hub of travel to three counties, it is also the heart of commerce and principal seat of political power to much of the north. The shops, the hospital, the doctors, the dentist, the powers that be—all are here. Atop a small building, and on the windows of an equally modest edifice directly across the street, a number of signs unabashedly attest to the importance of Emilio Naranjo, longtime *honcho mayor* of the north's Democratic party, and father of Río Arriba Sheriff Benny Naranjo:

NARANJO REAL ESTATE

U.S. MARSHAL

U.S. DEPARTMENT OF AGRICULTURE

DEPT. OF INDIAN AFFAIRS

FOOD STAMPS

JUSTICE OF THE PEACE

NO PARKING

Española serves a general area of about 8,000 square miles, with a population of around 60,000 persons, 60 percent of them of Spanish or Indian ancestry. Río Arriba County itself covers nearly 6,000 square miles and has a population of 25,900 persons, 70 percent of them of Spanish ancestry and 10 percent Indian, including 1,217 Jicarilla Apaches.

To those who know the country but do not live here, there is always a bit of a last chance feeling, leaving Española and heading on north up U.S. 84. The signs of man fall away quickly; there is a sense of being drawn helplessly onward. The dusty trees of San Juan Pueblo, then the scattered tin rooftops of Hernández are left behind and the highway narrows to two lanes, riding the edge of the shallow-running Chama, watched only by castled sandstone cliffs and the empty windows of abandoned adobes.

The road swoops up through a brushy pass, and suddenly there are a gas station, signs of sparse settlement through the trees, and another roadside historical marker.

ABIQUIU

Established on the site of an abandoned Indian pueblo, Abiquiu in the mid-eighteenth century became a settlement of *Genizaros*, captives ransomed by the Spaniards from the Comanche and Apache.

There were no other pueblos beyond this point. From here northward, none of the early Spanish explorers traveled, not Coronado, not Espejo, not even Oñate. On maps made as late as 1848, when the first Yankee traders came this way, the upper reaches of the Chama River were still labeled *Tierra de Los Indios Utah*, sometimes: *Apachería*.

And yet as early as 1814, two citizens petitioned the *alcalde* or mayor of Abiquiu on behalf of themselves and 70 others for permission to go north, and in 1832, José Manuel Martínez, his family and some 30 other families received a grant of land from the Mexican government and did go north to face the Utes and Apaches, and eventually to pacify, cultivate and settle the Valley of Yellow Earth—Tierra Amarilla.

Beyond Abiquiu, the road climbs sharply up the face of a cliff, crests a long timbered ridge, and suddenly the upper valley of the Chama is there below, spreading to the horizon in all directions, green and gray with grass and sage, red and yellow with wind-sculpted sandstone, rimmed all around with the low, smoky violet of distant sierras.

It is certainly one of the most breathtaking vistas in the world, with the highway virtually the only mark of man discernible as far as the eye can see. It is here that Reies Tijerina stood one afternoon with his arms spread toward the horizon and one hand pointing off across the vast stretch of grazing land, much of it owned by the Purina Feed Company.

"There is where I will build my pyramid, there! Not for me, but for justice. My *Monumento de La Justicia,* do you understand? And it will last for a million years."

At the far end of the valley, the road swerves suddenly, skirting the foot of a 200-foot escarpment of eroded cliffs banded in hues of red and yellow. A sign indicates that Ghost Ranch is hidden somewhere off toward the foot of the mesa. The Ghost Ranch Museum flicks past on the right, the enormous concavity of Echo Amphitheatre towers away to the left and the landscape squeezes into the brushy, bouldered climb up Arroyo Seco and into Carson National Forest. More timbered ridges, a sign that says Canjilón; another valley, some poor roadside stores and a sign saying Cebolla. One final ridge of rock and piñon, and below is the valley of Yellow Earth, where many of the descendants of José Manuel Martínez and his fellow pioneers still live.

The land is of a dull sulphurous tint where it is exposed in a freshly plowed patch or an eroded hillside. Off to the east, a timbered escarpment marks the western edge of Kit Carson National Forest, broken by a 300-foot heap of bald gray granite known as TA—Tierra Amarilla—Rock. Four miles to the north, the end of the valley is marked by a low rise, with the junction of the Brazos and the Chama beyond, then the town of Chama and the first dark slopes of the Colorado Rockies.

Little Nutrias Creek wanders in from the west, threading a broad basin of rolling meadows, clustered cottonwood and willow, and the scattered tin rooftops of small ranchos. On any day of a not-too-dry summer, the valley looks greenly fecund and untroubled under its flawless blue sky. But the town is something else again.

The visitor can almost smell the melancholy musk of long decay as he swings down off the new highway, past empty adobe shells crumbling amongst rank weed, fallen fencing and the rusty hulks of automobiles, five empty shacks, then the Río Arriba County courthouse.

Three-storied, plastered a lurid pink with a pale blue border around the top, it is the most substantial building in town. Next to it stand the delicate shambles of the old hotel, boarded up and empty except for a few occupied rooms at the back. Across from the hotel is another ramshackle frame building with a rotting outside balcony, D R U G S in faded letters over the boarded door and soft-drink signs rusting on their nails. Down either side of the main street stretch other closed-up Western buildings, complete with sun-bleached false fronts and short stretches of wooden sidewalk. BILLIARD HALL in three-foot-high letters is dim as its memory above blank and broken windows; and across the street, BIG DANCE TONIGHT clearly means long ago and never again.

The town is not all ghost. On any normal day there is bound to be some activity in front of the little post office-grocery store. Now and then a pickup truck travels through or a patrol car pulls into the narrow plaza in front of the courthouse. There is a new high school out on the edge of town, a new elementary school and a junior high school, all filled with children from the surrounding area. Tierra Amarilla has an official population of 1,097. (Town residents actually number about 450.)

Nonetheless, standing on the main street under the steady beat of the sun on a summer day, say, the day before the June fifth raid, or for that matter, the day after, the visitor could not help but feel the town's crumbling spirit. A way of life has been dying here, much of it within single human memory and recently enough to be sorely missed and sought again.

Just around the corner at the end of Main Street and out of sight of the courthouse there is a gas station, its sign the brightest thing in town, its double outhouse freshly painted lime green. It is here that Reies Tijerina allegedly stopped after the courthouse raid and calmly requested that the gas tank of the bullet-riddled deputy sheriff's GTO he was driving be filled with high-octane gasoline.

Next door rises the brown bulk of the second largest building in town. There is no pink plaster here, only the raw adobe, wattled with straw and flecked with chips of dung, with great gaping cracks meandering down its surface. The roof is of corrugated iron and has the steep, hipped pitch common to this area; the long front porch has unpainted wooden posts and broken boards in the flooring. There is a 1958 Buick out front with its hood gaping open, a treadless tire leaning against a corner of the porch, a small cardboard sign propped inside a second story window: A Future Farmer of America Lives Here.

This is the house of Juan Martínez, direct descendant of pioneer leader José Manuel Martínez, and one of the "closest living heirs" to the Tierra Amarilla Land Grant, which once included within its boundaries all of the valley of Yellow Earth, much of Carson National Forest and all of the upper Chama valley north to Colorado, with a portion extending 40 miles into that state.

Juan Martínez is janitor of the local high school and can be seen pushing a broom up and down its halls five afternoons a week. At heart, by upbringing and by his own quiet declaration, he is a man of the land, a farmer, a stock breeder. It is just that there is no more land.

In 1901, less than 10 years before Juan was born, a Missouri lawyer named Thomas B. Catron successfully completed the final legal maneuver in his brilliant campaign to gain possession of most of the 595,515 acres of the Tierra Amarilla Grant. The land on which Juan's great-grandfather, Francisco Martínez, built and maintained his *hacienda* had already changed hands several times, eventually to fall into the hands of the U.S. government as a fish hatchery site. The small rancho on which Juan was born was not an inheritance from the original Mexican grant, but a homestead of two quarter sections, acquired by his father under the United States Homestead Act of 1862. Juan had left the rancho reluctantly, but in the end there was no choice, since his homestead was not sufficiently large to raise cattle profitably, and the U.S. Forest Service had withdrawn his permits to graze cattle inside Carson National Forest, on meadows that had once been a part of his great-great-grandfather's fiefdom, and had always been open to the free use of all residents of the valley. When the Martínez family moved into the crumbling house in Tierra Amarilla, it had been abandoned for 17 years.

Juan Martínez stands nearly six feet in his best boots and is still lean for his years, with a closely trimmed mustache on a weather-worn face and eyes perpetually narrowed against sun, wind and human intrusion. Noted for a deadly quiet preceding sudden action, he has all the attributes of a man sure of his dignity and deadly to his enemies. Eight years ago, two of his sons, Félix and Moisés, found themselves outnumbered in a local bar and came home badly battered. Juan mustered the eight most mature of his 12 sons and sallied forth to route the 15 or so who had done the original job. He was 50 years old then. He is 58 now, and still not a man to be trifled with.

Fernanda Martínez is three years younger than her husband, with gray-streaked hair and a body grown bulky with the bearing of 14 children. But the beauty is still there in the broad mouth, the short nose, the thick hair finger-combed back from a handsome brow, and especially the large eyes.

"Oh yes, life was good when I was a girl," she says. "Things were changing, but we didn't know it. It didn't show so much at first, so we just went on living."

In 1913, when Fernanda was born in the village of Cebolla (Onion), just 12 miles south of Tierra Amarilla, life for the people of Río Arriba was still very much as it had been for a hundred years. The daughter of farmer and sheepherder Danué Gustos and his wife Elena, Fernanda grew into a world neatly circumscribed by family, village, race and the reassuring rigidity of customs adapted to frontier life from a social system 2,000 years old.

The father was the undisputed head of the family, as her husband would be someday. With paternal power came the obligation, born out of frontier hardship, to care for the women and children without stint or qualification.

"No, I was never hungry," Fernanda says. "My father always took care of me, and after him my husband. And there was always my family. No, I was never afraid."

Joseph, the *pater* but not necessarily the *genitor* of Jesus, was personification of an ideal and stood crowned in the church, with the infant on one arm and the other hand holding a flowering staff. A woman seldom was cast out or lost her chances to marry because of a baby born out of wedlock. In many cases the oldest child was the wife's by a lover previous to marriage.

"They say that up in Rosa once there was this man who took a young wife, but he find out she is already pregnant by her sister's husband. That man, he go ahead and marry her, but he refuse to go to bed with her anymore, and all his kids he have by his wife's sisters and make her raise them like her own."

There were jealousies and there was righteous vengeance, but the children were nonetheless cared for, and sustained on all sides by a network of traditional loyalties.

First came the *sangrelidad* or blood ties of the kinship cult, the "extended family." From the father, the family reached out through the village to cousins, uncles and grandparents—*primos, tios* and *abuelitos*—each beholden to the others in relative degree, all a part of and loyal to the whole. Families reached from village to village, but it was the home village of the father and grandfather that held the strongest attraction, and it was there that men and women alike were required to honor accepted custom and standards of decorum.

"I remember once this man denounce his wife to the justice of the peace for bringing her lover into the house, and that judge, he sent all three out of town and tell them not to come back until they get some sense and can behave better."

When the young men went out to sow their wild oats, they always went to another town. When they went off to work, across or out of the state, they invariably brought the money back to their home village and looked there for a bride.

There was another cohesive force within each community and between communities: *compadrazgo*, the selection of godparents. Spanish settlers often functioned as godparents at baptisms of Indian children and adults, and for a time a large number of godfathers were chosen by fathers from the ranks of their fellows in a secret brotherhood known as *Los Hermanos Penitentes*. Godparents were expected to provide guidance and, if possible, other aid for the godchild. If the parents died and there was no other family, the godparents often took responsibility for the child's support and upbringing.

The entire system of loyalties—racial, religious, familial and commercial—was formalized by ceremony. While life consisted in the main of the hard daily life of house and field, there were special times when it was celebrated through ritual, sometimes joyous, sometimes mournful, sometimes ecstatic with the pain of mystery.

"In Cebolla we had the fiesta of Santa Rosa every year. Everybody would go to a special Mass, and then there would be a procession. I remember the statue being carried through the *placita*. But best of all, I remember the dance at night; everybody dressed up, and even the old men would get up and dance."

Young men would sometimes come from other villages, and sometimes there would be fights, hopefully broken up in time by the *bastonero*, appointed by the community to keep the peace. Sometimes there was bloodshed, for as the young men always went to another village to sow their oats, they would clash with young men waiting in that village to protect its honor and women.

"I remember the horse races on the feast of Santiago, those *corridas de gallina*. They would take this rooster and bury him in the sand with just his neck sticking out, and the first one to lean down from his horse and pull up that rooster and get away with it was the winner."

They were great and wild horsemen, and up through the 1920s and beyond, the great majority of the cowboys working on the ranches of the Southwest were of Spanish blood. In one Río Arriba village church the tall statue of the warrior saint, Santiago, was mounted on a mule and wore the complete outfit of the *vaquero*.

"I remember this old man, he refuse to teach his son to ride because

27

it would ruin him. He say it is horses that make men wild. He say, 'I myself am another man with a horse under me, like a Comanche.' "

Death was celebrated too, and there was plenty of it. Many women died in childbirth, and all the men went armed. There were three kinds of *velorios*, or wakes. One was for the recently dead, another for the dying crops of a dry year. And there was the wake of all wakes, when the white-and-blue dress of the Blessed Virgin was changed for the black of Our Lady of Sorrows, and all the long week of *Semana Santa*, the *Penitentes* sang and scourged themselves in their *morada* and the women prayed and mourned in the church. Finally, on Good Friday, the men emerged, dragging the huge crosses, their brows wreathed in wild rose thorns, moving slowly to the shrill fifing of the *pito* and the ratcheting clatter of wooden *matracas*, on the way to the Calvary or *calvario*. There they tied one of their members to the cross until his limbs turned black for lack of blood, his body wrapped in a clean white sheet so that he could not be recognized later by the pattern of his scars. His sobs came muffled from the black head bag: "*¡Ay! ¡Cómo estoy deshonrado!* Not with the ropes! Nail me! Nail me!"

"Sometimes the women would come and sit with my mother and gossip. And at night sometimes the men would be there, and some relatives, and maybe somebody from Las Nutrias, which was the name of Tierra Amarilla then, or even from as far away as Española. Sometimes the *sala* would be full of people, and there would be stories and songs, and those old men, they would tell us how it had been and how it should be."

These were the *tertulias*, unplanned, informal gatherings, usually in somebody's house. Perhaps there would be word of a miraculous cure by some local *curandera*, who might also be suspected of occult meddling in some local affair of love or business. Sometimes the local *cantador* would recite one of the old *inditas* or *décimas* in the melancholy wail of the ancient music, or sing a modern *corrido*. Sooner or later there would be talk of the adventures of *los viejitos*, living and dead, who had colonized this land, and of the long-gone *conquistadores*, those fierce and determined *hidalgos* who had come north from New Spain in search of gold in the name of God. Then someone, very likely an elder, might be inspired to remind the company that they were members of *La Raza Santa*, the Sainted Race; *custodios de las costumbres de nuestra gente*, custodians of the venerable and proper way of life; and *herederos*, inheritors by right of sacred, ancient and natural law to the land their forefathers had first broken to the plow—land which had been stolen from them, and which they must get back, if they had to burn every gringo haystack and barn in Río Arriba, if they had to string up every *vendido* politician by his lying tongue.

"Those old men, they would get so mad," says Fernanda. "And then the young men would get all excited too and talk about using their guns. I was frightened and couldn't understand it then, because I was only a little girl, and I didn't know how much things were going to change, were changing even then. But I know it now and I know they were right, those old men."

Fernanda Gustos grew up within an intricately structured social system which, while it tended to restrict the individual and ws far from perfect, did guarantee virtually every one of its members the loyalty, protection and support of a great many others and gave all a sense of unity through common race, religion and language, enabling her to say with honesty, "No, I was never hungry; no, I was never afraid."

Things had, of course, been changing all along, but the changes had been so gradual at first that they had for the most part gone unnoticed. Even as late as 1933, when Fernanda and Juan were married, life in the villages of northern New Mexico was still what the sociologists call viable. It took a nationwide depression to finally bring home to the *Hispanos* of Río Arriba the fact that for 50 years they had been living in the past, and that the present was about to overwhelm them.

"It really started to change after 1935, I think," says Juan Martínez, sitting stiffly upright in the dim shade of the sitting room of his crumbling house. "That was when the government started to close in on us. The Forest Service. Also, big men like Ed Sergeant, T. D. Burns, Miguel González, they started selling land. Like Ed Sergeant, he sold that land that is run by the Chama Land and Cattle Company. There was another man by the name of Heron. He took the rest of the common land, then Billy Mundy came, and they started putting up the fences, fencing all that land that had been *ejido* for so long, that had been free."

In the late 1940s and early '50s, Juan Martínez, like his father before him, began to take a more active part in the affairs of the Abiquiu Corporation, a land grant organization some 40 years old at the time. Its cultural roots ran back through the *Penitente* Brotherhood and other clandestine organizations, including *La Mano Negra* or the Black Hand, sometimes called by the popular press "The Mexican Mafia."

Juan was not alone. A number of such organizations had sprung up around the turn of the century, some of them designed to administer land grants still in the hands of original heirs, others devoted to the restoration of lost lands, ostensibly through legal means, actually by any means possible. Throughout the Southwest, predominantly in New Mexico and in the forgotten villages of the north, thousands of others shared the conviction that their rights as sainted race and rightful heirs had been flaunted. They represented a potential force of rare cohesion and determination, needing only the pressures of increasing harassment to fire them in their common cause, and a leader to bring them together for battle.

There was even a legend among them that such a man was destined to come, that he would be a man of exalted spirit, indomitable courage and dazzling legal acumen.

Reies 4

IN early 1958, nine years before the raid on the courthouse, a group of heavily bearded men in flowing white robes appeared in the logging town of Lumberton, 30 miles northeast of Tierra Amarilla. They were of *la raza*, "the race"; which is to say they were *Hispanos*, or Spanish-Americans, as the more politic prefer to say in New Mexico. To those who would listen, they confided that they were Heralds of Peace and had come from a place called *Valle de la Paz*, or Valley of Peace, in Arizona. One of them, apparently their leader, was a preacher of Pentecostal bent and considerable persuasive power: a solidly built man in his early thirties, with thick black hair and glinting gray-green eyes, a personal presence which seemed forever on the brink of some cataclysmic ecstasy and a speaking style that could compel the most skeptical sheepherder to come forward with at least a dollar in his hand and his eyes agleam with yearning for instant transmutation from damned to delivered, from lost to found.

The stranger preached mostly to those of *la raza*, always in Spanish, most often in private homes, sometimes in ramshackle rented halls. He and his disciples were nicknamed *los barbudos*, the Bearded Ones, and there were jokes about what they did or did not wear under their muslin robes. But the local *Hispanos* were nonetheless impressed by the preacher; more than a few thought they detected the passionate abandon of a true saint. They were even more impressed when he began to salt his fiery sermons with talk about something that interested them fully as much as did any prospect of the pastures of Heaven: the land under their feet, which they believed had been stolen from them and was theirs by right of divine inheritance, royal decree and natural law.

Those not of *la raza* were equally impressed, although to a far less charitable degree, and were not surprised when a series of petty thefts appeared to coincide with the comings and goings of *los barbudos*. Bill Crane, then Sheriff of San Juan County, did some investigating, but he could not come up with any evidence to justify arrests. Nonetheless, non-Spanish-speaking residents of the area remained convinced that the strangers had been more than a little sticky-fingered. The conviction would deepen into bitter regret through the next five years, as the beards came off and the robes fell away to reveal *los barbudos* as heralds of something distinctly other than peace.

"By God, if we had known who they were and who he was," one of them recently fumed, "we would have run them out of here on a rail and floated them down the San Juan right back to Mexico, where they belong. To think that four separate times I was face to face with him and once at night and dead alone. My wife says I've got so soft in the head I wouldn't recognize the Devil if I met up with him, and I think she's right."

Devil or saint? A difficult if not absurd polarity to apply in judgment of any man. But Reies Tijerina inspires and even courts such extremes of opinion. There is evidence that he would judge himself and others in terms that leave little room for compromise. His own account of his early years describes the making of a man hungry for absolutes.

But his story also gives dramatic form to the dilemma of a people sorely disadvantaged by history down to the present day. It is true in its essentials, and is a useful exposition of a number of psychological as well as social truths.

By his own account, Reies López Tijerina was born to a pious and Christ-loving woman just north of the hemisphere's bloodiest border on September 21, 1926. Reies says the birth took place on a heap of cotton sacks in a one-room adobe shack at the edge of the fields outside Falls City, Texas, 120 miles north of the Mexican border.

Called king-like after the King of Kings, the infant was swaddled in sacking and left in the care of his four-year-old brother Ramón, while his mother Herlinda returned to the fields with her husband and their oldest son, Anselmo, who was seven. In all, Herlinda delivered 10 children without the aid of a midwife, three of them dead within the first year of life. Five sons and two daughters survived and were all baptized in the Roman Catholic Church. Their mother is remembered as big-boned and strong-willed. "Once, when there was no food in the house, she made a bow out of an automobile spring and an arrow out of scrap metal, and she shot a jackrabbit for us to eat."

But most of all, Reies remembers her as deeply and fervently devoted to *La Religion*. To the people of Spain and Mexico, and to most of the Spanish-speaking people of northern New Mexico, there was for a very long time only *The* Religion, the mother faith, as there was *España*, the motherland.

"The nearly eight years that my mother lived after my birth, all she taught me about was God and religion," Reies Tijerina says. "She read the Bible a lot. She prayed before meals and in the evening. When I was frightened and cried, she would take me up in her arms and pray and soothe me by asking me to tell again about the dream, about what I had seen in heaven."

31

The dream had happened when the boy was around four. The family was picking pecans then, so the tea at table was made from the bark of the pecan tree. Even then there was only enough for half a cup for each in the morning, and the boy wanted more. "I couldn't understand why there wasn't enough. I was only four. I became so . . . how do you say . . . *sentido,* hurt. And so I went from the table and to bed and stayed there. I was there 24 hours, and I was dead. Anselmo remembers, they were sure I was dead, and they had the coffin and everything there, and then I got up and I had this dream.

"You see, right from the beginning my mother gave me too much belief in God, and this dream that I had might have been part of her teachings. But again, it's still in my mind that it was not a dream in a way, but I like to say dream, because people don't believe. I saw Jesus, and he took me by the hand and was showing me great green pastures and a garden full of flowers, a beautiful place, and then he was pulling me along in one of those small little toy wagons, a red one, you know—I never did have one—he was pulling me along in that."

Again and again the mother would urge the child to tell the dream, sometimes just to her, sometimes to the whole family, sometimes for the neighbors. The boy's frights often came in the night from another, recurring dream.

"We were working on the Stevens ranch five miles from Poth, and this car would come driving toward our house by itself, without any driver. It would come closer and closer without a driver, and I would begin to tremble. I was afraid Stevens would think we had stolen it and would come and shoot one of us. I would wake up shaking and crying, and then my mother would come and remind me of the other dream and that would soothe me."

The father, Antonio, had already buried two wives. He was a sharecropper, planting wheat, barley, corn, cotton, beans. Three times when his crop was ready his debts were ready too, and three times the landowner came to take all of the crop away. Once he had been a landowner himself, and sometimes he told his children of how he was a Laredo land grant heir and had had his land taken from him, and would tell of others who had been run off their land and worse. Now, with his third crop demanded, he protested and was ordered off at rifle point by a man named Albert, who had two sons who arrived on horseback to rope him and drag him from the land.

He went to the judge in Poth, and the judge said, "Tony, Albert is an outlaw, no law can control that man. Don't make trouble, just take your chickens and hog and go, or you will lose them too." He had already been slashed in the thigh once before by a mounted man, hamstrung and crippled so badly that sometimes now Herlinda had to hoist him on her back and carry him to the fields in the morning and carry him back at night. With his third crop gone and the burns of the rope on him like stripes, Antonio fell silent and stayed silent, so much so that his son would say of him later with impatient regret, "Once he began trembling he never stopped. He lives in Wichita Falls on Social Security and is a very religious man now and terrified all the time, too timid to even speak out."

However, according to Reies, there was another member of the family who was to remain unbroken to the day of his death. He was Antonio's father Santiago, who steadfastly insisted that he was legal heir by grant of the Spanish king to the Laredo land he had lost, and told his sons and his grandsons so again and again. He also told them tales of murder, lynching, burning and other countless wrongs done to his people by the Texans, the *Tejanos*. He told of the three times he had fled across the border to escape the Texas Rangers. He was fondest of telling of how he had been strung up by vigilantes once, only to be cut down at the last minute by order of a Mexican border judge who had said simply, "That's not the one."

Whether the tales were entirely accurate as he told them and as his son and grandsons later told them does not matter, for one such tale was as reliable as another and all added up to one side of the truth in that stretch of land above a border that had known only blood and misery for a hundred years. To understand the history of that border is to begin to understand both Reies Tijerina and his cause.

In 1810, 40 years before old Santiago was born, Father Miguel Hidalgo had issued his proclamation of liberty from the village of Dolores in New Spain. The *Grito de Dolores* marked the beginning of Mexico's long struggle for independence. Nine years later, the United States signed a treaty with Spain, receiving Florida in exchange for cessation forever of all claims to Texas and the long Río Grande boundary, thereby infuriating the land-hungry Yankee adventurers lingering in Louisiana, and setting the stage for a century of strife between invading *Tejano* and entrenched *Mejicano*.

In 1836, about the time Santiago Tijerina was born, Santa Anna, commander-in-chief of the armies of the Republic of Mexico, surrendered at San Jacinto and acknowledged that the boundary between Mexico and the new Republic of Texas was the Río Grande. However, for the 12 years that preceeded the Treaty of Guadalupe Hidalgo and for many years afterward, the area for 150 miles north and south of the great river was a no man's land of continuous struggle between those who had first settled the land and those who had come to take it from them. While the Republic to the south progressed slowly through revolution and counter-revolution, its orphaned blood brothers north of the river gradually lost power, purpose, property and heart.

However, in the 1850s and '60s when Santiago Tijerina was growing up, the tide of battle along the border still favored the *Mejicanos*. They represented at least 80 percent of the population and they had sometimes the official, always the unofficial favor of the various turbulent governments to the south. In the late 1850s, *Hispanos* were still doing much of the freighting in Texas, hauling goods to the value of millions of dollars annually in ox cart caravans from San Antonio to Chihuahua and other points in Mexico. In 1857, Texas freighters set out to take over the trade, and dozens of *Mejicano* freighters were found spread-eagled to the spokes of their cartwheels and riddled with bullets, their goods gone and their oxen shot. But then as now, the *Mejicanos* worked for less than the Texans, and Texan business interests eventually ended the Cart War. In the little town of Goliad, just 50 miles from where Reies Tijerina was born, old-timers still point out the live oak tree from which several Texan ruffians were hanged.

It was about this time, when the United States was too preoccupied with the Civil War to bother with the disordered and bankrupt new state of Texas, and Benito Juárez was struggling to maintain his revolutionary regime against the French invasion of Mexico, that certain men of brilliant and frequently murderous inspiration arose to take advantage of the border's chaos. They rode magnificent horses saddled in gear worked with silver and gold. Their immense sombreros were also worked in silver and gold thread, their velvet jackets and fine buckskin trousers gleamed with silver *conchos* and they bristled with weapons, with power. They were the conquistadores come again, true *hidalgos* of the border hell, expert in everything they did, elaborately mannered as they murdered and remorseless in their hatred of the gringo. They quickly became, and remain today, the *Hispano* folk heroes of the Texas border country.

In the early '70s, with the Civil War over, the tide began to turn in favor of the Texans and old scores were settled with a ferocity which equaled and sometimes surpassed that of the most bloodthirsty of the *bandidos*. In 1874, Captain L. H. McNelly formed his famous company of Texas Rangers and in defiance of United States orders crossed the Río Grande and successfully attacked *bandido* Juan Cortina in his hide-out in Mexico. In 1876, President Porfirio Díaz of the Mexican Republic took Cortina prisoner and kept him under surveillance until his death in the '90s. Meanwhile, the "Mexican troubles" continued through the '70s. The terms *pelado* and "greaser" came into increased use north of the border, and a dead *Mejicano* dangling from a tree outside of town became a common sight. In March 1875, a well-organized band of 150 Mexicans crossed into Texas near Eagle Pass and split into four divisions, one of which attacked Nuecestown, killing several people, including one "good Mexican," taking 25 new saddles from the store and fleeing south again. For a month after the raid, every *Mejicano* found riding with a new saddle was killed.

In another typical case, a sheepman named Thad Smith and his wife were found hacked to pieces. A posse trailed three *Mejicanos* who had been seen near the Smith house, and while the sheriff watched, shot one of the suspects, rode another down and 'cut the throat of the third. Two other *Mejicanos* who were also said to have been seen near the Smith place were jailed, and that night taken out and strung up from a gate pole.

This took place in and around Refugio, about 70 miles south of Falls City, where Reies Tijerina was born. His grandfather Santiago was in his mid-twenties; his father, Antonio, was not yet born.

In the 1880s and '90s wholesale depredations from south of the border decreased drastically as the Yankees began to consolidate their holdings by dint of superior force and laws designed and administered predominantly in their favor. But a tradition of chaos haunted the land, the habit of violence was in the blood of the men who ruled it, and racial hatred was in Texas to stay. For every "bad Mexican," there was now a "white hardcase" to carry on the tradition. Many of them were Rangers, never known to honor any discipline beyond raw courage. The boot was simply on the other foot, and now it was the Texas cattlemen who were dealing in "wet stock," stolen in Mexico and smuggled north across the river. Now the *bandido* was replaced by the "stomper," often gathered into a band as well organized as the legions of Cortina had ever been. Among them were men like King Fisher and Billy the Kid after him, who tallied their killings with the disdainful qualification, "not counting Mexicans and Indians." Fisher, as a matter of fact, is credited with having done away with 19 *Mejicanos* before he and Ben Thompson were shot to death in San Antonio in 1884.

A kind of peace gradually came to the border with the beginning of the new century, but underlying it was the deathless heat of vendetta, with the Texans now completely in power and the *Mejicanos* being ground slowly into resentful peonage.

For a time new figures appeared in the Republic to add to the pantheon of folk heroes. In 1910, General Díaz was overthrown by Francisco Madero and the new revolution proclaimed. Two years later, Madero was assassinated, but the road to revolution was kept open by men like the mounted *caudillo*, Emiliano Zapata, and Doroteo Arango, better known as Pancho Villa. Villa led raids across the border for four years, armed with guns sold to him by American manufacturers. Santiago Tijerina was in his sixties then, and his son Antonio was 25. In 1917, the new constitution of Mexico followed the spirit of Father Hidalgo's *Grito de Dolores* a hundred years before by decreeing that all land and water was the property of the nation, including all minerals, subsoil and petroleum. The Church was also to be divested of much property and power, and in 1926, the year of Reies Tijerina's birth, masses in Mexican churches were suspended for two years. In 1934, General Lázaro Cárdenas became President, and on March 18, 1938, the Republic of Mexico expropriated all British and American oil interests and declared them the property of the Mexican people.

Much of this happened when Reies Tijerina was a boy, and the rest was told by the old man, Santiago, who had once escaped hanging and liked to boast of bare-fisted fights with Texas Rangers. The old man favored others of his grandsons, especially Anselmo, and didn't like the younger Reies, who listened saucer-eyed to the bloody tales and then had dreams of the pretty pastures of heaven.

Reies says that in his early years he was little affected by his grandfather's tales and their implications and by the poverty and bitterness around him. "It was the way of life and I was just a little boy. I didn't know any better. All my friends were the same, and I was content. I only had about six months of school in all, because we were always on the move, and the only books I read were Jack and Nancy and so forth. I didn't think anything of going with my brothers to the garbage cans of the rich people, and we would find half a loaf of bread and meat and make our own lunch and go to school."

In 1934, when Reies was seven, Herlinda died, 11 months after giving birth to her 10th child, taking with her an unborn 11th.

"My father never did marry again, he didn't seem to even want to talk. When he talked to the ranchers he would forget the few words of English he had and would tremble and limp away. Anselmo was really the father. From his paycheck of about 20 dollars for 15 days of pick and shovel work, he would keep a nickel. My father didn't want him to smoke, but once Anselmo bought a pack of cigarettes from his money."

There was little talk of getting the family land back now, and no woman to pray before meals. "We moved from town to town looking for work—Poth, White Face, Lubbock, Wilson, Levelland, Forestville. We picked beans and melons. We picked cotton, 25 cents a hundred pounds, chopped cotton, 10 cents a row, topped turnips and hoed onions and cultivated broom corn and shelled pecans . . ."

It was the Depression, and they were legion, but they were not the only ones in the fields in those days. There were the dust bowl immigrants from Oklahoma who came through in their old cars, nearly half a million over a period of four years, most of them heading for California. Many stopped off to work and quite a few to stay in Texas and southeastern New Mexico, eventually to prosper and quickly forget, exchanging old memories of hard times for the more comfortable conviction of natural superiority of gringo over greaser.

"I remember when we were working near Fredericksburg and had been paid for our work, my father and the other men would have to guard the road so our money wouldn't be taken away from us. I remember the dark night and those model Ts going by on the road and the men whispering, 'the Klan.'"

Anselmo went away to work on the WPA and sent money home when he could. "That left Margarito as the oldest. He was the humblest of all. He couldn't talk until he was seven. When Anselmo would leave the chicken coop open, my father would ask, who did it, and Anselmo would say, Mario, and poor Mario would just stand there with his mouth open."

There was Ramón. "He learned reading and writing at 19 and was always the best-looking and chased by all the girls, and yet he turned out to be a good-living man and straight in his family life. When we collected junk he was always the one to gather the money into some cloth and give it to my father."

There were the two girls, María and Josefa, and there was Cristóbal, the youngest, born 11 months before Herlinda's death and sent early to be raised by a man named Nasario Vásquez. "Almost a full-blooded Indian and nearly a hundred years old now, he was very straight and good-looking like those people."

It was the Depression, and one learned to live on pecan tea and beet tops, to trade scrap iron and to bale and sell rags, and to steal. Memories of past glory and gringo outrage were cherished and feverishly elaborated in the mud *jacales* and tin-roofed shacks at the edges of the fields and in the back alleys of the Texas towns. The men would gather around fires of smashed strawberry crates to talk, and in the morning a boy could tell how many there had been by counting the slashes in the ground where the cane knives had been buried in a circle. Sometimes there was talk of the legendary 429 land grants of Texas, given to the people by the Spanish Crown. Again and again one heard the tale of the time Texas Rangers poured kerosene on the two *Mejicano* children and set them afire. One could be goaded into consuming rage by the nightmare, or one could remember a mother's arms and another kind of dream.

In 1939, Antonio Tijerina took his family north to Michigan to work in the beet fields, and there they stayed for five years. Despite his dreamy nature, Reies had begun to make another kind of reputation in his family. They called him jokingly *abogado sin libros* or prairie lawyer—literally, lawyer without books—and they noted how stubbornly he could stick to an argument once he had taken it up, regardless of all reasoning or even threats of violence against him. In Michigan, he once argued with a rancher named Waite over how well the family had weeded a field, and later his father fearfully scolded him for having talked back. The boy was 15 and changing. And then, in 1942, a Baptist preacher named Samuel Gallindo gave him a New Testament.

"I didn't leave that book that night until I had read it all. Then I got my brothers and read it to them a second time."

Blessed are the poor . . . Blessed are they that mourn . . . Blessed are the meek: for they shall inherit the earth . . .

"I found all those words to reach my heart, and learned that mercy and truth could meet, and it was like an echo of the times when my mother had read from the Bible and held me in her arms and prayed."

Blessed are ye, when men shall revile you, and persecute you . . . Ye are the salt of the earth . . . Ye are the light of the world . . .

"Then I read the rest of the Bible, about Abraham, David, Ishmael and Moses, who led his people to the Promised Land, and there through the prophets I saw satisfaction for the yearning of my heart for justice and peace. I found the word justice used as many times as words like love. I began to talk to Protestants and especially to Baptists and

Methodists there in Michigan, and that was when I began to decide on the religious life and made plans to go to Bible school."

Let your light so shine before men, that they may see your good works . . . it hath been said, An eye for an eye, and a tooth for a tooth: But I say unto you . . .

There has been much speculation as to why, in the first half of this century, so many Spanish-speaking people of the American Southwest left their native church and turned to the Protestant church, especially the Pentecostal and Evangelical sects. It has been suggested that the change is the result of a profound sense of racial failure and of the natural inclination of the conquered to take on the lineaments and talismans of the conquerers. On the other hand, it has been pointed out that the Pentecostal sects have always been popular in frontier agrarian societies, where there is invariably a need among the people, regardless of race, for a more personal, more vigorous and more emotionally satisfying attempt to comprehend and control the natural forces so close around them.

There is a further explanation applying especially to the case of the *Mejicanos* of southern and central Texas, where by 1946, when Reies Tijerina started Bible school, the Spanish-speaking segment of the population had long been divested of all land and negotiable property and for the most part of any real political power, and were rapidly losing the last remnants of their cultural identity. Without special skills, deliberately ignored by the educational system, they remained visible to the Texans only as a vast brown pool of cheap labor. As individuals, they were invisible, as negligible as the adobe walls against which they crouched, little more than mud upon mud.

The one thing they were allowed, which was even pressed eagerly upon them, was formal conversion. The one book they were urged to read and were given free was the Bible. And it was there in the New Testament, previously withheld from them by many of their priests, that they found the solace of the utterly destitute: that as grains of sand, they were the elect; that as the salt of the earth, they would yet see the light; that the meek would someday, somehow, in some apocalyptic reversal of social law, inherit the earth.

"So I went to Bible school," says Reies. "Ramón went with me. And my grandfather, that old man, he wouldn't speak to me after that, he didn't speak to me for years."

Reies entered the Bible school run by the Latin American District Council of the Assemblies of God Church in Isleta, Texas. He says he was 19 then, in 1946, and that within the year he was rebuked by his Anglo-American sponsors and suspended from the school.

Brother Kenzy Savage, who was superintendent of the school at the time, says that Reies was 23 when he began his studies, and that "He was fanatical, more peculiar in his thoughts, I guess—he was not orthodox. When he went to school he was a very sincere student. I don't know, when he left school, he began to get these rather far-out ideas about how people ought to conduct themselves."

Brother Savage does not recall anything about a girl. He says that Reies was graduated as a preacher and joined him for some "pastoring" in the Santa Fe area. "He was a very good speaker, with a lot of spunk and spirit. I appreciated his ministry at that time."

The record does show that Reies married a pretty fellow Bible student of his own age named Mary Escobar, whom he prefered to call María. His brother Ramón also took a fellow student for his bride, making it a double wedding. But Ramón's was to be a far more stable marriage than that of his volatile brother. Three months after the wedding, Reies gave away all his possessions and left Mary, telling her he would be back when God had shown him his duty.

"We didn't have much, a radio and some chairs, but I gave it, you know, to the poor. Because I kept on having a struggle with my conscience, my soul. I was not satisfied, I was always finding that the Bible rebuked me. I found things, not outright things, but that I was a hypocrite, that I was not doing what I could do."

For that which I do, I allow not; for what I would, I do not; but what I hate, that I do.

"That urge had been building up in my soul for months, building up and building up, and every time I would stop to think or pray or read the Bible, I would feel that urge, that I was way back, way behind, that I had to overcome everything."

For I delight in the law of God after the inward man; but I see another law in my members, warring against the law of my mind.

"So I told my wife that I was going to seek the light, a better opening, and I built this place all by myself, this cave in El Monte, California, up on top of a hill all covered with brush. I lined it with cotton I pulled out of an old car seat, and I had to crawl like a snake to get in there. I had in mind that it had to be so that I couldn't turn back, that I wouldn't get out of there unless I could find something better, and if I died, I wanted it to be where they wouldn't find me.

"I don't know how long I was there, but it was some days, and I had great illuminations. I found that there were not so many religions as they had taught me in Bible School, there was just the two strong powers of good and evil. I saw that those of different religions were all the same, they all wanted new automobiles, they were all full of pride and coveted the same things, and so I learned that there was no difference between Protestant and Catholic after all. Being subject to certain pressures, they would all act the same. And so I went back to my wife with a new interpretation for the Bible, just literally, the way it was, and I started out preaching again."

In that first year of apostolic mission and young marriage, Reies began to put together a book of his sermons which he called ¿*Hallará Fe En La Tierra?*—Can Faith be Found On The Earth?—asking, as always, the same question of the world which he asked of himself.

The next year, 1947, the first of six children was born. They named him Reies, Jr., but the new father liked to call him David. Late in that year, word came from Texas that old Santiago was dying and that he wanted to have last words with Reies in particular.

"I was so surprised. You know, that old man didn't like me when I was a kid. But he must have heard from Ramón about how I had talked back to that rancher, Mr. Waite, and the others in Michigan and about how I was beginning to fight injustice."

Reies decided to go, but first he once again felt the need to cleanse himself of wordly possessions. "I used to take the Mexican nationals, the ones who came to hoe the beets, into town in my car or wherever they wanted to go and lend them my car and let them use the gas. So I gave them my new watch and three suits, so as to feel at ease with my heart's desire. When I read that Socrates' wife threw a bucket of hot water on him when he wouldn't make money, I rejoiced, because my wife was always angry at me for doing the same thing and giving my things away to the poor."

Thus unburdened, he set out from Chicago with his wife and one-year-old son to walk to Texas, often refusing rides along the way, "because I wanted to feel really close to the prophets of old, to Moses and Saul and Isaiah and Paul, those men who had defended justice in the world and suffered for it."

At the end of the long trek, they found old Santiago still alive, and he called Reies to his bedside and kept him there. "I thought maybe that now he was dying he would want me to tell about the dream and help him pray, but I was wrong. All he wanted to do was tell me the old tales again, to print them in my mind, how he had been hung and cut down, what the Texas Rangers had done. He lasted two days and didn't want to be with anyone but me. That old man, he was a lion right to the end."

Though the lion was dead, the tiger was yet to be born. "I wasn't ready to leave my religious work, you see, I was still looking for a way to bring mercy and truth together into justice with the Bible, and so I became the pastor of that Assembly of God Church in Victoria, Texas, and tried to bring, you know, the word of God to the people."

Ramón was following his brother's lead in El Paso, working hard at a job, raising a family and preaching as a lay minister when he could. Cristóbal, the youngest, was to have no more than six encounters with members of his family for the next 10 years. He had left his Indian godfather, had gotten married and was driving refrigerated trucks for a living, always different from the others in certain elusive ways, even to looking somewhat different. As for the two oldest, Anselmo and

Margarito, they had been out in the world long before the others and were to come to the final faith from the underside, as it were.

For many, the hardest of worlds had gotten only harder since the Depression. True, the Big War had brought boom, and for a time there were opportunities for all, even for the unskilled. For a few years there was no need to follow work and wages from field to field and suffer the fluctuating whims of growers and the weather. One could find decent wages and learn a skill in the factories, or one could enter the armed forces, where living conditions amounted to luxury; there were possibilities for glory and even advancement, and the subtle promise was held out of acceptance in a world which seemed to value individual courage and initiative above exclusivity of language, culture, race. On May 28, 1943, Anselmo López Tijerina volunteered for service in the United States Army, but was turned down as 1-Y, insufficient education. Five months later he tried the navy, with the same result. On December 1, 1946, he was arrested and given 20 days in jail for assault and battery in Port Huron, Michigan.

Before the war, there had been at least the WPA, to this day remembered fondly by countless middle-aged *Mejicanos* of the Southwest. Tenant farmers had received some aid in bad years through the Farm Security Administration. After the war, there was almost nothing for the unskilled to do. Because of the brief wartime manpower shortage, the federal government had allowed the growers to initiate the *bracero* program, importing Mexican nationals to do field work formerly done by domestic labor.

The *bracero* was recruited from the Mexican rural poor by contractors in Mexico, checked for good health by the U.S. government without charge to contractor or grower and shipped into the United States to live under prison camp conditions and work for slave wages. He was invariably illiterate and was without language or rights in this country. He was a chattel, and a productive one, paid on a piecework basis, seldom making more than 80 cents an hour for back-breaking work. After the war, the powerful lobbies of agribusiness managed to get the *bracero* program continued. The growers didn't relish the return of domestic workers who had acquired a taste for better treatment and conditions in the armed Forces and had perhaps been tainted with ideas of unionism in defense industries. Even in a year of recession and unemployment, almost 450,000 *braceros* were allowed into the United States.

In addition, small tenant farms were rapidly disappearing, since the abundance of cheap *bracero* labor made the operation of large plantation farms once again feasible. Mechanization also went ahead rapidly, although some growers found the *braceros* to be cheaper even than machinery. In 1951, when the Korean War brought on another brief manpower shortage, Congress took the excuse to extend the *bracero* program and even to codify it as Public Law 78, which provided minimal standards of housing and food and a minimum wage for the *bracero*, but no such control over wages and abuses for the domestic field worker. The overall effect of the *bracero* program was to worsen working conditions for both Mexican national and domestic field worker and to depress wages. While most workers improved their living standards during the postwar years, the ratio of wages received by hourly paid farm workers fell from 54 percent of the wages received by factory workers in 1948 to 46 percent in 1956.

For those who had managed to attain a skill during the war, things were no better with the curtailment of defense work and the firm resistance of practically all Southwestern industry and business to unionism.

This was the way it was for Anselmo and Margarito Tijerina and tens of thousands of others like them through the "boom" years of the '50s. They waited and are still waiting in the crumbling houses and outbuildings of another century, down the back alleys of a thousand rural villages in Texas, Arizona, New Mexico, Colorado, California, in shoestring communities of tin-roofed shacks out along the highways, in the *barrios* growing like tumors in the flanks of the cities: La Rana in Torrence, South Dos Palos and Oxnard, all in California; Goat Hill in Denver; San José, Martínez Town and Barelas in Albuquerque; and El Cuerno and La Tripa in San Antonio, the last meaning "guts" and referring to the slaughterhouse that long dominated the area.

Long before, when there had still been a patch of land left to the Tijerinas, Margarito had plowed the 200 acres by himself. "With a middle buster plow and four horses," Reies says. "He would go to the nopales cactus and collect pigeon eggs and after working he would cook his own meals and eat alone, because it was hard for him to talk and always would be. After 17 he went out on his own. He wandered from El Paso to Michigan. He was picking tomatoes in Indiana . . ."

In an Indiana bar, Margarito got drunk and became convinced that another, equally drunk man was taking liberties with his female companion. He killed the man with one blow. His court-appointed attorney advised him to "just say you're guilty and hope for the best." He was tried without a jury, convicted of manslaughter, and sent to the penitentiary. In the pen he learned to write and read a little, and was paroled 10 years later, but restricted to the state of his birth, Texas. Anselmo met him when he got out of jail. They worked and drank together. They were brothers, the two oldest, and they had both been in jail.

In the meantime, Reies was preaching in the Assembly of God Church in Victoria, Texas. A girl was born to the Tijerinas in 1948 and called Rose, although her father preferred to call her Rosa. While on a trip to Mexico that year, he gave in a second time to the compulsion to strip himself down to his soul, giving away his car, his clothes, everything he had to the nearest and hungriest. Mary was furious; there was a third child on the way. But the struggle was out of her hands. It always had been and always would be.

One afternoon in 1949, after Reies had concluded a sermon, the little hall emptied of all but an elderly stranger, white-haired and gaunt, pale-skinned and blue-eyed. He wanted to talk to this fervent young Mexican; he had been wanting to talk to such a one for a long time.

"He had been frightened by a miracle and he knew horrible things. According to his tale, he had never been a real God-fearing man, and one time he got angry with God because he was hungry, you know, and he cursed the holy spirit and he said, if the God of Elijah is alive, let him feed me right here while I'm walking, as he fed the prophets of old. And just then there was a bunch of crows flying overhead and at his words they started fighting and they let loose the nuts and pecans that they had in their claws and they rained on him. After that he was like a cursed man, always sad and wanted to die, but he couldn't die, and so he told me that to redeem his curse, his sin, his great big sin against God, he was going to tell me the truth about his people.

"He told me that he was not supposed to say anything, and he made me promise not to release his name, and then he told me these tales, horrible, these horrible tales. He told me about how when he was a kid in Cuero, Texas—that's about 20 miles from Victoria—his father and his uncles would murder and destroy women and children and do horrible things. And how an Anglo would go about getting hold of the land grant of one of the big *hacendados*, the Spanish owner of the big *hacienda* and the land. How this Anglo would burn and destroy at night, and then during the day he would come and pretend to be the *hacendado's* friend. At night he would send out his rangers, his pack of, you know, bandits, to burn the barns and kill the workers of the *hacienda*, so nobody wanted to work for Mr. Francisco. And then during the day he would come and give Mr. Francisco whiskey, and have dances and let his daughter dance with the *Mejicanos*, the Spanish, to really prove his friendship. And he would express his sympathy for all Mr. Francisco's troubles and would offer to buy the grant for a good price in gold.

"But Mr. Francisco could not sell, you see, because he had promised his father on his knees by the bed that he would never sell it, never let it out of the family. That was traditional. But then after a while all his barns were burned and his cattle shot or stolen and nobody would work for him, and finally he thought he had to sell, for gold, and he gave in. Then the Anglo came to help him pack. There were lots of things and people, maybe 30 or 40 families to get packed, and the Anglo would ask casually, 'Which gate are you leaving by?' Because the grant was big, you know, 20 or 30 miles to get out. And the *hacendado* would say, 'Oh, by the south gate.' And they would never get off that land, none of those people, they would be caught and killed before they got off the land and buried beside the road, and that way the Anglo would get the deed to the *hacienda* and his gold back too. He told many other tales, that Anglo, we were five hours in that city park of Victoria, Texas. Well, I was the minister and I had the influence of the Bible and the Pentecostal type of thinking, and for a while it did bother me, all those things he said, but I got rid of it, or I thought I got rid of it, and I went on preaching here and there and holding campaigns."

After nearly three years as a pastor in Victoria, Reies was becoming noticed as a fiery and effective speaker and a dedicated but troublesome worker. He says that in 1950 in Isleta, he was offered his long-deferred graduation diploma from the Bible Institute, but turned it down. "I told them no, that a piece of paper wouldn't change the past, or the future either."

Brother Savage says that Reies did graduate from the Bible school, but that in 1950 his ministerial license and credentials were revoked, with "unorthodox attitude" given as the reason. "He started out trying to be a minister," Brother Savage says regretfully, "but he didn't last with us."

Reies says that he began instructing his flock to cease paying tithes, assuring them that the church was there to help the poor, not to take from them, and that he took a hammer and beat the collection plate flat before their eyes. A month later he was relieved of his ministry and asked to leave the church.

He set out on his own, preaching in tents, halls and storefront tabernacles, from Tennessee to California. On the road, there was much more to see, and much more to think about. In Stockton, California, there was the Farm Placement Service's pre-dawn shape-up. In front of the farm labor office on Skid Row every morning are thousands of men, black-, white-, but mostly brown-skinned, milling about, waiting. It was and is a slave market, worked on the "day haul" system, with workers required to show up for selection daily, hired on in the morning, laid off at night. Some are selected, some are not, the number needed depending on the crop. A few at least are always left over, often hundreds. Those selected are loaded into dilapidated buses and driven off to the fields; those not selected stand about, slip into the saloons, flop down in a vacant lot to peel the seal from a pint of cheap wine, or go home to the shack, the cup of coffee and the crawling, crying kids.

"I saw and heard so many things in those years that I was preaching from place to place that I can't remember them all, only the ugliness and hopelessness, and how a man could preach the word of God forever and never change a thing. I was in New Mexico, and the people there talked a lot about how the land had been taken away. Colorado was bad, and Texas was the worst of all. Another man, an Anglo, picked me and my wife and kids up when we were on the road and took us to his house. He said he didn't like preachers, they were hypocrites. He was a kind of good-doer, a kind of Baptist. His wife was a Methodist.

"He said that religion was all right, but that it wasn't enough, that I should study history and law and do more to really help my people. Well, I was getting a following and I had an idea. I wanted to create a community of justice and harmony, with our language and our customs. A place—well, a *pueblo*. Do you know what that means? Do you know all of what that means in Spanish?"

Born in feudal times out of the Latin word for people, its indigenous meaning is rooted deep in the communal memory of the Spanish peasant. Modern dictionaries say: town, village; people, race, nation; populace; common people. In practice it can mean either the village or its people, alternatively; or simultaneously, both in one breath. In the beginning, in the towns of feudal Spain, it also meant quite literally *los de abajo*, the ones below, since the fortress home of the lord was most often built on an eminence, with the huts and fields of the villagers clustered below.

As a result of the unbridgeable gulf between *castillo* and *pueblo*, between *los de arriba* and *los de abajo*, the *pueblo* tended to develop independently, constructing its own subculture, fostering folklore and cherishing memory, and ultimately producing an independent, integrated and eminently satisfying society. To be part of the *pueblo* was to be a part of an organic whole which could be seen by the eye, felt by the heart and encompassed by the mind.

"A *pueblo*, you see. Not just a place, but a place of people living in harmony, and our kind of place, our kind of harmony. I had read Plato's *Republic* and other things. I knew that others had tried it and failed. But we would not fail, I told my people. All we needed was determination and faith."

If ye have faith as a grain of mustard seed, ye shall say unto this mountain, Remove hence to yonder place; and it shall remove; and nothing shall be impossible unto you.

There were 17 families in all, and between them they got together enough money to buy 150 acres of the former multi-million-acre Peralta Land Grant in Arizona. It was desert land, worth about nine dollars an acre then, located south of Phoenix between Casa Grande and Eloy, and just north of the Papago Indian Reservation.

"We had permission from the State of Arizona," Reies says. "And we had trustees. I picked the wildest spot I could find so that we wouldn't trouble others and wouldn't be bothered ourselves."

They built a church, then dwellings, then a small store. The land was held and worked in common, but at first they had to do outside work for wages, driving out to the nearest field work, driving back at night. They called themselves the Heralds of Peace and their community, *Valle de la Paz*. The Valley of Peace was later described by Lois Ott, chief identification officer of the Pinal County Sheriff's office as "nothing but a gypsy camp over at Peter's Corner." At any rate, there was to be precious little peace at Peter's Corner.

"At first it went well," Reies says. "We built, we worked, we were happy. It really seemed as though we were building a new life of mercy and justice, a real Kingdom of God. But they didn't like us there, the Anglos up in Casa Grande and over in Toltec. I used to help people. Some boys got in trouble, and they were going to send them to jail for a long time, and I helped them, you know, to beat the court, and that was when the sheriff, Lawrence White, began to hate us.

"Teen-agers started coming around and wrecking things when we were off picking cotton, and one of our girls was raped. We started our own school. Then all of a sudden, to our astonishment the surrounding teachers objected and the school board got involved. We had permission, but still they didn't like it. That was when they began to burn our buildings down, and the FBI agent, Dan Pelton, and the sheriff wouldn't investigate."

That is how Reies describes it. There was no official recognition of any trouble at the Valley of Peace until March 18, 1957, when a Frank Shedd, Jr. reported that six wheels and tires had been stolen from two feed trailers at the Rodney De Lang ranch near Toltec. Officers Kinard and Davis of the Pinal County Sheriff's office at Casa Grande reported tracing the tires to *Valle de La Paz*, where they allegedly found two of the stolen tires already mounted on a truck owned by Reies Tijerina, Margarito Tijerina and Sevedeo Martínez. The three were arrested and the next day charged with grand theft. FBI agent Dan Pelton was called in when five U.S. Forestry Service hats and a Forestry Service purchase order book were found. The order book bore the stamp: Taos, New Mexico. A number of other articles were reportedly found, some in a dry wash nearby, some down at the bottom of a dry well, including two more of the missing tires and wheels, 11 canteens, three Coleman lanterns and five Forestry Service axes. That is how the sheriff's office describes it.

As for the court, it dismissed the charges of stealing tires and wheels for lack of evidence. However, in the process, it was discovered that Margarito had jumped the Indiana parole confining him to Texas. He was arrested and jailed and preparations were made to return him to Indiana authorities.

Eighteen days later Reies was charged with grand theft again, this time for the assorted hardware found in the dry well and elsewhere. On April 5, after a hearing, he was released on a thousand dollar bond.

"That was really the beginning of the end," he says. "You see, it was just like that Anglo told me, when they wanted to get the *Mejicano*, to get the law on him, they would take a horse, a nice horse, see, and put it in his corral at night, and then in the morning they would get the sheriff and come and say, Aha, he stole the horse, put him in jail. That is what happened, and when the judge threw the first case out of court, that was when they decided to get us out for good. By that time all that Rockefeller money was going into the Arizona City project, and land near us had gone up to $1,500 an acre. Almost all our buildings had been burned, and then that high-flying airplane crashed on our property, and because of that, one pregnant girl lost her child and an old woman went crazy."

If the supposition that their enemies would sacrifice an airplane as a tool of persecution indicates a degree of imbalance in the attitude of the Heralds of Peace, paranoia was not exclusive with them. In July of that year, every visitor to Tijerina's home and every letter received by him was carefully noted by officers of the FBI and the sheriff's office. In a letter he was to write seven years later, Bill Ballard of the Pinal County sheriff's office would warn Santa Fe District Attorney Alfonso Sánchez that "Subject Tijerina should be considered extremely dangerous and is known to be an escape artist."

On July 7, Reies and three others were charged with having attempted to break Margarito out of Pinal County jail. Sketches of the jail layout and hacksaw blades were found. When the attempt failed, Margarito was swiftly shipped back to Indiana for reimprisonment, and Reies and the other three were required to post bond of $5,000. In August, Reies appeared for jury trial, but during the noon recess he walked out of the Florence County courthouse and failed to return for the judgment.

That was it, the end of another beginning. The Valley of Peace remained little more than rubble and a few charred remains; its prophet was on the lam, to remain a fugitive for the next three years. So much for faith, as a grain of mustard seed.

But the mysterious makings of the messianic personality are not so quickly shed, a mother not so easily renounced. While he was hiding out in California that fall of 1957, Reies again felt the need to seek retreat and ask God for instruction.

"I left my warm bed into the cold weather because I wanted to pray, you know, in the open. I felt very sick about all the trouble in Arizona, and I wanted to ask God to show me the future of my life. I fell asleep, and I saw frozen horses and this old kingdom with old walls, you know, and these tall pines. The horses started melting and coming to life, and three angels came in my dream to my house to help me, and my wife got angry and she left me. And she did too, later, in Albuquerque.

"In the morning the sun woke me, and the dew had covered me all over, but I had that great dream. Only I gave it more of a spiritual interpretation then, because, you see, I was still clinging to my religious feelings. I thought the dream was of heaven, the kingdom of God and things like that. So I went secretly back to my friends in *Valle de la Paz*, and I told them, 'Well, what about New Mexico? I recall now that in 1945 somebody invited me to join a land grant question, something about the land.'

"So we got into our cars, seven of them, and we drove to New Mexico."

The Tierra Amarilla Grant 5

I N 1951, seven years before the arrival in northern New Mexico of *los barbudos* and their leader and 16 years before the raid on the Río Arriba County courthouse, a lean, blue-eyed cowboy named Bill Mundy rode up the timbered shoulder of Brazos Peak with an old friend, bear hunter Bill Dogget.

There was 10 inches of snow on the ground between the straight white trunks of the aspen and the dark conglomerate of spruce and ponderosa. Toward the top of the mountain they stopped and edged their horses to the icy lip of a rock shelf. They could see all the way across the valley, all the way north to Chama, and all the way south to where the Chama River met the Brazos, with the town and valley of Tierra Amarilla beyond. It was a lot of land. Much of it was for sale, and more of it could be counted on as sooner or later available, in one way or another.

"I decided right there on the spot," Bill Mundy says. "It was what I had wanted all my life."

He was born in 1917 in Hatch, New Mexico, way down in the southwestern corner of the state. His father was one of those hardy souls who had come west to New Mexico at the turn of the century, exchanging the hard life of the Texas dirt farmer for the even harder life of the desert dry land farmer and stockman, but for a reason. In Texas he had been a tenant. In New Mexico there was a chance to own the land that daily soaked up his sweat. From the beginning, ownership of land was a dream and a determination in the blood of the Mundy clan, passed on from father to son.

"He was up to his headstall in debt," Bill Mundy says of his father, "and had just scraped everything off and was getting ready to plant, when the Depression caught him with a $35,000 note and wiped him right out. It took us 23 years of sharecropping that farm, taking in other people's cattle and so forth, but we got it back. Twenty-three years, but finally it was ours, free and clear."

That was when the blue eyes had turned north, hungry for other land to be held free and clear. So Bill Mundy had come to Río Arriba, where he had heard there was land to be had, if you were willing to fight for it.

48

"Oh, I knew the place hadn't been worked right for 16 years and never fenced. I knew why the owners hadn't lived on it all that time, that they were just too damn scared to. I knew I had bought a fight. But I also knew that the only way I would ever get the spread I wanted was going to be through a freak deal like this one. So I took it, freak deal, fight and all."

The land that Bill Mundy arranged to buy in 1951 from an absentee landlord, Carl Brueselbach of Denver, was the last unfenced major holding in the valley of the upper Chama. The *Hispanos* of Tierra Amarilla had been grazing their sheep and cattle and gathering wood on the land for more than a hundred years. They considered it to be all that was left of their natural right, the *ejido* of the Tierra Amarilla Land Grant, the last remnant of their common inheritance. They had managed to keep it free through a combination of legal harassment, political coercion and outright violence for a century, but with Mundy's arrival the tide had finally and irrevocably turned against them, and the ancient tradition of custom and law that had created and sustained the *Merced de Tierra Amarilla*, in fact for only 16 years, in spirit for a century, was once and for all banished from the Chama valley. But its heirs were not to accept defeat so easily, and Bill Mundy, as the latest in a long line of living symbols of their disinheritance, was to suffer more than his share of their vengeance.

Merced means favor, present, gift. It also means mercy. It was the term used to describe the grants of land by the Spanish crown or its representatives to colonists in the New World, since such grants represented either gifts to the already notable and wealthy, or mercy for the impoverished and land-hungry.

By Spanish law and papal decree, all of the land in the Americas touched by Spanish sword, scepter and cross was held to be the exclusive property of the crown itself. At the time of Columbus' discovery of America, Ferdinand and Isabella were creating, through the government of Castile, an absolute patrimonial monarchy, freed from the scattered feudal rights of the medieval nobility and supported by the Church as divinely appointed. Columbus' first expedition was authorized and financed as a private venture of Queen Isabella, and the profits of the venture accrued to her and her heirs as sovereigns of Castile. Possession of the new lands was confirmed to the crown of Castile by the papal bull of 1493. From the outset, the Indies were neither Spanish nor colonies, strictly speaking, but were considered the direct and exclusive possession of the crown. The king was the absolute proprietor and sole political head of his American dominions, and it was as such that he bestowed grants of land upon individuals or groups of his choice. By virtue of his royal, divine and exclusive dominion, he could grant this land conditionally, under statute or by proclamation, as the royal interest moved him.

However, early in the development of the Spanish colonial policy, three types of land grant became standard: the *sitio*, the proprietary grant, and the *pueblo* or community grant. Tens of thousands of such grants were made during the four centuries of Spanish domination in the West Indies, Central America, South America and in the southern portions of North America, including present day Florida, Louisiana, Texas, New Mexico, Colorado, Nevada and California.

In colonial New Mexico in particular, the nature of the grants tended to change with the passing of time and the gradual increase in population.

Originally, the *sitio* was the predominant type of grant, given by the king to an individual strictly for personal exploitation. Virtually all of the initial exploration, conquest and early settlement of Spanish America was the result of individual enterprise, under commission of the crown. As inducement to investment of time and money, the crown rewarded individual entrepreneurs with land as well as political title and power. The *sitio* was usually a vast tract suitable for establishment of a large plantation or livestock ranch, given to a notable personage of privileged name and lineage, usually as a reward for service to the crown.

In later years *sitios* were sometimes sold outright by the crown to the highest bidder. In South America, the *sitio* grants have tended to remain intact in the hands of individual families down to the present day. But in New Mexico, due to the general low quality of the land and the fluctuating fortunes of the large landowners in the last years of Spanish and Mexican sovereignty, the large *sitios* tended to fall into disuse and neglect, allowing increasing numbers of squatters to move in and establish small farms and villages, which, once established, were difficult to dislodge, and quickly became integral to the local economies.

The second most frequent type of land grant was the proprietary grant, also made to an individual, sometimes as reward for special service to the crown, but often only in exchange for the proprietor's promise to further the task of colonization. This type of grant was often made to help deepen the zone of settlement and was prevalant in such frontier buffer zones as New Mexico.

In exchange for formal proprietorship and other economic and political advantages, the grantee was required to attract settlers, build a village community, erect a church, secure a priest, put in an irrigation system and provide military protection. This type of grant tended to become, by degrees, more and more of a rural village community, with the grantee often compelled by force of both legal and social custom to relinquish reasonable shares of his property and privilege to the other inhabitants.

Thus it was that in the free and open frontier society of colonial New Mexico, the land granted by the crown of Spain and later by the government of Mexico often tended to gravitate to the people, regardless of how it was originally granted.

The third type of grant, the *pueblo* or community grant, was given directly to a community of petitioners. More prevalent in northern New Mexico than in most of the other colonies, it was made to a petitioning group of at least 10 village families for the purpose of establishing a rural farming community, often at the edge of Indian country. When the grant was made, the village site was selected, centering on a central plaza. The families drew lots for their house sites and then set about constructing an irrigation system, building a church and dividing the arable land among the families. Around the village site and the irrigated plots stretched the *ejido*, or common lands.

Ejido is from the Latin *exitus*, "outside," and means common and unalienable land most often found outside of or on the edge of a village or town. In feudal Spain, it was the custom for the lord to grant a plot of land for the exclusive use of the villagers. It could be neither sold nor exploited by any one individual, being granted to all by the will and through the power of the one. The lord's motive was often less than altruistic, his usual objective being to establish a central place for the gathering of the crops and the separating out of his share, sometimes as high as 60 percent.

But in time the *ejido* gained broader use. When it was not being used for the sorting of crops or as a communal threshing plot, it was grazed by the sheep, goats and cattle of the town. As the village grew, the *ejido* was often gradually encompassed and became a kind of public park and place for community meetings, much like the English village green or common. As times changed and the power of the feudal lords diminished, the people of the villages came to think of the *ejido* as theirs, unalienably and forever, and the customs and laws of land usage tended to support them through several centuries, culminating in a decree to that effect by Charles IV in 1798.

The *ejido* of the community land grant in colonial New Mexico was by Spanish law and custom available to all members of the *pueblo* for grazing, hunting and the gathering of firewood and timber. Since the outer perimeter of such a frontier grant was often vague and indefinite, being determined only by geographical barriers and the fluctuating limits of the Indian threat, the *ejido* was usually considered to consist of all that land surrounding the village and not in use by individuals as house or family garden plots.

On April 25, 1832, José Manuel Martínez, "together with eight male children and others who may voluntarily desire to accompany him," petitioned the Constitutional Corporation of Abiquiu for a tract of land, "for cultivation and pasturage, situated on the banks of the Chama River, and known as Tierra Amarilla . . ."

It happened that the Mexican Republic had been declared in 1821, and certain reforms had been instituted, so that Manuel Martínez and the other families did not petition an *alcalde* responsible to the crown of Spain, but petitioned an *alcalde* and town council elected according to Mexico's new constitution. But such "democratic" reforms had little real effect on the conduct of land affairs in New Mexico. The Mexican constitution had contented itself with proclaiming "equal rights" for all, Indians as well as Spaniards. In the matter of land ownership, it favored continued observance of the laws of Spain "to the extent that they are not contrary to the particular conditions of the country."

Following a three-month exchange of petitions and letters, the Mexican Territorial Deputation in Santa Fe approved the Tierra Amarilla Grant and directed the constitutional justice of Abiquiu to "proceed to make said grant, delivering to each one of those who may unite with the petitioners a certain number of *varas*—executing them to the grant therefore."

It was further directed, "that the pastures, watering places and roads shall be free, according to the customs prevailing in all settlements."

Thus it was that the Tierra Amarilla Land Grant was established after Spanish law and custom, and under the Mexican constitution which recognized that tradition, as an essentially communal grant, complete with *ejido*, land common to all, unalienable and perpetual. The *ejido* existed independently of any concept of private property. It could be neither sold nor exploited by any individual, being the property of all, living, dead and yet to be born. It became part of the communal continuity implied in the word *pueblo:* people, village, land—past, present and future.

However, with the final collapse of the feudal system and the gradual disintegration of the national monarchies, the merchants and speculators of the growing cities began to cast hungry eyes upon the common lands. Since then, there have been continual and unrelenting efforts by individuals and governments to alienate and make private property of the *ejidos,* both in Spain and her colonies, and, in fact, throughout the world, wherever the concepts of private and communal property, and of parochial and absolutist government came into inevitable conflict.

By the beginning of the 19th century, most municipal, provincial and national governments had begun to allow the *ejidos* to be broken up and made off with piecemeal. In Mexico, *ejidos* were reestablished only recently, after several revolutions, through expropriation and by governmental decree. In modern Spain, *ejidos* have remained intact mostly in the small villages in the provinces of Navarre (where they are still called *exidos*) and Catalonia, both provinces noted for their stubbornly individual and often separatist tendencies.

One early dispute involving the *ejido* system in Spain occured in the town of Deva, where certain influential individuals were allowed to plant trees on the village common, and thereafter sought to exclude other villagers from the *ejido*, claiming that since the trees were private property, all the land covered by them was private, and their shade was private and exclusive also.

Manuel Martínez and his fellow pioneers could never have dreamed that their descendants would one day suffer a similar prohibition against enjoying even the shadow of their common inheritance. The entire valley of Tierra Amarilla was thick with virgin timber in 1832, the shade was plentiful as far as the eye could see and all the land north of the Sierra Colorado was theirs, peopled only by roving bands of Navajo, Apache and Ute.

They divided up the best bottomland along Nutrias Creek and allocated family plots, but repeated Indian raids prevented them from immediately setting up their *placita* and building a church. The town of Las Nutrias, later to be called Tierra Amarilla, was not permanently established until the late 1850s. But by the 1840s there were a number of small sheep ranches in the canyons at the north end of the valley and some 50 families on the grant, including the families of Manuel Martínez and his son, Francisco.

And then, beginning in the late 1840s, the Yankees came, bringing with them a different attitude toward property, a new system of law adapted to that attitude, a vigor and determination that bordered on the ruthless and a hunger for land that led inevitably to corruption and outright lawlessness.

Long before the military occupation, Yankee traders had been working their way into New Mexico from the north. Fur trappers like Kit Carson had been harvesting the beaver-rich streams of the Sangre de Cristo mountains for a decade, occasionally dropping down into the little village of Fernando de Taos for supplies and relaxation. In addition, a few astute outlanders had managed to settle by ingratiating themselves with the native elite or *ricos*. But they were few and barely tolerated. In 1846, when General Stephen W. Kearny marched into New Mexico on behalf of the United States, there were around 70,000 Spanish-speaking people in the province, but only a few hundred "foreigners."

On August 15, Kearny stood in the plaza of Las Vegas and addressed the populace through an interpreter, saying, "We come among you for your benefit, not for your injury." Four days later he stood in the plaza in Santa Fe and added: "We come as friends, to better your condition. I am your governor. Henceforth, look to me for protection."

Eighteen months later, representatives of the United States met with representatives of an abjectly beaten Mexican Republic in the city of Guadalupe Hidalgo in Mexico to draw up a treaty ending a war described at the time by army Lieutenant U. S. Grant as "unholy," and years later by Woodrow Wilson as "predatory." As terms for peace, Mexico was required to accept the loss of Texas in return for $15 million and to hand over California and the territory which later included the states of Utah, Nevada, and most of New Mexico and Arizona. The remainder of New Mexico and Arizona would be annexed by the United States through purchase under the Gadsden Treaty of 1853.

The Treaty of Guadalupe Hidalgo, signed on February 2, 1848, has been called a "bonus freedom paper." Actually, it is merely consistent with that traditional sanction of the law of nations reflected some years later in an opinion written by Chief Justice Marshall of the United States Supreme Court that, " . . . it is very unusual, even in cases of conquest, for the conquerer to do more than to displace the sovereign and assume dominion over the country. The people change their allegiance, [but] their relations to each other and their rights of property remain undisturbed."

The treaty guaranteed the civil rights and property of Mexican citizens within the ceded territories and gave them the right either to become United States citizens or to return to Mexico, their property to remain inviolate in either case. Concerning property, the key paragraph of Article VIII reads:

> "In the said territories, property of every kind, now belonging to Mexicans not established there, shall be inviolably respected. The present owners, the heirs of these, and all Mexicans who may hereinafter acquire said property by contract shall enjoy with respect to it guarantees equally ample as if the same belonged to citizens of the United States."

High-sounding promises, but keeping them was not to be so simple. Military occupation with its usual excesses lasted for nearly five years. On March 3, 1851, a territorial government was installed, to last for 62 years. The territorial governor and other high officials were appointed by the President of the United States, and every act of the territorial legislature was subject to review by the governor, who had veto power and used it frequently. Legislation that got past the governor had to be approved by the United States Congress, a restriction which was not applied to other territorial assemblies, such as those in Colorado and Wyoming. But then, neither of those territories contained such a vast majority of *Hispanos*.

Harper's Weekly summed up the contentions (and the fears) of those who opposed New Mexico's admission to the Union, openly admitting obligation for their information to "two gentlemen resident in the Territory, with the best opportunities of knowing what they say":

> "Of the present population, which is variously estimated, and at the last census was 111,000, nine-tenths are Mexicans, Indians, "greasers" and other non-English speaking people. About one-tenth part of the population speak the English language. The nine-tenths are under the strictest Roman Catholic supervision. It is virtually an ignorant foreign community under the influence of the Roman Church, a community almost without the characteristic and indispensable qualities of an American State . . ."

For the six decades of territorial government, the English-speaking one-tenth of the population ruled New Mexico virtually unopposed. With the cooperation of the fast-weakening former Mexican elite, the Anglo-Americans managed to control the vote so well that only once in 60 years was the *Hispano* majority able to elect a territorial delegate to Congress. Allergic to taxes and sending their own children out of the territory to school, the *ricos* and Anglos neglected to provide schools of any sort outside the few church schools. As a consequence, New Mexico had no public school system of even minimal standards until well after statehood was granted in 1912.

But territorial government offered its greatest advantages to the ruling minority in the matter of land acquisition, the primary preoccupation of the time. As someone soon said, "Captains of Industry are at best second lieutenants in New Mexico; the land's the thing!"

At the time of the occupation virtually all of the arable land in New Mexico was in *Hispano* hands, vast tracts belonging to the *ricos*, the rest occupied by communities of common sheep herders and irrigation farmers. Although their property had been ostensibly guaranteed by the Treaty of Guadalupe Hidalgo, the creating of machinery for confirmation of ownership under the laws of the United States had been left up to the U.S. Congress. For some eight years Congress did virtually nothing, and during that time some of the most blatant land steals were accomplished, often by force of arms. In the Mesilla valley more than 200 native families fled to Mexico after receiving abuse and threats of violence at the hands of Anglo settlers who set themselves up near the natives' farmhouses, then proceeded to claim all the adjacent land as theirs.

Finally, in 1854, Congress created the office of surveyor-general under the Secretary of the Interior. The first appointee to the office, William Pelham, was charged with surveying the territory and establishing the basis for a system of orderly ownership and transference of land titles. He devoted himself to the first task with professional vigor and against considerable odds. Not only did he have to deal with a suspicious and hostile *Hispano* population, but he risked losing his survey parties to Indian arrows. He early became aware of the fact that most of the population lived on narrow strips of irrigated land along some river or stream, which they held by right of possession, handed down from father to son. This strip pattern of land ownership was not compatible with the rectangular mode of United States surveys. In addition, it was the custom of the people to live around a community plaza for protection against Indian attack, and not often on the land they worked. United States land laws called for actual residence upon the land as a requirement for the confirmation of possessory rights. Finally, there was no allowance at all in the national land laws for recognition of the communally held pasture and woodlands back of the irrigated areas—the *ejidos*.

Pelham let these problems slide and concentrated on the task of establishing a general survey. However, he was supposed to report on all private land claims, every one of which, no matter how large or small, had to be reviewed and either rejected or confirmed by Congress. This included all the Spanish and Mexican land grants. During his six-year term of office he actually surveyed the exterior boundaries of very few of the grants, but he did hear testimony of ownership and recommended confirmation of many, including the Maxwell Grant, soon to be the largest single piece of privately owned real estate in the history of the United States, and the 595,515-acre Tierra Amarilla Grant.

To the isolated villagers of Río Arriba, the changeover from Mexican to United States sovereignty had been scarcely noticeable at first. It is true that Yankees and *Tejanos* began to appear in larger numbers, but almost all of them settled in the south and east of the territory at first. Those who came into the far north most often came to trade or freight goods along that extension of the Santa Fe trail that passed up along the Chama on its way through Colorado and on to California. The new things the freighters brought were welcome, and the strange values they carried with them were diverting and even instructive. There had been some bad droughts and the old markets for agricultural products to the south had been cut off abruptly by Mexico's surrender of the territory to the Yankees. The people of the north had turned to stock raising along with those of the south, and newly opened markets for mutton and beef in the eastern United States were welcome and necessary.

Probably none of the native farmers and stockmen living along the upper Chama were aware that as early as 1848, the year of the Guadalupe treaty, Manuel Martínez's son Sixto had signed all his "right and title" to land in New Mexico over to his brother Francisco before leaving for California. Certainly few of them were aware that six years later Francisco Martínez had, in petitioning the U.S. Congress through Surveyor-General Pelman for confirmation of the Tierra Amarilla Grant to himself in the name of his father, taken the first step toward divesting them of much of the land upon which they had built their houses and cultivated their crops, and all of that *ejido* which they considered their common property.

Not even as late as 1866, when a charming foreigner named Thomas B. Catron came to live briefly among them, did they fully realize what was happening. They obligingly helped him learn their language and sent him on his way to the territorial legislature, unaware that in a few short years he would not only own all their land, but that, along with several other equally astute gentlemen, would to all intent and purposes also own them, lock, stock and barrel.

It was after the Civil War, celebrated only by brief and minor action in New Mexico, that the first real flood of land-hungry Yankees began to arrive, led by a breed of enterprising, shrewd and resourceful men, many with legal training and all with political acumen.

The Sergeant brothers settled on the Chama River shortly after the war, where one of their sisters joined them. Among her sons was Tom Burns, knows as T. D., an Irishman of enough charm to court and marry a daughter of the *rico* Gallegos family of Abiquiu. Stephen Benton Elkins arrived in 1863, was admitted to the New Mexico Bar a year later, learned the Spanish language and was elected to the territorial legislature in 1866. In that same year he returned to the east to get his former University of Missouri classmate, Thomas Benton Catron. As a former Confederate officer, Catron had been proscribed from practicing law in Missouri and willingly joined Elkins in the drive across the plains to the promising prospects of territorial New Mexico. These men, along with others and with the cooperation of various surveyors-general and other federally appointed officials, were to be known, hated, admired and envied for 50 years as the Land Grant (or Santa Fe) Ring, and to the extent that their various families remain active, are so regarded to this day.

The prime plums of the early 1870s were the larger land grants, and life in the territory quickly became centered around traffic in these grants. The basic method of relieving the native owners of their property was simple enough. Although the process of guaranteeing title was not complicated in theory, it could be difficult in practice. The surveyor-general could be recalcitrant in passing on his recommendation to Congress, and Congress was often dilatory in rendering a final decision, unless, of course, someone representing the claimant had friends in that august body. If it was sometimes necessary to exaggerate the complexity of the confirmation process, it was not difficult to assure the claimants, few of whom even spoke English, that one who knew the ropes in Santa Fe and Washington could best guide the claim through the intricacies involved.

The natives, *pobres* and *ricos* alike, were used to such reciprocal practices. And besides, what could they do when they knew neither the language nor the laws suddenly in dominion over their property? They had an old saying, *En pais de los ciegos, El Tuerto es rey;* In the land of the blind, One Eye is king.

When it was explained to them that in the absence of cash, which was extremely short at the time, the Yankee lawyers would accept their fees in land—and as it became apparent that by the time the process was finished the fees for such services could be high indeed, sometimes as much as half the land confirmed—they had no choice but to shrug again. *Mejor tener medio de algo que todo de nada;* Better to have half of something than all of nothing.

In addition to lawyer's fees, there were now real estate taxes, of which there had been little if any under the former governments. More than one grant owner or community of heirs lost half the grant to attorney's fees in the process of getting the grant confirmed, only to lose the rest to taxes, the land then going to the highest bidder for as little as $1.25 per choice acre. The unfortunate fact was that the wording of the old Spanish and Mexican grant documents was often vague and the descriptions loosely worded, leaving plenty of room for an ingenious man to interpret them to his advantage, especially if he had influence in the territorial courts and with the surveyor-general.

After Pelham, two Civil War appointees briefly held the office of surveyor-general, and then, in 1869, Dr. T. Rush Spencer took charge of the office. Spencer made very few surveys during his three years of office, but he made a lot of friends among the Republicans in political power in the territory. In 1871, Spencer was visited in Santa Fe by William Blackmore, one of a number of British land speculators who came to New Mexico in the 1870s, representing large amounts of Dutch and British capital. Through the good offices of Spencer, it was arranged for Blackmore to make a buying tour of the territory. In Taos, Blackmore was approached by a Captain Simpson, who had married a daughter of Don Seldón Valdez, claimant of the 30-mile-wide, 90-mile-long Los Conejos Grant in southern Colorado. A tentative arrangement was made, without consulting the 3,000 or so *Hispano* settlers living on the grant at the time. Blackmore had dealings with a number of other men, and by the time he returned to Santa Fe, he had made arrangements to purchase 760,000 acres on the Cebolla, Lucero and Mora Grants, and had also dickered for the purchase of land on some 12 other land grants, including the Tierra Amarilla Grant, for a total of over two million acres.

After further discussions, he and Surveyor-General Spencer bade one another farewell, and Blackmore headed back to Washington where he spent several days consulting with Senate and House members of various public lands committees "relative to pending land grant legislation." Blackmore had been in the United States less than eight months when he sailed for London on December 13, but he left as the principal owner-to-be of 500,000 acres of the Los Luceros Grant, 138,000 acres of the Mora Grant and 120,000 acres, or approximately half, of the Cebolla Grant.

Consideration of the last-named grant was hurried through by Spencer with unprecedented dispatch and recommended to Congress for confirmation early the following year. The attorney for the grant claimants was Thomas B. Catron, with whom Spencer had secured a fifth interest in the Mora Grant two years previously, in company with Stephen B. Elkins and others. That same year Spencer had been an official of the Maxwell Land Grant and Railroad Company, along with Lucien B. Maxwell, Catron, Elkins, William A. Pile, territorial governor, and others. Elkins had been appointed United States district attorney in 1868, and in 1871, the year of Blackmore's visit, had been elected president of the First National Bank of Santa Fe, succeeding Lucien Maxwell. Catron had been appointed district attorney two years before Elkins, who was appointed attorney general a year afterwards, and was elected to the bank board the same day his old Missouri schoolmate became bank president.

James K. Proudfit was appointed surveyor-general on September 30, 1872. Three weeks after he took office, the Consolidated Land, Cattle Raising and Wool Growing Company, of which he was a partner along with Stephen Elkins, Thomas Catron and others, was incorporated. He openly propagandized for the cattle industry and strove to secure increased appropriations from Congress to accommodate the industry's needs for surveys. Most of his surveys were in the northeast part of the territory and the Pecos valley, all strictly cattle country.

By far the most audacious of the surveyors-general was Henry M. Atkinson, who took office in 1876. In one typical use of his office for the benefit of himself and his friends, he contracted with John T. Elkins, brother of Stephen B., and R. T. Marmon for the survey of the Maxwell Grant in 1878. Not only did Stephen B. have a major interest in the grant, not only was he bondsman for the surveyors as well, not only did the surveyors take only 21 days for a job that should have taken at least two months, but they surveyed the grant at nearly twice its legal size, said survey being promptly approved by Atkinson.

Atkinson was instrumental in securing final confirmation of the Tierra Amarilla Grant to Thomas B. Catron. By the time Atkinson became officially concerned, the problem was ostensibly one of determining the final boundaries of the grant. But a more basic issue was involved, going back to the original petition of Francisco Martínez for confirmation and patenting of the entire grant in his name alone, as his private property.

All of the surveyors-general found themselves faced with an annoying variety and number of claimants to the land of most grants. In many cases, especially those involving proprietory and community grants, there was also the frustrating issue of the *ejidos*. The expedient resorted to in many cases was a simple one: the property was arbitrarily converted to private property by decision of the surveyor-general, leaving it then free to be converted to its often predestined ownership.

In 1856, after hearing testimony from four men that Manuel Martínez and his son Francisco had lived on the TA Grant "off and on" for the 22 years since 1832, ·Surveyor-general Pelham had written to Congress that ". . . the grant made to Manual Martínez, of which Francisco Martínez is the present claimant, is deemed by this office to be a good and valid grant."

No mention was made of the other settlers who had accompanied Manuel Martínez north into *Apachería*, and whose descendants were then living on the grant. Nor was there any discussion of the problem of the *ejido*, despite the fact that in outlining the history of the grant, Pelham had quoted the entire wording of the original grant document, including this explicit proviso:

"That the pastures, watering places and roads, shall be free, according to the customs prevailing in all settlements."

On June 21, 1860, Congress confirmed ownership of the grant to Francisco Martínez as son of Manuel Martínez, and authorized a survey to be made and a patent to be issued. Almost immediately, Francisco Martínez began to make conveyances of tracts within the grant, transferring it in bits and pieces to other hands. At first conveyances merely confirmed resident settlers in their individual holdings of house and garden plots and specified the traditional *ejido* rights of each allotee, including, "range, water, firewood, watering places and free and open roads without prejudice to third parties nor to allottees, as in all established grant settlements." No doubt Martínez exacted a charge for this service, but at least he made an initial attempt to see that his fellow heirs were protected.

Then suddenly he began to leave *ejido* rights out of his conveyances, and then to eliminate all references to any ownership of any kind other than that of himself and his family. Simultaneously with this development, he began to make conveyances to wealthy residents in Santa Fe, most of them Anglo-Americans. In 1864, a year after confirmation of the grant to Francisco, another Martínez brother, Julián, together with his wife Refugia, signed over to Frederick Muller of Santa Fe, "the undivided ⅛ of the tract known as the Tierra Amarilla Grant." The assumption apparently was that since Manuel Martínez had eight sons, ownership of the grant was held equally among them. Again, the other settlers were ignored, and there was no mention of *ejido*.

There is no way of knowing who had the original idea to simplify things by converting the entire grant to the Martínez family, but the odds are that it was the inspiration of one of two men, either Tom Burns or Tom Catron.

Around 1866, T. D. Burns sent to Santa Fe for copies of the grant documents and began to seek conveyances from Martínez heirs, working together with the aforementioned Frederick Muller and Elias Brevoort of Santa Fe. But a far more astute practitioner was soon to enter the picture and put Burns and his cohorts into the shade.

In 1874, Francisco Martínez died.

In July 1876, Surveyor-General Atkinson contracted for a survey with his old friends and associates Sawyer and McBroom, who put the grant at 594,515.15 acres, 80,000 of which lay in Archuleta County, Colorado.

In September of that year, Thomas B. Catron negotiated for a conveyance from María Guadalupe Martínez, whose father had been a brother of Francisco Martínez. Her uncle, the renowned New Mexican patriot-priest Padre Martínez of Taos, attempted to dissuade her, but the advice of her husband, Tomás Lucero, prevailed, and Catron received the first of 88 key conveyances eventually acquired from Martínez heirs.

Five years later he received the most important conveyance of all. A story of long standing among the *Hispanos* of Río Arriba has it that Paz Martínez, son of the elderly widow of Francisco, had killed an Apache and had been jailed in Tierra Amarilla. On advice from T. D.

Burns, Mrs. Martínez had gone to Santa Fe to talk with District Attorney Tom Catron, who had prevailed upon her to sign some papers. Before the old lady had returned to Tierra Amarilla, her son was free.

There was a Martínez son named Paz. Conveyance of his rights to Catron was made in 1881, along with those of his widowed mother and nine brothers and sisters, putting Tom Catron within a legal hairsbreadth of final and complete control of the grant.

Two days later, the grant was patented by authorization of President Rutherford B. Hayes in the name of Francisco Martínez, "his heirs and assigns."

Shortly thereafter, Catron initiated a quiet title suit against "all unknown heirs of Manuel Martínez, Eusebia Martínez, Sixto Martínez and all other persons claiming interest in the Tierra Amarilla Grant."

In that same year, despite the fact that the grant was not yet legally his, Catron conveyed to the Denver and Rio Grande Railroad Company a right-of-way across the northern tip of the grant and sold 14 house lots in Chama to railroad employes. The following year, he secured $200,000 worth of mortgage bonds against the grant. He next formed the Southwestern Lumber and Railway Company in conjunction with his many friends and associates in the territory, secured a loan and in 1897 began logging.

By 1901, when all adverse claims on the grant had been decided in Catron's favor, the upper Chama valley had become treeless grassland and Thomas Benton Catron had become the largest single landowner in New Mexico and a very rich man.

Not even Congress could ignore the land abuses in New Mexico forever, and irregularities under Atkinson brought repercussions while he was still in office. Among other things, it was discovered that many of his surveys were inaccurate, having been accomplished by such exotic methods as tying a red rag to a wagon wheel and counting the number of revolutions. In many instances resurvey revealed that no original survey had been made at all.

However, it wasn't until the Democratic administration of Grover Cleveland came to power in 1885, a year after Atkinson left office, that large-scale investigation of fraudulent practices began.

In that same year, Cleveland appointed George W. Julian surveyor-general of New Mexico. Seventy years old at the time, Julian threw himself into his duties with the zeal of a crusader, and was promptly dubbed "Old Malaria" by the Republican press of the territory. One of the few surveyors-general who could not be bought at any price, he was a passionate exponent of the homestead principle and particularly concerned that the public domain was being harvested at an alarming rate by a few men who were amassing enormous landed estates through fraudulent enlargement of land grants.

One such case was that of the San Joaquín de Chama Grant, which had been bought by the Englishman Blackmore, sold to the Río Arriba

Land and Cattle Company and approved by Atkinson at 400,000 acres, almost 300 times its originally granted size.

The Maxwell Grant had been similarly enlarged, and Julian wasted no time in pointing out that it had been "limited by the law under which it was made to about 96,000 acres," half the size for which it had been surveyed and patented in 1879. The Maxwell land grab was, he wrote, "an inexcusable and shameful surrender to the rapacity of monopolists of 1,662,764 acres of public domain, on which hundreds of poor men had settled in good faith and made valuable improvements." Going after the Santa Fe Ring, he said, "They have hovered over the territory like a pestilence. To a fearful extent they have dominated governors, judges, district attorneys, legislatures, surveyors-general—they have confounded political distinctions and subordinated everything to the greed for land."

However, as it turned out, the doughty Julian was able to actually change very little. Most of the damage had already been done, and the presence in the territory of one or two honest men was too little and too late. Between 1891 and 1894, the U.S. land commissioner's investigators filed 641 criminal cases involving land fraud. Only 15 received a jury verdict of guilty. In 82 cases the U.S. marshal was either unable or unwilling to locate the defendants. Virtually all of the jurors were native *Hispanos*, reluctant to return a verdict of guilty, sometimes out of instinctive sympathy for anyone accused of a crime, sometimes out of fear of reprisal, often because they had been bribed. Only one member of the Santa Fe Ring was indicted. Max Frost was adjutant general of New Mexico and had held the office of registrar at the Santa Fe Land Office through most of Atkinson's term as surveyor-general. His business activities included mining interests, connection with four newspapers and involvement in several cattle companies along with Atkinson, McBroom, Catron, Elkins and others. In 1880 Atkinson had let a contract to Frost to conduct a survey, although he was not a qualified surveyor and in fact had such bad eyesight that he later went stone-blind.

Frost was indicted by the grand jury for official misconduct in receiving a bribe, along with 14 additional charges, including subornation of perjury and conspiracy. Tried in 1887, he was convicted by a jury of 11 *Hispanos* and one Anglo, but appealed and was granted a retrial. In August of the next year, he was acquitted by an all-*Hispano* jury, immediately after which a series of other cases against him were dismissed. Five more cases against him were dismissed the following day when it was discovered that the official files had disappeared from the office of the court clerk.

The territory's leading newspaper, *The New Mexican*, hailed the clearing of Frost's name as a triumph of justice, which was not surprising considering that he was the newspaper's president, manager and editor. Thus ended the Santa Fe Ring's darkest hour.

Surveyor-General Julian's efforts did lead to reduction of the San

Joaquín de Chama Grant to a more reasonable size, but the Maxwell Grant was never carved back to legal proportions, and eventually it passed into the hands of an Oklahoma oil magnate, who passed it on to the Boy Scouts of America, making that organization one of New Mexico's largest landowners today.

At the time of the Treaty of Guadalupe Hidalgo, the estimated area of Spanish and Mexican grants within the United States had been 24,000 square miles or something over 15 million acres, equal in extent to the land surface of four New England states: Rhode Island, Connecticut, New Hampshire and Vermont. (This is conservative; some authoritative estimates are as high as 35 million acres.) During the 14 years between 1854 and 1870, the surveyors-general submitted 222 land grant claims to Congress. Congress confirmed 45, 22 of which were finally patented for a total of about five million acres.

In 1870 Congress suddenly changed its policy and declined to act on New Mexico land grant claims, except for a few isolated cases. In 1890 Congress moved to take the impossible burden of adjudicating private land claims from the shoulders of the surveyor-general, creating the Court of Private Land Claims.

The court first met at Denver in 1891, adjudicating land claims and recommending them to Congress until 1904, when it closed for good, having validated only about two million acres of grant claims out of a total of nearly 35 million submitted.

Between Congressional patenting of grants recommended by surveyors-general and grants validated by the Court of Private Land Claims, a total of 6,715,880 acres was confirmed—less than half of the original 15 million.

By 1910, when the court closed, over 70 percent of the Spanish and Mexican grants in the United States, among them the Tierra Amarilla Grant, had been lost to their original owners.

In 1912, Thomas Catron sold a large part of the north end of the Tierra Amarilla Grant to the Arlington Land Company for sale to cattlemen, and the first fencing began. Only then did the natives of the valley really begin to realize what was happening. Only then did they wake up and find One Eye triumphant and themselves fenced off and increasingly alone in the Land of the Blind.

In that same year, which was also the first year of statehood, various descendants of the original Tierra Amarilla settlers began to seek redress in the courts. At first it seemed they might have reason for hope. Antonio Joseph, territorial delegate, had filed a memorial with the Department of the Interior on behalf of "a large number of persons who represent themselves to be descendants of those who originally went upon said grant with Martínez and who complain that they are being deprived of their rights to free pasturage, to wood and watering places by the present grant owners."

Surveyor General Julian had also written to the Secretary of the Interior, noting that during the original negotiations in 1832, Manuel Martínez, already a wealthy man at the time, had objected to the *ejido* provisions and had asked that the land be "reduced to private property" in his name, but that he had been flatly refused by the Mexican Territorial Deputation, which had explicitly declared *ejido* rights as a condition of the grant.

Julian pointed out that the four witnesses appearing on behalf of Martínez before Pelham in 1856 "were not questioned severally, but jointly, the questions being leading," that they could none of them so much as write his name, that they were not cross-examined and that their statements confirming Martínez ownership bore "the evident marks of machine testimony." He further reminded the Secretary that members of the Congressional committee which had confirmed the grant in a parcel with thirteen others had admitted that they had "no time to scrutinize the evidence and the applications made by the surveyor-general of the Spanish and Mexican laws and usages to each of them in detail." He had written further that, "the people of New Mexico are not at all pleased to be compelled by law to submit their rights of title to one man, whose fitness for surveying is not supposed to qualify him particularly for discharging the duties of a judge . . ."

In conclusion, he had recommended the institution of a suit to set aside the Martínez patent—the basis for Catron's claim to ownership—as "clearly fraudulent."

Julian's recommendation was declined by the Secretary of the Interior on February 21, 1881. The Secretary cited the U.S. Supreme Court's two previous refusals to declare either the Sangre de Cristo or the Maxwell Grant fraudulent. "It is unimportant," he wrote, "whether the 'pastures, woods and watering places were left free and common to all.' " Congress' confirmation "being absolute and unconditional, we must regard it as effectual and operative for the entire tract."

In regard to the memorial filed by Territorial Delegate Joseph, the Secretary reminded claimants of the language of the 1881 patent, which seemed to conditionally leave the door open through the lower courts: ". . . these Patents shall only be construed as a Quit Claim or relinquishment on the part of the United States and shall not effect the adverse rights of any other person or persons whomsoever."

"These are matters with which this Department cannot deal," the Secretary concluded. "But said parties must obtain redress, if entitled to any, from the Courts."

"I was in and out of court seems like half the time those first few years," says Bill Mundy. "Adverse possession, every other thing you can think of. Payne versus Archuleta, Mundy versus Martínez . . . they're all on file down there at the courthouse, if you want to go see. These people could have had a good case on adverse possession, some of them, but they didn't act fast enough and weren't smart enough, or their lawyers weren't."

"Cost us a lot of money, and we didn't have it to throw around in those days. I had a note on this place and $20,000 payment to make every year for four years. And the place wasn't even fenced, hadn't been worked for 16 years. The owners had been scared off. The people were just using it, grazing it, cutting wood. It had been out of control all that time."

Living alone in a tent the first year, while his wife taught school in nearby Chama, he discovered that a large lower pasture had, in lying fallow for 16 years, become rich in nitrogen. He planted wheat and got a phenomenally good crop, enough to meet his first payment and buy a trailer for himself and his wife to live in.

"But the next year this land grant stuff started, and the trouble, and it was in and out of court and so on, and I didn't make it with the whole wheat crop and had to get an abeyance. Then the third year I had more trouble."

In 1951 several haystacks and two barns had burned in Río Arriba. In 1952, more haystacks, all belonging to large landowners, had burned. In 1953, a good deal of fence, including Mundy's, was cut.

"It wasn't just cutting here and there to let their sheep through. That you just figure is like a tree falling across your wire. Kinda gets your back up, but you have to catch them at it to get anything done. But in the winter of '53 they took a half a mile out on me, cutting every few yards. After that I began to waste more time riding shotgun on my property than I did in court. Then Tijerina and his gang showed up, and things really began to get hot."

The Abiquiu Corporation 6

BACK in 1925, there were two stores in El Rito, a small village 30 miles southeast of Tierra Amarilla. One was owned by Ed Sergeant, uncle of the T. D. Burns of Santa Fe Ring fame; the other belonged to Tobías González, a feared and respected *político* in his own right and said to be at the time *honcho mayor* of the *Mano Negra*, or Black Hand.

One night in late winter, the Sergeant store caught fire and burned to the ground. Self-styled private detective Bill Martin of Santa Fe was asked to investigate and arrived on the scene while the ashes were still warm and the canned goods still popping. Prompted by conviction and encouraged by rumor and some evidence, Martin arrested old Tobías's son, Emilio, then out of the penitentiary on parole.

During the preliminary hearing on the arson charge some weeks later, Emilio was inadvertently left alone in a ground floor room of the Tierra Amarilla courthouse and took the opportunity to slip out a window and disappear into the hills. After a hunt lasting months and involving several shooting skirmishes, he was finally run down along with nine other young members of the Mano Negra. Emilio González spent much of the rest of his life in jail, but his adventures, and particularly the casual style of his escape from the courthouse, assured him a permanent place in the pantheon of folk heroes still remembered fondly amongst the *Hispanos* of Río Arriba.

The basic elements of Emilio's story are classic: ethnic conflict between natives and invaders; a secretive native cult dedicated to resistance; violence by a native leader who is immediately named outlaw by the dominant invaders; repression, arrest and daring jailbreak; chase, capture and often tragic ending; final enshrinement of the native leader as martyr, or at least hero.

Such elements have been detected in the folk traditions of such widely scattered places as Scotland, the Ukraine, Mongolia, Andalusia, Sicily and Sardinia, and, most recently, in many isolated places in South America. They reach back in history through the revolutionary days of the United States to the times of Robin Hood and before. In the century and a quarter following the Treaty of Guadalupe Hidalgo, they have appeared repeatedly in the history of northern New Mexico, and they were to appear yet again with astonishing adherence to the classic pattern beginning with the arrival of Reies Tijerina and *los barbudos* in Río Arriba in 1958.

Reies says that he did not hide his face with a beard like others of *los barudos*, despite the fact that he was then a fugitive from Arizona law. Regarding charges that the Heralds of Peace tithed certain citizens of Lumberton without their permission, several times to the tune of hundreds of dollars worth of property, he will say only that his own most serious stealing was done as a boy in Texas, when he would fashion a hook from a coathanger, reach in through the junkyard fencing and snag out auto parts, then run around front to the office and sell them back to the dealer.

His first months in New Mexico were mostly a return to the evangelizing of previous years, when he and Mary had traveled from church to church and town to town, preaching when they could, doing other work when they had to. "He was always too fast and nervous," Mary Escobar says. "Once we worked in that Pontiac engine factory in Michigan, and he fainted there. Maybe that had something to do with it, because he was even more in a hurry after that, as if he just had to get something done. And he was even more like that after the trouble in Arizona, when we first came to New Mexico. As though he was looking for something."

Sometime late in 1958, Reies met Higinio Martínez, a notary public of the town of Chama, just east of Lumberton. Through several long evenings Martínez recounted a detailed history of the TA Grant from his point of view as an heir. Reies asked questions. Higinio arranged for him to meet other heirs, among them stern and wary Juan and his great uncle, José María Martínez, in his early sixties then, still tall, but frail as a bundle of reeds except for hands so hard-worked they resembled many-rooted turnips.

The old man brought out a small suitcase and showed Reies a much-thumbed copy of · the surveyor-general's plat, showing the northern border of the grant reaching up into Colorado. The court had recently asked him to deposit the map and other documents in evidence, he said, but he had known they just wanted to take them away from him, so he had refused to let them have them. Hadn't T. B. Catron conveniently lost an entire trunk full of other people's documents during his infamous stagecoach ride from Cimarron to Las Vegas back in 1878? Hadn't Territorial Governor Pile sold some of the Spanish archives for wastepaper as many years ago? Hadn't the clerk's records disappeared when Max Frost was being tried for fraud? Hadn't the Mora County courthouse burned down mysteriously only a few years back, leaving only Felipe Sánchez with copies of all the land documents, for which he had since been charging outrageous prices? Oh no, the old man said, he was no fool, and he cited northern New Mexico's ironic paraphrase of the bird-in-hand proverb: *mejor una hijuela in el colchón que cien en Santa Fe*—better one deed in the mattress than a hundred in Santa Fe.

He showed his visitors two *hijuelas* or written conveyances of individual riverside plots, one dated 1832, the other 1864, both from Francisco Martínez, conveying plots to Juan Manuel Martínez, grandfather of José María Martínez, great grandfather of Juan. The *hijuela* stipulated in Spanish that the recipient should have this land together with access to whatever land, pasture wood, water and roads he might need to support his family.

Then the old man got out a copy of the original grant of the Mexican government to José Manuel Martínez "together with eight male children and others who may voluntarily desire to accompany him," of all that land "situated on the banks of the Chama River, and known as the Tierra Amarilla, bounded on the east by the range of mountains, on the north by the Navajo River, on the south by the Nutrias River . . ."

The words leaped out in Spanish, black against the photostated texture of the smudged and ancient parchment, the clean, quilled strokes sure and venerable in age, the scrolled rubrics regal and strange, the whole an undeniably authentic artifact and emphatic reminder of another and better time, a time of their language, their customs, their law, their rights, their power.

"I tell you, I hadn't had much faith in a long time, but I was excited that night," Reies says. "I could see that this land had been stolen from these people, without right, without justice. They had been tricked out of it and run off it, just the way we had in Arizona, and my father before me, and his father before him. I knew about the land grants, of course, but not all of it, and I wanted to know more. I started to talk about it, you know, in my sermons. And I began to talk to the people and to find out all I could. That was when I began to meet the people in the Abiquiu Corporation. These people still cared. They still had faith. They still had fight in them."

As Juan Martínez had said; life for the people of the northern villages had not taken its crucial turn for the worst until the 1930s. It is true that the region's traditional agricultural base had begun to deteriorate before the turn of the century, but many of the wheat and corn farmers of Río Arriba had become stockmen, grazing their sheep and cattle on pastures they still considered to be their *ejido*. Despite the immense holdings of the few, there remained enough uncontrolled range and land of either uncertain or indifferent ownership on which a man could run his few cattle and from which he could take his firewood and now and then cut roof beams for the house of a newly married son or daughter. If most of the land was technically owned by various of the conquerers, it was still nearly as wide and wild as ever, and it seemed there was room for all.

Although there was an increasing need for cash, the coming of the railroads in the 1870s and '80s brought easily accessible wage labor. Juan Martínez, Sr. worked on the narrow-gauge Denver, Rio Grande and Western until it was finished in 1881. Later he worked for the lumbermen who contracted with T. B. Catron to clear the thickly wooded valleys of San Joaquín de Chama and Tierra Amarilla. A man could supplement his living from his small garden and herd and get the necessary money for cash purchases by going out to work not far away on the railroad, in the mines which supplied the engines with coal or with the logging crews, and still be able to return to the vital reassurance of family, home and village.

The people of *la raza* were still very much in the majority in northern New Mexico, and although they did not have commensurate political power, they had more than in the territorial years, and they had developed other, less visible institutions for making their majority effective.

For the most part, in isolated and forgotten Río Arriba, the customs held firm, the language was supreme and life seemed proper and good, if no less difficult that it had always been on the wild frontier.

There were still weddings and wakes, fiestas and fights, dances in the *placita* and ritual in the church. There was still time to fill the sala with neighbors when one of the renowned *trobadores* came to sing for his wine and supper. He was sure to sing the tragic romance of Delgadina, imprisoned for the crime of womanhood by a lustful father; and inevitably there would be the ballads and *corridos* celebrating the daring deeds and bloody deaths of the fearless leaders of *gavillas,* the roving bands of *bandidos.* There was Ruperto González, who was said to have boasted on the threshold of death, *"Yo soy,"* "I am." There were Joaquín Murrieta, Antonia Ramas, Feliciano, Rubén Leyba, Río Arriba's own Emilio González, and, invariably, Pancho Villa.

> *Desde la Revolución*
> *De don Francisco Madero*
> *Villa fué de los primeros*
> *Un valiente verdadero . . .*

And then, beginning in the second decade of the new century, there began to appear those ditties in which English and Spanish were mixed with a humorous irony that reflected a bitterness growing deeper year by year.

> Jariru, my fren,
> *Nos dice doña Inés,*
> *Pues pronto aprenderemos*
> *A hablar el idioma inglés.*

> *Para decir diez reales*
> *Dicen* dolen ecuora;
> *Para decir mañana*
> *También dicen* tumora

Váyanse, americanistas,
No se vayan a quedar;
Los machos que las trajieron
Que las vuelvan a llevar.

Joking in song helped ease the growing sense of loss and quieted the rage, but the fact was that the pale *americanistas* and their lean, bony men would not be leaving, a "dolen ecuora" would remain a dollar and a quarter and would not again be 10 *reales,* and *mañana* would increasingly become "tumora." And tomorrow belonged to the tall, blue-eyed *Tejanos,* moving with sure vigor into power and ownership in the south, east and west of the old kingdom and now beginning to filter north in bothersome numbers.

What was more, times were getting harder. With the railroads finished and the timber gone, wages had to be hunted further and further afield. The young men began to leave the north and eventually the state for longer and longer periods of time. Skilled *vaqueros* ranged the South-west and went as far west as California and as far north as Montana looking for seasonal work on the big ranches. Others were forced to join the migratory labor force, competing with hordes of Oklahoma immigrants in the cotton fields and pecan orchards of Texas, in the beet fields and mines of Colorado and all the way west to the vineyards of California's San Joaquín valley, returning when they could, always to less land, reduced herds and flocks, villages slashed by the highway and invaded by the artists and tourists, and a way of life that was grudgingly but surely crumbling away from its people, many of whom were too eager to flee its somber restrictions and increasing difficulties.

In the Great War of 1917, volunteers of *la raza* so drained the state of its population that there were not enough young men left to fill the draft quota. Those who went away came back with new ideas and new ambitions and often found themselves impatient with the old life. They left again, never to return, often hastily selling their land to the nearest bidder. The land continued to go, often sold parcel by parcel to pay taxes, based upon acreage rather than on annual crop yield, as had been the case under Spanish and Mexican law. Virtually all such small lots eventually fell into the hands of the larger owners who often in turn sold out to the state or federal governments at substantial and often politically bolstered profits.

In 1916, enactment of alcoholic beverage prohibition just across the line in Colorado helped boost the economy in the Río Arriba villages for a time. The manufacture of bourbon was something a man could do with his hands and on his own, and dozens of stills sprang up and were kept busy in the old adobe *jacales* of the mountain sheep camps, providing much-needed cash income for many families. National Prohibition, coming seven years later, brought more demand for illicit booze, but it also brought federal agents, local gang warfare, a deepening corruption at all levels of life and new inspiration to the old tendency to resort to violence whenever purpose, pride or just plain hot-blooded propensity could be served.

And then came the Depression and the difficulties which to the nation at large were primarily economic, but which threatened total cultural destruction to the villagers of northern New Mexico. In one fell swoop they lost all sources of supplementary income, with all mines and construction shut down, their migratory cousins already out of work and starving in distant Texas and California and Prohibition shortly to be repealed. More important, with reduced consumption of beef and mutton in the East and the closing down of the packing plants, there was no market for livestock and some of the larger landowners began to sell land on the one hand, while on the other, those who had the cash to buy hastened to take advantage of the small and undercapitalized. A great deal of land changed hands, and a lot of it passed into the hands of the state and federal governments during the 1930s.

It was also in the 1930s that the Abiquiu Corporation was founded as the Tierra Amarilla Land Grant Corporation, with its membership drawn from heirs and claimants to the TA Grant. About that same time, the haystacks and barns of the valley's larger landowners began to burst into flame with a frequency that was not to abate from that time onward.

Fiercely nativistic, secretive and rebellious organizations were not new to New Mexico. One of the first, the best known and for a time the most effective was the *Confraternidad de Nuestro Padre Jesús Nazareno*, or *Penitente* Brotherhood.

Throughout the Spanish colonial period there existed a number of lay brotherhoods of the Catholic Church in the parishes of New Mexico. These organizations were devoted primarily to the maintenance of churches and the statues of saints, conduct of religious services in the absence of priests and provision of mutual aid in times of crisis. The *Penitente* Brotherhood began as just such a passive, nonsecretive religious aid society.

But at the beginning of the 19th century, the new government of Mexico forced the Franciscan padres to abandon New Mexico, leaving the province with a serious shortage of priests. The sick died without rites, corpses remained unburied for days and children went unbaptized. Out of frontier necessity, the Brotherhood became increasingly involved in lay services.

In 1883, a bishop named Zubiria made the first episcopal visit to New Mexico in 73 years and complained of a certain "Brotherhood of *Penitentes*, already existing for a goodly number of years, but without any authorization," and protested against "the excesses of very indiscreet corporal penance which they are accustomed to practice on some days of the year, even publicly."

The origins of the Brotherhood's self-flagellation rites are obscure, but such practices are neither new to the Church nor to Spanish culture. Until just before the Spanish Civil War, it was the custom in one small village in Andalusia for criminals to allow themselves to be trussed to crosses on Easter Week in exchange for their freedom.

There is evidence that New Mexico's *Penitente* Brotherhood originated in the village of Chimayo, about 30 miles south of Tierra Amarilla. Chimayo is known for its colorful blanket rugs, woven in a style introduced by weavers from a town called Esquipulas in southeastern Guatemala. The patron saint of the *Penitente* Brotherhood is Esquipulas, whose image appears among golden leaves on a dark green cross in the *santuario* at Chimayo. The natives of Esquipulas in Guatemala are mostly Indian. To this day, the majority of the natives of Chimayo in New Mexico are of mixed Spanish and Indian blood, mostly Pueblo. The Pueblos, like most American Indians, have long included self-flagellation in their religious purification rites.

Whatever their origins, the Easter Week rites of the *Penitentes* included several days of secret meetings in the village *morada*, with the fasting penitents kneeling on rough stones and cactus and, later, glass; cutting themselves with obsidian knives and, later, steel; chafing their bodies with cactus and, later, plaques pierced with nails; lashing themselves and each other with scourges of leather and cholla cactus and, later, barbed wire; and rubbing their wounds with salt. Holy Week culminated in the trek to *calvario*, a hill somewhere near the village, where one or more penitents were raised on the cross. George Martin recalls giving medical aid to men who had actually been nailed. In later years, the penitents were usually tied with rope, but often insisted on hanging long enough for blood poisoning to have its chance. When a crucified penitent died on the cross, his shoes were left on his widow's doorstep.

The development of the Brotherhood into a secret organization can be traced back to its suppression as a religious cult, but its development into a covert political force began with the coming of the Yankees.

Before returning to Mexico, Bishop Zubiria issued an order forbidding further "reunions" of *Penitentes*. But he failed to send any new priests to the neglected province, and his order was ignored. The Brotherhood continued to gain adherents, particularly in the northern villages and especially among the poor, although the *ricos* found it increasingly to their advantage to at least tolerate the movement. There were even sympathizers among the clergy; perhaps the most renowned was the patriot priest, Padre Martínez of Taos.

Antonio José Martínez was born in 1793 of a well-to-do family of Río Arriba, related to Manuel Martínez of the Tierra Amarilla Grant. Married young, he lost both wife and child and went to Durango to study for the priesthood. Returning in 1822, he was given the church at Taos, where he established a school, bought New Mexico's first printing press from its Santa Fe owner, and began to print church rituals, textbooks and a newspaper called *El Crepúsculo*, or The Dawn. It is a matter of record that Padre Martínez was sympathetic to the *Penitentes*. It is strongly suspected that he was a key conspirator in the single organized attempt by the natives of New Mexico to repel their invaders.

After his curiously bloodless conquest of the province, General Kearny hastily set up a territorial government under Charles Bent of Taos, then left for California, leaving a Colonel Donophan in military charge of the region. Donophan was compelled to chase some marauding Navajos across the Continental Divide and while he was gone, a well-organized revolt took shape, with several prominent *Hispano* families among its leaders. Last-minute betrayal of the plot in Santa Fe did not prevent its going ahead in the north, where the rebels included Indians from Taos Pueblo. Governor Bent, in Taos for the Christmas holidays, was caught in his house and scalped alive, and the skin of his head nailed to a board and carried through the plaza to great rejoicing. At least 16 other Yankees were killed, among them a newly appointed U.S. district attorney, who was shot with arrows and thrown to the hogs.

Colonel Sterling Price of the United States Army headed north from Santa Fe with 350 troopers, battling some 2,000 rebels and Indians along the way. After a week-long running battle he arrived in Taos to find the remaining insurgents holed up in the pueblo's church, which he bombarded with 12-pound howitzers. One corner of it still stands amidst rubble which has not been touched to this day. In suppressing the revolt, Price lost 10 men killed and 52 wounded. During the fighting 150 rebels and Indians were killed and an equal number wounded. An additional 30 were executed for "treason," and a great many Indians were flogged.

Padre Martínez was never officially implicated in the uprising, but he was known to be friendly with leaders of the original plot, and he sheltered several rebels in his house during the uprising. Many of the rebels had been out-of-work frontier fighters from such settlements as Abiquiu and Las Nutrias, and most had been *Penitentes*. This did not enhance the Brotherhood in the eyes of the conquerers, nor did it bring the priest much favor. In 1856, Martínez was unfrocked by Bishop Jean Lamy for such "irregularities" as the frequent presence of attractive ladies in his home, but mostly for his continued tolerance of the Brotherhood.

The French-born Lamy arrived in New Mexico in 1851, virtually on the heels of the invaders. He understood nothing of frontier problems and little of the Spanish tradition, but he was acutely sensitive to the mood of higher authority, civil as well as ecclesiastical.

With the passage of civil control into the hands of the United States, the number of priests in New Mexico further dwindled. Those who remained were frowned upon by the authorities, most of whom had a distaste for "papists and popery."

The Protestant newcomers were particularly horrified by the Brotherhood's corporeal recreation of that event they so doted upon in the abstract, and there was fierce opposition to the annual crucifixions, including attempts to stop them by force. One little old lady of Río Arriba recalls standing as a young child in the *placita* of San Pedro on the

Sangre de Cristo Grant during the Good Friday celebrations and receiving the shock of her life when the call to colors sounded and the United States cavalry thundered in to "save" a highly indignant penitent from the cross.

Equally strong opposition came from the Church itself, in the person of Bishop Lamy, who sought to deny the Brotherhood standing as a religious society and forbàde parish priests to celebrate mass in *Penitente moradas*. He later instituted the practice of "verification," instructing all priests to ascertain of the dying whether or not they were *Penitentes,* and if they were, to withhold the sacraments until Penitentism was renounced. In 1888, he denied the sacraments to those who insisted on observing the wakes for the dead, which had been traditional in the Río Grande villages for centuries.

On the other hand, there were the Anglo-Protestant evangelizers who, with the encouragement of the civil authorities, had been paving the way for native conversion with lavish distribution of Spanish-language Bibles. In the 1880s, the Reverend Alexander Darley, "The Apostle of the Southwest," made several whirlwind tours of New Mexico, and was followed by a steady stream of other "Bible-benders." A number of natives succumbed and became, as they are still called in Río Arriba, "Hallelujahs."

But most clung to their frontier mode of faith and traditional means of mutual aid and protection, their dedication only deepened by repression, their religious fervor increasingly augmented by ethnic resentment. Driven underground and compelled to conduct their ceremonies and business in secret, the *Penitentes* continued to grow in numbers and soon became a silent but powerful force in the affairs of the territory and later the state, their influence lasting throughout the 19th century and well into the 20th.

At the height of their influence they had chapters as far north as Denver and as far south as Socorro. Their numbers were concentrated in the northern counties. In San Miguel, Mora, Taos and Río Arriba they represented up to 80 percent of the *Hispano* population, which meant a firm majority of the voters. In some villages membership included virtually the entire population. At one time in Talpa in Taos County, four *moradas* or chapter houses could be seen from one spot. As late as 1936, there were 38 *moradas* in San Miguel County and nearly as many in Río Arriba.

Although the *moradas* tended to remain independent of one another until later years, and therefore could not be reliably delivered up by any one individual or party, they were predominantly Republican throughout that party's period of ascendency in the northern counties and were worked upon by both parties to swing many an election, from the county level on up to state senator. Initially forced into secrecy, they soon found secrecy an advantage. Politicians who could not have accepted their public endorsement benefited from their unvoiced support. For a time they determined the election of virtually every northern representative to the state legislature, and their approval was crucial to the election of many a New Mexico congressman.

Within the *Penitente* community, membership guaranteed mutual protection and aid. The *morada* sometimes served as a communal storage house and emergency clinic. The *hermano mayor* of the local chapter was often called upon to settle a local dispute, and the *Penitente* hierarchy even passed judgment on such serious questions of law as murder. Food was distributed to the needy, feed and farm machinery communally purchased and used, widows and cripples cared for. By nature of its membership, the Brotherhood tended toward a strong ethnic bias. As a mutual protection society, it demanded unwavering loyalty of its members to the organization and to each other.

For decades it was an accepted fact that no *Penitente* indicted for a crime against an Anglo could be convicted, simply because the odds were that the entire jury would be members of the Brotherhood. In the 1870s, Captain William B. Haines of the state militia wrote to Adjutant General Max Frost, complaining that he had failed to get an indictment against a cattle rustler named Sandoval and adding bitterly, "No more prisoners will go to Tierra Amarilla to be tried by Mexican *Penitentes* (don't know if spelt right) and get off."

Reaction by the ruling minority was, however, prompt, and as usual the expedient was simple, direct and effective. It became customary for the predominantly Anglo judges to excuse a juror from service if it was so much as alleged that he was a *Penitente*.

On occasion, reaction was even more direct. In the early 1880s, an active rustling operation was being conducted out of Durango, Colorado, by former riders of the McSween Regulars of the recent Lincoln County Land War, together with such renowned "stompers" as Charlie and Clay Allison of Taos. Much of the stolen stock was being taken from the herds of the Archuleta brothers, the richest stockmen of that era, one of them a Colorado state senator, thanks to *Penitente* support.

The situation finally came to a head in Bloomfield, 60 miles west of Lumberton, when a man named Blanchard was shot and killed by Justice of the Peace Guadalupe Archuleta. Archuleta claimed he had been trying to arrest Blanchard as a member of the rustling gang. The dead man's brother Moses claimed it was murder. The town immediately split into Anglo and *Hispano* factions, but the former turned out to be the stronger, and by the time the militia arrived, Justice of the Peace Archuleta was swinging from a cottonwood limb as notice to all that neither a wealthy *Hispano* family nor the *Confraternidad de Nuestro Padre Jesús Nazareno* could forever stay the hand of the conqueror.

After the turn of the century, *Penitente* power began to steadily wane. The Brotherhood continued to be a factor in state politics well into the 1930s, but the economy of the north had begun to fail by the 1920s, and the long disintegration of village culture had begun, with its attendant discouragement and desperate attempts at ethnic defection, reflected in the increasing number of "Hallelujahs" enlisted by the endless stream of Pentecostal evangelizers tramping Río Arriba. Following the Depression, the young people began to leave in droves. Those who did not leave were increasingly impatient with the old ways. Without young initiates, the society could not grow. The last *hermano mayor* of the *morada* of Los Martínez, southwest of Tierra Amarilla, died in 1918, and there was no one to replace him. The carved wooden *santos* of the *morada* of nearby Arroyo were removed in 1929. The *morada* of Ranchos de Taos was closed up in the 1930s. In 1960, there were possibly 135 *moradas* in New Mexico and Colorado with a combined membership of from two to three thousand. But the membership consisted mostly of old people, and the *moradas* were no longer vital to the conduct of village affairs.

In 1947, the Catholic Church restored its blessing to the Brotherhood, with the caution that it proceed "with moderation." Nonetheless, the hostility of parish priests has not abated, nor has the Brotherhood's fondness for secrecy and its determined resistance to outside interference. To this day, should the curious tourist wander too close to the small grilled windows or iron-bound door of the *morada* in Chimayo or Abiquiu or Ensenada, a man is sure to materialize, indicating by his mere ominous silence that the stranger would do better to seek local color elsewhere.

The truculent and secretive tradition of the Brotherhood has remained, to be handed on like the night rider's mask. There has been a variety of similar organizations, developing parallel with and beyond the heyday of the *Penitentes*. In the 1890s the *Gorras Blancas* or White Caps were operating in San Miguel County, their main efforts devoted to discouraging Anglo homesteaders from settling on grazing lands. The *Mano Negra* (Black Hand) first appeared in northern New Mexico during the Prohibition era and has been sporadically active ever since, in name at least, serving various causes, groups and leaders. Countless other marauding apparitions throng the folk memory of Río Arriba, some with names, some known only by the name of the family or families involved. Beginning around 1935, the Albeyta family organization of Parkview was a power in Río Arriba for some 14 years, electing state senators by day and burning haystacks by night, until its powerful patriarch, Midalgo Albeyta, died in 1949.

Some of these organizations have been more blatantly criminal than others, some better organized, some more successful; but they all have had in common a tendency to secrecy and violence, a passionate distaste for the invader and his ways, and a fervent yearning to return to the ways of the past. They are all, to one degree or another, examples of what sociologists call nativistic cults. Taken altogether, they indicate a strong tendency toward what is called a revitalization movement; that is, a deliberate effort to construct a more satisfying culture, tending toward reinstitution of the past, with a strong emphasis on the elimination of alien customs, values, persons.

There have always been other, nonsecret and ostensibly less truculent local institutions in New Mexico. There are the governments of the irrigation systems, tracing their tradition back to Spain, where the system serving the rich Valencia valley is still administered by a council of eight elders, equivalents of the New Mexican *mayordomo de acequia* or ditch boss. There are the governments of the community land grants, recognized along with the ditch associations by territorial statute as early as 1894 as "bodies corporate, with power to sue or to be sued as such."

But with the steady grativation of the land out of the hands of the small landowner and the *Hispano* in general, the ditch associations have tended over the years to fall into the hands of the larger and predominantly Anglo-American landowners, and, most recently, to come under the indirect but persistent control of various arms of the United States government.

Although all of the land grant organizations are public corporations and some are devoted primarily to the administering of lands still in the hands of their original owners or their heirs, some of them administer no land at all, but are made up of individuals who feel that their land was unjustly and illegally taken from them and who have banded together to secure return of that land, by one means or another.

What is more, many of the land grant organizations, particularly those in the northern counties, are passionately if not publicly devoted to the stubborn fostering of the dream that time and fortune have not passed them by, that as the land is their inheritance, so is the life they once lived on it, and both must be restored.

The Abiquiu Corporation of Tierra Amarilla had been in existence under one name or another for some 40 years when Reies Tijerina first arrived in New Mexico in 1958. For four decades the organization had been involved in litigation on behalf of various of its members, represented by many lawyers, before many judges in various courts. Like most such organizations, the Abiquiu Corporation had also involved itself in politics, sometimes publicly, sometimes as one of the hidden factors that have been a part of the rat's nest of New Mexican politics since the heyday of the Brotherhood. Very little had been gained in those 40 years, more had been lost.

"Bill Mundy was fencing the last of the grant land," Juan Martínez says. "The lawyers had all double-crossed us, including Alfonzo Sánchez, and we couldn't get anywhere in the courts. So we were ready to listen to just about anybody who had a good idea of what to do, just as long as we could be sure he was with us and would stay with us. Of course, Reies wasn't from here, and at first a lot of the members thought he was trying to take over. That he was just another politician trying to use us for a stepping-stone to the district attorney's office or the legislature."

Early in 1958, Uvaldo Martínez, then president of the Abiquiu Corporation, invited Reies Tijerina to address the membership. Reies was accompanied to the meeting by Anselmo, who had come up from Texas, and a half dozen of *los barbudos*. No sooner had Reies begun to speak to the hundred or so men and women present, when one Juan Mares, a grant member, stood up and demanded expulsion of all nonmembers. There was an argument, followed by push and shove, followed by an out-and-out brawl, during which the guest speaker had his scalp laid open with a hickory club by the sergeant at arms. Anselmo seized the club and threw himself into the melee. At one point, an old man was clubbed to the floor.

Eventually Sheriff Emilio Naranjo's deputies arrived, and all of *los barbudos* were arrested except Reies, who had been taken away bleeding to the home of a friend. The others were released, but Anselmo was kept in the jail in the basement of the Tierra Amarilla courthouse for 11 days without being charged. The old man refused to identify him as his assailant.

On the twelfth day, when his cell door was ajar and the trusty's back turned, Anselmo slipped out of the Tierra Amarilla courthouse and headed for the hills.

He was arrested 10 months later, crossing the border from Mexico with Reies, and was extradited to New Mexico by Texas Governor Eugene Connally. Early in 1959, he was tried in the District Court in Tierra Amarilla, convicted of assault and sentenced to one to five years, of which he served 18 months.

In Río Arriba it was not entirely a drawback to have a brother who had slipped out of the Tierra Amarilla jail as handily as had Emilio González 25 years before him. Nor did it hurt to have a three-inch scar on your scalp as a token of your determination to speak your piece.

It has long been tradition and is still the custom for a young initiate of the *Penitente* Brotherhood to receive instruction for weeks before his initiation, and finally to be sent after dark to the *morada*, there to knock upon the iron-bound door and recite:

"God's child knocks at this chapel door for his Grace."

"Penance," speaks a voice from within. "Penance is required by those who seek salvation."

"I ask this Brotherhood," recites the novice, "who gives this house light?"

"Jesus," answers the *hermano mayor* from within.

"Who fills it with joy?"

"Mary."

"Who preserves it with faith?"

"Joseph."

Then the door is opened and the initiate taken in, to suffer the obsidian knife, the leather scourge and salt in the five wounds of Christ.

"It was a mess, all that trouble," says Juan Martínez, stern and stiffly upright in the shade of the Martínez sitting room. "But when it was over, we knew he was a man. And we were pretty sure that he was one of us and not one of them."

"Those first years were like prospecting," Reies say of the time between his arrival in New Mexico and the founding of the *Alianza* in 1963. "I traveled all over, I went to meetings, I talked to everyone I could. Not just in the north, but in Río Abajo too, all over the state."

Typical of the villages he visited in the lower river country is the fragmented, dying little town of Rowe, which lies in the long valley of the upper Pecos, 30 miles southeast of Santa Fe and a hundred miles south of Tierra Amarilla. This is the eastern edge of Río Abajo country, with long stretches of grazing land separated by forested ridges and vast mesas, the whole drawn and quartered by a network of paved highways far more complete than in the mountainous north. There are more people here, and a smaller percentage of them are *Hispanos*. To the south is that part of New Mexico called Little Texas, where the Anglo-Americans have been in the majority for over 40 years. Eighty percent of the businesses along these highways are Anglo owned and operated; the juke box music in the bars is Country & Western.

This is no rare pocket of cultural retardation; this is what it is like in the rest of the Southwest. The conquest has been established for nearly a century and nears completion. *Las costumbres de neustra gente* barely exist; the old way of life has been infiltrated by the conquerer's concepts. Only language, the old adobes crumbling into disrepair, and the memories of *los viejitos*, the old people, are left.

Never much more than a whistle-stop and company store in its present location, Rowe has been even less than that since the four lanes of new superhighway 84 came down the valley five years ago and sheared half the town away, leaving the church, the post office, two stores and a dozen or so residences clustered in the triangular squeeze of old highway and new. Inside the church one hears the tires whistling on the blacktop a hundred yards away, and on a warm day the smell of burning rubber and baking tar cuts through the rank tang of the weeds. Seen from a passing car, Rowe is nothing more than a flash of brown rubble, a glimpse of tin church-spire and scabrous backsides of unpainted hovels. The actual current population is less than 100 and steadily declining, yet the village has an unbroken existence that goes back 200 years, and once had a golden bell hanging in its church tower. From Rowe and nearby Pecos, Reies Tijerina eventually drew a good dozen loyal followers.

"I talked to them all," Reies Tijerina says. "I went to meetings, I read the books and the laws and I dug and dug. Because I had to be sure. I didn't want another tragedy again like we had in Arizona. I kept asking questions of professors and lawyers and the old-timers. I went to Texas and to Mexico. I looked at the deeds and papers the people had, and I studied the old Mexican laws and the Spanish laws.

I began to see how very much land had been stolen, how many people had been robbed and were angry. And how the law was there, written down, and it had been broken by lies and deceits."

On one of his early exploratory trips to Mexico, he found the book which was to become the basic text for his new gospel of divine inheritance. Commissioned by Philip II of Spain in 1570 and called the *Recopilación de leyes de los reynos de las Indias,* or *Recompilation of the Laws of the Kingdoms of the Indies,* it contains most of the basic legislation pertaining to Spanish colonial policy. Its 6,400 laws include statutes encouraging intermarriage of Spaniards and Indians, and others intended to guard against wanton speculation in land, absentee landlordism and reduction of native peoples through forced labor. Among its many laws regulating the ownership of land are those concerning land grants and those ordaining that each frontier settlement should have its *ejido,* or common and inalienable land. There are even laws reflecting the crown's attempt to incorporate into its legislation some of the juridical customs of the Indians.

The *Recopilación* has long been recognized as one of the more notable and humane documents of modern colonial legislation, which is not to say that actual administration of the colonies was either so orderly or so humane. The differences between the policies as dictated at home and as administered abroad were often as wide and deep as the ocean which separated crown and colony. The *Recopilación* notwithstanding, entire tribes of Indians were forced into virtual slavery, thousands dying in the mines of Peru and Mexico. The legal obligation to give native labor religious training was often satisfied only by perfunctory baptism, and the duty to feed, clothe and protect them was often fulfilled at minimal levels of bare existence. Absentee landlords owned and speculated in huge tracts of land without ever seeing it, and even the Indians were bought and sold in large numbers without ever being seen by seller or buyer. Despite efforts by certain elements of the Church, native beliefs and customs were often attacked and destroyed, whether or not they interfered with civil administration.

But the *Recopilación* did have considerable effect on the conduct of affairs in the colonies, and its intent was clearly to write upon the *tabula rasa* of the New World an outline for a more rational and equitable mode of life. It was this intent that excited Reies Tijerina when he first discovered the book in Mexico, and he was further impressed by its legalistic phrasing, orderly air and tone of absolute moral conviction.

> *Que los pobladores y sus hijos y descendientes legítimos sean Hijos-dalgo en lat Indias . . .*

> That the settlers and their sons and legitimate descendants shall be gentlemen-*hidalgos* in the Indies . . .

As a masculine noun, *hidalgo* means gentleman or "nobleman"; as adjective it means noble and courteous, with an additional connotation of generosity. Broken into its primary parts, it becomes *higo de algo*, literally, "son of something."

The *Recopilación* promised that, inasmuch as settlers going to the New World were giving up various degrees of social status and security at home, they should by royal decree be declared *Hijos-dalgo* in the New World.

> ". . . and [they] shall be conceded all honors and privileges properly possessed and enjoyed by all *Hijos-dalgo* loyal to these Monarchs of Castile, under jurisdiction of the Laws and Customs of Spain . . ."

The royal pledge was clear: those who braved the rigors of America were to be rewarded with land and honor, to be conveyed by laws and customs of lineage to their children, heirs, successors and assigns. They were to be landed men and *hidalgos* all—"sons of something" for evermore.

Reies wasted no time in obtaining a copy of the book and taking it back to New Mexico with him. Set against the Treaty of Guadalupe Hidalgo, it became basic documentation of the thesis he was building. The land had been given; it had been taken away. Knighthood had been bestowed; it had been ignored. The laws had been created by royal and holy decree; they had been broken.

"When I read the *Recopilación* and thought about the hypocrisy of the Treaty of Guadalupe Hidalgo, and when I saw the true and perfect titles that the people had, I began to realize what a great big injustice had been done. And I began to talk to them about it, to tell them they must do something."

He crisscrossed New Mexico from north to south and east to west, staying in the homes of those who were sympathetic, living from hand to mouth, and preaching when he had to. But now his sermons were increasingly filled with talk of the grants.

"I discovered that there are 1,715 land grants in the United States, and they are all over, in Texas and Arizona and Colorado and California and Louisiana and even in Florida. As I went from place to place and as I read the books and talked to the people, I began to realize what a big thing this was."

In New Mexico alone, grants recorded and recognized by the United States cover roughly a million acres. These include 12 grants of less than 1,000 acres, 35 grants of from 50,000 to 100,000 acres, and 19 grants of more than 100,000 acres. A map of them, including those never recognized or confirmed by the United States, would cover at least an eighth of the area of the state, probably more, and certainly all of the best farmland.

"It was a hard life and there was no stopping, but I had to talk to the people and see their papers and study the law and make sure there was a good case and enough of the people who really did want, you know, justice to be done."

He talked with thousands who had lost their land, but he also talked with those still in technical possession. A number of confirmed grants were still legally owned by descendants of original grantees and administered in the names of legitimate heirs by land grant organizations. He soon discovered that the resentment of the unlanded ones was sometimes shared by their seemingly more fortunate cousins. In some cases, the discontent was the result of conflict between rival factions within the grant, but in other cases the grant organizations had come under extralegal control of one kind or another.

The land owned and administered by the Antón Chico Land Grant Corporation lies at the bottom of the Río Abajo country, on the Pecos 35 miles southeast of Rowe, 60 miles southeast of Santa Fe, 160 miles south of Tierra Amarilla. Santa Rosa lies further east in Guadalupe County, and further to the south lies Fort Sumner in Lincoln County, where Billy the Kid became famous in an earlier struggle over land.

The land is about as flat as land can get, broken at 50-mile intervals by long mesas several hundred feet high, but forever dwarfed by the vast stretch of the horizon. This has always been grazing land; first there were the buffalo and antelope, then sheep, and now cattle. For most of the Spanish colonial period this region, like the vast *Llano Estacado* east of Rowe, was divided up into large sheep ranches, each the semifeudal domain of a rich and powerful *patrón*, who was lord and protector of those settlers who gathered to live and work on his land.

Despite the fact that the word is derived directly from the Latin for father, the English equivalent for *patrón* is often given as "boss." But the *patrón* was not simply an employer. The health and welfare of his paid workers was essential to his own well-being, and what was more, as a brother in race and religion and facing the same hostile environment, he was very much one of them. Locked in feudal containment in his *hacienda*, he and his family usually lived an essentially sober and regulated life, little different in its strictures than the lives of those outside its wall. Although he was rich and had power, the *patrón* was not free, but was intimately responsible to those who depended upon him, and upon whom he depended. His was far more a paternal than a dictatorial role, with duties and obligations to fit that role.

Throughout the first half of the 19th century, half the Spanish population lived out in the country in the *haciendas*, which began as the residences of one or two rich families. From the beginning, the *hacienda* of the *patrón* was the center of the community, not only as fortress in time of peril, but as acknowledged depository and idealization of a way of life and a set of attitudes common to all.

But as the dominant families grew, the families of those who supplied the labor grew: the servants, soldiery and artisans. As the population grew, the *hacienda* grew, burgeoning into an elaborate complex of buildings and eventually into a little village, with detached houses and garden plots and a separate church. Gradually most members of the labor force were able to separate themselves to a degree, becoming independent artisans and small farmers. Eventually they were either given land outright or were able to buy it from the *patrón*.

In most cases, some and even all of the land eventually devolved to communal ownership. A proprietary grant, and sometimes even a *sitio*, eventually became a community grant. A few such cases were recognized by the United States authorities. The *Merced Real de Antón Chico* is one of those, granted to certain settlers "their children, heirs, successors and assigns," by Governor Fecundo Malgares, representing the King of Spain, in 1822. After many years of litigation, the grant was confirmed "to the town of Antón Chico" by United States patent in 1891.

But even in such cases, the habit of *patronismo* remained. This traditional, reciprocal relationship between *patrón* and *peón* and all that it implies was eminently suited to the administration of large ranches and the settlement of a wild frontier, but it lasted long beyond its usefulness and tended to produce a people too accustomed to the restrictions and amenities of patronomial peonage. *Patronismo* remains a prominent facet of *Hispano* psychology to this day, and continues to be exploited by politicians, merchants and landowners, *Hispano* and Anglo alike. The *Merced de Antón Chico* has been under the patronizing control of a single Anglo family for three generations. Although Reies Tijerina did eventually gather a dozen or so followers from among the dissidents on the grant, for the most part grant members remained content to relinquish complete control over their political and financial destinies in exchange for the aid, protection, guidance and, most of all, credit offered by their blue-eyed, store-owning patrons.

As one of the dissidents put it: "The fact of the matter is, we have a different problem here. We have the land, at least technically, so we don't need Tijerina to help us get it back. We sympathize with him, some of us, but our real problems are right here on the grant, and it's up to us to solve them. We're in his boat, at least in some ways, but he's not in ours, if you get what I mean."

"I was not really looking for members so much those first two years," Reies Tijerina says. "I was only trying to find out all I could. And I found out that even the people who still had the land didn't really have it. I found out all the injustices and the way these people were being cheated too and how angry many of them were. I found lots of others who saw that our people and our language and our way of life were being destroyed. I went everywhere, and I learned that the people in the south were as angry as those in the north, although they had lost more and were not so sure of themselves."

It was true, the people in the shattered villages of Río Abajo had long been nearer total surrender than had those of the northern villages. While many of them would eventually join the cause, they were for the most part a weary and cautious people, suspicious of strangers, skeptical of improvement and even wary of the beguilements of their own past. It was fine enough to hear the ancient words declaring them *Hijos-dalgo* and heirs by royal decree, but to many it seemed better to dream upon it than to act and bring even the fondly preserved dreams crashing down into grim reality with all the rest.

It was in the north that Reies would find the hardiest of his supporters and the shock troops of his cause, those he would come to call his *"valientes."* Cris Tijerina put it succinctly one night long after the raid: "We knew that if we were ever going to get anything done, it would have to begin in the north. They still had guts, but they didn't have the land, so they had the least to lose."

Before leaving Río Abajo, Reies reviewed his findings and made his decisions. "I thought about all that I had found out, and I decided that this was what I had hoped it was, this was my life's work, like a mission. And that was when I understood that dream that I had in California. Those tall pines, they were in New Mexico. And the old kingdom, well, I had found out that New Mexico used to be a kingdom. The three angels were the angels of the law coming to tell me what I should do and how I could do it. And the frozen horses, they were the land grants, the *mercedes,* and when I found the true and perfect titles of the grants and common lands that belonged to the *pueblos,* and the president confiscated them, just like that, I realized they were not dead. They could be brought back to life. I tell you that when I realized that, it was one of the biggest moments of my life."

The prospecting years were over. In late 1959, Reies returned to Río Arriba to spend the winter in the house of Juan and Fernanda Martínez, there to consult the angels of the law and to plan how he might best set about thawing the frozen horses and restoring the ancient kingdom.

The *Alianza* 7

SOMETIME in 1960 in an Albuquerque supply house, a chain hoist fell, setting in motion a series of ironies that continues to this day, and which could have maintained momentum only in the Byzantine little world of northern New Mexican politics.

The falling tackle happened to strike and crush the hand of Félix Martínez, son of Juan Martínez of Tierra Amarilla. Two fingers had to be amputated, and Félix engaged a lawyer. The lawyer, who diligently set out to get compensation for Félix, was Alfonso Sánchez, soon to be district attorney of New Mexico's first Judicial District, and archenemy of *Alianza Federal de Mercedes* and its founders, among whom would be his former client, Félix Martínez.

But the refinements were already more intricate than that, and there were even grander ironies in the making.

Shortly after his accident, Félix went home to Tierra Amarilla to recuperate. There, in his parents' house, he met Reies Tijerina for the first time. That night there was the first of many long discussions between Reies, Félix, Juan and others of the Abiquiu Corporation.

"Oh yes, they all got along fine," Fernanda Martínez says with wide-eyed gusto. "That night we knew we were really going to do something about those gestapos that have been running things around here for so long."

In her tiny front room, in the shaded sitting room next to it and in the dining room there are photographs, dozens of them, on the shelves, on the tables, hanging from the walls. "That one is Eugene when he was in the navy, and that is Valdemar, the next oldest. That's Virginia and her husband, he's a guard over at the forestry camp of the penitentiary; and that is Julia, married to a boy in Phoenix. Here is Ramón—they called him Ray when he was in the air force—and here is Félix when he was a kid. You know the story of the little boy with his *burrito?* When they asked him what he wanted to be when he grew up, he said President, and his *burrito* would be Vice-President. That's Félix. When he was four he wanted to be President. But he looks different these days, with his beard. Like Ché Guevara, no?"

Félix, who was 21 in 1960, with only the faintest beginnings of a mustache, was 12 years younger than Reies and a product of another time. Nonetheless, although there were contrasts in the personalities and outlooks of the two men, they understood each other immediately on certain mutually vital matters. They quickly became friends, and during the several weeks of Félix's visit, information was shared, policies were generally agreed upon and plans were projected.

Among Fernanda's photographs there is a wedding picture in a tooled-leather frame. "Yes, that's him, Reies, and his wife then, Mary; and Félix and his wife. They just got married. Reies married them because he was still a Pentecostal preacher then. Sometimes that winter he would preach and go to the meetings and talk to people here, but most of the time he listen to the radio and read all the time those law books. He was always a very quiet and respectful man, you know. He only get mad when he talk about Catron and T. D. Burns and how the federal government take away our land and the Forest Service take away our grazing permits. Yes, that's Reies. He never drink, never swear, just work and work."

Shortly after the wedding, Félix moved back to Albuquerque with his new wife, planning to begin pre-law studies at the university. The study of law has long held strong attraction for the more intelligent and ambitious young members of *la raza* in New Mexico. As heirs to the legalistic side of the Spanish culture, they are attracted to the law's ordered vagueries and promise of manipulative power; as members of a minority group disadvantaged in the face of alien law, they seek education in the enemy's weaponry.

Shortly after Kearny's arrival in 1846, so the story goes, the young men of Taos asked their priest what kind of government the United States would bring them. "A republic," Padre Martínez replied, adding that a republic was "a burro on which lawyers will ride better than priests."

The canny padre's comment was not only astute as prediction, but was underlaid by an older irony long familiar to the people of northern New Mexico, to whom all outside government has always seemed to resemble that plodding, mean-minded and arbitrary beast of burden, the jackass.

The long-standing political cynicism of the New Mexicans can be traced back to before the coming of the Yankees. From the beginning, one of the most difficult problems of Spanish colonial administration had been distance, not only the expanse of ocean between crown and colonies, but the vast overland distances between colonial governments and such outlying settlements as those in northern New Mexico. It was these great distances, coupled with the crown's jealous insistence upon maintaining control over the smallest details of colonial administration, that led to indifference and corruption on the part of many colonial administrators and profound and long-lasting distrust of authority on the part of the colonists. The further away the settlement from central authority, the less responsible were the officials, and New Mexico was one of the most remote frontiers.

As history continued through the years to keep the northern areas isolated, the people continued to be sustained by dire experience in their knowing disdain for absentee civil control. Coupled with their native distrust for authority was a profoundly cynical attitude toward the spoils system which always accompanies corrupt government, reflected in such ironic bits of folksay as, *No tengo política, sólo tengo bolsa:* I don't have politics, I just have a purse.

If the people of New Mexico were justified in their political cynicism by the failings of the Spanish and Mexican colonial systems, they were only further fortified in their opinion with the coming of the Yankees, who proved even before their arrival to be as adept as any *alcalde* or *patrón* at corrupting the public interest.

Kearney's celebrated "bloodless occupation" had actually been engineered far in advance by a former Kentuckian turned Santa Fe trader, James Magoffin, who had so firmly entrenched himself in the hearts of the Mexican authorities and local *ricos* that he was known affectionately throughout the province and even in Mexico City as Don Santiago. Shortly before the invasion, Don Santiago traveled to Santa Fe and had a private talk with Mexican Governor Manuel Armijo, who was suffering from an empty treasury at the time.

Immediately after Don Santiago's visit, Armijo displayed all the signs of sudden affluence. When word came that Kearny was on his way, Armijo took steps to see that there would be no armed resistance, then slipped quietly south to Mexico. Shortly after the Occupation, Don Santiago Magoffin asked the United States Congress to reimburse him for $50,000 spent "for secret services rendered during the war," and got it.

Sixty-two years of misrule and land thievery under the United States territorial government did nothing to change the native attitude toward vested authority. The best they could do was adapt themselves to the new regime, and in the end the basic lesson was not new after all, but only the old cne disguised by new pretense. *En país de los ciegos, El Tuerto es rey.* In the land of the blind, One Eye was still king, except that one no longer spoke of kings and patrons, one spoke of Presidents and senators, of leading citizens and dedicated public servants. One no longer sought out a priest for guidance and intervention with the powers that were. One got a lawyer.

Those *Hispano* leaders who were to survive quickly learned their lessons. The *rico patrón* usually stayed aloof from public office, but he quickly learned to vote his employes, his dead relatives and his sheep if necessary in the long and losing battle to retain his pride and position. But with the loss of his property he was soon forced to give way before the more adaptable among his fellows, and the belated arrival of statehood in 1912 found the first of a new breed of astute and purely political leaders already active among the *Hispano* population. These were the men who were canny and effective enough in 1910 to make sure that the new state constitution contained provisions which were relatively favorable to the Spanish-speaking population. They wasted no time in forming a series of complex alliances with the Anglo Republicans, already known as the Old Guard and destined to retain the controlling edge in state politics well into the 1930s.

The study of law soon became a prerequisite for the politically ambitious *Hispano*, primarily because it continued to be true that "the land's the thing!" By virtue of a New Mexico phenomenon which might be called "Catron's Law" or "The Santa Fe Ring Syndrome," the longer the conquest continued, the more *Hispanos* there were who had lost land and who sought restitution as legal clients and as voters. Many a young attorney of *la raza* started out as a land grant lawyer and ended up in the state legislature or other public office, often having come by a piece of land or two along the way.

It was not illogical for Félix Martínez to have engaged Alfonso Sánchez to represent him, despite the fact that Félix was a member of an organization generally suspected of being prone to do violence to haystacks and other property. Sánchez was well known to members of the Abiquiu Corporation, and, according to them, he had on at least one occasion heartily encouraged them in their less legal activities. He was also a land grant heir himself, born in 1928 in Belén, on the Tome Grant just south of Albuquerque.

"But there was no land left, it was all divided up by the family," he says with a small shrug and turning aside of the head. Sánchez is a neatly made man with a pleasant, dark-jawed face, given to an expression of pained earnestness. "I have just a little bit of land down there, good for nothing. No, I didn't start out ahead in this world, believe me."

His mother died when he was seven, leaving his father, a Santa Fe Railroad mechanic, to raise seven girls and three boys. He graduated from Albuquerque High School and in 1946 volunteered for the air force to serve in Korea. The GI Bill helped pay for his law studies at the University of New Mexico and the University of Denver. Since then, he has been a member and active supporter of the GI Forum, an *Hispano* veterans' organization.

Sánchez passed the bar examination in 1957, and one of his first cases was on behalf of members of the Abiquiu Corporation, fighting court action by the Payne Land and Livestock Company, which was seeking to quiet title on some 5,200 acres of land, some of it along Nutrias Creek. Descendents of Thomas B. Catron retained a major financial interest in the Payne organization, which had also been the victorious party in suits confirming Bill Mundy's title claims. The land along the creek included the strip farms of around a hundred grant heirs, including Juan and José María Martínez, and had been used by them as family garden plots and pasturage for a hundred years.

"The Payne Cattle Company suit was for the whole tract, you see," explains Alfonso Sánchez. "So what I wanted these people to do was to take out their own individual quiet title suits on those strips along the creek."

His brow wrinkles in the customary expression of pained pleading as he recreates the dialogue, explaining to beloved, but sadly misinformed cousins.

" 'This way you are defendants,' I told them. 'You are being filed against. File your own suits for those strips.'

" 'But why should we file for them?' they said. 'We know they are ours.'

" 'The law is such that you just cannot sleep on your rights,' I told them. 'You are being filed against. You are in a better position if you file back.'

" 'But the rest is ours too,' they said. 'We want to file for that. It is part of the grant.'

" 'There is no grant,' I told them. 'The Supreme Court says there is no grant. You will lose the small plots along with the rest.'

" 'We want it all,' they said. 'It is all one grant. We want to file for it all, all together.' "

He throws up his hands, shakes his head sadly, turning away. "What could I do. The Supreme Court is the Supreme Court, the law is the law. I told them I couldn't help them, not the way they were going, and I withdrew from the case. I don't know what happened, but I think they went to Tiny Martínez then." (Tiny Martínez was another up-and-coming young *Hispano* lawyer, soon to become district attorney of San Miguel County.)

At the time that Alfonso Sánchez had taken the case, he was in private practice, but by the time he dropped out in December of 1958, he had been appointed assistant district attorney in Santa Fe. He had also acquired scattered property in the Tierra Amarilla valley, part of it belonging to his wife, the rest of uncertain origin.

He shakes his head in saddened denial. "No, I did not tell them to cut those fences. Reies came to me later, after they had formed the *Alianza*, sitting right there in that chair, and they wanted me to represent them for something, I don't remember. But I said, 'Reies, you cannot do it with these violent means. You have to do it through the law, through the courts. You listen to me, I'm right, I have to be right, because the law is right.' "

This mild outburst is the closest he comes to vehemence. He sighs, subsiding into his chair. "Reies, I admire him, he has built up this tremendous organization from nothing. He could really do things for the people, but he tells them they can have something they cannot. 'These are my people,' I told him, 'and I have to do what's right for them.' And then I told him, 'Now get out.' "

He shakes his head. "No, I did not counsel them to violence or any other illegal activity. I know that some of them say that, but it is not true." He looks away, aggrieved, but not bitter, the mildest and most forgiving of men.

And yet, even disregarding the fact that there are 20 people willing to swear to the event, it is not so difficult to picture him standing before the assembled membership of the Abiquiu Corporation, pointing out into the chill Río Arriba night and advising them to go out and cut the fences and let their cattle through, to light the haystacks as torches of defiance against the common foe—all in that hushed, aggrieved and saddened voice of righteous rue and fevered moral compulsion.

These are my people, I told him, I have to do what's right for them. . . .

By February of 1960, the same winter that Reies Tijerina spent in the Martínez house in Tierra Amarilla, Bill Mundy had put up about 40 miles of barbed wire fencing on the land he had bought from Carl Brueselbach back in 1951. In the nine years since then, his fences had been cut a dozen times and he had lost several haystacks to fire, but he had allowed nothing to interfere with the progress of his campaign to bring the land under his control. His third wheat crop had come in profitably in 1954, and he had immediately begun pulling stumps, 2,000 of them from one field alone, to clear more bottomland. When he had enough fencing for reasonable control of stock, he began to run registered cattle and brought the son of his father's foreman, Alberto Teraces, up from Hatch to help out.

"The Teraces family has been with the Mundys for two generations. I learned my Spanish from Alberto's father. That old bandit still rides every day down there in Hatch. Alberto's one of the best men I've ever had work for me, and that makes him rare."

He put up corrals and a loading chute, erected a large Quonset hut barn, added other outbuildings over the years. Eventually he built a house, doing much of the work himself, aided by his two sons and Alberto.

"It was a pretty good house if I say so myself. No adobe, all frame, except for a stone chimney you could nearly walk into. Had a main room big enough so that four squares of young people could dance and still have room left over for the old folks to sit around and watch."

By 1957 Mundy was ready to start buying more land; by 1960 he had 25,000 acres.

"It wasn't perfect, but it was just about the spread I needed, and I had that note paid off. Then things started getting hot again, and it wasn't just fence and baled hay this time. They started shooting my stock. They got a few of my registered steers, and then they got my best stud horse, worth two thousand."

He carried a 300 Savage in a saddle scabbard off and on after that, and a friend from the State Patrol provided him with a riot gun to be kept in the house for his wife. Things seemed to settle down after the District Court refused to review its decision in favor of the plaintiff in the case of Mundy versus Martínez. 1959 had started out quietly. When the elk season closed, Bill Mundy and his wife decided to take a quick trip down to Las Cruces to visit her family. Their two boys were away at college. They left late in the afternoon on February 29. That night their house caught fire and burned to the ground in sight of a handful of helpless neighbors, leaving only the 35-foot brick chimney standing above smoking rubble.

"It was arson, there's no doubt about it," Mundy says. "There was a big center pole in the main room, and I had this Chimayo blanket hanging there. One of the neighbors that came up said to himself, 'I can at least get that rug out of there for Bill,' and he dove in through a window, but all he got was oil on his pants. They had piled all the stuff up around that center pole and then scattered oil and kerosene all over. And they had broke all the windows out.

"Oh, they knew what they were doing all right. But there was a good clean snow on the ground, and we found tracks, three sets, and the place down there across the highway where they had been laying up behind a bank, ducking down everytime a car passed, waiting for us to leave. The trouble was, we left one light on, same light every time, and they had got used to that. They knew our comings and goings all right.

"Of course, nothing was really done about it. Somebody found a rifle in the snow over by Chama. It belonged to my son Jimmy and once in sheep camp he left it too close to the fire and the stock had got burned, so we identified it all right, and they took it in for deposition. I think it was that Freddy Martínez who came and got it, but nothing ever came of that either. They kept it so long we finally had to go down and get it back ourselves. It was the damndest investigation I've ever seen, and the insurance man said the same thing."

As part of the investigation, about a hundred individuals were asked to take a polygraph test, among them Bill Mundy and his foreman, Alberto Teraces. One of the questions asked was, "Do you know who burned the house?" Mundy answered, no, and the machine indicated that he had not answered truthfully. The same happened with Alberto. All the others were asked the same question, but none of them registered as having lied.

"Well, hell, what kind of a question was that?" Mundy protests. "I knew who had done it, but I couldn't prove it. Either way I answered, I came out a liar. The second time they did it, me and Alberto came out okay."

Whatever the truth of the matter, a new tale of Anglo deviousness was added to the *Hispano* folklore of Río Arriba. The rifle, it was said, had been found by a Chama motel owner known to be friendly to Mundy. Most of the furnishings had been moved from the house to the barn before the night of the fire, it was said. The tracks in the snow on the other side of the highway had been seen only by Mundy's friends and had been obscured by everyone else's footsteps by the time the police had arrived.

Bill Mundy had burned his own house, said the tale, for the dual purpose of getting the insurance money and casting suspicion on the natives, in particular members of the Abiquiu Corporation and their new friends, the Tijerinas.

Most of those questioned were *Hispanos,* many of them members of the Abiquiu Corporation. Only one of the Tijerinas could be found for questioning: Anselmo, who was still serving time for assault and jail-break. All the *Hispanos* questioned were repeatedly asked, "Where was Reies Tijerina on the night of February 29? Where is he now? What do you know about Reies Tijerina?"

Reies says that he had left the Martínez house in late January of 1960 and was in Mexico in late February researching land grant matters with Cristóbal, the younger brother who had been raised apart from the family. The previous year, Reies had met with the then President of Mexico, Miguel Alemán, to discuss the possibility of some kind of public recognition by Mexico of the land grant demands.

Reies and Cris left Mexico sometime in May of 1960, Cris to return to his job driving refrigerated trucks out of San Antonio, Reies to return to New Mexico filled with a new determination and a plan.

Upon his return, he immediately threw himself into a furious evangelic campaign that was to last, virtually unabated, for the next seven years. Athough he had help, it was essentially a one-man campaign and always would be, carried along by an incredible energy and personal insistance. His objective was to enlist the sympathy, understanding and eventually the commitment of every man, woman and child of *la raza* that he met, and he left no stone unturned.

"He would talk to anybody," Félix Martínez says. "If he stopped for gas, he would talk to the man on the pump. At the store he would talk to the customers. And the owner. I once saw him try to convert a state cop while the guy was making him out a ticket."

He spoke at meetings of land grant organizations, meetings of ditch associations, in rented halls, in churches, wherever listeners might gather. He went from house to house, speaking to the men in the fields and the women in the kitchens, preaching to the families far into the night, exhorting the informal gatherings, the *tertulias,* like the legendary poet Apolinario Almanzares before him, who was said to have been a Comanche slave sold to the settlers for a blanket and a horse.

> *Lo mismo es pobre que perro*
> *Para que lo tratan mal.*
>
> *Al pobre le dicen, ¡fuera!*
> *Y al perro le dicen ¡sal!*
>
> Poor man and dog are the same
> In the treatment they both receive.
>
> To the poor man they say, Get out!
> Beat it! they say to the dog.

Reies also sang to them of expulsion from paradise and the bitter taste of poverty, lashing them with the staccato rhythms of his preacher's voice, goading them with a mind gifted with metaphor and trained to the single, compelling phrase.

They took your land away and gave you powdered milk. They took your trees and grazing away from you and gave you Smoky the Bear. They took your language away and gave you lies in theirs. They took your manhood away and asked you to lie down and be a Good Mexican. They told you you were lazy and cowardly and backward, and you believed them....

It was strong stuff, but it was for a purpose. They could not deny what he said, and he had books, sometimes opening them and pounding the dust up from their pages, sometimes holding them on high, large and venerable, bound in leather.

There are 1,715 land grants in the United States, given to you by the King of Spain. To all of you, to those who have no papers, even to those who have no memories. This book proves it. You are Hijos-dalgo, de la Santa Raza. The law is with us, justice is with us, God is with us!

It was heady and even fanciful, but it had the ring of history, warming the hearts of the old with memory, exciting the young to incredulous fascination. At least it was not the familiar promises of the *políticos,* to come to nothing beyond scraps of patronage for the few, the detested 10-pound brown paper bags of powdered milk for the many. At least it was not the earnest pledge of the welfare sociologist offering aid in adjusting to an alien way of life. It was a beguiling and truly impressive dream: the promise of return to their own way, their own power. And it wasn't as though he didn't have a plan.

This book proves that your land was stolen from you. In their own words at Guadalupe Hidalgo the gringos promised. By their own words they are liars. But they have lied before and had to give way before justice. The Indians have their land back, and we will have ours. We shall form an alliance of all Hijos-dalgo and heirs of all the grants, and we shall demand our rights under God. We will go to the Supreme Court, and if they don't listen, we will go to the United Nations, and if they don't listen, we will go to the International Court in Holland. If they won't listen to us, we will take direct action ourselves. Justice is mightier than their guns, and we fight in the name of justice.

Many of them were first attracted to the man by curiosity and later by fascination. Most were drawn to the meetings as they always had been to any promise of diverting performance, religious or political or preferably both. However, they were impressed and excited in increasing numbers.

But they were not very many, as yet, and most were wary and watchful, not ready to commit themselves beyond attendance at a few meetings and perhaps the contribution of a dollar.

In 1962, Alfonso Sánchez appeared before Judge James M. Scarborough and had no trouble in getting a $2,000 settlement for his injured client, Félix Martínez. Félix gave $200 to his wife and immediately headed north to Río Arriba, where he placed the remainder of the money in the hand of Reies Tijerina. The money paid for another fact-finding trip to Mexico and provided the financial base for the organization which was to make the life of Alfonso Sánchez hell for some years to come.

"Poor Al," Félix says with a grin. "If he had known what was going to come of it all, he and Scarborough would have cut two more fingers off my hand instead of giving me that money. But he was still friendly then. He was getting ready to run for district attorney."

"I even offered to let Félix have that hall on my property in TA to hold a dance in," Alfonso Sánchez says with an aggrieved sigh. "Rent free, to help finance his law studies. But he was too busy making trouble."

By the end of 1962, Reies was known by name to most of the *Hispanos* of northern New Mexico, and many of them had heard him speak. His reputation among those on the dismembered farms and in the dying towns of Río Abajo was uneven and scattered, but growing rapidly as he continued to make forays south, moving from village to village and grant to grant, expounding his message in the kitchens of the crumbling adobes.

He was only vaguely known to the majority of state officials and virtually unknown to the Anglo residents of Little Texas in the southernmost regions of the state. But many law officers were already acutely aware of his presence, and the Anglos of Río Arriba had long ago decided that he was the Fiend personified.

He was not the only one to suffer that year. The Ramon Spill ranch burned a month later. Another large landowner's barn had burned in January. Fences continued to be cut, cattle were slashed and, with the coming of spring weather, haystacks began to burst into flame up and down the valley of the Chama.

There is no doubt that such events did much to enhance Reies Tijerina's reputation in the eyes of many *Hispano* residents of Río Arriba, and they certainly earned the dark ire of the Anglos of Chama. He was not only a man of impressive and inflammatory words, but he also seemed to make things happen. Although he never publicly advocated violence, and always spoke of himself as "a man of peace and justice," his increased activity did coincide with increased activity by the night riders. It was difficult to disassociate the fiery passion of his preaching from the fires springing up in the night.

Freddy Martínez, detective lieutenant of the State Police in charge of criminal investigation in Río Arriba, began to put together what information he could on Reies and his brothers, consulting with his old friend Emilio Naranjo, sheriff of Río Arriba. Interest was expressed by numerous others, including Senator Joseph Montoya, who had always been able to count on a solid vote from the northern counties. The longtime *honchos* of the democratic establishment were coming awake to the possibility that there was something more dangerous in the wind than the usual aimless outbursts of anonymous violence and the floundering efforts of the Abiquiu Corporation.

The predominantly Anglo residents of Chama, most of them merchants, hotel and motel keepers and highly skilled workers employed by the various federal projects in the area, began to become increasingly anxious, alerted by rumor, speculation and their own uneasy instincts.

A new folk figure was in the making. A new name was catching the imagination of the majority in the north; a new nemesis was coming to haunt the minds of the minority, leaping to their lips with increasing assurance and anger.

"I know who burned that house," says Bill Mundy. "I can't prove it, but I know who did it."

However, despite a steadily increasing notoriety, his name was not yet a household word in New Mexico. He had gathered a small group of faithful lieutenants by the end of 1962, but they were few, and none of them able to work full time at organizing. Anselmo was out of jail but working at a job, serving as silent companion and bodyguard when he could. They were about eight altogether: two in Albuquerque, one in Bernalillo, one in Canjilón, one in Española, three in Tierra Amarilla.

Félix was the only one with a steady income at the time and supplied most of the petty funds for the effort. He had not been able to start at the university as planned and had been working full time as a vacuum cleaner salesman, supporting his wife and child and helping with the organizing when he could.

One night they heard that some *Hispanos* had been beaten up in the little town of San Luis across the border in Colorado, and they piled into old cars and headed north. Arriving in town, they circulated, made their contacts and called a meeting.

"That was really when the *Alianza* began, that night," Félix says. "Reies, he was beautiful, he brought them right off their chairs. He told them what we were going to do, and they listened. They couldn't help it. He has that fire, the pure and simple fire, right? The mayor was there and the sheriff too, and I'm telling you, they were scared. Because the way we'd set that town up, they *had* to be there. They *had* to listen to us."

Apologies were made by the town officials for the beatings and a promise was made to find and punish the offenders. It was a small triumph, but a significant one. San Luis is a tough mining and cow town and Anglo controlled.

"When we left there, we had decided," Félix says. "The thing to do now was to announce ourselves, give ourselves a name."

That same year, Reies and Mary Escobar decided to break up their marriage, which by then included six children.

"He didn't care about luxuries," Mary Escobar remembers. "All he wanted to do was preach. Preaching, reading, fasting. When we were traveling, I had to wash clothes on the rocks sometimes, and when the car broke down, we would just leave it there. But when the kids were growing up I started to want to settle down, and that's when our arguments started. I like to laugh, he does not much. He's too fast and nervous. Maybe that's why we didn't make it together, because he's so fast, and I'm so slow to think. I married him because I believed he was chosen by God for a special purpose. I still do, but now I think he was chosen for this cause, for the poor of the earth."

Cristóbal arrived in 1963 and joined Reies and Anselmo in a house on Fourth Street in Albuquerque, the first *Alianza* headquarters.

The first formal meeting of the *Alianza* was held in Alameda north of Albuquerque on February 2, 1963, and was attended by 34 members. The newspapers were informed, but did not send reporters.

The first *Alianza* publication was issued in September, 1963. Mimeographed in smudged ink on cheap paper and entirely in Spanish, it was the first popularly available printing of the Treaty of Guadalupe Hidalgo in the Southwest and probably in the United States in either Spanish or English, although editions would soon proliferate in both languages. The newspapers still took no notice.

The first convention was held in a high school gymnasium on September 21, 1963. Representatives of some 50 land grants were there. A constitution was drawn up declaring the objective of the organization to be the restitution of all lands and rights of all Royal Heirs to grant property guaranteed by the Treaty of Guadalupe Hidalgo, including all roads, highways, railroads, cities, banks, factories and Christmas trees.

The *Alianza Federal de Mercedes* or Federal Alliance of Land Grants applied for incorporation in Albuquerque on October 7, 1963, and was legally incorporated the following day. The objects and purposes of the corporation were stated to be:

"To organize and acquaint the Heirs of all the Spanish Land Grants covered by the Guadalupe Hidalgo Treaty . . . Thus providing unity of purpose and securing for the Heirs of Spanish Land Grants the highest advantages as provided by the afore-said Treaty and Constitutions (of the United States and State of Mexico)."

Article VI of the bylaws said: "All Heirs or members suspected of treason against the *Alianza Federal de Mercedes,* or communist affiliation are prohibited to vote or perform any activity. . . ."

Still the newspapers took no notice. In reporting that winter's session of the state legislature, the Albuquerque *Journal* did note that Representative Albert Amador had pushed through a memorial bill asking the federal government to appoint a commission to look into the land grant problem. The *Journal* did not bother to follow up later with the news that nothing had come of the memorial, since such grandstand plays were a standard part of the political repertoire and their ineffectuality a foregone conclusion.

While they ignored the founding of the *Alianza* completely, the newspapers did give full coverage to the election of Alfonso Sánchez as district attorney of the First Judicial District at Santa Fe, pointing out that Sánchez had won handily, thanks to the support of the Democratic establishment of Río Arriba, but no thanks to certain dissidents in the north, particularly members of the Abiquiu Corporation.

Alfonso Sánchez's first year in office began with comparative quiet in Río Arriba. Only a few fences were cut and a few cattle shot that winter. But in April, Don Graham of Chama was informed anonymously that "when trouble starts the best thing to do is leave town."

Similar anonymous phone calls and letters were reported by Anglo residents with increasing frequency as the summer wore on. Around the 10th of July, Leo Smith, foreman of the 33,000-acre Texas-owned Chama Land and Cattle Company operation, was working on a fence he had started the previous fall when seven of his *Hispano* neighbors walked up and told him to stop, that the land was theirs and they didn't want any more fences on it. Smith identified two of the men as trustees of the Abiquiu Corporation.

And then, in late July, at least 40 individuals, some of them ranchers, large and small, some not, most of them Anglos, received a neatly typed three-page notice headed with the name of the Abiquiu Corporation and entitled EVICTION ORDER.

> To All Whom It May Concern:
> In the name of the Almighty God, and by virtue of the legal land title given to Manuel Martínez, by the Mexican authorities in the year of our Lord on 20th day of July, 1832, we, the heirs of Manual Martínez, acting under the power invested in us by the above-mentioned Land Title, do hereby serve notice to all those non-heirs now possessing either small or large tracts of land within the Boundaries of the Tierra Amarilla Grant, that on the 20th day of October, 1964, we are determined with firm and resolute action to take possession of these tracts. . . .

The notice concluded:

> All Non-Heirs now possessing either large or small tracts of the Tierra Amarilla Land Grant are hereby given the vacating time prescribed by law, which in this case would be the maximum, to leave the premises on or before the 20th day of October, 1964.

"This is ridiculous," said Leo Smith of the Chama Land and Cattle Company. "I was born here. Nobody is going to run me out."

The next day he found one of his cattle shot and killed. Shortly afterward a Chama Land and Cattle Company barn burned to the ground, with an equipment loss estimated at several thousand dollars.

The new district attorney was informed of these alarming developments in his bailiwick. Whatever might have been his thoughts on the irony of it all, he wasted no time in declaring his intention to find and prosecute the culprits responsible for the damages and the threat.

But even the best proverbs can be turned about; and the blind would have their day, however brief, in the land of One Eye.

File 43-1 8

THE years between the founding of the *Alianza* in 1963 and its third national convention in 1965 mark the beginnings of Reies Tijerina's swift rise to national prominence. During this same period, there was an equally rapid proliferation of confidential reports concerning him and his organization.

Two days after the Anglo residents of the upper Chama valley were ordered to vacate their homes, Alfonso Sánchez began a file which started out as number 43-1, but which quickly became known as the *Alianza* or Tijerina file.

The file was begun with notes from the State Police file on the Tijerinas, which went back to the 1958 brawl which had landed Anselmo Tijerina in jail. Much of the material was the work of Detective Lieutenant Freddy Martínez and included the report of an informant within the Abiquiu Corporation, who had provided the names of 32 members of the Ensenada-Tierra Amarilla chapter.

Noting that the first 10 on the list were "The ones that are doing the sabotaging," the informant added "They beat the hell out of (an older member) last night . . . tried to make him swear that he would help them out regardless of what happened. So he left the meeting and two overtook him and beat him up."

The report concluded with the plea, "Please keep this out of public for they might catch me here at night and beat me up to scare the gringos. If I can be of help, come around. During the week days, for my wife will be in [a nearby town]. If she knew about this it would scare her. . . ."

On the same day that he began his file, Alfonso Sánchez wrote to Sheriff Naranjo regarding "Reyes [sic] Tijerina, alias King Tiger, Alias Reyes Tijerina López":

"Dear Emilio:

I understand that the above referred to individual is the person responsible for the recent threatened acts of violence involving the Tierra Amarilla Land Grant. Would you please investigate."

Also on the 22nd, he wrote to "Hon. J. Edgar Hoover, Director, Federal Bureau of Investigation, Washington, D.C.":

"Dear Sir:

Would you please forward to this office an FBI kickback with reference to the above referred to individual . . . [who] is allegedly involved in communistic activities and inciting some of the Northern local residents on land grant matters . . ."

The file included a copy of the eviction notice then in the hands of some 30 Anglo residents of Río Arriba, with a particular paragraph circled for emphasis:

"We want to have it clearly understood . . . that this ACTION OF OURS is sanctioned by hundreds of thousands of workers and Peasants in the WHOLE of Latin America . . ."

A report obtained by telephone from a number of sources, including Walter Kegel, former district attorney of Río Arriba, noted of Tijerina that ". . . he is considered as a crackpot by many who have come in contact with him. The original rumor was that he and another man were up here at the instance of the Communist Party. The United States Attorney's Office, Walter Kegel, State Police Headquarters and others . . . indicate that he is a far left radical . . ."

However, the compiler of the report concluded that among his informants it was agreed that Tijerina was not directly active in the current troubles in the north, and, in fact, was in Mexico at the time.

Three months before, in April, Reies had traveled with Amaranto Serrano of the Abiquiu Corporation to Washington, D.C., intending to confront the Secretary of the Interior with various land grant matters, including the corporation's claim to the TA Grant. They were presented to a representative of the department, who Reies later claimed had suggested that he was after a cash settlement "to shut up about the grants."

At the Department of Justice, Reies had surprisingly little trouble getting to see the then Attorney General, Robert Kennedy. "I told him," Reies says, "that the day was coming when no man would be able to be elected President of the United States without the approval of the Spanish-speaking peoples, here, but especially in Central and South America. I said to him, 'Listen, you think you are having trouble with the Negroes now, wait until we get started.'"

Kennedy was apparently receptive and sympathetic during the short interview, but he made no concrete promises, and the meeting was never called to the attention of the Washington press.

Representatives of the State Department were even less sympathetic than those at Interior. Following Reies' visit, a State Department representative commented to newsmen that Tijerina's claims were "so fantastic that it is difficult to form a defense in reasonable words."

The few news stories that appeared took the statement at its face value and for the most part lightly dismissed the visitors from faraway New Mexico. Nonetheless, it was Reies' first national publicity.

Within two months he was in Mexico, attempting to arrange for an automobile caravan to Mexico City, ostensibly to seek encouragement from "the poor people of Mexico," but more hopefully to attract international publicity for *Alianza* demands. Together with his then 15-year-old daughter, Rose, and four of his loyal followers, he set out from El Paso to prepare the route, making arrangements along the way for the marchers to camp in the fields and use the water of those who could be encouraged to help.

Arriving in Chihuahua, 150 miles south of the border, they discovered that several local dissidents had been recently jailed. Reies addressed a crowd in the city plaza, demanding the release of the prisoners, and was promptly arrested and jailed by Chihuahua State Judicial Police for holding a public meeting without permission. Reies says that a phone call to the capital secured his immediate release. Mexican official records say that he was ordered to return to the United States, and that he continued on to Mexico City instead, and that police subsequently kept an eye on him, waiting for his 30-day visitor's permit to expire. On August 8, the official records show, he was found shirtless in Mexico City, working on his car, was taken into custody and expelled from Mexico for "violation of the general law of the people."

Reies says that he was taken into custody by two plainclothes policemen without warrants and hustled to the airport so precipitously that he had no time to say goodbye to his daughter and had to borrow a shirt from the hostess of the plane. He was flown directly to Tuscon, where his brother Ramón, alerted by a telegram from the others, met him. He says that he had been encouraged in his project by a personal secretary to Adolfo López Mateos, President of Mexico at the time. He claims that he had advised the State Department of his plans, and that the Justice Department had sent FBI agent Gordon Brown to try to discourage him. He points out that coincidentally with his sojourn in Mexico, the Presidency passed from the hands of López Mateos to Díaz Ordaz, who was shortly to announce a five-year plan which he promised would "leave private initiative intact." Díaz Ordaz, Reies said, was instrumental in his eviction from Mexico, where he was already known for his friendship with such restless elements as the group gathered around the widow of Pancho Villa in Chihuahua.

Whatever the cause, the *Alianza*'s first attempt at a peaceful bid to draw public attention to their cause had failed. "Not many of us were going to go anyway," Fernanda Martínez says. "All those poor people down there, we didn't want to see them. And besides, it would cost us too much." A third and perhaps more pertinent reason might have been that the men of the Abiquiu Corporation were busy with their own project at the time, and it appeared to be far from peaceful.

As soon as the shower of eviction notices had descended on the startled outlanders of Río Arriba, District Judge Scarborough ordered a hearing for members of the Abiquiu Corporation and set the date for October 16, just four days before the eviction deadline.

A few days later, the state attorney general received a letter informing him that the members of the Abiquiu Corporation could not consent to such a hearing within the state of New Mexico, since in doing so they would be contradicting their own eviction notice, which had clearly stated that no court in the United States—federal or state—had jurisdiction over the Tierra Amarilla Grant, "or any other land grant in the United States." "Furthermore," the letter concluded ominously, "we shall proceed to carry out our work as stipulated in our eviction notice." It was signed by Amarante Serrano, president, and by the directors of the corporation, among them Juan Martínez.

Judge Scarborough talked to Amarante Serrano on the telephone and explained to him that the case was not to try the title to the land, but to consider restraining the Abiquiu Corporation. Serrano protested that justice was not being done and that he had sent copies of everything to Attorney General Kennedy and President Johnson explaining why the eviction notices had been sent and insisting that the Tierra Amarilla Grant belonged to members of the corporation under the Treaty of Guadalupe Hidalgo.

Scarborough promised to let members of the corporation testify concerning their land claims "so as to avoid any appearance of being unjust," according to a report in file 43-1.

Meanwhile, harassment continued in the north. The owner of a plumbing company in Chama received threatening anonymous phone calls, and he reported being advised by the *Hispano* town marshal that he was likely to get his tractors burned if he "resisted." The clients of a fishing lodge outside of town protested to the owner that while wading in the Brazos after trout, they had been informed that they would have to purchase fishing licenses from the Abiquiu Corporation at a rate identical to that charged by the state. Rancher Rex Sawyer found one of his steers missing, traced it to the house of one of the Corporation trustees and was told he couldn't have it back until he paid a seven-dollar grazing fee, an amount which, it was pointed out to him with gleeful irony, was in line with what the Forest Service was charging.

Such mock emulation of bureaucratic fee-gathering had a significance beyond mere harassment of local landowners. It was directed, not so much at its immediate victims, as at particular agencies of the United States government, which has for some time been the largest landowner in New Mexico and, as such, one of the principal targets of *Hispano* animosity.

Beginning in 1892 with the creation of the Santa Fe National Forest, the federal government had by 1960 gained possession of roughly 10 million acres or about one-eighth of the total land area of the state. It is one of *la raza's* fondest ironies that this area approximates that of the land once owned by the *Hispano* population.

Much of the land was acquired by purchase, usually at a healthy price paid to Anglo-American land speculators who had previously acquired the land from original native owners. Some of the larger tracts have become federal property by Presidential fiat, beginning with Theodore Roosevelt's creation of Carson National Forest by proclamation in 1906.

Carson covers 1,225,408 acres of northern New Mexico in three sections, the largest taking a good sized bite out of Río Arriba County, which is nearly 70 percent federally owned. The forest includes all or portions of a dozen Spanish and Mexican land grants and entirely encloses and consequently claims the *ejido* rights of several small villages, including Las Trampas, Placitas, Vallecitos and Canjilón.

Together with the steady buildup of federal ownership of land came increasing government interest in overall land management, reflected in the increased activity of its own and state and federal agencies, including the Bureau of Land Management, the Bureau of Reclamation, the Park Service and the Forestry Service. Beginning in the 1930s, this increased federal activity began to draw the attention and resentment of those to whom most of the land had once belonged.

Land management was and is needed. The ecological balance of the region had already been thrown badly out of kilter by the turn of the century. The cutting of timber had led to too-rapid runoff and consequent floods and erosion. By the 1930s, surface water was being drained off at an alarming rate, artesian wells were drying up east of the Pecos and in the lower Pecos valley the water table dropped 32 feet in 25 years, and as much as 200 feet in places. A tremendous buildup in the number of stock animals had led to serious overgrazing, which was destroying the natural grass and shrub cycles and leading to widespread erosion of topsoils.

To some extent this disruption of nature's natural balances was due to carelessness and ignorance on the part of the native population, to the villagers' casual habit of taking firewood and logs from the forests whenever they pleased and particularly to the enormous sheep herds of the *haciendas*. However, conditions were not bettered by wholesale removal of entire forests, such as that contracted by T. B. Catron in the Chama valley in 1897. The vast herds of cattle run by such Anglo stockmen as John Chisum of the Pecos valley exceeded in numbers and gluttony the herds of the richest *patrones*. Until the Yankees brought the first windmills in the 1870s and later the first motor pumps, all irrigating in New Mexico had been done with natural overflow, after the ancient Spanish law of water usage inherited from the Moors. The water belonged to him who could first put it to beneficial use; first user in time was first in right. Without wells and pumps, this meant that no water was used that could not be made to overflow onto the land by force of gravity. To the *Hispano* as to the Indian, this meant that nature could be pushed only so far, and in the end, if there was no water there, one could only pray for it. Such an attitude, often refered to scornfully as *fatalismo*, is offensive to the Anglo-American turn of mind which most often sees nature as something to be engineered.

When the wells began to go dry and the windmills to pump sand and the Río Grande to silt up and flood the suburbs of Albuquerque, the Bureau of Land Management took over and reclamation agencies and projects began to proliferate. This growing bureaucracy, joined by the legions of various "atomic and space" agencies, eventually made the government not only the largest landowner, but also the largest employer in New Mexico, thereby putting it in a position of advantage envied by many an individual entrepreneur.

The final outcome of such massive, integrated attempts to control the forces of nature is still in doubt and is likely to remain so. The water table continues to drop in New Mexico, and it is still impossible for Albuquerque landowners to get flood insurance.

There is no doubt as to the effect of the large reclamation projects upon the fortunes of the small stockmen and farmers in New Mexico, most of them *Hispanos*. Between 1910 and 1920, an extensive reclamation project was carried out in the Mesilla valley through the construction of Elephant Butte Dam, immensely improving the lot of the large-scale commercialized cotton farmer, but divesting virtually all of the small farmers of their land through tax foreclosure and throwing them into the migratory farm labor population. As a result of the Middle Río Grande Conservancy District Project of 1937, conditions were considerably improved for the large landowner near Albuquerque, but in the process thousands lost their land titles because they were unable to pay assessments which they had not even been allowed to vote on. Since few of them had the skills or for that matter the inclination to seek employment in stuffy government offices, they were also thrown into the rapidly overcrowding farm labor population. Of the great number of *Hispanos* forced to leave their land and accustomed way of life, quite a few eventually became followers of Reies Tijerina or are privately sympathetic to his cause.

In gathering its vast holdings through the first half of this century, the government has not always been entirely politic in its handling of those people it happened to find on or about its new domains. This was especially true in New Mexico, where title to much of the land acquired was still in question, at least in the minds of the natives. Not only was title frequently unclear, but there were often people living on the land when it was purchased, and they were perforce "sold" with it.

Through the first few decades of its existence the Forestry Service was content to let well enough alone, following an unofficially permissive policy regarding the many scattered farms on its land and allowing the villagers of adjacent communities to go on gathering firewood and grazing their sheep there as they had been doing for two centuries.

But beginning in the 1930s, a change took place, reflected in a policy referred to in land management circles as "multiple use." Justified by the increasing concern of conservationists and in keeping with the trend toward more careful management of the public domain, this policy was officially explained as a program to extract the most from the forests for the benefit of the many, while at the same time protecting and conserving the land for the use of future generations. In practice, it amounted to parcelling off the fruits of the land on a not always democratic basis, while at the same time tightening all restrictions, often with the blind zeal of machine bureaucracy.

The forests were mapped and trails were built for the rapidly increasing annual flood of out-of-state recreationists. From strategically located signboards, Smoky the Bear warned hikers and campers to break their matches in two and drown their campfires, and the public was happy to do so, secure in the knowledge that the land was theirs and the trees would be there forever, just as long as they did what Smoky said. In the meantime, the sportsmen were developing a system of strong lobbies to insure their right to fish the streams and kill the animals. Logging rights were let on a sustained-yield basis and ostensibly under strict controls. If the small logger found himself at a disadvantage in both getting the contracts and circumventing the controls, bigness was the national trend and there was strong sympathy for it in the agencies of Big Government.

When there were complaints in the Española valley that the Forest Service had helped the Duke Lumber Company set up in business by providing it with certain legal services, the reply was that the new operation was not only more efficient, but it brought 100 new jobs into the area. No mention was made of the fact that quite a few of these jobs were filled by men from other areas or from out of state. When a number of smaller outfits were put out of business by the Duke operation, it was explained that they were "inefficient." The small outfits eliminated by the larger company had supported a total of some 300 men, many of whom were thrown onto the welfare rolls.

Also beginning in the late '30s, the growing career force of the Forestry Service began to exhibit an increasing bureaucratic fussiness, reflected in an unrelenting campaign to tidy up the forests, which meant getting all interlopers out, the humans along with the livestock. Fences were built, animals were ear-tagged, and those animals belonging to owners without grazing permits were held until their owners paid trespassing fines. There were also fines for cutting trees and gathering firewood. The problem of removing the human beings living on federal land was a more delicate one and progress was cautious but steady, while the intent was unmistakable.

The Santa Fe National Forest includes all the Polvadera Grant and encloses a tiny community called Cañones, which the Federal government has been doing its best to forget for 30 years.

Back in 1937, Antonio Lucero of Cañones was approached by agents of the government and representatives of Emmett Wirt of Santa Fe and asked for proof that he owned the 25 acres he had been farming for some 20 years. He produced tax receipts and an ancient conveyance, but was informed that these were questionable proof of title. Eventually he was induced to sign his X to a quitclaim deed to the land and in return was given a 10-year use permit with no guarantee of renewal, all improvements to go to the government when his time was up. Immediately afterward, the government bought the grant from Wirt for $42,121 and made it part of the Santa Fe forest.

As a requirement for the sale, Wirt filed affidavits swearing that Lucero was the only person farming on the grant at the time. It was not true. In 1937, there were at least 25 families, some of whom had been there since the 1880s, farming some 34 tracts along Cañones Creek. Only Lucero was living on his land at the time; the rest lived nearby in the village of Cañones. But it is unlikely that either the government agents or Wirt were ignorant of the well-known custom of the people of the frontier settlements to live together for mutual protection, going out to work the land only during the day.

Three years later, in 1940, local land management director E. D. Eaton "discovered" the remaining Cañones farmers, and a chain of correspondence followed which reflected the sincere concern of some officials, but in the end only confirmed the tendency of machine bureaucracy to reduce the human and grind away the small. Eaton wrote to his chief asking for advice, his concluding sentence revealing an acute awareness of local bad feeling toward his bureau.

> ". . . we do not wish to evict any of the present occupants. They are definitely dependent on their small farms and if evicted will be unable to support themselves. Moreover, any such action would arouse general public opposition and would lead to endless trouble."

W. F. Dickson replied from Albuquerque, recommending that attempts be made to induce each family to sign quitclaim deeds in exchange for use permits to be issued yearly. If this did not work, they were to be offered life leases "only for the duration of the natural lives of the heads of the family." If that didn't work, Dickson acknowledged that "as a last resort . . . the lands may have to be deeded to the families."

Two years later, area conservationist Lewis Korn interviewed each claimant and reported that "Every claimant has warranty deeds, tax receipts or uncontested occupancy over a long period in his favor. Moreover, no purpose could be served by eviction . . . the lands concerned are mostly irrigated; their management would be expensive and would not improve the status of any dependent operators. . . ."

But a year later, Solicitor Robert Shields reviewed the cases of four claimants and after a great deal of technical discounting of proofs of ownership concluded that "we do not believe that any of the claimants is entitled to a quitclaim deed from the Government."

Closer to the scene, an officer of the regional division disagreed. "We can, of course, give the parties concerned some form of long-term use of the lands but this would not solve their problems, since I understand they use these lands as a basis for loans and treat them as deeded property, and therefore as collateral." And he concluded: "Another course that might be followed—although I hesitate to put this in writing—is that if the matter is stalled enough some office or another may forget about it and the thing can go along as it is. . . ."

By 1960, no direct action had been taken against the people living along Cañones Creek. But the threat of eviction that had hung over their heads for 23 years remained. Similar situations existed in the equally small and threatened villages of Vallecitos and Placitas in Carson forest. These villages would supply Reies Tijerina with a number of enthusiastic followers.

Finally, as a part of its efforts to tidy up its premises, the Forest Service, in cooperation with the Bureau of Land Management, began after World War II to drastically reduce the amount of animals allowed to graze in its forests. To do this, they had to reduce the number of permits in existence, and although the expressed purpose of the reduction was to lighten the drain on forest resources, the effect of the withdrawals was not indiscriminate.

The Taylor Grazing Act had been passed by Congress in 1934 for the express purpose of setting up mechanisms to protect the rights of small stockmen. Permits were issued, based on the number of animals already owned. Under the Grazing Act, the permits could not be sold, but they could be "given away" with the sale of each animal. By hanging on to his permits, the small owner could maintain his share of free use of the forest pastures, even if he was temporarily without animals. But in the 1940s, the Forest Service began to withdraw permits not in immediate use. In addition, a waiver of transfer could be demanded upon the sale of the animal under permit. Under certain conditions, the Forest Service could simply eliminate permits across the board.

From 1947 to the early 1960s, the number of permit holders in New Mexico was cut from 1,628 to 986. The cut in the number of permits was more drastic. On the allotment which serves the village of Vallecitos, total permits were cut by 40 percent. On the El Rito allotment, 70 free milk-cow permits were eliminated, along with 80 free horse permits, 200 cattle permits, 4,000 lambing permits and 2,000 sheep permits. Both villages are predominantly *Hispano*. In those 20 years of reduction, the number of sheep and goats grazed in New Mexico forests fell from 81,-806 to 37,075, while the number of cattle and horses stayed at about 21,000 head. This was partly due to the steady decrease in the market value of sheep during that time. But it is no secret in New Mexico that the grazing of sheep and goats had long been an *Hispano* preference, especially among the small ranchers.

Not only was the smaller stockman steadily losing out to the larger, but that loser was very likely to be a member of *la raza*. The village economies of the north had long been based on family ownership of a milk cow, a few sheep, a horse and maybe some beef cattle. They had a saying: *Mientras que la hierba crece, el caballo ño muere*—as long as the grass grows, the horse will not die. But the grass was no longer theirs. Instead, it was increasingly forbidden to them.

In Canjilón, there was eventual loss of 1,000 cattle permits, along with 20 free milk-cow permits and all free permits for horses and bulls—a reduction of 31 percent of the grazing. This in a town with an actual population of less than 500 persons whose economy had been based on livestock, grazing and timbercutting for a hundred years.

Canjilón was where Forest Ranger Smith had been in charge for 20 years. He never spoke a word of Spanish, but was always quite willing to say in his own language that he favored the large owner, that a man could run a hundred cattle a helluva lot more efficiently than five, that it only made that much less paper work for him and that as far as these locals were concerned, a few of them were all right but the rest were not much good, and if they gave him any trouble, they were just liable to find their cattle out on the highway trying to live off the yellow line.

Canjilón was to provide Reies Tijerina with the boldest and wildest of his shock troops. Canjilón was where Tobías Leyba had been born and lived all his life; where his nephew Baltazar Martínez had come to live with his mother after being asked to leave the Marine Corps; where Salomón Velásquez had been born; where Juan and Tony Valdez sometimes did some logging with their cousin Moisés Morales, who was fond of spinning his pickup truck around on the raked gravel of the Forestry Service parking lot and calling out to Ranger Smith cheerful but possibly obscene remarks in a foreign tongue.

Ranger Smith was not all Forest Rangers, but he was chief ranger at Canjilón in the fall of 1954 and one of the first of various federal officers in Río Arriba to receive the Abiquiu Corporation's eviction notice. Trustees of the corporation were apparently unable or unwilling to distinguish between individual and public landowners. The United States government was ordered along with the other outlanders to be out by October 20, or else.

There had been a number of small fires in the northern forests during the previous two or three years, none of which had got badly out of hand, but several of which were privately considered by Forestry officials to have been arson. Government fences had been cut a number of times within forest boundaries, and some animals belonging to larger permit holders had been shot. As the eviction deadline approached, rangers at the Canjilón station began to go to and from work discreetly armed.

Other recipients of the notices were no less apprehensive. Most of them had been informed indirectly that if they did not leave on October 20 they would be escorted out and compelled to leave with only personal belongings and one vehicle, the rest to be left behind as partial payment of back rent. There were more threatening phone calls and one landowner had his tires slashed and his gas tank sugared. Victims of the continuing incidents complained that an earlier date should have been set for the hearing and were scornful of the explanation by law enforcement agencies and the district attorney's office that arrests could not be made without adequate evidence.

Alfonso Sánchez was painfully aware of what a delicate situation he had on his hands. He knew that the harassment was not entirely indiscriminate and that many of his constituents in the north, while not active, were sympathetic to such action, especially as taken against certain individuals. His file 43-1 contained a note about one such Anglo resident and local representative for the Minnesota-based landholding corporation financially connected with the surviving family of T. B. Catron:

> ". . . has a long record of selling tracts of land with water rights which either are not present or which do not cover the represented acreage and in addition had a cute little trick of selling tracts on conditional sales agreements and then, when practically all the money has been paid, finds some way to claim a breach and takes the land back and keeps the money . . . he apparently has nothing but enemies and understandably so."

To make matters worse, the district attorney knew that, should trouble start on any large scale, there were those capable of violent reaction. One such group was said to make its headquarters at the Elkhorn Lodge in Chama. File 43-1 contained a report submitted in July which noted of the north, "People generally in the area are not involved in any violence but there are a few individuals, primarily the Mundys, the Herons and their employees . . . who might be."

There was one arrest which the district attorney was by now convinced would be well worth the risk in the long run, and which it seemed might even solve the immediate problem.

Unfortunately, the FBI "kickback" on Reies Tijerina, which arrived at the end of July, listed only the three arrests and charges filed during the Valley of Peace troubles back in 1957. A letter to the chief of police of Casa Grande returned the police version of events there, along with the information that the charges had been dropped. It seemed there was nothing to do but wait for the hearing and hope for the best.

Around October 15, large signs appeared within full view of several large-landowners' houses and opposite several government installations, notifying all and sundry that road blocks would be set up, all outlanders stopped and questioned, all hunters and fishermen required to purchase licenses. The notices were signed: Trustees, Abiquiu Corporation.

The opening day of hunting season was only weeks away. Heavily armed hunters would be flocking north in station wagons filled with yapping dogs. It was not hard to imagine the look on their faces as they were flagged down one by one by the raggle-taggle militiamen of Río Arriba and informed that, contrary to what they might have read in their history books, this was not their country—not this part of it, anyway. . . .

Armed guards appeared around the construction site of the giant tunnel being built as part of the San Juan-Chama Transmountain Diversion Project outside Chama. Several federal employees at the trout hatchery in Parkview joined their fellows of the Forestry Service and armed for self-defense. Residents of Chama began moving their wives and children out of town and readied their own armaments. Bill Mundy went about his work as usual, but with the 300 Savage close at hand in its saddle sheath. The Abiquiu Corporation set up a headquarters on the highway between Tierra Amarilla and Chama.

"There is going to be bloodshed," Freddy Martínez is reported to have said from behind the dark glasses he never removes.

"We will defend ourselves," declared Leo Smith, foreman of the Chama Land and Cattle Company.

The hearing was held on schedule in District Court in Albuquerque, Judge Paul Tackett presiding. One hundred and fifty men and women were named as defendants, along with "unknown heirs" of several deceased persons, including Francisco and Manuel Martínez.

The defendants, choosing not to be represented by an attorney, were represented by Amarante Serrano and other trustees, including Juan Martínez. They presented their cases, which consisted of documents, citations and opinions to sustain their claim to the land, a matter which Judge Tackett explained to them was not at issue. After five hours, during which they couldn't seem to get this through their heads, they were sent home.

Six days later, on October 20, the exact day of the eviction notice deadline, Tackett issued a Final Decree and Restraining Order, stating that "in view of the numerous federal and New Mexico decisions holding said grant [of Tierra Amarilla] to be a private grant instead of a community grant . . . the Corporation of Abiquiu is not and cannot be a duly licensed land grant corporation as contemplated by the laws of the State of New Mexico; that the Corporation of Abiquiu . . . [is] adjudged an invalid corporation and permanently enjoined from existing as such."

The night of October 20 was a tense one for many, certainly including District Attorney Sánchez. But beginning the following day, the signs were one by one removed, the corporation's highway headquarters disappeared and by week's end, good citizens, state and federal governments and red-capped hunters were once again in possession of the Tierra Amarilla Land Grant and could return to "peaceful enjoyment of said land."

It was not the first time the state's legal machinery had been enlisted in an attempt to decree the organization out of existence. As recently as 1951, District Judge Carl A. Hatch had ordered a permanent injunction forbidding the election of a board of trustees to an organization calling itself, in those days, the Tierra Amarilla Land Grant.

"I tried to tell them," sighs Alfonso Sánchez, wistfully exhorting his misguided charges *in absentia*. "You can't go taking over land like that. You have to go through due process, and to do that you have to have a case. There is no case here. Tijerina is lying to you about these grants. This man is dangerous for you, for all of us."

By now he was not the only one convinced that Tijerina had been behind the Abiquiu Corporation's actions, nor was he alone in his fears for the established order. State Attorney General Stewart Hatch began a file on Tijerina and the *Alianza*, as did the FBI and other official agencies, both state and federal, on the scene and in Washington, D.C.

There is little doubt that Reies was one of the driving spirits behind the Abiquiu Corporation's effort of 1954, but he was not alone and certainly not entirely in charge. There is evidence that there was considerable internal conflict between the *Alianza* and the Abiquiu Corporation, then and at other times.

However, whatever the degree of his involvement, he benefited enormously from the affair. Not only was it the talk of the *Hispano* grapevine, but it received press coverage statewide and was mentioned in newspapers throughout the Southwest and even as far away as California. Not only had the land grant question been brought to greater public attention that ever before, but the name Tijerina was well on the way to becoming synonymous with it.

. Meanwhile, the furious pace of his campaign to enlist the *Hispano* populace had not abated. By now the *Alianza* had a headquarters, a cement block building on Third Street in Albuquerque, with an office and a hall with 200 folding chairs. The building had been paid for with funds from the sale of the *Valle de la Paz* land in Arizona, with full agreement by all former Heralds of Peace, Reies says. "That was always what we decided, that the money should in some way go to further the cause."

To go with the new building, a new letterhead was printed with the slogan, *La Tierra Es Nuestra Herencia y La Justicia Es Nuestro Credo* (the land is our heritage and justice is our creed). The constitution approved at the first convention had been printed, entirely in Spanish, stating that, "The cardinal principles of the *Alianza Federal de Mercedes*

111

will be: Justice, Judgment, Compassion and Truth. Justice for the oppressed; Judgment for the oppressors; Compassion for the forgotten and Truth for all."

A rubber stamp was acquired which proclaimed with each smudged impression that the *Alianza* represented five million land grant heirs in Texas, New Mexico and California.

If a large percentage of the five million were not yet aware they were being represented, several thousand were, among them an increasing number of urban *Hispanos*, many of whom had entertained a scholarly interest in land grants for years.

"I had been reading up on the grants up in Utah," says 55-year-old Alfonso Chávez. "Professor Ernie Wilkinson of the university suggested I write to Congressman Peterson, who helped to get a million-dollar settlement for the Utes. But Peterson just referred me to the Justice Department. So when I came to Albuquerque in 1962, I heard about what Reies was doing and in 1963 I talked to him and I found out we practically speak the same language."

"I am an heir to the Cubero Grant," says Mrs. Adella García Meyers, a middle-aged California lady with silver-blue hair. "We had been declared heirs by the court, but people had been using our land and the state was trying to assess us for taxes and improvements all the way back to before we were born. The judge and lawyers were trying to get us to hand over 400 acres in payment. I met Reies in California in 1964, and he promised to help me."

"Reies looked me up in Albuquerque in 1963 because of my activity in trying to straighten out the Atrisco Grant," says gray-haired, dapper Eduardo Chávez. "Ricardo Griego of the other grant party had called Reies a Communist wetback over at the Lions Club, and anybody that Griego gets that excited about, I'm interested in. I was night watchman at the West Mesa Airport then, but I've been full-time with Reies ever since."

There were many others who felt their land had been stolen. Some made no claim at all, but joined for other reasons, of which the land was only a symbol. Margarito arrived, still under sentence for killing the man in Indiana. Reies would later say that his brother had claimed that his parole officer had remanded him to Reies' custody.

The *Alianza*'s second national convention was held at Seth Hall in Santa Fe on August 29, 1964. Attendance was not numbered in the hundreds this time, but in the thousands. Guest speakers came from as far away as Mexico City and Chicago. This time the New Mexico press was well represented. Also unofficially present were agents of the various law enforcement agencies and other interested parties, including the office of Alfonso Sánchez.

Although much of the general public, particularly in Anglo circles, was still reluctant to take Tijerina seriously, and was so encouraged by the press, official attention was thoroughly alerted, for the most part to alarm and apprehension. From 1964 on, *Alianza* conventions would be faithfully attended by law officers and investigators of widely varying loyalties.

The *Alianza* and its fiery leader were noticeably quiet through the last months of 1964 and the first of '65. Then, on August 27, 1965, the District Court at Santa Fe received a registered letter written in Spanish announcing that the militants of Río Arriba were once again "disposed to take possession of the land." On the edge of the paper, the legend *COLONIA MEXICANA* had been typed above a name that had been defaced, but not so thoroughly as to prevent the curious from making out beneath the row of Xs the name of the organization only recently enjoined from existing, the Abiquiu Corporation.

"The ogre has reared its head again," commented the Santa Fe *New Mexican*.

"Tijerina," the *Hispano* grapevine reported excitedly, and the news was bitterly seconded by state officials.

However, a report in file 43-1 indicated that the *Alianza* leader appeared to have had a falling-out with grant leaders in the north and to have transferred operations to the Pecos valley and San Miguel County. The report added that a theft ring was operating in the area "similar to Tijerina's operation in Arizona," although no charges were made to connect Tijerina with the thefts.

"Reies first come here, I think, in 1965," says Pula Padilla of the crumbling highway town of Rowe. "He speak over in Tecolote, and after that I join the *Alianza*. My father and my uncle too. Reies, he stay over on the Tecolote Grant in the house of Cruz Sánchez for a while. Cris, he came here to the house first, then Reies. I say to him, 'You like fish?' He say yes, so I go down to the river and I catch 10. He eat six. Oh, he love to eat, just like he love to talk."

This was the period during which Reies was busy increasing his following south to Antón Chico and broadcasting for a time from a radio station in Las Vegas as the "Voice of Justice."

The north was not, however, without an energetic champion that winter. Félix Martínez had managed to complete two years of college, thanks partly to a $1,000 scholarship received in 1964 for selling more Electrolux vacuum cleaners than anybody else in the United States. At the same time that he studied and worked, he had been organizing for the *Alianza*.

"I was selling two things. Every time I sold a vacuum cleaner, I also made a convert."

Then, in early 1965, his marriage broke up. He left his wife and child, quit school and "drove anywhere I could drive a car, just throwing my money away for three months."

One of the places he happened to visit during his travels was the Watts ghetto outside Los Angeles, where, according to him, he "learned where it's at."

In the late summer of that year, two events took place which, while

113

they were of the broadest national interest, would each have a profound effect on the *Alianza* and its leader and ultimately upon untold others within the *Hispano* community.

On August 11, the black people of Watts revolted and sustained a riot which lasted for five days, resulted in the death of 35 persons, most of them black, and caused property damage estimated at $200 million.

Three weeks later, about 700 Philippine migrant workers following the grape harvest in California, found that growers in their home area of Delano refused to meet the $1.40 per hour wage paid by the Coachella Valley growers and were moving in temporary Mexican immigrant workers in hopes of reducing the wage to 90 cents. Organized by the Agricultural Workers Organizing Committee of Delano, the field workers were refused even discussion of collective bargaining by the growers and decided to strike. On September 16, they were joined by 1,100 Mexican-American migrants, organized by the National Farm Workers Association. Under the leadership of César Chávez, the *huelga*—strike—of Delano remained steadfastly passive and within the law, despite floods of strikebreakers and increasing incidents of violent provocation by growers and police.

To Reies Tijerina and his *Alianza*, and to many of the more than six million *Hispanos* of the United States, the contrast between the two events would eventually come to symbolize an increasingly urgent choice. Was it to be the benign patience of Our Lady of Guadalupe, symbol of the Delano strikers, or was it to be, "Burn, baby, Burn!"?

Félix returned to Río Arriba a different man. He was 24, and he had talked with the younger *Hispano* leaders in California, who called themselves *Chicanos*, and with black militants in Watts. He came home with a beard and mustache modeled after that of Ché Guevera and a new phrase on his lips: "Revolution speeds up evolution."

No doubt he had a hand in the formation of the new *COLONIA MEXICANA* and contributed to the resounding air of manifesto distinguishing its letter to the District Court. Judge Tackett wasted no time in instructing the district attorney's office to announce that if this new "alleged corporation" violated the restraining order of the year before, its members would be charged with contempt and "dealt with accordingly."

"We just won't stand for any monkey business up there," added the district attorney's assistant, E. E. Chávez.

Nothing more was heard of the *COLONIA MEXICANA*. The rift between the northerners and Tijerina proved to be of little consequence, and Félix was soon busy helping prepare the *Alianza's* third annual convention, which was held in Albuquerque in September.

The convention was attended by 3,000 enthusiastic members and supporters, and a large corps of reporters, several from out-of-state. Guest speakers had come from as far away as Mexico, San Antonio, Denver, Los Angeles and Chicago. In his keynote address, Tijerina an-

nounced that the *Alianza* had retained lawyers to challenge the authority
of the Middle Río Grande Conservancy District, the same flood control
authority which had put so many small *Hispano* farmers and stockmen
out of business. A highlight of his address was his impassioned denunciation of the land. The Senator had been invited to attend the convention
ests and to the Anglos in general.

The previous year, Reies had contacted Montoya and asked him
to look into *Alianza* claims and initiate Congressional action for restitution of the land. The Senator had been invited to attend the convention
but had not appeared. His reaction to Tijerina's denunciation was to request renewed FBI investigation of Tijerina and the *Alianza*.

The success of the 1965 convention deepened the growing enmity
of established forces towards the *Alianza*. Among certain politicians and
officials both state and federal and of widely varying stripe, a quietly
frantic campaign was taking shape, its objective to discredit the *Alianza*
and its leader and possibly to destroy them.

A lengthy memorandum from State Attorney General Stewart Hatch
soon found its way into file 43-1. It noted that in a recent speech
Tijerina had referred to the Watts riots and according to informants had
promised "another Watts from the middle Río Grande to the Colorado
border, if members of the *Alianza* do not get their 'rights.' " It further
noted that "in personal conversation T. speaks approvingly of F. Castro's
'land reforms' and other Cuban programs"; that "T. finds it necessary to
make trips to Mexico for 'medical care' "; that he "allegedly receives
funds through *Banco de México*"; that although the Immigration Service
reported no evidence of illegal entry, there was "doubt about T.'s origins
[which appear to be] Spanish, not of N. M. or Tex."; that Professor
Clark Knowlton, "usually friend of left wing groups," had delivered a
speech at the convention; that the recent convention had been described
by the manager of the Albuquerque Civic Auditorium as the "best dis-
ciplined and best run convention" ever held there; that Tijerina spoke
on the radio "daily at 6 A.M. on KABQ, Albuquerque, 9:30 A.M. Sat.
and Sun."; and that the *Alianza* allegedly had "$144,000 in the bank and
82 suits ready for filing to reclaim title to the land [from Spanish
grants]."

Accompanying the memorandum were several membership lists and
a map. Reies' name appeared at the top of a list entitled "informal hierarchy," with Anselmo beneath him and Cristóbal third in command. The
map of New Mexico bore the written note at the bottom, "location of
agents, Sept. '65," and had seven towns circled, apparently the location
of law enforcement agents, and 24 towns underlined, apparently locat-
ing *Alianza* members.

The memorandum concluded with the information that "T. claims to
control 14,000 votes" and Attorney General Hatch's opinion that " . . .
political dynamite . . . potential danger to maintenance of order . . . may
be controlled by accused and possible actual Communist."

The attorney general's final question was "What to do about this (so-called) Communist Wetback . . . any legitimate role state play decrease power prevent increase?"

On October 2, an event occured which seemed sure to do much toward solving the attorney general's problem. Late that evening an old model station wagon pulled up in front of a store run by Robert Wilson and his wife in Rutherton, a few miles northeast of Tierra Amarilla. A woman got out, then a man, who entered the store, hit Mr. Wilson over the head with a blunt instrument, stabbed Mrs. Wilson with an ice pick or similar instrument, then fled with $300 in cash.

Shortly thereafter, Anselmo Tijerina was arrested. Several weeks later, he was released, and Margarito Tijerina arrested in his place and charged with felonious assault and robbery.

The Republic of San Joaquín de Chama 9

THE first public confrontation between Alfonso Sánchez and Reies Tijerina took place on the stairs of the Río Arriba County courthouse during Margarito's trial in July, 1966. The raid was 11 months into the future, but many of the participants were present to witness the rehearsal of some of the more personal passions behind the violence to come. The exchange was brief and the words ludicrous, but the musty wooden walls echoed back other unspoken and older ambiguous conflicts.

"I told him he had called me a Communist wetback in the newspapers," says Reies. "I told him that was slander and if he didn't watch out I would sue him, and then he would have to find a good lawyer."

"I told him that I had not called him that," says Alfonso Sánchez. "I said, 'But what you are advising these people to do, that is Communistic. Overthrow of the government and all this about taking back the land and setting up your own government and *pueblos*, that is Communistic.' "

"I told him he had lied in *Newsweek* magazine when he said I tried to hire him to help the *Alianza*," Reies says. "I told him, 'We didn't want you then, we do not want you now, we do not want you in the future!' "

"I told him that he knew darn well he had come to me, sitting right in that chair," says Alfonso Sánchez. "I told him that he might be needing a lawyer himself pretty soon if he didn't stop inciting to violence and illegal acts. When the jury went out, I said to him, 'You've been sitting here in that front row all this time, now you can see how our system works.' But when the jury was ready, guess who came running down those stairs with his hands to his face, saying, 'I can't do it, I can't listen to what they are going to do to my brother!' "

Anselmo was twice positively identified by the Wilsons as their assailant. He was charged with assault and battery, arraigned and his bail was set. When further investigation revealed that his alibi was airtight, he was released and Margarito was picked up. The Wilsons now identified Margarito as their attacker, and he was charged, arraigned and denied bond by request of Indiana authorities.

The two brothers do not look dissimilar, but they do not look identical, either. Margarito's defense rested on the testimony of a number of people who said they had seen him in Albuquerque at the time of the crime. By the time he was brought to trial on July 17, 10 months after the assault, all the witnesses had disappeared into the migrant stream in search of summer work, with the exception of one man named Márquez. At the last minute, Reies' 19-year-old son David came forward to say that he too had seen his uncle in Albuquerque, but that since he had been with a girl in the trees at the time he had not come forward earlier out of embarrassment and a desire to protect her. The district attorney was quick to point out to the jury that the boy had taken a long time before "deciding to become a witness." Dismissing other incidental witnesses as "a bunch of liars," he asked that they be impeached, but the jury declined.

Defense witness Márquez claimed to have cracked a rib before the trial and asked to be excused from making the trip from Albuquerque to Tierra Amarilla, testifying by deposition instead. The district attorney reminded the jury that he was thereby denied his right to challenge this witness' testimony by cross-examination. A woman named Bea, who had been living with Margarito, was found in Chicago and brought back, presumably to be charged as Margarito's accomplice. However, she did not testify, nor was she charged.

The trial lasted for three days, with the jury being let out each night. On July 19, Margarito was convicted, sentenced to from 10 to 50 years and put in the New Mexico penitentiary, with an Indiana parole violation waiting for him when he got out. The next month, Alfonso Sánchez charged him as a second offender and habitual criminal, which would increase his term to 25 to 100 years, if convicted. Perjury charges were brought against David Tijerina and he was required to post a $1,000 bond. Appeal of Margarito's conviction, which required a $1,500 cost for a trial transcript, was not made before the deadline.

"Mario was always . . ." Reies squints, shakes his head impatiently. "Well, I told you, he didn't talk until he was 11, and he drank so much sometimes, *so much*."

"Poor Mario," says Fernanda Martínez, who was a defense witness. "He had a job working on gardens for that Anglo in Albuquerque, but that woman, Bea, she got mixed up with the man. And the man took Mario to the John Birch bookshop and kept saying things about Reies, and Mario got mad and lost the job. He tried to live out at the ranch for a while, but there is no electricity and no water and only that old house trailer we have. He was so mixed up sometimes, and he had a terrible temper. Poor Mario. But maybe it's for the best."

Margarito's conviction undoubtedly brought second thoughts to some of those who had no interest in the land but were sympathetic to the plight of the *Hispano* in general. Many such were Anglo liberals, who are small in number but vigorously active in New Mexico. However, those who had hoped that public discredit of one Tijerina would do fatal damage to the rest of the Tijerinas and their organization were to be sorely disappointed. On the contrary, the summer of 1966 saw the fortunes of the *Alianza* mounting steadily, both in terms of membership and rapidly broadening public attention.

Back in November, 1965, the Denver *Post* had carried a lengthy article crediting the *Alianza* with a membership of 14,000, telling Reies' version of the troubles at *Valle de la Paz* in Arizona, and quoting him as saying that the United States government was the party responsible for making good on past wrongs.

In April, 1966, the *Post* ran another story, this one with a photograph of Reies posed in front of the *Alianza* headquarters in Albuquerque. Clearly visible was the motto, "The Land Is Our Heritage," and the article quoted Reies as declaring passionately, "I saw the miserable situation of my people. Their cries and needs. I give my life to them."

It is true that the *Alianza*'s claims to millions of acres were usually dismissed as without basis, most often with the quotation from the State Department official about being unable "to form a defense in reasonable words." (Curiously enough, in the same year that Reies travelled to Washington, some of the documents sold as newspaper by Territorial Governor Pile back in 1869 had turned up in the possession of a Kansas City book and document dealer named Kenneth D. Sender. Sender was offering the documents, dated between 1697 and 1845, for sale in New Mexico for a reported price of $50,000, when the Attorney General reportedly stepped in to claim ownership on behalf of the Department of the Interior, and whisked all that wastepaper quietly away.)

But it was the very enormity and seeming audacity of Tijerina's claims that guaranteed him an attentive, if amused press. In May an article in the small San Diego *Independent* credited the *Alianza* with a membership of 15,000, pointed out that the *Alianza*'s claims included thousands of acres of San Diego and quoted a local member as saying that he himself had no claims in San Diego proper, but adding, "However, my family does claim Newport, Santa Ana and a good portion of Los Angeles."

Early that same month, Reies and Cristóbal had made a trip to Spain, ostensibly to research land grant matters. After looking into Spanish land law at Madrid's *Biblioteca Nacional,* they moved on to Seville, where Reies was interviewed by a newspaper which referred to him as "the Martin Luther King of the Spanish-Americans."

In the interview Reies reiterated the charge of cultural rape which had long been a part of his gospel, then introduced two significantly new themes. For the first time, the *Hispano* cause was related to that of the American blacks then in revolt in a dozen urban ghettos, and for the first time oblique reference was made to the war in Vietnam.

"The Anglo absentee landlords are not content to just steal the Spanish-American lands, but wish to wipe out their culture and language," Reies told Seville reporters. He said he was prepared to lead "five million members" of the *Alianza* to a takeover of vast portions of the United States, "and to reinstitute the Spanish culture and language there."

"Americans," he charged, "want nothing to do with anything Spanish and hope to keep Spanish-Americans in a second-class category of citizenship, worse than that of the Negroes, for at least the Negro problems are talked of, while the Spanish-Americans are regarded only as potential soldiers to be sent to fight in other countries."

The interview appealed to an officially suppressed but long-standing popular resentment of American air bases in Spain, which had recently been aggravated by the dumping of three hydrogen bombs on the Spanish coast. State Department officials labeled Tijerina's statements "strongly anti-American" and charged him with doing "the U.S. image a great deal of harm."

However, Tijerina's 30-day journey to Spain impressed the *Alianza* membership and that organization continued to grow, watched now, no doubt, by the CIA as well as other national and local government agencies.

By the middle of 1966, Reies was claiming an *Alianza* membership of 20,000 in four Southwestern states and California. Police estimated the figure as closer to 5,000, but it was becoming increasingly difficult to tell who were members and who were not. The membership files were closed to public examination, the *Alianza* leadership saying that secrecy was necessary in recruiting those who had reason to fear reprisals.

Furthermore, there was an increasing number of semi-secret members and sympathizers, shy of being known as such and still not fully committed, many of them hesitant as a result of charges made by *Alianza* critics and echoed uneasily among the general *Hispano* population.

There were those who said that Tijerina was only using the land grant question for his own benefit and profit. They predicted with bitter assurance that he would in the end turn out to be just another self-seeking *político*. They said he was salting the money away in a bank in Arizona. And they asked why he had not yet managed to get an actual court suit in motion for legal restoration of even one land grant.

Among the state's 33,000 *Hispanos*, the doubters were by far the majority. But the margin was narrowing.

Alianza membership dues were only a dollar a month per family, and although there were frequent calls for voluntary contributions, it was generally agreed that these barely covered the cost of such projects as the trip to Spain, which had been approved by the membership. A one-page *Alianza* "progress report" sent out shortly before the trip repeated a desperate appeal for back dues three times, but probably got very little cash return. All of Tijerina's lieutenants acknowledged that only Reies could get appreciable amounts of money out of members and that it had to be done in person, preferably with a moderate-sized crowd upon which he could work the magic of his speaking style.

He repeatedly and heatedly pledged that he would never run for public office, and there was little evidence of the usual back-door overtures to established politicians. On the contrary, he had pleased the people no end by vehemently and persistently attacking the powers that were, one and all.

The charge that was taken most seriously, especially among those of the membership with strong claims to the land, was that no case had as yet reached court. But Reies had repeatedly assured them that cases were being prepared, and he made clear that his plan was to force the general question of the land grants into court, as he had already brought it forcefully to national and even international attention.

Perhaps most reassuring of all to a clannish, Catholic and essentially conservative population, was the fact that it was a matter of common knowledge that Reies neither drank, smoked nor gambled, was singularly restrained although always gracious in the presence of women, drove an old model, moderately priced car and lived with notable frugality in a three-room apartment at the back of *Alianza* headquarters.

As for the continuing charges that he was a Communist, a few were conventionally alarmed, but many were inclined toward the instinctively pragmatic spirit reflected in a comment by Eddie Chávez: "I'm not sure what a Communist is, but I get a feeling that a lot of the time it's anybody who causes trouble for the people in charge."

A far more pertinent cause for suspicion to many was the fact that Tijerina was not a native New Mexican. But even they had to admit, when pressed, that in the ways that counted most to them, he was more nearly a native in spirit than many an Anglo then branding him as an interloper and alien.

While many were suspicious and most were unsure, an increasing number were sympathetic and inclined to approve, if not to join. He was one of them, not only in language and blood, but as equally disadvantaged and disinherited. As they were a minority, so he seemed a minority of one in the face of the same overwhelming odds. He had dignity and passion and style. To many, especially to the old and those of the north, he had become the old and proper ways personified, and was a living promise of return.

In addition, the *Alianza* also served as a social club, and its headquarters became for many a home away from home. Food was served after every meeting, there were *tamaladas* and dances, wedding receptions and engagement parties, and on religious holidays statues of the saints appeared among paper flowers on makeshift altars in the meeting hall. On quiet afternoons, old men sat talking or dozing in chairs along the walls. Behind the small speaker's platform a mural was being painted. A brilliantly hued rainbow lettered *Alianza Federal de Mercedes* arched above a rich and verdant landscape, where a strange, narrow-headed bird tore at the guts of a snake and a brown-skinned man and a red-skinned woman walked hand-in-hand at the foot of a towering pyramid, at the peak of which was incised the word: Justice.

The symbolism of the mural was of Reies' choosing, and reflected a quality of his campaign that drew perhaps more adherents than any other: it was colorful, it was imaginative, it had flair. He made drama for them—their kind of drama—and so far it was drama staged well within the law.

Late in June, Reies announced a march "to the capital to demand our rights." The march would be orderly and peaceful, patterned after the civil rights marches led by Martin Luther King. Reporters were there on July 2 when a hundred *Alianza* members set out from the Albuquerque headquarters to walk the 65 miles to the state capital in Santa Fe, carrying canteens, cooking outfits, bedding and placards, a large one in front declaring: "William A. Pile, Governor of New Mexico, Destroyed Spanish Archives."

There were women, children, a bearded man on a burro. Two days later, they entered Santa Fe and marched toward the capital grounds, hand-sewed flags flapping, hand-lettered placards held on high. They were met by two members of Governor Jack Campbell's staff, who explained that Campbell was in Los Angeles attending a governor's conference.

"We will talk only to the governor," Reies declared. "He could get on a plane and fly here. It would only take him 15 minutes to talk to us, then he could fly back.

The governor returned when the conference was over, six days later. He received the *Alianza* leader in his office and was offered a petition to President Johnson demanding executive action on behalf of land grant claimants. Choosing the better part of political valor, Campbell accepted the petition and promised to send it on to the President and the state's congressional delegation. In conclusion, he complimented the *Alianza* on the order and cleanliness of its march and demonstration and said that he was glad to see the group exercising a basic American right in such orderly, democratic fashion.

From the steps of the capitol building, Reies assured a diminished crowd of his followers: "This will start a chain reaction of similar events until the Spanish-American receives justice."

The only result, beyond brief stories in Albuquerque and Santa Fe newspapers, was a letter sent to the governor from State Archivist Dr. Myra Ellen Jenkins, outlining her opinion on the *Alianza*'s land grant claims, implying that she thought the organization was a con game, and concluding, "I fear that there are outside influences which are reopening this old issue for pecuniary gain."

At the next formal meeting of the *Alianza* it was voted to sue Mrs. Jenkens together with the state for two million dollars. "The suit was for slander," Reies explains, "but to defend herself, she would have to produce proof from the state archives. She would have to prove that we were wrong, that there is no case for return of the land. It would have become a land grant case, you see. We would have taken it all the way to the Supreme Court!"

A month later, Mrs. Jenkins filed for dismissal of the case on grounds that the suit "fails to state a claim . . . upon which relief can be granted."

The District Court concurred; no relief was to be granted.

As for President Johnson, he failed to reply. Reies scornfully suggested to the *Alianza* membership that the President was taking petty vengeance on him for having claimed that the LBJ Ranch was a part of the Pedernales Land Grant, swindled from its original Spanish owners at the turn of the century. He pointed out that the President's land holdings in Texas had been steadily mushrooming at a rate denied to the public, but reported to have reached 14,000 acres, with another 26,000 acres being bargained for. He reminded them that as a junior Senator, Lyndon Johnson had consistently backed legislation to sustain the *bracero* program. And then he read to them from the President's 1965 civil rights address to Congress, in which he had recalled his first job as a teacher in Cotulla, Texas, noting that few of his students could speak English and that he couldn't speak much Spanish, and adding that, "They never seemed to know why people disliked them. But they knew it was so. Because I saw it in their eyes. I often walked home late in the afternoon after classes were finished, wishing there was more I could do."

"There is much more you can do, Mister President," Reies railed to the weekly gathering in the cement block building in Albuquerque. "You can learn our language if you want to teach us. You can get off our land. You can answer us when we write to you!"

But the membership had heard this before and would hear it again. The results of the Santa Fe march had been disappointing.

Senator Montoya had made a tentative offer to introduce a bill into Congress to create a commission to investigate land grant claims, and two state representatives, both Democrats and *Hispanos* like Montoya, had agreed to support such a proposal.

But there was a gubernatorial election coming up and a strong Republican in the running, and as was often the case, the vote in Río Arriba could tip the balance.

Republican David Cargo had an impressive record as a lawyer and in the state legislature. Fond of referring to his *Hispano* constituents as his *coyotes*, a term of casual endearment implying healthy rebelliousness, he was in turn considered by many of them to be an honorary *primo*.

The word means literally cousin, first, second, third and on into the infinity of blood relations existing at the far end of the *Hispano* family. In use, it becomes that kind of outwardly casual address which is actually governed by strict and subtle rules of decorum, defined by the social context in which it is employed. The nearest English equivalent might be "pal" or "buddy." Like them it can be used as a formal term, as one of intimate confidence, in condescension or in derision. Mistakenly used, it can be taken as intrusive presumption, and as such, can be dangerous to him who misuses it. *Coyote* can also become an insult if improperly employed. It is a measure of David Cargo's disarming political style that he was able to use the word so casually in his campaign to secure himself a reception amongst *Hispanos;* difficult for an Anglo, doubly difficult for a Republican.

For the first time it was rumored that Reies Tijerina was entertaining private conversations with a politician: Cargo. When informed of Senator Montoya's proposal to enter a land grant bill, Reies replied with uncharacteristic vagueness that "We don't feel the time is right yet."

To many *Alianza* members it smacked of the same old game of trading favors at the expense of principle. What could the Republicans fail to do for them that the Democrats had not already failed to do? After the failure of the Santa Fe march, they were in need of reassurance that there was more promising drama in the making than the tired old ballet of the ballot box. In September, they got it.

The fourth annual National Convention of the *Alianza* was held in Albuquerque's Civic Auditorium and had an attendance of more than 3,000. Gubernatorial candidate David Cargo appeared briefly, but the highlight of the first day's doings was the introduction to the gathered membership of their future king and emperor, a roly-poly little man with the voice of a friendly eunuch, known familiarly as Jerry Noll. The highlight of the final day was the creation and proclamation of a new city-state, free and independent of the governments of New Mexico and the United States and called the *Pueblo de San Joaquín del Río de Chama.*

The two events were related, not only as equally unlikely and startling, but also in the anachronistic spirit with which they were hailed by those present, and which graced them both, little man and big idea, with a touchingly fragile reality.

Gerald Wayne Barnes, as Jerry Noll had called himself in those days, had first appeared in New Mexico back in December of 1960, when he had wandered into the offices of the Socorro *Defensor-Chieftan,* down in the south-central part of the state, and let it be known that his sister's air force was going to shoot down President Eisenhower's plane during an impending Presidential flight over Brazil.

He had just visited his sister, Doña Anita del Castillo, in New York, where she was living incognito as plain Irene Gray. Doña Anita had complained of continued harassment by certain agents of the United States government, apparently the same who had previously been persecuting her in a variety of ways in Seattle, including stealing her 10-month-old infant and putting plaster-of-paris in her Metrecal diet supplement.

On his way home to report his sister's troubles to their mother in Seattle, Jerry had decided to stop off and look into an attempt by heirs of the Socorro Land Grant organization to set up something called the Socorro Free State. The 1953 Socorro attempt to establish a city-state loosely styled on the Greek model had met with nothing but trouble, the United States being distinctly unfriendly to such attempts to set up sovereign and independent political units within its borders, no matter how democratic their precepts. However, Jerry made it clear to the editors of the *Chieftan* that he was not at all interested in establishing an egalitarian utopia, but intended to restore an absolute monarchy, with himself and his sister at its head. He was, he explained, Don Barne Quinto César, direct descendant of a Hapsburg noble and thereby King Emperor of the Indies, which included all the Spanish land, granted and otherwise, in North and South America. He intended, he said, to file suit in the U.S. District Court in New York for the restoration of the Socorro Free State under his sister's sovereignty, and to demand restitution of all the gold taken by the Yankees from California. Claiming that the Mexican government had had no right to give up the Southwest and other Spanish possessions to the United States, he warned that his sister was angry with President Eisenhower for violating her territorial sovereignty by sending an atomic submarine into her waters off Patagonia, and had ordered her air force to make short work of him.

Beguiled as they were by the cherubic stranger's erudite ramblings, the editors of the *Chieftan* must have been a bit ruffled by his frequent references to "Anglo invaders" and "land-grabbing gringos," since his enormous eyes behind the thick lenses were a flawless blue and his skin as pink as a baby's.

It would never have occurred to them that a descendant of the German Hapsburgs was likely to be blue-eyed. And they certainly did not know that Gerald Barnes had spent some years of his youth in the Monroe State Reformatory in Washington State and had later been apprehended while attempting to rob a bank while wearing a lady's black silk stocking over his head.

As it was, they considered him a harmless lunatic, wrote a scornful little piece about him and sent him on his way, hoping never to hear of him again.

However, a copy of the *Chieftan* article eventually reached the hands of Adella García Meyers, the same blue-haired California lady soon to join the *Alianza* in hopes of getting help with her Cubero Grant. After an exchange of letters, during which she learned from Gerald Barnes that he was an attorney in addition to "being a historian of international law," Mrs. Meyers arranged a meeting at her home in California, told Jerry her troubles and perhaps paid him a small retainer, although he was getting an allowance from his mother at the time. Jerry set out for New Mexico, where he immediately became embroiled in the legal squabble over the Cubero Grant.

"The way the court had it set up on this one deal," he explains, "they were going to declare Mrs. Meyers and the others heirs, but they wanted to assess their land for back taxes. I found out that LaFollette, attorney for the heirs, Tibo Chávez, attorney for the trustees, and Judge Tackett were all working secretly together to get about 400 acres right on the edge of the biggest uranium mine in the world. Well, I put a stop to that."

He did manage to tangle proceedings up enough to bring them to a temporary halt, but in his zeal he drew the searching attention of the court and was discovered to be practicing law without a license. He decided to temporarily vacate the land of his destiny.

Back in Seattle once again with his mother, he became increasingly impatient with attempts of hostile agents to stamp out the last of the Hapsburg line. "They kept doing things to my mother's brakes, and finally they fired a shot through the living room window and hit the chair right where I would have been sitting." It was during an attempt by one such hired assassin to enter the house while representing himself as a health inspector that Jerry lost his temper and attempted to stab the invader with a dinner fork. He was convicted of third-degree assault and spent six months in Walla Walla prison. Upon his release early in 1966, he abandoned Seattle, leaving behind him $500 bail and an outstanding bench warrant for shoplifting. In California in May, Adella Meyers introduced him to Reies Tijerina, who took him back to New Mexico and installed him as Secretary-Historian of the *Alianza*, where he soon came to be called *primo* and was regarded with particular affection by the wives and children. Four months after his arrival, he was introduced to the convention as "Don Barne Quinto César, Jerry our favorite king," and received a standing ovation.

Reies waves a hand irritably when asked why he became involved with royalty. Does he believe that Jerry is really a Hapsburg and a king?

"How would I know? No, probably not, of course not, I don't know. I liked him, and he knew all about the land grants, things even I didn't know."

Jerry had a small independent income and was a dedicated worker, and, despite his record for attack with a dinner fork, he remained consistently amiable in the face of what some said were difficult conditions. "Tijerina has a complex personality," says Eunice Myrick, who was elected secretary when the *Alianza* was formed, but left after three months. "He's pretty hard to know. He had his own methods, and I didn't think I was getting an opportunity to do my job correctly."

Many would come out of curiosity, some would volunteer to help, but for a long time Jerry would be the only blue-eyed one to stay among them, and in the end his loyalty would be submitted to the supreme test and would hold firm. He was their Anglo.

For his part, there was nowhere else where he could anticipate that ultimate recognition he had dreamed of ever since his fourth birthday, when a terrible and marvelous thing had happened.

Had it been a dream? Whose dream? His father took him on his knee and told him that he, a common aircraft worker in the Boeing plant in Seattle, was in reality Don Barne Cuarto César, and he, Jerry, was *Quinto*, the royal heir.

The father died when Jerry was 13. The king was dead; long live the king, who was short, round, nearsighted, and who had a voice that would never descend to the lower registers.

Life can be lonely for a king, even more lonely for one waiting to be crowned. Jerry was loyal. Jerry worked for nothing. Jerry could write clear English, and he had a phenomenal memory for recondite legal language and a gift for proclamatory, regal prose that seemed so instinctive it could almost have been hereditary.

Immediately following the 1966 convention, a document issued from *Alianza* headquarters, entitled:

FINAL NOTICE TO THE UNITED STATES OF AMERICA AND TO THE STATE OF NEW MEXICO

BE ADVISED that FINAL NOTICE is hereby being
given unto you that, the HEIRS of the various
Royal Land Grants in Nuevo México are fully
resolved to exercise their lawful rights to
their lands and authorities . . .
NOW THEREFORE, these repeated violations of
international law by the United States of
America and its political subdivision the State
of New Mexico must cease once and for all time . . .

Toward the middle of October, another proclamation appeared, this one serving notice on the United States that a new republic had been declared within its borders.

BE IT KNOWN THAT, with the royal blessing of Don Barne Quinto César, KING EMPEROR of all the INDIES, the PUEBLO DE SAN JOAQUÍN DEL RÍO DE CHAMA is hereby declared by royal decree and grant to be a fully constituted INDEPENDENT FREE CITY STATE, with full rights to establish on and defend those lands granted to it in 1806, by OUR royal predecessor . . .

A professional process server was called to *Alianza* headquarters, given four one-dollar bills and directed to deliver the proclamation to the Regional U.S. Forest Service offices in Albuquerque, where he attempted to give it to Regional Forester William D. Hurst, a solidly built man with steel-rimmed glasses, a bulldog jaw and the rueful truculence of an unwilling bureaucrat. Hurst refused to touch the document, but fired off an immediate reply to *Alianza* headquarters:

"The property you propose to claim in the *Pueblo San Joaquín* belongs to the U.S. government and full resources will be used to protect it."

The San Joaquín de Chama Grant is the same that was enlarged to 300 times its legal size by Surveyor-General Atkinson in 1872 in connection with its sale, through Antonio Joseph of Taos (the same who had filed the foredoomed memorial on behalf of TA settlers), to the Englishman Blackwell. Surveyor-General Julian later saw that the grant was reduced to its legal size of 1,400 acres, but congressional representatives of T. D. Burns' Río Arriba Land and Cattle Company persisted in their attempts to have the enlargement verified, the most recent congressional bill having been thwarted by protest of the Department of Agriculture in 1944. A portion of the grant had eventually become part of the Presbyterian-owned and operated Ghost Ranch complex, and the remainder had been acquired by the government and made a part of the Santa Fe forest. Shortly after the founding of the original *pueblo*, the settlers had been plagued by floods and many had moved north to Canjilón, where their descendants still live.

The *Alianza* plan was to symbolically occupy the grant by setting up a camp in the forest's Echo Amphitheatre picnic area which was near the site of the original grant settlement. At the convention, a town council had been elected by 39 families of *vecinos* or "member-neighbors" who claimed to be heirs to the San Joaquín land. They had elected as their mayor elderly José Salazar, a sheepherder and direct descendant of the original leader of the grant community.

On the weekend of October 15, a motorcade of nearly a hundred cars made the 120-mile trip from Albuquerque to Echo Amphitheatre, where they set up tents, built fires, posted six armed guards and sat down to wait. Not a single law enforcement or Forestry official attempted to interfere. By the next evening all but 30 of the campers had left. By Monday morning there were only smoking campfires.

Despite Forester Hurst's threat to use "full resources," the Forest Service had decided, upon advice of certain other agencies of government, to treat the whole affair as casually as possible in the hope of minimizing the possibility of violence and limiting public attention.

The policy had been successful. A confrontation had been avoided, newspaper coverage had been minimal and public reaction had been mostly indifferent. However, during the following week there was a subtle shift. Chief Forester Hurst made it publicly known that next time the one-dollar entrance permit would be required of all persons entering the picnic area. There was a distinct air of challenge about the announcement. If it was a trap, the bait was eagerly taken. Reies Tijerina announced that there would be another takeover the following weekend. Both sides were obviously agreed that there would be an "incident." They had, however, quite opposite ideas of what kind of a "case" could be extracted from such a confrontation.

On the morning of October 22, Rangers Walt Taylor and Phil Smith stood waiting at the entrance to Echo Amphitheatre. Behind them, the huge wind-sculpted concavity loomed above the small area of stunted pine and juniper, winding paths and scattered picnic tables. The two rangers had been instructed to demand payment of the entrance permit from everyone. If refused, they were not to attempt to stop anybody from entering but were only to write down their license numbers. They were specifically instructed to carry no firearms. Cristóbal Zamora, a Forest Service staff officer, waited near two white Forest Service pickups in the nearby parking lot.

First to arrive was a pickup bearing 72-year-old Baltazar Apodaca of Canjilón and his friend Pablo García. They parked near the entrance and passed the time arguing with the rangers. Other *Alianza* cars arrived and parked nearby, but made no attempt to enter.

State Police Captain Martin Vigil arrived, in command of several patrol cars. The officers ranged themselves along the opposite side of the highway at a discreet distance from the entrance. Their radios informed them that Tijerina was four miles south, rallying his forces opposite the entrance to Ghost Ranch.

At about 11 A.M. the convoy appeared, a long string of more than 50 vehicles, horns honking, flags flying. The lead cars swooped so close to the State Patrol cars that Captain Vigil had to throw himself out of their path. They passed Taylor and Smith and squealed to a stop inside the Amphitheatre parking lot. The rest followed, their drivers ignoring the rangers' shouts for them to stop. Men, women and children tumbled from the cars and trucks and thronged the gravel lot.

Taylor and Smith moved toward the crowd and were quickly surrounded. They again demanded payment for entry permits and were hooted down. The uniformed State Police remained across the road, but State Police and FBI plainclothesmen quickly infiltrated the crowd and busied themselves taking pictures along with the several television cameramen present.

There was a good deal of pushing and shoving and shouting into the faces of the two rangers. Suddenly Taylor, a one-time professional boxer, broke free and ran toward one of the white pickups. Several men ran after him. Taylor reached his truck on the driver's side. At the same moment, the opposite door was opened, and a man reached in and flipped open the glove compartment to reveal a loaded .38-caliber revolver.

Whether or not he had been after the gun, Taylor had no chance to reach for it. He was clutched from behind and turned, to find himself facing Cristóbal Tijerina, who grasped his tie and shirt before he could speak and said, "Shut up, you son of a bitch."

To which Taylor replied, "Look, *primo*, you don't have to talk to me like that."

He could have chosen no form of address more likely to worsen his already delicate circumstances. The crowd closed in, shouting and clutching at him. Somebody grabbed his arm and told him he was under arrest. It was Alfonso Chávez, wearing a badge and trying to drag Taylor through the excited crowd.

"I felt I was in big trouble," Taylor later testified. "They began to grab at me and tear my clothes. Women were dancing and shouting, 'Get him!' I thought I was a dead man, I really did."

According to Reies, he nearly was. "When they saw that he had that gun in his car and was going for it, those people wanted to lynch him," Reies said later. "Cris and Alfonso, they stopped it by getting him away from there."

Ranger Smith had already been led by Esequiel Domínguez up to one of the picnic shelters under the looming cup of the Amphitheatre. Cristóbal Zamora was also being dragged along, when someone shouted, "Release him, let him go. Don't harm him, he's one of us."

Zamora was released, making it clear who was *primo* and who was not.

Taylor was pushed the rest of the way to the picnic shelter and made to stand beside Smith. Facing them was a group of leathery, solemn-faced elders ranged behind a rotund seated figure who looked more like a Kewpie doll than a judge, yet had a peculiar kind of magisterial dignity about him all the same.

"I, Don Barne Quinto César," intoned Jerry Noll, "Have been appointed magistrate by the *alcalde* and *pueblo* council of the free city-state of *San Joaquín del Río de Chama*. Hear ye, hear ye, you are brought before me on charges of . . ."

He hesitated. Taylor would later describe Jerry as "nervous as a whore in church." The charge was supplied vigorously from all sides: "Trespassing!"

"Trespassing," intoned the magistrate. "Do you have an attorney?"

"You damn right I do . . ."

"Never mind. You are hereby found to be trespassing without permission on the property of the *Pueblo Libre* of San Joaquín, and furthermore, have been found to have a firearm in your possession in defiance of the edict of the council of the *Pueblo de San Joaquín de Chama* . . ."

It was, Taylor later protested, "the stinkingest farce" he had ever seen, a travesty of justice. He and Smith were fined $50 each, given suspended sentences of 11 months and 21 days and told to leave. Taylor and Smith turned to go to their trucks, but were told the trucks had been impounded. Taylor asked for and was given permission to remove personal belongings from his pickup. He was handed back his now empty gun, then the handful of bullets that had been removed from it.

It is at this point that Reies and other *Alianza* members say they gave Taylor and Smith permission to take the trucks after all, and that the keys were handed to the two men, who handed them back and refused to take possession of the vehicles. Taylor and Smith deny that the truck keys were returned to them. At any rate, they left the trucks where they were and walked the several hundred yards down the highway to where the police were waiting and with them, *primo* Cristóbal Zamora.

Zamora heard and later translated the speech delivered by Reies Tijerina atop a picnic table to the gathered mass of from 400 to 500 *Hispano* land granters. Reies said many of the usual things, slashing the air with his hands, holding the dusty old books on high, while his words rebounded in endless echo between the vast bowl of the Amphitheatre and the sandstone cliffs on the far side of Navajo Canyon. But the words which were to echo longest, in the press and eventually in U.S. District Court in Las Cruces, came toward the end.

"Fidel Castro has what he has because of his guts. There are a lot of guns out there across the highway, but don't be afraid. Because we are strong. Castro put the gringos off his island and we can do the same."

The crowd cheered, federal and state officials watched silently from the road, the only sound the scratch of busy pencils. Eventually night reached its long, chill shadow down the canyon, and all of the official cars moved away but one. Tents took shape in the darkness at the foot of the concave cliff, fires flickered, armed guards patrolled and the *Pueblo de San Joaquín del Río de Chama* settled down for its first night of actual communal existence in nearly a hundred years.

At the convention the month before, how many had thought or hoped that it might somehow be more than a symbolic occupation? How many dreamed tonight in their tents and beside their flickering campfires that it was not a mere legal charade, but a genuine and lasting restitution of the misplaced past?

Reies had many times exhorted them to visualize the new Old World they would build and the pueblos they would found and people. Each man and his family would have enough land for a house and garden, and all the rest of the land would be common and free, as it had been in the old days, as it still was in the Indian pueblos. No one would have more personal property than he actually needed. There would be barter, but no selling for profit. Government would be by a council of elders and exclusive to each pueblo. As they saw harmony in nature, they would recreate it in their institutions, their homes, their villages, their customs, their worship. The land would be *ejido* and belong to all, and they would be a true *pueblo:* people, village, landscape; past, present, future.

What would Reies himself have dreamed, if he slept at all that night?

"My belief in land is that it belongs to God," he was wont to say. "We cannot, we should not fence it nor post it or say it's mine."

But he was also fond of saying, "This land belongs to the Spanish and Indian people. It was given to us by the king of Spain in the name of God, and we want it back."

And upon occasion he also said, "Moses led his people out of slavery, and Joshua. Just like the Bible says in the Book of Joshua, where he distributed lands to the Israelites, the Hebrews. Well, that's just the way it is in our case."

It is more likely that he did not sleep and that, in his role as his people's Moses and Joshua, he reviewed the more immediate purposes of the *Alianza* occupation of Echo Amphitheatre.

One purpose was, of course, to secure further publicity for their cause.

The other was to force a confrontation that would hopefully provoke a major land grant case. They had deliberately trespassed on government land. Surely it was common as well as written law that the party which charges trespassing must prove ownership of the land. Surely this was the way to get the Supreme Court to review its two previous, century-old decisions concerning land grants. Surely there would be no way out for the government now.

While waiting for the U.S. District Court in Albuquerque to issue a restraining order, all Forestry officials, federal officers and state police kept their distance outside the Echo Amphitheatre area. With teen-agers wearing sidearms and deputy badges standing desultory guard over the camp, the number of occupants steadily dwindled through Tuesday, then Wednesday.

Wednesday afternoon, 12 state, Federal and Forestry officers moved in. They found the *alcalde*, José Salazar, seated on a rock in front of his tent boiling potatoes and coffee. Baltazar Martínez, in red beret and with his shirt unbuttoned to the waist, carried the camp's last weapon, a 30-30 rifle.

The last 20 squatters packed up, drifted to their cars and pickups and drove away. A few yards down the road from the entrance, rangers and officers tore down the lopsided, hand-stenciled sign reading, *"Pueblo República de San Joaquín del Río de Chama*, 1806," revealing once again the tidy green-and-yellow lettering underneath: "Santa Fe National Forest."

Asked by Albuquerque reporters why the *Alianza* had attempted such a patently foredoomed occupation of federal property, Reies Tijerina smiled and said, "Publicity. This time the whole world will know of our dilemma. This time they will have to charge us with trespassing and take us to court, and then we will see whose land it really is."

Charges were carefully prepared by U.S. Attorney John Quinn, and late in 1966, federal Judge Howard Bratton of the U.S. District Court in Albuquerque charged five *Alianza* members—Reies and Cristóbal Tijerina, Jerry Noll, Esequiel Domínguez and Alfonso Chávez—on five counts each, including converting government property to their personal use and assaulting Rangers Taylor and Smith, the latter to be eventually changed to "conspiring to prevent by force, intimidation or threats" the two Rangers from carrying out their duties. There were no charges of trespassing and never would be.

Seven cities had been torn by riots that summer, whole blocks of Detroit had been reduced to smoking ruin, seven Negroes had lost their lives and scores of policemen had been injured. Cleveland, Ohio, and Gary, Indiana, soon had their first black mayors.

That same summer in Delano, as part of their peaceful *huelga* against the California grape growers, César Chávez and his followers had carried Our Lady of Guadalupe all the way to Sacramento on their shoulders. But Governor Ronald Reagan had refused to so much as see her or them, and nobody appeared to be on the point of nominating César Chávez for mayor of anything.

H.E.L.P. 10

AMONG the interested bystanders at the Echo Amphitheatre takeover in October had been a museum researcher named Don Devereux. On May 7, one month before the raid, he included some observations in a letter to an associate.

"About 400 *Alianza* members were there, most were armed, and the atmosphere was both spirited and tense. It was the first *Alianza* activity of real magnitude and it obviously was a vast learning and therapeutic experience for the *Alianza* people. I have never seen so much ethnic pride and self-respect among the villagers before or since, not to mention the obvious new knowledge of how much impact they could have through collective and determined action."

Devereux, slim, bearded and in his thirties, knows the north better than many outlanders, having lived in El Rito for several years and traveled the mountain roads as a peddler, trading and selling out of the back of an ancient pickup truck which he still drives. Of the "prospects for violence," he wrote:

"One thing I do know from my experiences in the villages of northern New Mexico is that when old men I respect vow 'to burn and raise hell,' they probably will."

Devereux was soon to become research and development adviser for the state office of HELP, the Home Education Livelihood Program, a division of the government's War on Poverty. In the months before the raid, HELP and other poverty agencies would do their best to arrest the polarization of forces then building toward explosion in northern New Mexico. For its pains, HELP, along with the poverty program in general, would suffer a series of nearly fatal setbacks, proving once again that when the shooting starts there is no room for those in the middle.

Only a few years before, in 1964, Congress had enacted legislation under the Johnson administration setting in motion a series of programs called the War on Poverty. They were related to concepts and programs developed previously during John Kennedy's administration and were based on what was claimed to be a new and better approach to social welfare.

Traditional welfare in New Mexico, as elsewhere, followed the old New Deal philosophy which, partially excepting the WPA, was generally paternal and manipulative and designed to keep the poor in their place. Government told the poor what to do and, if they could prove they were hungry enough and thwarted enough in their search for work, it fed them at subsistence level and created jobs for them. But to qualify for the make-work jobs, a poor man often had to sell his property. To qualify for the handouts, he often had to quit his job. The net effect was to place power in the hands of those administering the programs, while sustaining a system which was really designed to perpetuate poverty, not cure it.

According to the War on Poverty creators, there was to be no paternalism in the new programs and as few out-and-out handouts as possible. The initial assumption was that nobody knows the problems of the poor like the poor. Consultation with the poor tended to bear out one of the basic concepts of Russian anarchist Michael Bakunin, who believed that every man desires to do worthy work, that it is man's nature to wish to stand on his own two feet, guard his home and provide for his family. The poor seemed to agree—they wanted jobs, not handouts, education, not stagnation, opportunity to do something, not encouragement to do nothing. In accordance with the American Dream, they wanted to make something of themselves, to rise from the ranks of the poor and enter into the ranks of the secure and satisfied, the capable and skilled, the comfortable and advantaged.

The new concept appealed to liberals on humanitarian grounds, and the rest of the unpoor could hardly argue with the American Dream. Congress approved, and the various agencies set out, each in its own way, to establish bootstrap programs designed to encourage the poor to develop ideas, institutions and leadership of their own.

HELP was sponsored by the Council of Churches in New Mexico and was designed to aid the migratory workers of the Southwest, encouraging them to take a more active part in their home base communities, offering them basic education in English and consumer and credit education and aiding the women to develop profitable home skills.

Under HELP supervision, migratory workers living on off-season stipend wages had built a dozen community centers in the state, one of them at La Loma on the Antón Chico Grant south of Rowe. La Loma Community Center was formerly an unfinished school building, given to the community by the state school board and remodeled by HELP employees and volunteers. It is a simple one-story building made of cement blocks with a single decoration to distinguish it as a community structure: a tiny cupola on the roof, curiously echoing the double spires of the church in Antón Chico.

"We had a good priest here when I was a little kid," says Pacomio Ortega, who began work as a carpenter on the community center shortly after returning from the army in 1958. "He was a German, and he used to get the people together and send a wagon to Las Vegas to buy groceries so we wouldn't have to pay Abercrombie's prices. He was killed in an automobile accident in 1937. This priest we have now is French and won't have anything to do with the community center. He preached against it, but we went ahead, even when the money ran out."

Pacomio was named director of the center during reconstruction of the building. When there were no funds for mortar, he and his "stipends" put several walls together with Antón Chico mud mixed with straw and dung to make adobe. In early 1967, most of the rooms were still unfinished inside, but there were a hundred folding chairs in the meeting room, pots and pans in the kitchen, several old sewing machines in the activity room and two battered desks in the office area. Two rooms in the back corner of the building were used by the county health department nurse several days a week and once a week by a visiting doctor and a dental hygienist.

"They were going to put the clinic in a building in Antón Chico," Pacomio says. "It was owned by the Abercrombies, and the rent was going to be $125 a month. They nearly swung it, because they were already in control of the CAP [Community Action Program] here, with David Abercrombie as director. But the rest of us managed to hold off the decision until the center was finished, and now we have our clinic here and it's rent free.

"After that, we made them have a meeting of the water association, the first one in 16 years. Georgia Abercrombie was treasurer, and we found out there were a few thousand dollars missing. That made them pretty mad. But the real trouble didn't start until we got to talking about the German priest and decided to start a co-op. HELP doesn't officially have anything to do with the co-op, but I have to admit that building the community center got us started thinking in that direction. Once you start doing things for yourself, it's pretty hard to stop."

It had not occurred to many of those who had given qualified approval to the War on Poverty programs that in changing the poor from mere welfare recipients, paid to stay out of the way, into active, competing participants in society, they would be putting them very much in the way. Gradually it began to dawn on those of the unpoor with the most to lose that it was one thing to give the yearly $10-bill to the Community Chest and allow a percentage of the tax dollar to be handed out to sustain the aged and unemployable at minimal subsistence, and that it was quite another thing to find your labor force suddenly equipped with the means to resist exploitation through a HELP employment office; to discover your traditional political hold on the community threatened by the appearance of an alarmingly apolitical CAP development committee; to begin to lose your advantage of superior capitalization to a HELP agricultural co-operative; to see your retail business slipping due to the establishment of a CAP credit fund or the ominous appearance of a co-op store and gas station. It was one thing to help the poor to go on being poor, and it was quite another to suddenly find yourself competing with them at evened odds and on equal terms. It was particularly galling to see the poor encouraged in their rebellion by highly educated and fairly well-paid professionals.

It was becoming increasingly clear to the unpoor that the War on Poverty was a war on the status quo. This fact was openly acknowledged by Robert García, who was in charge of the state Office of Economic Opportunity and administrative head of the War on Poverty in New Mexico. A priest who let it be known that he did not like to be called padre, García was on indefinite leave from his small parish in southern New Mexico and was the first United States Catholic priest to be given his archdiocese's permission to wear lay garb and work at a salaried secular job.

Lean and intense, the 32-year-old García wore an adman's black-rimmed glasses, drove a red sports car and had sky-diving as a hobby. He was intelligent, emotional and eloquent, quick to speak his mind, quick to take offense, and by all evidence was almost entirely without that tempered inner guile and instinct for self-preservation that makes for political longevity. As soon as he took charge of the state OEO he assured himself of permanent characterization as "the controversial priest" by announcing that he believed that "religion is sterile in effecting real social change . . . the pulpit is a failure."

Of his intentions regarding the poor, he stated flatly that "We are teaching them to live without the *patrón*. For years, the politicians have been using them. Now they want to use the politicians."

Of the War on Poverty, he declared that it was creating a new "poverty force" which was beginning to challenge the middle class and all government, down to the city councils and the school boards. He assured critics that any efforts to curb this power would be hopeless once the poor had the habit of active participation in deciding their own fate. If thwarted, he promised, "the poor will become even more forceful in making social demands upon the government. They have had a taste of freedom."

Bold and honest words, but likely only to deepen the conviction among the established merchants, employers, landowners and politicians of the state that the War on Poverty was really a war on them.

Certain politicians and bureaucrats felt themselves to be particularly disadvantaged by OEO national policies, designed to keep federal funds out of the hands of the state authorities. In New Mexico, a long patrimonial social tradition combined with the inherent obligations of the extended family and a large state bureaucracy had tended to create a complex patronage system, with welfare often bestowed in return for political commitment rather than on the basis of need.

According to its creators, the War on Poverty had been set up so as to keep both funds and their control as free of local pork barrels as possible. State government had been given virtually no voice in requesting funds and only an indirect advisory capacity regarding their use. The programs were funded from Washington on the basis of budgets submitted directly to the national OEO offices from state administrators of the various agencies. The programs were coordinated by Robert García's state OEO office, which was directly responsible to the OEO office in El Paso, which in turn was responsible to Sargent Shriver's office in Washington.

In the first three years of the poverty program in New Mexico, state branches of the various agencies were funded for a total of over $50 million, with a theoretical $55.09 for each of the million-plus residents. Of that amount, 10.2 million would be spent by December, 1967. It was a lot of money to be bypassing the filter of the state patronage system. To some it seemed to be passing into the hands of over-paid out-of-state OEO employes. Others felt that it was flowing too indiscriminately into the hands of the poor, not merely as money, but as nascent power. Such a situation was generally intolerable to local politicians, petty bureaucrats and others accustomed to their cut of the federal pie. In bars and barber shops and up and down the corridors of the halls of state, those who felt that their rights were being ignored and their advantages threatened exchanged mutual complaints and readied themselves for battle, rallying for an as yet undeclared war on the War on Poverty.

What was needed, of course, was a scandal, some specific and convincing provocation to justify open hostilities.

As early as 1965, the state OEO office had begun its own file on the *Alianza* and Reies Tijerina. Early in 1966, García's office had received a report that Tijerina was allegedly planning to infiltrate the Community Action Programs in certain villages. Informants noted the names of several CAP directors said to be sympathetic to the *Alianza* and perhaps even members.

OEO officials were uncomfortably aware of the threat that the *Alianza*'s extremism posed to the progress of their own reformist policies, which were not strictly radical, being directed at correcting abuses rather than changing the system itself. Their mission was to reach what Don Devereux called "in-system solutions"; to better the lot of the disadvantaged without causing drastic disturbance to the basic economic system.

Poverty workers were acutely aware that the *Alianza* could undermine them with the local units of the program's army, the poor themselves, while at the same time feeding grist to the mill of their enemies on the right, who would waste no time in branding poverty workers as secret *Alianza* members, or at the very least, guilty by association of ideals.

Late in 1966, shortly after the Echo Amphitheatre takeover, word came in from the local directors of HELP community centers in La Loma, Mora and Canjilón that there would be worse trouble soon if something wasn't done. CAP Director Cris Trujillo reported the same from San Miguel. In nearly every community in which the CAP was represented, the *Alianza* was active also, and reports agreed that one by one the more vigorous and often the more intelligent among the "hard-core" poor were publicly or secretly crossing over to stand under Tijerina's radical and more racial banner.

These were the people upon whom the entire War on Poverty ultimately depended. One of the OEO's principal missions was to enlist and pacify potential activist leaders and to integrate them into the system before they began to move toward the kind of violent reaction already underway among the blacks. It was for this reason, among others, that the OEO had the encouragement and support, sometimes directly financial, of such organizations as the Council of Churches, the Ford Foundation and others, all of them anxious to prevent gravitation toward "out-of-system" solutions.

The situation was reported to be particularly delicate in the northern villages, with the grazing season coming up and so many of the small stockmen now entirely shut out of the federal forests by withdrawal of their grazing permits. Tijerina and other *Alianza* organizers were said to be moving from village to village, recruiting for a variety of rumored projects, all potentially violent.

In late January of 1967, Don Devereux discussed the matter with his friend, Alex Mercure, state HELP director. In mid-February, the two got together with State Representative Milnor Rudolph and Larry Prentice, administrative assistant to the new governor, David Cargo. All agreed that the issue was essentially between the local population and the federal government. The stumbling block to an in-system solution was that the government agency most directly involved, the Forest Service, would not take the land grant question seriously at all and was reluctant to discuss specific grazing problems. Officers of the service refused outright to talk to *Alianza* leaders or members. The problem for the state was to maneuver the two hostile forces into serious discussion and negotiation. The solution decided on was the creation of a temporary commission of investigation and recommendation, to include an important figure from New Mexican religious life, another from public life and a third "significantly placed in federal government," hopefully a representative of the Department of Agriculture concerned with Forest Service matters.

OEO personnel throughout the northern counties were directed to organize meetings of grazers in crucial areas and encourage them to elect delegates to come to Santa Fe and air their grievances before the commission and in the presence of Forest Service representatives. The Most Reverend James P. Davis, Archbishop of Santa Fe, was invited to serve on the commission and accepted immediately. As part of an already scheduled trip to Washington, Alex Mercure hoped to interest an appropriate official of the Department of Agriculture. Devereux suggested inviting former Governor Jack Campbell to serve as the third member of the commission. It was thought that his participation as a major leader of the state's Democratic party would obviate any charges of political opportunism. However, it soon became apparent that David Cargo planned to chair the commission himself.

The youngest governor in the state's history, Cargo, at 38, had defeated his Democratic opponent, Gene Lusk, by patching together a coalition of hard-core Republicans, progressive-minded Independents, labor leaders and dissident Democrats, including a numerically small but vitally important bloc from the little Byzantium up north.

In the summer of 1966, just before "Little Joe" Montoya made his offer to introduce a land grant bill in Congress, Reies Tijerina declared that the *Alianza* represented a potential voting block of 30,000. In a state with only 256,000 registered voters, that was considerable. A third of that amount equaled Cargo's winning margin of 10,000 votes; a sixth was enough to tip the balance in Río Arriba, and apparently did.

In an incidental note of political irony, it was rumored that the *Alianza* had been "delivered" for Cargo through the efforts of one Joe Benites, who had worked for Barry Goldwater in 1964.

However, Cargo had proved himself to be capable of winning *Hispano* approval on his own. It helped that his wife, Ida Jo, was a daughter of the noted Anaya family of Belén. Cargo also had a way with the press. Looking like a smaller, glossier Steve Allen, he had impressed reporters with his air of absent dedication and a soft-spoken wit rare in New Mexican politics. And in a state where political success depended heavily on personal contact with the voters, Cargo had managed to project a sympathetic image to a surprising number of renegade Hispano voters, those whom we called his *coyotes*.

"He came right here to Rowe," says Johnny Trujillo. "He shook my hand and said, 'Do you need a job?,' and when I said, 'Yes,' he said, '*Hijo*, I'll see that you get one.'"

At inauguration, Cargo's promises had been the usual ones of "quality" government, with reduction of patronage, no toleration of conflict of interest and "equal opportunity" for all ethnic groups. By February of 1967 it had become obvious that he actually did intend to do his part toward reform of the horse-and-buggy machinery of the state government. Wholesale issuing of new liquor licenses had always given a festive air to the inauguration of new governors in New Mexico, but Cargo issued no new licenses and even seemed bent on revoking a few, particularly those of several bars on or near Indian reservations, noted for turning drunken Navajos out into the snow to freeze to death.

However, Cargo was above all an astute and quick-footed politician and particularly jealous of his delicate margin of approval among the *Hispanos* of the northern counties. The plan to invite Jack Campbell to head the HELP emergency grazing commission was put aside. Cargo would stand at the head of the table.

In the meantime, Alex Mercure had arrived in Washington in late February and had contacted an Assistant Secretary of the Department of

Agriculture named Baker, who agreed to attend, pending formal invitation. Regional Forester William Hurst was in Washington at the time and was notified of the planned commission. It was Hurst who had refused to accept the *Alianza*'s proclamation of the Republic of San Joaquín de Chama and had issued the indirect challenge that had helped precipitate the second Echo Amphitheatre takeover. Alex Mercure arranged to fly back to New Mexico with him, and Hurst warily agreed that the planned commission might do some good. However, he stipulated that he, rather than Governor Cargo, should formally invite Baker. The matter was left in his hands. Baker never arrived.

A preliminary hearing was arranged and held on March 8 in the capitol building at Santa Fe. It was a sight to warm the heart of any in-system advocate. Present were Governor Cargo and his administrative assistant, Larry Prentice, Archbishop Davis, Mercure and Devereux, and 25 grazing delegates representing some 250 small grazers, all *Hispanos*, many of them known or suspected *Alianza* members. The picture was, however, incomplete. Conspicuously absent were the heather green uniforms of the U.S. Forest Service.

Nonetheless, those present went through with the "dry run." One by one, the grazers expressed their grievances, and one by one they were questioned with evident concern and sincerity by the governor and the archbishop. The meeting lasted for two hours, and Don Deverex wrote: "The delegates left feeling optimistic and efficacious. It seemed that afternoon that events had taken a promising direction." Forestry officials had promised to attend the official hearings, set for May 1 and 2. "We hoped that then real progress would be made."

However, polarization of opposing forces was already running ahead of efforts for conciliation and compromise. The District Court and U.S. Attorney John Quinn had set July 31 as the date for the criminal trial of the accused offenders at Echo Amphitheatre. In Santa Fe, District Attorney Alfonso Sánchez was busy at his law books, determining to what extent the state could contribute to the punishment of the same offenders. State Attorney General Boston Witt had applied to the state legislature's finance committee for a special appropriation to finance an investigation of the *Alianza*, with emphasis on the Tijerinas and their alleged Communist connections.

In mid-March, a half-mile of fencing was systematically cut at Ghost Ranch near Echo Amphitheatre. It was as yet too damp for fire to get a purchase in Santa Fe or Carson forests, but it would be warm enough soon.

On April 17, the *Alianza* staged another protest march. About 500 men, women and children, many carrying banners and placards and several on horseback, paraded to the plaza of Albuquerque's Old Spanish Town. Asked if the red flags carried by many of the marchers had particular significance, Reies told reporters that "the red is for warning, danger."

In his speech he pointed out a recent news item in the Albuquerque *Journal* stating that relative to their proportional representation in the state, there was a larger percentage of *Hispanos* in Vietnam, a larger percentage in combat and a larger percentage getting killed and wounded. "They are sending your children to die in Vietnam and won't give you a decent living here. They have attempted to destroy your culture, now they are sending your boys over there to destroy another culture. They are not satisfied with having stolen all the land from us here, they send our boys to bloody death so that they can take more land away from the poor people over there."

Coinciding with his emphasis on the relatively new Vietnam theme, there was a new face at Reies' side that day. Rudolfo "Corky" González was a young-looking 38 and well built, given to wearing two-tone sport shirts and white sweat-socks. Raised in Denver, González recalls his first day in school, when the teacher told him his name was not Rudolfo, it was Rudolf. Forbidden to speak Spanish in school, he says he soon came to the point where he could speak neither language and had to go to special classes, where they taught him English. Raised in the city, he was boxer and bondsman and dabbled in conventional politics. Then, in 1965, he was appointed head of Denver's War on Poverty program. He resigned after a short time because, he says, he was disgusted and wanted to do more and do it faster.

In 1966, he founded the Crusade for Justice, a Denver-based militant *Hispano* organization. He was writing a play called *The Revolutionist* and would soon publish an ambitious epic poem entitled *I am Joaquín,* with such mellifluous and uncompromising calls to arms as:

"The Villages

The Mountains

The Streams

belong to *Zapatistas*

Our Life

Or yours

is the only trade for soft brown earth and maize."

City-made, formally educated and thoroughly modern, González was an indigenous *Hispano* revolutionary who did not speak Spanish. Like Félix Martínez, he was among Reies Tijerina's earliest contacts with that fast-growing complex of *Hispano* organizations to be grouped under the general heading of *La Causa*, the Cause; and of which, all unknown as yet, Reies would soon become the first bonafide hero.

Leading the marchers into downtown Albuquerque to the federal buildings which housed the offices of Regional Forester Hurst and U.S. Attorney Quinn, Reies paused to tell reporters that that day's march was the "last human warning" to the federal government.

Later that same day in Santa Fe, he led another group of some 200 demonstrators to the steps of the capitol building and demanded to see the governor. Cargo eventually emerged in his shirtsleeves and agreed to meet with Tijerina on the following Friday. The two parted amicably, but shortly afterward, when a reporter asked the governor what had been said, the Cargo wit took a particularly acrid turn.

"He said he wanted to know if I have any objection to him taking over New Mexico," the governor said. "I told him to come up and talk about it."

That Friday, April 21, the Santa Fe *New Mexican* reported that a meeting between Governor Cargo and *Alianza* representatives had been friendly and productive. Tijerina was quoted as having said afterward, "This is the first time we've ever been given such satisfactory attention. We learned the modern way to approaching the government in a united manner. We feel this is a war of words, of law, of interpretation."

In fact, the meeting had been extremely tense and the results ominous. Cargo had kept Tijerina and a dozen *Alianza* men, women and young people waiting for five hours. Because it was suspected that some of the *Alianza* men were armed, a number of State Police officers were present and remained ranged around the wall of the office throughout the interview. When Cargo promised to take pertinent documents with him to Washington in June, Reies protested that Governor Campbell had made a similar promise the year before, but that nothing had come of it. He made it clear that there were plans for another takeover in the north, and that unless land grant claimants received more immediate satisfaction, the plans would be carried out. "If anybody is found trespassing on these land grants, they will be arrested and punished!" Reies declared.

While he pounded the table, the governor rested his cheek on his fist and drew circles on a notepad. Afterward, outside the capitol building, Don Devereux circulated among the demonstrators and overheard more than one muttered pledge to "burn and raise hell." That afternoon he talked it over with Alex Mercure. They felt that the grazing commission hearings coming up in 10 days could right the balance or tip it.

That weekend, Forest Service signs along the Chama highway were defaced and tourist facilities at Echo Amphitheatre suffered damage eventually estimated at $3,000. On the following weekend at Yeso Tank in the Carson forest near Echo Amphitheatre, a fire sprang up in a 30-mile-per-hour wind and might have become a major forest disaster, had it not been discovered almost immediately and held to 10 acres by fire fighters.

The first commission hearing was held on May 1, and the heather green uniforms were present. However, Regional Forester Hurst's first act was to announce that he and his fellow rangers could not take part in the entire two-day conference; they had to fly to Phoenix for official business late that afternoon.

In addition, there had been some last-minute trouble in rounding up the grazing delegates. Erroneous information had been spread by some-one the day before the hearings, directing the delegates to Albuquerque instead of Santa Fe. A number of the last-minute dropouts were known to be *Alianza* members. Moreover, in several districts of Carson forest, the Forest Service had announced May 1 and 2 as the dates for tagging cattle, thereby tying up several delegates out of Santa Fe.

Proceedings did begin with about 15 of the expected 50 delegates present. The Forest Service officers listened to a few of the delegates' grievances, but they seemed much more concerned with explaining their multiple responsibilities under federal law, their hopes for economic development through forest resources, their efforts to improve range, forest and especially recreational and tourist facilities. By the time they had finished, it was time for them to leave for Phoenix. The room emptied of heather green, leaving behind the tailored dark serge of the clergy and the governing, and the dull earth colors of the governed.

A planned two-day meeting had lasted less than a day. Governor Cargo had been in and out most of the time. Half the scheduled delegates had been absent. Not one of the thousands of grazing permits withdrawn through the preceding years had been reinstated, not one new permit had been granted, not one blade of grass had been offered to the men who had come in need of it. They put on their battered old hats and went home.

On May 3, Don Devereux had occasion to spend a few hours with a CAP director who had been present at the abortive commission meeting and who now reported that on the evening after the meeting, he had sat in on a gathering of San Miguel grazers and had heard serious discus-sion of plans for setting fires and using dynamite on Forest Service installations.

On May 6 a fire developed with incredible speed at Barranca Mesa on the outskirts of Los Alamos. By nightfall, through the efforts of a small army of firefighters, it was under control, but not before it had come close to spreading into the outskirts of the atomic city, threatening gov-ernment installations there. The fire chief reported that two additional small fires had been discovered in the same area. Investigators examin-ing the terrain said the fires were definitely arson.

Five days later, Devereux wrote the letter in which he predicted vio-lence for the north. "We are drifting back to dangerous poles—the extreme demands of the *Alianza* and the total rigidity of the federal government, with scant intermediate alternatives."

On May 8, two days after the Barranca Mesa fire had threatened Los Alamos, another fire broke out in Ratito Canyon inside Carson forest. For two days black smoke palled the sky. Over a hundred firefighters fought the blaze with shovels and backfires, while Forest Service and

143

State Police helicopters crossed and recrossed the surrounding area, descending with a shuttering roar on anybody found wandering the forest, instructing them via bullhorn to report to the nearest patrol car for questioning, and trailing overhead to see that they got there. Investigators, including the FBI, decided that the fire had originated from three separate blazes and called it arson.

Shortly thereafter, HELP Director Alex Mercure received a phone call from Regional Forester Hurst, asking him to set up a meeting between Forest Service officials and key anti-poverty personnel in the northern counties. Mercure tentatively scheduled a meeting for May 23. But it was too late for that sort of in-system solution. If it had not been too late all along.

Coyote 11

BACK in March, 10 days after his "last human warning" to the federal government and the tense meeting with Governor Cargo, Reies Tijerina had written to fellow militant Corky González in Denver. The letter, written in Spanish, congratulated Corky on the continuing success of the Crusade for Justice and then got down to business.

"This summer the *pueblo* will take possession of San Joaquín del Río de Chama once and forever. The *pueblo*, or as they call us, 'the sons of San Joaquín,' are firing up and full of an ardor and *CELO* [ardor, zeal—R. G.] such as has never been seen before in the history of New Mexico. The entire population of New Mexico has been stirred up to a miraculous degree; which pleases the soul of the natives, but causes great astonishment and terror in those foreigners who arrived in New Mexico only yesterday. The takeover of San Joaquín will take place around the 3rd of June. Those Valiants of Denver who wish to come and personally witness the valor of 'The sons of San Joaquín' are invited . . . please reply and let me know. Because it could be that this will precipitate and happen before the 3rd of June . . ."

Concluding with the suggestion that the planned event might last for many days, the writer declared his heart to be with those in Denver and signed himself: Reies López Tijerina.

Beginning around May 12, word began to spread through Río Arriba that the *Alianza* was planning something big. Rumor set the date as Saturday, June 3, but nobody seemed quite sure of what was going to happen, except that Reies Tijerina was letting it be known that it would be a showdown between the *Alianza* and the federal government.

On the 19th, in the U.S. District Court at Albuquerque, Judge H. Vearle Payne ruled favorably on a motion of U.S. Attorney Quinn ordering *Alianza* officers to produce for copying the organization's complete membership roster. Instigation of the motion was laid to the Bureau of Internal Revenue, which reportedly wanted to look into the *Alianza*'s tax situation. Nobody doubted that once the list was in official hands it would be put to a variety of uses.

OEO officials had also been alerted to the impending showdown by alarmed reports from CAP directors in the northern villages. Still convinced the situation might be solved by in-system mediation, Don Devereux and Alex Mercure arranged a meeting with Governor Cargo and urged that they be authorized to get the help of one or more social troubleshooters experienced and professional enough to, in Devereux's words: "First, find out what exactly the *Alianza* was up to. Second, contribute toward immediate steps to break the impasse. Third, help design a long-term approach, perhaps including the establishment of some kind of advisory staff to work with the *Alianza* and steer them along a reasonable and law-abiding course . . ."

Cargo agreed and authorized them to look for such a team in his name.

In the meantime, the job of delivering Judge Payne's court order had fallen to Emilio Naranjo, who had recently been appointed U.S. Marshal. Although it was known that on the 14th, Reies Tijerina and several *Alianza* members had spent an afternoon posing in and around the Río Arriba courthouse for CBS Television, it took Emilio six days to locate Tijerina. Handed the order, Reies handed the marshal back a copy of his letter of resignation as President of the *Alianza*. "Now I have no responsibility to hand over the names of my people," he said.

The same day, Don Devereux received a reply to his letter on behalf of the governor requesting professional outside help. The reply was from Dr. Ralph C. Guzmán, long a prominent *Hispano* social scholar and activist in California, past assistant director of UCLA's Mexican-American Study Project and at the time chairman of the Socio-Economic Studies Foundation, a nonprofit educational organization specializing in research projects among the *Hispanos* of the Southwest.

The letter suggested that Devereux contact Warren Wiggins, Guzmán's former boss in the Peace Corps, who was at the time chairman of a private foundation located in Washington, D.C., calling itself Trans-Century. Guzmán said that Trans-Century hired ex-Peace Corps volunteers and suggested that two such men would be capable of carrying out "the task of trouble shooting and redirecting energy" in northern New Mexico.

Devereux and Larry Prentice, the governor's administrative assistant, set about negotiating with Trans-Century for the loan of two such men.

A few days later, a hastily arranged meeting of the *Alianza* took place in Albuquerque. Reies Tijerina emerged to announce to reporters that the *Alianza Federal de Mercedes* had been disbanded by its membership, which had then voted to regroup under a new name, the *Confederación de Pueblos Libres*, or Confederation of Free City-States. "Now we have no responsibility to hand over the list," he said again. He announced that the new land grant organization would hold its "first national convention" in the tiny northern hamlet of Coyote on Saturday, June 3, the date of the rumored showdown. Then he disappeared, not to be seen again in public for the next eight hectic and fateful days. It was May 28.

District Attorney Alfonso Sánchez was immediately alerted by Tijerina's announcement of the June 3rd meeting at Coyote and was determined to stop it. His notes in preparation for indictment of those already under Federal charges for the Echo Amphitheatre takeover included charges of carrying deadly weapons, unlawful possession and transportation of explosives, obstructing justice, concealing identity, disorderly conduct, unlawful assembly, vagrancy, loitering, aggravated assault and battery, sabotage and disloyalty, defacing an official symbol, insulting the flag, transporting stolen livestock, causing damage to an animal—to wit, a cow—and trespassing.

Unimpressed by the *Alianza's* assumption of a new name, Judge Payne issued another order for Reies Tijerina to show cause why he should not be held in contempt of court for noncompliance with the first order, and dispatched U.S. Marshal Naranjo to deliver it.

Convinced that official efforts to abort the Coyote meeting were snowballing dangerously and would only frustrate last-minute efforts to reach a compromise, Devereux and Larry Prentice urged the governor to arrange an emergency conference with the district attorney's office, State Police and others. Cargo declined.

That afternoon, Devereux went to Bill Feather, editor of the Santa Fe *New Mexican,* and asked for a reporter to act as observer of the rapidly developing situation. None of the regular reporters was interested, so a young cub reporter named Peter Nabokov was given the assignment.

Emilio Naranjo was up all night on the 30th, trying to chase down Reies Tijerina, but he could not locate him. Naranjo had previously driven the few miles north from Española to Anselmo Tijerina's house in Hernández, which served as the *Alianza's* northern office. But he had found only two pretty young girls doing office work, Valentina Valdez and Josephine Tijerina. Other federal officers located Reies Tijerina's new nineteen-year-old wife, Patsy, in Albuquerque, and tried to hand her Judge Payne's order, but she refused to accept it. Saying she did not know where Reies was, she slammed the door in their faces.

Three loosely defined complexes of power were now maneuvering purposefully in northern New Mexico. They were Reies Tijerina and an undetermined number of *Alianza* members and sympathizers, Governor Cargo and the advocates of in-system solutions and the U.S. Attorney, DA Alfonso Sánchez, the Naranjos of Río Arriba, and, to a qualified degree, the State Police. Not only were they working increasingly at odds with one another, but communication was rapidly breaking down between all three.

On the same day that Emilio Naranjo and other federal officers were trying to serve their court order on Reies Tijerina, Don Devereux learned from Larry Prentice that fees and expenses had finally been agreed upon with the Socio-Economic Studies Foundation for the hiring of two special agents. Prentice was vague on the question of where the funds would come from, but the two troubleshooters were on their way. Their names were Robert Aragon and Hector Burgos. It was May 31, a Wednesday.

By Thursday, Reies Tijerina had still not been located. Anselmo had returned to his house in Hernández and was being watched closely by police. As yet unknown to the police, Ramón Tijerina had arrived from San Antonio to join Eddie Chávez, *Alianza* secretary, in the Albuquerque headquarters. Membership records and other documents had already been removed from the office.

Rumors flew along the *Hispano* grapevine from Río Arriba to Río Abajo. It was said the *Alianza* planned to dynamite the Forestry building at Canjilón and the Parkview fish hatchery, that *Alianza* assassins were looking for Alfonso Sánchez, that federal assassins were looking for Reies Tijerina, that the Black Hand was behind it all, that the Chama Minutemen were mustering to attack the adobes of Canjilón. All agreed that there was going to be big trouble this time.

Emilio Naranjo decided to cancel his weekend fishing trip and be on hand with four deputies at Coyote on Saturday, and he suggested that his 29-year-old son, Benny, who had inherited the sheriffship of Río Arriba from him, do the same. Under instructions from Colonel Joe Black, State Police Captain Martin Vigil arranged to have at least 25 patrol cars in the area. On Thursday afternoon, Alfonso Sánchez made his first move, filing a complaint at District Court in the Tierra Amarilla courthouse against the five defendents of the Echo Amphitheatre takeover. Reies and Cristóbal Tijerina were now wanted on criminal charges, along with three others, Jerry Noll, Esequiel Domínguez and Alfonso Chávez. Warrants were issued for their arrest.

That evening, Hector Burgos and Robert Aragon arrived in Santa Fe. They immediately went into conference with Devereux, Mercure, Prentice, and Joe Benites.

Aragon was young, cool, well educated and well spoken. He had been with the Peace Corps in Chile. Burgos was an older man with little formal education; an ex-labor organizer in California's Imperial valley. He reportedly had been sent by the State Department into the Dominican Republic in 1965 with a Mexican passport, his mission to save as many liberals as possible from the CIA-backed reaction.

There were some awkward moments over money. Burgos and Aragon were to be paid $1,500 for the job, which included a report and recommendations to be submitted later. They requested an advance payment of $750. There was a state law against expenditure of state monies in advance. Larry Prentice arranged to borrow the money personally from the First National Bank of Santa Fe.

The two men had already been briefed. They were given the latest details by their hosts. They had seen the situation many times before, they said, particularly in Latin America. There was talk of classic components and right-left drift. Tijerina was the rebel leader and *Alianza* members were the revolutionary rabble. The U.S. Attorney Alfonso Sánchez and the Naranjos were equivalents of the overreacting right, the army and/or state police. Solutions were discussed in terms of the redirection of energy and "deputizing the opposition." Phone calls were made and contact established with Joe Benites, the same person who had reportedly "delivered" the *Alianza* for Cargo eight months before, and who now offered to act as intermediary between the governor and Reies Tijerina.

Theirs was not the only unpublicized meeting that night. In his office a few blocks away across Santa Fe's old town plaza, Alfonso Sánchez was meeting with Río Arriba law enforcement officers and State Police, outlining his plan to abort the Coyote meeting with a sweeping series of arrests the next day.

Approval was not immediately unanimous. Representatives of the State Police, in particular Captain Hoover Wimberly, protested that such mass arrests looked too much like preventative law, and pointed out that a good many of the district attorney's warrants were questionable and would likely be judged defective by the court.

The district attorney argued that his primary and immediate objective was to keep the peace, and that this was the only way to do it. The argument lasted two hours, but in the end State Police officers had to concede that when warrants were issued with the approval of the court, it was the job of law enforcement to make the arrests. In fact, it was Captain Wimberly who was charged with field coordination of the State Police share in the operation.

There was a third and equally furtive conference that Thursday night. It took place in the back room of an old adobe house in Río Arriba. Black oilcloth from the kitchen table covered the window and the women sat in the front room talking quietly, ears cocked for any whistled alarm from the boys sitting in the deep grass out by the road. Word had come that there were now warrants out for four others besides Reies, but beyond that they couldn't be sure. It was decided that in the morning word would be sent out reassuring as many as possible that the meeting would be held at Coyote on Saturday. Arrangements were made for transferring the membership records to a place which some among them took distinct pleasure in referring to as field headquarters.

Early on Friday morning, June 2, Burgos, Aragon and Joe Benites drove north from Santa Fe, through Española and on to Anselmo Tijerina's house in Hernández. Reies was not there, but Anselmo was. While the four men were talking, a Mountain States Telephone Company truck drove up with a State Police patrol car in escort and stopped on the highway. A service man began to climb the pole. Aragon hastily called the governor's office in Santa Fe. From the capitol building a call was made to a contact within the State Police organization. An order was radioed to the patrol car to remove the tap from Anselmo's phone. The service man climbed back up the pole, made an adjustment, then climbed back down again. The lines of communication had to be kept open as long as possible to facilitate deputation of the opposition.

In Santa Fe, Alfonso Sánchez was speaking with repressed passion over the radio. "As district attorney I wish to give notice to all *Alianza* members who plan to be present and participate in the meeting at Coyote tomorrow, that meeting is versus the laws since it is planned to take over private property. Criminal charges of unlawful assembly will be filed against all persons who attend."

Afterward, the district attorney explained to newspaper reporters that in this case, unlawful assembly was "Three or more persons assembling with intent to unlawfully take over lands of the United States government by force and violence." Those not charged with unlawful assembly, he said, were likely to be charged with extortion, and he added that the extortion charge promised a sentence of up to 10 years in the penitentiary and a fine of up to $5,000. He promised to file charges for any other violation against the state, adding, "there's a long list of them." He reminded *Alianza* members that "attempting to take over by force is a Communist philosophy," saying in conclusion, "and I'm not kidding."

In the meantime, efforts to slow down the rapidly accelerating pace of reaction went on. It was suspected that U.S. Attorney Quinn was preparing to issue warrants of his own. It was an educated guess that he had failed to backstop himself in Washington. Shortly before noon, a phone call was made to the Justice Department in Washington. Some time after noon, U.S. Attorney Quinn received a call from Attorney General Ramsey Clark's office, urging Quinn's restraint. No federal warrants were issued.

However, there is no way to go over a district attorney's head. Early Friday afternoon Alfonso Sánchez met again with State Police Chief Joe Black, Captain T. J. Chávez and half a dozen other law officers, planning strategy for the next 24 hours. On his desk were warrants for everything from unlawful assembly to public drunkenness. He expressed the feeling that the federal authorities were failing in their duty, indicating that he had been in touch with U.S. Attorney Quinn. Roadblocks were planned for that night and the following morning. In the meantime, officers were to proceed with the arrests. Sánchez says that he called the Capitol building and spoke to Cargo at 4:30 that afternoon, telling the governor that he was going ahead with the arrests.

"I told him that there would be trouble if Tijerina and the others weren't captured. I told him that I had information that they had 15,000 rounds of ammunition, that I had receipts for carbines *Alianza* members had purchased. 'This man is dangerous,' I told him, 'and it's my duty to have him and the others in custody.' "

At 4:45 the meeting broke up. Sánchez headed north to Española to swear out more warrants. His car probably passed another heading

1832. A grant of land called Tierra Amarilla to Manuel Martínez, "and those who should wish to accompany him; the forests,
roads and watering places to be kept free, according to custom."
University of New Mexico

Tierra Amarilla (above). "I saw these men come into the courthouse, then I heard a shot and saw the State Policeman fall. And that is when the war began."

Big Dance Tonight means long ago and never again; the courthouse at the end of TA's main street. PHOTOS: *Author*

Bill Mundy atop his mountain. "It was around 200,000 acres then. I knew it was the only way I would ever get the kind of spread I wanted, so I decided to take it, freak deal, fight and all." PHOTO: *Jamison*

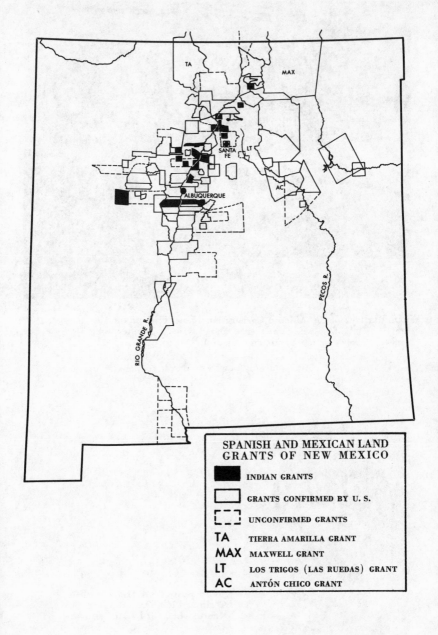

SPANISH AND MEXICAN LAND
GRANTS OF NEW MEXICO

INDIAN GRANTS

GRANTS CONFIRMED BY U. S.

UNCONFIRMED GRANTS

TA   TIERRA AMARILLA GRANT

MAX   MAXWELL GRANT

LT   LOS TRIGOS (LAS RUEDAS) GRANT

AC   ANTÓN CHICO GRANT

Juan Martínez of the Abiquiu Corporation (Rose Tijerina on his right). "At first we weren't sure about Reies, but after the trouble, we knew he was a man, and one of us."

Signs posted on trees in Río Arriba, 1968-69. "Tierra o Muerte—Land or Death." PHOTO: *Author*

Reies Tijerina. "They took your land and gave you powdered milk, took your grazing and gave you Smoky the Bear, took your language and gave you lies in theirs. There are 1,715 land grants in the United States, and we will get them back."

Four sons of Herlinda: Cris, Reies, Ramón, Anselmo. "She was strong and pure; she gave us everything." PHOTO: *Jamison*

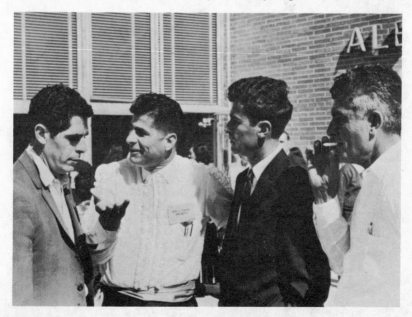

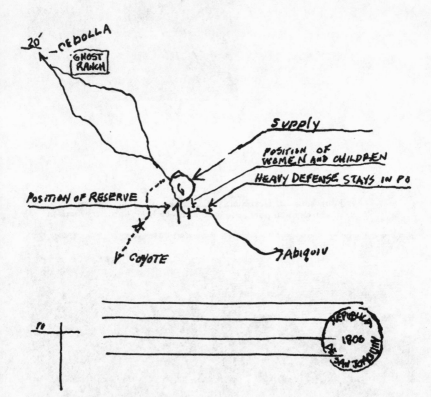

Author's rendition of captured battle plans. "To take over most of northern New Mexico and establish a new Cuba."

Canjilón. The empty house of Tobías Leyba. "Throw your guns out and come out with your hands up. We're coming in." PHOTO: *The New Mexican*

Baltazar Martínez and his mother. "The most dangerous of the bunch, a nut. That boy was raised in these mountains; he could live under a rock." PHOTO. *The New Mexican*

Ralph Featherstone of SNCC.
"¡Poder negro! ¡Poder negro!"
PHOTO: *Jamison*

Jerry Noll, King Emperor of the
Indies.   "I am ready to die for
my people. It is part of being
king; all in a day's work."
PHOTO: *Jamison*

Tomás Banyacya of the Hopi Nation, Ralph Featherstone of SNCC, Ron Karenga of U.S., Reies Tijerina. "A new alliance of the people of color."

Tijerina and Governor Cargo. "He said he wanted to take over northern New Mexico. I told him to come up and talk about it." PHOTO: *The New Mexican*

General Kearny, 1846:   "I come among you for your benefit, not your injury."

Canjilón. General Jolly: "20,000 rounds won't last long if we start shooting." PHOTO: *The New Mexican*

Canjilón. "Hands on top of your heads. Keep moving."
PHOTO: *The New Mexican*

Alfonso Sańchez examines the body of Eulogio Salazar. Chief Black: "The worst goddamn beating I've seen in 30 years as a police officer." PHOTO: *The New Mexican*

Canjilón. D. A. Sánchez: "Now what do I do with these people? How do you do this and not make them bitter all their lives?"
PHOTO: *The New Mexican*

Canjilón. Roundup of noncombatants.

south and bearing two men, who, unknown to the district attorney, were determinedly bent upon redirecting his energy.

Burgos and Aragon returned to Santa Fe a little after 5 P.M. and reported to the governor's office that the *Alianza* strategy for the Coyote meeting involved three phases, beginning with signs to be posted as token roadblocks. If the signs were ignored, guards would be posted to keep police and officials out of the area. If the guards were resisted, there were plans for an all-out fight.

It was a hair-raising prospect. However, Burgos and Aragon also reported that word of police plans for a massive clampdown had quickly spread north, and that Cristóbal Tijerina had told them that Reies was alarmed. Their observations led them to believe that Tijerina felt he could not back down in the face of Sánchez's challenge, but that he knew he was in a bad bind and was looking for a way out. There were potentially violent elements within the organization, but Tijerina still had them under control. However, if he was not given the means of saving face, he would be under severe pressure from the militants and would be himself inclined to fight, especially since he had apparently become convinced that certain federal agents had been assigned to kill him.

Burgos and Aragon suggested that the governor have breakfast with Reies the next morning, with no police present. Cristóbal Tijerina had indicated that if the arrests could be called off, the Coyote meeting would be held peaceably, and perhaps the governor would attend the barbecue to both seal the peace and demonstrate his sympathy.

Cargo agreed to the early morning meeting and set about trying to forestall the arrests. U.S. Attorney John Quinn assured the governor on the phone, that he had no plans at all for arrests. The conversation with District Attorney Sánchez took considerably longer. The governor says that Sánchez agreed to drop the warrants and to call off the police at least until the next day. The district attorney says he promised no such thing.

Cargo emerged from the conference at 7:30 and mentioned to a reporter that he had held off federal and state arrests and that he was in the process of arranging a meeting with Reies Tijerina to negotiate a permanent solution to the impasse. He was, he said, optimistic.

The governor's negotiating team increased its efforts to arrange a meeting with the rebel leader. Don Devereux, Burgos and Aragon continued to hear from Joe Benites, who was circulating in the Albuquerque area, calling in a new number each time he moved. Within an hour, he called to say that he had conveyed Cargo's assurance to Reies that the arrests would be suspended, and he added that a time and place for the breakfast meeting were now being discussed.

But roadblocks were already in place in the north and the arrests had begun. At 8:10, State Police spotted a late model Cadillac moving along a back road near the Chama canyon just north of Coyote. After a short chase, the car was forced over to the side of the road. In the front seat was Félix Martínez; in the trunk were several pistols, a high-powered rifle with a cutaway stock and telescopic sight, a sleeping roll, a walkie-talkie and eight gas masks.

"I told them I wanted to see my name on a warrant before I'd give them the keys to the trunk," Félix says. "Damned if they didn't pull a bunch out, thumb through until they found one for a firearms violation and hand it to me. I was on a hunting trip, I told them. The gas masks? Be prepared, that's what they told me in the Boy Scouts."

He was taken to Santa Fe and booked, not on the firearms charge, but under Alfonso Sánchez's blanket conspiracy charge. He was shortly joined in the Santa Fe jail by his father's great-uncle, tall, frail José María Martínez, and then by his father, Juan.

"They took him from work and wouldn't even let him come over here for two minutes and tell me what was happening," says Fernanda. "Somebody came by and tell me that he thought he seen Freddy Martínez in a patrol car at the high school. I went right up to the courthouse, but it was locked. I went around back and banged on the jail window, but those two men in there said they were sorry, but they didn't know where my husband was, they were the only ones in there. They took him right to Santa Fe without telling me, those gestapos."

Word reached the governor's office of the first arrests and roadblocks. Cargo gave instructions for his private phone number to be given to Tijerina, then left for his mansion and dinner. Devereux, Prentice, Aragon and Burgos drove to Cerillos Road, selected a motel at random and began a series of phone calls that would go on all night and into the next day. Young Peter Nabokov of the *New Mexican* joined them at the motel. Joe Benites was contacted and asked to assure Reies that there was still room for negotiation and to urge him to contact the governor. Anselmo was reached at his home in Hernández and also given the governor's home number. A few minutes later, conversation was taking place between mansion and adobe. Anselmo complained that he had been into the hills up behind his house twice that night, driven out by police who kept bursting in, throwing the furniture around, then rushing out again. The governor apologized but explained that he had no legal way to halt the arrests at this point. However, if a conference with Reies could be arranged, they might at least prevent further trouble. Anselmo said that he was not at the moment in contact with his brother. He said that he would see what he could do, but that he didn't think he would have much time, since he could see through the window that the police were coming again.

Early on Saturday morning, Captain Hoover Wimberly and a fellow patrolman spotted a car moving down a back road north of Hernández, gave chase and forced it to pull over. As he stepped out from behind the wheel, gun in hand, Wimberly saw the driver of the other vehicle swing out to face him. He saw the swarthy face with its curly black hair and brooding gray-green eyes, and he saw the hand move toward the ivory handle of the Colt .45 in its silver-worked black leather holster.

"He was going for it, but I took a chance and waited," Wimberly says. "He decided against it. It was close. For both of us."

Cristóbal Tijerina was in custody, and the contents of the automobile's trunk were even more pleasing to the arresting officers. There was a rifle and what looked like rolled maps sticking up from a carton. There was another box containing pamphlets and a wedding picture, and there were two metal card-files. Cristóbal was hurried south to Santa Fe and jailed, but the files were held briefly at Emilio Naranjo's office in Española, where the little five-by-seven cards were thumbed through with mounting excitement.

Five others were arrested in the early hours of Saturday morning, including Anselmo Tijerina. Unannounced, the governor appeared at the Santa Fe jail and asked to speak to the two Tijerinas in custody. He was admitted to the windowless cell area and was alone with them for nearly an hour. They declined to tell him where Reies was and said they did not know what the *Alianza* leader planned to do now. The governor warned them that violence would not be tolerated and left. Shortly afterward, Cristóbal assured a state policeman, "I'll be out of here in three hours. Your boss [Cargo] will get me out. We got him 2,300 votes."

Just before dawn, Ramón Tijerina, driving north between Santa Fe and Española, was forced off the road, questioned briefly and arrested. Three of the Tijerinas were now in custody, leaving only Número Uno.

Dawn brought a dull gray light to the sky over the Sangre de Cristos to the north. It was Saturday, June 3, the morning of Tijerina's threatened Coyote showdown. At 8 A.M. Eddie Chávez was contacted at *Alianza* headquarters in Albuquerque. He agreed to line up those *Alianza* officers still unarrested, with the exception of Reies, if the governor would personally guarantee their safety.

In Española, preliminary examination of the captured membership files had been completed. "A lot of people," Emilio Naranjo assured reporters, "are going to be embarrassed."

One of the little cards bore the name of Ida Jo Cargo and credited her with a 1966 donation of $12 to the *Alianza*. This information was immediately leaked to the press, and followed up by notice to all *Alianza* members that their names were now in the hands of the authorities. Also that morning, Alfonso Sánchez went on radio and television to repeat his pledge to jail all who attempted to attend the Coyote meeting that afternoon.

Nonetheless, they set out, at least a hundred of them. Those from as far south as Antón Chico, Tecolote and Rowe had been up since dawn. "It made us mad. How could he throw us into jail when we weren't going to do anything against the law, only go to a barbecue? Besides, my wife had been cooking all the night before."

Racing at full speed from Albuquerque, the white University of New Mexico car had reached Santa Fe in record time, wheeling off the street and disappearing into the dark mouth of the parking lot beneath the capitol building, Eddie Chávez, Santiago Anaya, and F. M. Casadas in its back seat. This time the governor's word had been made good. There had been no roadblocks and no arrests. The three men were ushered into the governor's office, and this time there were no policemen lining the walls. They seated themselves opposite the governor's desk: Chávez, short, dapper, blue eyes alert; Anaya, tall and sober, hair brushed stiffly upright, wearing work boots; Casadas wearing dark glasses, square and short in his best suit. Cargo joked about his *coyotes* and nervously handed each a souvenir ashtray with his seal on it. Each thanked him politely, and there was a silence. Eddie Chávez looked up, worried. "Well, governor, what about this problem we have here, that is facing us?"

The governor said that he thought it was now too late to prevent the abortion of the Coyote meeting. He volunteered the opinion that Sánchez's announcements had probably violated the civil rights of all those forbidden to assemble, but there was nothing that could be done about that now. He suggested that they issue a joint statement explaining that the meeting would not be held until later. He offered to attend when a new date was set. No, he could not make it until Wednesday at the earliest, he was going to Michigan tonight. The immediate problem, he said, was to get the word out. He would go on the radio, and they would notify as many as they could by their own means. Didn't they agree that this was the best way?

The governor spoke over Albuquerque radio at 10:30, asking all *Alianza* members to stay home and suggesting that tourists avoid the Coyote area.

For many without radios in their trucks and cars it was too late, and for others it was only further challenge. One family reached Coyote about 10 A.M. to discover a number of members already gathered along the road outside the school yard where the meeting was to be held. There was an equal number of police cars and more coming. Two state patrolmen and a man who said he was from the FBI began searching the cars. "They said somebody tipped them off we had our cars full of dynamite and things. They gave me a little white paper that said anybody who wanted the land was a Communist."

Later arrivals found the gate closed with chain and padlock. "The policeman told us we didn't have any business on the premises and that we'd better leave. He was the law and he had a gun to prove it, so after a while we moved on."

Many never got there at all. "They stopped me near Gallinas and asked for my driver's license and where I was going. I said we were going to Española, and they told us to drive right on through and stay away from Coyote."

At noon, Benites reported that Reies wanted all warrants quashed and all those in jail released immediately, or there would be trouble. There were hints of some kind of mobilization, and there was a discernible note of real anxiety in Benites' voice that had not been there before. But when this latest development was relayed to the governor, he indicated that he thought that at this point Tijerina should be encouraged to surrender, and that he, Cargo, would do his utmost to see that everybody's civil rights were protected from that moment on.

After some discussion, he agreed to present this argument personally to Tijerina. Benites was contacted and given the governor's unlisted number again. The governor went home to pack for his trip to Michigan. Benites called around four in the afternoon to say that Reies would call the governor at the mansion around dinner time. Reies says that he did call, but that when the governor reiterated that he did not have the power to quash warrants or release men criminally charged, the discussion had broken off inconclusively. Cargo left for Michigan late that evening.

Far to the north at Coyote, it was getting chilly. State Police and sheriff's deputies kept watch over the few who had remained parked opposite the locked-up school yard. Al day there had been rumors that Reies was on his way. There had even been a persistent rumor that he would swoop down in a helicopter to address a few encouraging words to them before the police arrested him. But he had not appeared, nor had Governor Cargo. As darkness closed in, even the diehards gave up. Among the last to leave were Tobías Leyba and his nephew Baltazar Martínez, who were accompanied back to Canjilón by a number of others who had been invited to stay the night.

Sunday's newspapers would dismiss Tijerina's threatened showdown as an abortive failure with such headlines as COYOTE MEETING A BUST.

Probably among those who read the headlines with relief that night was Senator Joseph Montoya, who had, according to reliable sources, arrived in Santa Fe and checked into La Fonda, unnoticed by the press. Alfonso Sánchez says that he did not know that his Democratic colleague was in town that night and that they did not confer.

For his own part, the district attorney felt far from relieved by the results of Saturday's arrests. His dragnet had snared a dozen *Alianza* members, but had failed to net Reies. The tiger was still at large. All Saturday night and all Sunday morning the district attorney waited, but still no word came of the key arrest. At noon, he discovered that the State Police radio had ceased broadcasting Tijerina's description. He drove all the way to Española to make sure the warrant got back on the air. Sunday night passed, and still no word. Monday morning, he called the FBI in Washington and spoke to an assistant of J. Edgar Hoover.

"I told them to get down here," he says. "I told them about the maps and plans we found in Cris Tijerina's possession to take over the whole darned state. You just can't go and take over anybody's land."

He was told he would have to go through Justice Department channels.

"I called the Justice Department and told them about it too. They said they would take it under advisement. Then the rangers at Canjilón called in and said, 'Hey, there's a lot of activity up here.' They could see them all around Tobías Leyba's house, and they were armed. The police had scope rifles on them, but they didn't shoot. I told Chief Black that Tijerina had to be in there and to get him. Black wanted a search warrant. I got one, first time I ever gave my secretary a direct order. I sent Eduardo Escudero over there with the warrants. No, I didn't go up to the hearing at lunch time. I didn't want Scarborough to arraign them all up there in the first place. And then he released them, the Martínez people, Cris Tijerina. . . . When they didn't pick up Reies, I knew there was going to be something like in Arizona, I just knew it."

Reies later said that on Saturday night after the failure of the Coyote meeting, there was another meeting in the back room of an old adobe building, with women posted in the front room and youngsters out by the road. He says there were about 75 people present.

"The people was furious like never before. We decided that we should not publish our activities from then on. We decided to make a citizen's arrest on the person who was tampering and abusing our constitutional rights, Mr. Alfonso Sánchez. We had been told by a very competent lawyer from Washington, D.C., that we could as citizens arrest any officer, state or federal, whom we saw that was violating any particular law. We had in our possession official warrants of arrest given to us by that lawyer. But there was a great deal of confusion, the main leaders were being jailed and one of the plain members left for Albuquerque with the warrants. But we succeeded in getting hold of one for the person of Al Sánchez. People were selected by ballot to make the arrest. It was decided to do it on Monday, after Cris and Félix and the others were released."

Late Monday morning, Don Devereux walked the half-dozen blocks from his Santa Fe home to the capitol building and went to sit in the reception room outside the governor's unoccupied office. Something told him it was the best place to be. He had been there for about an hour when Joe Benites appeared, looking untypically pale and rattled. Pausing only long enough to learn that Lieutenant Governor Lee Francis was not around at the moment, Benites left immediately, indicating that he was on his way to Albuquerque.

Devereux remained where he was for another hour or so, getting hungry but unable to leave, fixed in place by formless apprehension and an irresistible fascination. The first call came in at approximately 3 o'clock and was taken by Lieutenant Governor Francis. It was Judge

Scarborough, who said that the lock on the doors to the United States District courtroom had just been shot off with a submachine gun.

Five months before, a paid announcement had appeared in the legal notices column of the Albuquerque *Journal*, entitled MANIFESTO.

We, Don Barne Quinto César, by the Grace of God, of the Americas and of the Eastern and Western Indies and Islands and Mainlands of the Ocean-Sea Continent, King-Emperor, Sacra Cesárea Real Majestad . . .

HEREBY ADVISE THAT We have made trial of our national destiny in appeasement and it has reaped Us a dire harvest. The enemies of Our repose and welfare have . . . plundered our commerce, mines and public and private property, imprisoned Our subjects and murdered them, refused Our subjects justice, repeatedly violated Our territorial supremacy and air space, sent and garrisoned troops within Our territorial jurisidiction without Our consent, drafted Our subjects to fight their wars . . . and numerous other acts of provocation, aggression and usurpation, which would justify in the eyes of all nations immediate war.

THEREFORE KNOW YE THAT We shall commence to liberate our kingdoms, realms and dominions . . . we shall not take any prisoners of war, but shall take only war criminals and traitors, and try these war criminals and traitors by a military tribunal and execute them.

CONSEQUENTLY, all able-bodied men, whether Our subjects or resident aliens or stateless persons, ready themselves for military duty, and be subject to call for active duty at all times.

LONG LIVE OUR INDEPENDENCE

DON BARNE QUINTO CESAR

THE KING-EMPEROR

Feb. 20, 1967

The sole notice taken of this announcement by any representative of government, state or federal, had been a motion submitted by U.S. Attorney John Quinn to the District Court at Albuquerque, requesting that Jerry Noll be ordered to submit to psychiatric examination.

Manhunt 12

"**B**ALTAZAR MARTÍNEZ was wearing a white coat and no hat and he had dynamite," Deputy Sheriff Pete Jaramillo would testify at the preliminary hearing for the courthouse raiders early in 1968. "He and the old man, Baltazar Apodaca, were put there to guard us. The old man said to us, 'You are a bunch of *vendidos*.' They took us out in the hall, and Reies López Tijerina came to my back, put something in my ribs and said, 'Where's Alfonso Sánchez, tell me, you son of a bitch, or I will kill you.'

"They took us back into the county commissioner's room and made us lay on the floor again. There were about 10 of us in there. Juan Valdez came in and kicked the phone. He stepped on it. Baltazar Martínez told Baltazar Apodaca to go get some wires. He said Reies had ordered prisoners. Baltazar Martínez said to me, 'You come over here.' He tied me up with the wires, then called Dan Rivera to come. Dan Rivera said, 'I got to go to the doctor.' Baltazar Martínez let him go. Somebody said, 'Take the *gringo*.' Baltazar Martínez tied up the reporter. I found out later he was Larry Calloway. Baltazar Martínez said, 'I want keys to a car.' Tony Córdoba handed Baltazar Martínez some keys and said he had a red pickup. Baltazar ordered us out ahead of him. As we were going down the stairs he said 'Stop.' We got aside, and Baltazar Martínez shot out of the door. It was closed."

("He shot at the lock and missed it by six inches," Calloway said later. "When I saw that, I knew I was going to be all right.")

"Baltazar Apodaca went down and opened the door, and Baltazar Martínez motioned us out of the courthouse to where a red pickup was parked. We got in, and Baltazar Martínez drove back to the courthouse. Baltazar Martínez said to Baltazar Apodaca, 'Let's take that State Police car.' Baltazar Martínez went to the car, but it was locked. Baltazar Martínez shot the window with his carbine, reached in and opened it. There wasn't any keys. He took a shotgun and give it to Baltazar Apodaca and got back in the pickup. Baltazar Martínez backed the pickup up to a house beside the courthouse and honked. He handed the shotgun to a man who came to the porch. It was Cerelio García. Baltazar Martínez stopped at another police car farther on to the south. It wasn't locked, and he took some stuff. A case, like a camera case, some uniforms and another shotgun and some shotgun shells. He loaded the shotgun and threw it in the back of the pickup. Baltazar Martínez backed the pickup across to another State Patrol car. Baltazar Martínez got out and started shooting the red light on the patrol car. He took some more stuff out of it. He shot his gun there quite a few times.

"Some people were standing 50 yards away watching. Baltazar Martínez said, 'What are you looking at?' He shot over there, and the people scattered. Then he drove back to where the first car was parked. He said to Baltazar Apodaca, 'Let's open the trunk and get the ammunition out.' Baltazar Martínez shot up the front of the car with his carbine. A fella was coming in a pickup north to south. This man handed him a tire iron to open the trunk. Baltazar Martínez tried to open the trunk. The man in the pickup said, 'I don't think you're going to open that trunk without tools. I gotta go.' Baltazar Martínez told Baltazar Apodaca to go to the back of the courthouse and find a tool. Baltazar Apodaca came back five or ten minutes later without a tool. Baltazar Martínez took a stick of dynamite and took a long thing, maybe a fuse, and was trying to put it in the trunk but it wouldn't go. Baltazar Martínez started pounding on the trunk, but it didn't open.

"Baltazar Martínez got back in the pickup and drove north. There was a car there. 'Is that your car?' he said to me. I said yes. He took the wire off my hands and handcuffed me with my handcuffs. Baltazar Martínez ordered Baltazar Apodaca to put the stuff from the pickup into my car. Larry Calloway and Baltazar Apodaca got in the back. Baltazar Martínez was driving, and I was beside him. We went north through Tierra Amarilla to the residence of Juan Martínez. A lady and two kids came out on the porch. It was Mrs. Juan Martínez. Baltazar Martínez told the lady, "Look what I got here.'

Baltazar Martínez drove to the main road. We were heading south now. Baltazar Martínez said to me, 'You're running out of gas, you got any money?' I said, 'No, but I got a credit card.' Baltazar Martínez asked Larry Calloway. He said yes. Baltazar Martínez took 10 dollars out of Calloway's billfold. There was nobody to give us gas. Baltazar Martínez got two cans of pop and gave the change back to Calloway."

"We kept on going to Canjilón. It was 22, 25 miles. We met a State Police car going towards Tierra Amarilla. It passed and turned around to follow. Another car was coming and stopped and three State Police got out. Baltazar Martínez said, 'Let me go or I'll kill Pete.' We went on through Canjilón. We passed the filling station and more State Police were there. Baltazar Martínez was watching them and drove the car into a ditch near the church. He ordered me out on the right side. He had a pistol on my neck. Larry Calloway and Baltazar Apodaca got out on the left side."

(Calloway had loosened his bonds by them. When 72-year-old Baltazar

Apodaca slipped in the mud, Calloway was able to grab the muzzle of the rifle. "He fell backward and I moved away," Calloway said. The old man managed to squeeze off two shots into the ground as Calloway scrambled to safety behind the nearest police car.)

"Baltazar Martínez had me in front of him. He was holding me by my handcuffs and had a pistol at the back of my head. Quite a few State Police were around there. He backed me across the church yard. In front of the post office there was a green Dodge with a kid and two other kids. He put the gun in the driver's side and ordered the kids to drive to the mountains. Baltazar Martínez's mother got into the car. It was five miles to the mountains. Baltazar Martínez got out and put the gun at my head. 'Don't kill him, give yourself up,' his mother said. His mother argued with him to give up. They argued for a good 15 minutes I guess. The kids got out of the car and ran across the road. Baltazar Martínez took me across the meadow and into the brush. Baltazar Martínez ordered me to run. He was running behind me, with the gun at my shoulder, pushing me. I said, 'I'm tired, I can't run any more.' He kept pushing me until we were in the trees.

"Baltazar Martínez was alert. He was listening and looking under the trees. He ordered me to run again. My mouth was dry. I needed water, but I kept running. Then I stumbled and fell down. Baltazar Martínez just kept running. I heard a shot. I was laying with my face down. The shot sounded further away. I lifted my face and saw him running. I got up and started running the other way."

It was a little over an hour later that the police moved in to round up the 39 men, women and children waiting passively in the trees. Twice during the night, Baltazar Martínez's 63-year-old mother tried to creep through the circle of National Guardsmen to reach her son in the hills. All night, State Police patrol cars and National Guard jeeps combed the unpaved back roads. Officers and guardsmen searched the villages systematically, house by house. In the morning, the two helicopters came sliding down the sunrise to begin their methodical, shuttling sweeps along the timbered slopes, one with two men riding shotgun, pointing their submachine guns down toward the trees.

Unknown to the army in the field, others were preparing their own search that night, their quarry the same, their objective somewhat different. Anti-poverty officials, together with the governor's office, were concerned with reopening communications with the insurgents in hopes of preventing further violence. All agreed that an intermediary was needed and that at this point it had to be someone whom Reies Tijerina knew and trusted.

During the abortive negotiations before the raid, Reies had mentioned one man several times. A call was put through to Clark C. Knowlton, sociology professor at Texas University. Knowlton had been "working behind the Tortilla Curtain," as he put it, since 1958. He had traveled through northern New Mexico extensively and had published a number of scholarly papers concerning poverty and cultural decay in the northern villages. He had known Reies Tijerina since 1963. He readily agreed to come, free of charge, expenses paid. Acting Governor E. Lee Francis was among those who talked to him, inasmuch as Governor Cargo was still enroute by jet from Michigan.

Another call was put through to the OEO office in Washington requesting a second intermediary. Anthony Tinajero of the OEO's civil rights branch agreed to come. He too had long been active in *Hispano* affairs in the Southwest and knew Reies Tijerina.

Knowlton arrived early Tuesday morning, checked into the Desert Inn in Santa Fe and made several phone calls to *Hispano* acquaintances, letting it be known why he was there and that he could be contacted either at the motel or at the offices of the OEO. Tinajero arrived several hours later. They were joined by Don Devereux. Several calls came in, but not the one which would put them in contact with Reies Tijerina, by now the principal subject of the largest manhunt in New Mexico's history.

A force of more than 500 men was scouring the northern mountains in search of an estimated 15 rebels still at large. In addition to 350 National Guardsmen, there were 60 State Policemen, many on horseback, several sheriff's deputies, at least four FBI agents, 35 members of the New Mexico Mounted Patrol, a contingent of Apache police and an unknown number of unofficially deputized vigilantes. In addition to the two helicopters, a small plane equipped with a public address system circled low over the hills, urging the insurgents to surrender. And there were the two Patton tanks, one hunched motionless at the entrance to Canjilón, the other pointing its twin snout up the ruts toward Tobías Leyba's house, where the noncombatants were still under guard.

Asked by reporters why such a large force had been brought out to capture little more than a dozen men, State Police Chief Joe Black was noncommittal, but General John Pershing Jolly indicated that he was in possession of certain classified information concerning an *Alianza* plan to take over some 600,000 acres of northern New Mexico.

In Santa Fe, District Attorney Alfonso Sánchez was more specific, first taking the opportunity to charge that Governor Cargo was responsible for the whole thing. "Maybe if the governor quits holding hands with them, maybe then they will know they can't take the law into their own hands," he said, and added with a touch of exultation, "Everybody's been glorifying Cargo. Well, by golly, it's finally happened."

He told reporters that in addition to the arms, ammunition and *Alianza* records seized in Friday night's arrest of Cristóbal Tijerina, there had been several pictures of Fidel Castro, some books on warfare and plans for taking over "most of northern New Mexico, including El Rito."

Although he did not exhibit them at the time, there were, in fact, five overlay maps drawn crudely in ball-point pen and pencil and looking distinctly like an exercise in basic tactics of the sort suffered and forgotten by most short-term servicemen. But apparently someone had paid attention in class, perhaps looking forward to the day when he would pit himself and his *primos* against the armed might of the United States.

The largest overlay was titled, "Face No. 1," probably referring to the "phase I" which Burgos and Aragon had reported before the arrests and the subsequent raid. Three of the maps were stamped with a round seal reading, "Republic of San Joaquín, 1806." An organization chart started at the top with "The President or Commander-in-Chief of Country or Nations," and descended through "Divisions, which should have 6,371 men," regiments, battalions, "Company, which should have 152 men or more" and platoons.

The overlays seemed to cover an area bordered by Canjilón on the north, Coyote on the south, Gallina on the west and Vallecitos and El Rito on the east. They were liberally sprinkled with such legends as, "Reinforcement Area and Supply," "Supply Rout," (sic) "Patrol all Roads," "Women and Children Here," "Preson" (sic) and, ominously enough for Alfonso Sánchez, "P. W. Compound."

No doubt these documents had a part in inspiring General Jolly to his mobilization of such a prodigious muster of personnel and armament. They probably account for the fact that Monday night and all morning Tuesday the search concentrated in and around El Rito, which lies 23 miles south of Canjilón along a muddy mountain road. In El Rito and nearby Vallecitos, natives were questioned and houses were searched. One man would report to the Civil Liberties Union that four State Policemen entered his home with warrants to search two other houses, but not his. When he objected, they entered, turned the place upside down, found nothing, arrested him without a warrant and took him to Tierra Amarilla and then to Santa Fe, where he was jailed for three days without charge and finally released. Doors were kicked open, weapons were confiscated, nothing was found.

Around noon, State Police received an anonymous tip that Reies Tijerina had gone to Hernández, 30 miles to the south, to pick up a cache of arms. Anselmo Tijerina's empty house was entered and searched again. By this time the place was a shambles. Police then went from house to house. Chief Black admitted to reporters that the locals were not being very cooperative, and many were downright hostile. Nothing was found. There were no arrests.

However, a prize catch was made by two men on their way to assist in the Hernández search. State Policeman Carlos Jaramillo and cattle inspector Julián Archuleta spotted a tubby figure scrambling along the lower cliffs of Chama Canyon and gave chase. After firing three warning shots, they were able to prod Jerry Noll out of a hole. He was unarmed.

"They made me lean against the car and searched me and found my bag of tortillas," Jerry says. "Then they started banging my head on the fender and asking who I was. I told them, Gerald Wayne Barnes, but they wouldn't believe that and just kept on banging, so I said, Jerry Noll, but they said, 'Oh no, we know who you are, you're that nut, the king.' And then they put me in the car and banged my head on the dashboard all the way to jail."

He joined 17 other men and a woman in the Santa Fe jail, all *Alianza* members and held on a variety of charges, including possession of deadly weapons, unlawful assembly and inciting to riot. The woman was Reies' 19-year-old wife, Patsy. Her six-month-old daughter had been taken from her and put in a foster home, and she had been charged with conspiracy to commit a felony, to wit, kidnapping.

"Their favorite question was, 'Where is Reies?' " she says of the police. "And I always answered, 'I don't know.' 'Does Reies have guns and ammunition hidden someplace? Are the people going to riot? Is Reies a Communist?' 'I don't know, I don't know, I don't know.' And then, just for variety I guess, 'Don't you think Reies is too old for such a young wife?' "

Interviewed by a reporter, she was described as pretty but sad-eyed and nervous, and quoted as saying that her husband carried a gun with him all the time, "because he is threatened." And she added, "People are seeking justice. Everybody, all over the world, is complaining of no justice."

During the interview, word came from Alfonso Sánchez that she was to be released and not charged with conspiracy to kidnap "because she is pregnant."

Nearby at the state capitol, Clark Knowlton and Don Devereux were meeting with Governor David Cargo. Outlining their plan, they asked the governor for a guarantee that their emissaries would be allowed to pass through police and National Guard lines. The governor gave his guarantee. Knowlton and Tinajero then went directly to the Santa Fe jail to talk to the prisoners, explaining to reporters and police that they were there to investigate civil rights violations. By late afternoon, with the help of Joe Benites, they had made the first of a complex string of contacts which would eventually lead them to their quarry.

Both the police and the press, with the exception of one reporter, were as yet unaware of the presence of OEO agents on the scene. Shortly after he had conferred with Knowlton and Devereux, Governor Cargo was invited by an Albuquerque reporter to react to Alfonso Sánchez's charge that he was holding hands with the *Alianza*. "Ridiculous," the governor replied. The whole thing, he said, was a result of "sheer stupidity" on the part of the district attorney. "He got on the radio and stirred them up . . . kept up a constant harangue at these people, telling them they were Communists and they'd never get out on bond. That wasn't the way to do it." He was not, however, planning to coddle the rebels, he said. "If either of the two shooting victims dies, the entire crew is guilty of murder, since they were a part of the conspiracy." As for Tijerina: "He'll be charged with a serious felony. The only thing he has coming is arrest and prosecution . . ."

In Albuquerque that afternoon, Judge H. Vearle Payne ruled that his show-cause order of May 19 against Reies Tijerina be dismissed, since it had been satisfied by the seizure of *Alianza* records the previous weekend. During the proceedings, the nearly empty courtroom was guarded by eight city police plainclothesmen, seven Federal marshals and an FBI agent.

In Albuquerque's Bataan Hospital, State Policeman Nick Sais lay with a bullet in his left lung, still listed as in critical condition. He was under 24-hour police protection. In Santa Fe, jailer Eulogio Salazar was reported to be improving. He too was guarded by police.

Sixty-five miles to the north in Canjilón, the tanks waited in their ruts and the pastures were dotted with National Guard pup tents. In the surrounding countryside, jeeps patrolled the back roads, mounted searchers traced logging trails, foot soldiers combed brushy arroyos and timbered hillsides. Only newsmen and tourists with confirmed reservations at motels and lodges in Chama were allowed to pass the roadblocks. A truckload of groceries bound for Baldonado's store in Canjilón had been held up, but at a word from General Jolly the relief supplies were allowed through and Baldonado was once again doing a land-office business in lunch meats, soda pop and potato chips.

Around 4:30 P.M., the captives in Tobías Leyba's meadow were released from "protective custody." They had been held for more than 24 hours without warrants and without being charged, quite possibly being used as bait. Baltazar Martínez's tiny mother hurried off through the village, followed at a discreet distance by police.

The helicopters disappeared again. Night fell. An anonymous phone call came through to Chief Black's Canjilón headquarters, warning that Chama was about to be raided by a heavily armed company of *Tijerinistas*. State Police cars raced north, but no insurgents were found. "If they know what's good for them, they'll stay away from Chama," a State Police officer observed dryly. "These people up there are armed to the teeth and loaded for bear."

"Right after the raid, Bill Mundy came driving past the house like crazy," says Fernanda Martínez. "He had a whole truck full of guns and he was handing them out to all the Anglos."

"I happened to be working cattle up on the mountain when it happened," Mundy says. "I was pretty unhappy when I found out I'd missed the shooting part. But afterwards I got to thinking maybe it was for the best. Because all you've got to do in a situation like that is move in fast, drop down on one knee and start squeezing. Take three of them out before they know what hit 'em."

By midnight, Professor Knowlton had received some 20 phone calls, some protesting civil rights violations, but not all. One call put him in touch with someone in direct contact with Reies Tijerina. He was told that Tijerina might be willing to surrender to the governor personally, but that the rebel leader was deeply disturbed by the presence of National Guard troops in Río Arriba.

At 9 o'clock Wednesday morning, the National Guard began to withdraw from northern New Mexico. "The military has probably outlived its usefulness," Governor Cargo explained in Santa Fe. "They are only scaring people up there."

The guardsmen sheathed their bayonets, hoisted their packs and decamped in trucks and jeeps. Hospital van and field kitchen were hauled out of their meadows and driven away. The two tanks lumbered up onto their flatbed trucks and were trundled off through the forest past signs that read, "Land of Many Uses." Thirty State Police left with them. Thirty-five members of the New Mexico Mounted Patrol in bone-white Stetsons and creaking gunbelts urged their spirited chargers into horse trailers and also left. Pausing to survey the battlefield, General Jolly told reporters that mobilization of the National Guard would cost the state an estimated $20,000. Pressed, he grudgingly confirmed the persistent rumor that all along there had been no ammunition for his tanks. Then he got into his command jeep and drove away.

"I think we've accomplished what we brought them in here for," Chief Black told reporters. "That was to show the people of Río Arriba County that we mean business." Adding that he was moving headquarters for the search to Tierra Amarilla and would be keeping 25 men in the area, he said, "I feel we can gather information better by moving freely in the villages and working through informants."

An hour or so later, in a small roadside store in Cebolla, a little old lady bought three gallons of wine and tried to buy a case of bread. Police were informed and discovered Mrs. Martínez with wine and groceries headed toward *Mesa de Las Viejas* or Mesa of the Old Women. Located a few miles south of Canjilón, the vast, rocky plateau is thick with mountain spruce and piñon and virtually without roads. Now a part of Carson forest, it had originally been considered part of the *ejido* of the San Joaquín de Chama Grant. For over a century the residents of Canjilón, many of them descendants of the original grant settlers, had been grazing their sheep and cattle, cutting fencing and gathering firewood there. At just about the time Reies Tijerina had arrived in northern New Mexico the Forest Service had removed the entire mesa from the Canjilón grazing allotment, had reseeded it and alloted it to outsiders.

And now, a dozen State Police, FBI agents and county officers were dispatched to *Mesa de Las Viejas*, there to search all afternoon and into the night for 23-year-old Baltazar Martínez, who was said by Chief Black to be "the worst one of the bunch," and was reported by the newspapers to have "dynamite strapped to his chest." They didn't find him, although he was there.

However, police did capture young Tony Valdez as he tried to slip back into Canjilón, and Salomón Velásquez bumbled into their arms while trying to reach his house in Coyote.

Of an estimated 20 raiders, nine were now in custody. An additional 11 men and women were in jail as a result of Alfonso Sánchez's flurry of warrants, and there would be more.

In Santa Fe that morning, the district attorney issued new warrants for the arrest of Reies Tijerina and 12 others, charging them on two counts of kidnapping, three counts of assault with intent to commit murder and one count of "dangerous use of explosives with intent to terrify others."

Seven of the 12 charged were already in custody, among them Tobías Leyba, Jerry Noll, the old man Baltazar Apodaca and Reies Tijerina's 19-year-old daughter, Rose. In New Mexico, conviction of kidnapping can bring death by gas.

That same morning, all unknown to Alfonso Sánchez, Governor Cargo was consulting with Devereux and Benites, who told him that they were now in touch with Tijerina. They warned, however, that the situation was delicate; Reies was convinced the State Police had orders to kill him. Cargo emerged from his capitol office to tell reporters that an intermediary had contacted him and that Tijerina was ready to surrender to him personally, if guaranteed safe conduct. "He will not be harmed, but he will be prosecuted," he said. Pressed, he admitted that the intermediary had asked that the National Guard be withdrawn prior to the surrender, "but my decision was not based solely on the surrender offer." He refused to name the intermediary.

However, reporters had noticed the two strangers with Devereux and hastened to question them. Knowlton explained that he was there as an observer and said that he and Tinajero were forming a Citizens' Committee on Human Rights. "We intend to find out if there have been civil rights violations," he said. Tinajero concurred. "I know Reies Tijerina personally," he said, "but our concern is with the children and mothers."

Father Robert García, of the OEO, was as obviously sincere in his concern for civil rights as the other two, but he was typically uncircumspect on the matter of arrangements for Tijerina's surrender. He had come to the governor, he said, to get assurance of a "free pass for our people" to cross police lines. He did excuse himself from naming "our people," but the seed had been planted. The politically astute were immediately alerted, some to alarm, some to delight—depending on personal interest and political allegiance.

It was then left to Joe Benites to convey word to Tijerina that the governor would guarantee his safety and that of any other fugitives who might wish to surrender.

Shortly afterwards, Governor Cargo received two visitors from Albuquerque, Rubén Darío Salas and F. M. Cassaus, who said they represented certain *Alianza* members and asked that a general amnesty be declared for all those still being hunted. "I can't grant general amnesty," the governor told them. "The person that shot the policeman can only be charged."

On his way out, Salas warned quietly that should anything happen to Tijerina, "Things are going to be a lot harder to handle."

That afternoon, Judge Scarborough held a hearing in the Santa Fe courthouse before signing warrants charging Rose Tijerina and six others with assault with intent to commit murder and kidnapping. Robert García and his Committee for Human Rights were present, as were "friends of the court," attorneys Lorenzo Tapia and Charles Driscoll. Also in attendance were 17 armed officers, a dozen outside the courtroom, five inside. Perhaps remembering their discomfort two days before on the second floor of the TA courthouse, both Judge Scarborough and his court reporter Mike Rice were armed, the judge with a frontier-model pistol in an elaborately tooled holster. The proceedings were meticulously legal and concluded with Scarborough ruling no plea for the defendants, denying them bond and remanding them to the penitentiary for safekeeping. Tapia and Driscoll protested against the sending of 19-year-old Rose to prison, but in the end Judge Scarborough concurred with the district attorney's assertion that she in particular should be put away, "in view of her relationship to the head of the movement."

All of this was, of course, broadcast on radio and television and published in the newspapers.

Late that afternoon, a three-page typewritten "news release" arrived at the offices of two news services in Española and was immediately relayed to police. The governor was also informed, since the document evidenced particular hostility toward him. Charging him with responsibility for the arrests before the Coyote meeting, it said that the people of the "free city-states" were "fed up with aggressions, usurpations, encroachments and frauds of the U.S. government and of the state of New Mexico," suggested that "Cargo plans on building concentration camps" and concluded with the implied threat: "The officers and agents of the U.S. government and of the state administration should realize that their families are in a vulnerable position . . ."

In certain definite ways, the wording of the pronouncement was not consistent with Tijerina's style, but the document was signed with his name, and the signature checked with those already in police and newspaper files.

Cargo's immediate rage reflected a more profound disappointment and impatience. "If he wants to come to my house, let him," the governor said. "He has threatened my family. I'll meet him in my front yard and he won't get a chance to explain."

A planned trip to Tierra Amarilla to examine the site of the raid was canceled. The governor's mansion was put under police guard, and that evening Ida Jo Cargo and her three small children were driven secretly to Belén, where they remained with her family under round-the-clock police protection.

Cargo told reporters that word from an intermediary had now punctured any hopes that Tijerina or his followers would surrender. "They will fight it out," he said. "He thinks he's right, and he will carry it to the bloody conclusion, I guess." Asked if he thought Tijerina's decision was absolutely final, the governor would only comment, "He has a mind that's difficult to predict. He may change it yet."

Devereux and Benites had not given up and were still in contact with Tijerina through their telephone intermediary. Around dinner time they were informed that Reies would talk to one of them and a newspaper reporter, if they were willing to come to him. They agreed. Arrangements were made. They were then told to wait.

Alfonso Sánchez was still issuing warrants. Dolores Domínguez was arrested in Bernalillo and rushed to the Santa Fe jail. Ramón Tijerina was picked up at Reies' Albuquerque home, and Abelicio Moya was taken from his home. While the two men were being booked, policemen roamed the corridors with submachine guns.

To the north, the search continued, coordinated now from the TA courthouse, where broken glass still crunched underfoot and blood still stained the floor beside the radiator and the earth outside the sheriff's window. Word had come through that afternoon of "large-scale shooting" near the Mundy ranch. Officers raced to the scene but found only two boys target shooting.

Rumors persisted of an impending raid on Chama, and as darkness fell, armed Anglo residents prepared to sit through the night in shaded front rooms and stores and the offices of motels and hunting lodges. A reporter pulled into a darkened service station in Chama and got out to clean off his windshield. The door of the station opened to reveal a man with a pistol who said, "Get moving boy. I mean it."

In Santa Fe, Professor Clark Knowlton and reporter Peter Nabokov were visited by an armed man who blindfolded and handcuffed them, then led them to a car and put them in with two other men. They were driven northeast for an hour, then southward, then northward again. The journey lasted five hours. They were switched from car to truck and back to car again. The roads grew progressively worse. Finally they were jolting up a mountain track, pressed back into the seat by the steepness of the climb. The car stopped and the blindfolds were removed. They could see nothing but mountain blackness.

They were taken through a thick stand of mountain piñon to a small shack and ushered in. Beneath a single bare bulb at a rickety kitchen table, Reies Tijerina sat waiting in his shirt sleeves.

"He was calm, confident," wrote Nabokov, who was meeting the man for the first time. "His voice never rose, nor was he ever hysterical. His eyes did not whirl in their sockets. I never felt my life was in danger. His shirt was ironed, his face was clean shaven. Before we began to talk he ran a comb through his wavy black hair a few times. He began by saying the problem did not begin with the *Alianza*'s inception in 1963. He talked about the succession of 19th century agreements and treaties and the land grants. I was incredulous. We were meeting in the dark of night, an armed guard stood outside. But he was taking pains to brief me on other, more distant events, so I would understand."

Pressed about more recent events, Tijerina told about the *Alianza* vote to make a citizen's arrest of Alfonso Sánchez at the courthouse on Monday. "The shooting of anyone was prohibited," he said, but "when our arresting party reached Tierra Amarilla, two officers of the opposition made resistance and went for their guns. There was someone, it wasn't me, that apparently wasn't capable of controlling all the armed men."

What had they planned to do with Alfonso Sánchez if they had succeeded in capturing him?

"We would make him admit to the public that five years ago he told the people of the Tierra Amarilla Grant to go out and cut fences and let their cattle through and take their land back."

And if he had refused?

Reies' eyes glinted gray-green, and there was the hint of a smile. "There are a lot of old sheepherder shacks like this one. We would just move him from place to place until he died of old age."

Had Reies led the raid? Had he been there at all? "I am not going to say I wasn't, because I don't want my people to think I'm going to let others be punished without me, but I'm not going to say I was and incriminate myself."

He agreed with Professor Knowlton's urgent suggestion that further violence should be avoided. But when asked if there were any conditions under which he could be induced to surrender and submit to legal process, he said no. Not to the governor or anyone else. "One thing the public doesn't know," he said, "is that for several months there has been a well-organized plan to assassinate me." He became somewhat excited as he explained that he had stayed out of sight during the Coyote arrests because "the state police were supposed to kill me and later give the reasons to the public that they shot me because I resisted arrest or had tried to run away."

He said that he had considered giving himself up in exchange for an amnesty and suspension of charges against all except himself, but the governor had made it clear that afternoon that there would be neither suspension of charges nor amnesty.

What did he plan to do next?

"All depends on the opposition," he said. "If they continue to harass, depriving us of our rights and reducing justice to mere welfare and powdered milk, then they shouldn't expect us to continue as caged servants. Are we not human? Are we not equal?"

How long did he think he could hold out?

He was not afraid, he said. At the courthouse the state police "ran like coyotes. If they really thought we were criminals, they should have made a good stand." Despite the arrests, he still had 400 men ready to take up arms at a word from him. "I've got a thousand places to hide in New Mexico, there are tens of thousands of families to whom I'm a faithful representative. If I'm a fugitive to the federal government or to some poor state officials, to my people I am not a fugitive."

He said that he would consider Knowlton's advice against further guerrilla action, but he said that he could make no promises. "Our creed is justice, the land is our inheritance. My people demand satisfaction."

Knowlton and Nabokov were taken back to the car, blindfolded, handcuffed and then driven back the way they had come, arriving in Santa Fe at eight Thursday morning. Shortly after Nabokov's story appeared in that afternoon's *New Mexican*, Alfonso Sánchez sent for the young reporter.

Otherwise, Thursday was slow. Anselmo Tijerina was arrested late in the day at Hernández and arraigned in Santa Fe on charges of kidnapping and assault in connection with the raid. That left four suspected raiders still at large: Reies and Cristóbal Tijerina, Baltazar Martínez and young Moisés Morales, both of Canjilón. Four others would eventually be added to the list: Juan Valdez, José Madril, Reies Tijerina, Jr., and the fugitive to be known for months only as El Indio.

To the north in Río Arriba, 25 State Police and sheriff's deputies continued to concentrate their search on *Mesa de las Viejas*, looking for Baltazar Martínez and Moisés Morales, but without results.

Roadblocks had been removed, and tourists and natives once again moved freely up and down US 84. However, store owners along the highway and in Chama kept their weapons at hand. A waitress reported having seen three men with rifles moving along the road the previous night. "I don't know who they were, but I was scared."

In Canjilón, only sheep and cattle now occupied Tobías Leyba's meadow, and rain had all but obliterated the tank tracks along the rutted roads. Asked if local residents feared a return of the raiders, an elderly villager replied, "Why should we worry? These people are our neighbors."

"You hesitate to strike up a conversation about what happened," said a loyal official at the courthouse. "You don't know which side they are on."

Friday was more of the same. No arrests were made. When Reies Tijerina was reported to have been seen in Coyote, 10 policemen converged on the area and conducted another house-to-house search, but got little assistance from villagers and found nothing. Chief Black mentioned to reporters that there might have-been a lot of blank ammunition fired at the courthouse during the raid. Jailer Eulogio Salazar was reported to be in satisfactory condition in Santa Fe. Surgery had removed the bullet that had punctured the lung of State Policeman Nick Sais. He was listed as still in critical condition but "definitely improving." Asked in Santa Fe if he thought Tijerina would surrender, District Attorney Alfonso Sánchez said, "Not him."

A few minutes past midnight on Saturday, June 10, an unmarked police car trailed a brown '60 Ford into the outskirts of Bernalillo, just north of Albuquerque. Coming from the opposite direction, a patrol car swerved in front of the Ford, and officers from both pursuing cars tumbled out. The two men in the front seat of the Ford offered no resistance. The man lying on the back seat was Reies Tijerina. He made no attempt to pull the .38 automatic from his back pocket. He knew that he had been recognized by a service station attendant 10 minutes before when he had left the car to get a drink of water.

"I was going to tell my son and Ubaldo to let me off," he says, "but honest to God I fell asleep. I had in mind to ask Cargo through negotiations to drop the charges of the men who had been arrested for unlawful assembly and I would turn myself in to clarify the whole situation. The officer who arrested me said in the newspapers I hadn't shown no surprise, no resistance. But honest to God I fell asleep. I had heard them say that car is following us pretty close. I knew it, I knew it then. That's why it was the will of God."

A profoundly relieved Alfonso Sánchez complimented the police and expressed heartfelt thanks that King Tiger had been caught "without anybody at all getting hurt."

State Police Chief Joe Black coined a curiously expressive metaphor, describing the capture of Reies Tijerina as, "a jewel that dropped out of its setting, and we picked it up."

¡Viva Tijerina! 13

O N the morning of his capture, Chief Black's "jewel" was rushed under
heavy guard to Santa Fe to appear before a magistrate. Reies now
denied that he had participated in the courthouse raid. "I was in
the Coyote area at the time, and heard about it on the radio."

Signing a poverty affidavit, he explained to a reporter, "I owe a hospital $1,000 for my baby."

Asked about the "press release" that had threatened the lives of state
and federal officials, he said that he had signed it, but that he had not
written it and had intended it only to explain *Alianza* demands and to
protest the Coyote arrests. "I felt very, very bad," he said of the threats.
"I'd like someday, if my future permits, to offer my apology to the
governor."

Asked why he had been carrying a gun when arrested, he replied,
"because the State Police have organized a plan to get rid of me for
good."

Asked if he styled himself after Emilio Zapata, he said, "I admire his
work, but I admire the work of Moses more."

He was then rushed off under guard to the state penitentiary, which
stands out on the treeless high plain some 15 miles south of Santa Fe.
Reporters and television cameramen were there to record the chorus of
shouts from the cells as he was admitted: "*¡Viva Tijerina!*"

"For the first time in my life I feel a deep satisfaction and conviction
that I am serving and giving to my people *all* of my life," Reies wrote
from his cell in an article intended for publication in the *New Mexican.*
"In my reflections, I see that the whole world knows the problem of New
Mexico for the first time in history."

There was no doubt about it, the *grito* of Tierra Amarilla had been
heard halfway around the world. Reporters had come from all over the
country for the manhunt. Television viewers across the nation had
glimpsed Canjilón's crumbling adobes beyond the lumbering silhouettes
of National Guard tanks. National publications of every stripe had already or would soon tell the story, from the *New York Times* to the *National Inquirer,* from *Newsweek* to the *New Republic,* from the *People's*

172

World to *American Opinion*. The foreign press would take due note of the incident in Río Arriba, with a particularly lively interest shown by the press south of the border, including Mexico City's *Excelsior* and *El Mexicano*, a Juárez daily. Mexico's *El Día* would soon begin a lengthy series of articles about the Southwestern land grants and their disgruntled heirs.

Long neglected books such as George Sánchez's *Forgotten People* would be hastily reprinted. There would be a sudden increase in demand for little-known statistical and sociological studies of the northern villages and the *Hispano* in general. The first popular-priced English language version of the Treaty of Guadalupe Hidalgo would soon appear. Researchers would shake the dust from ancient volumes of land grant documents in the State Archives at Santa Fe, and in the library at the University of New Mexico the microfilm reels would roll and the names would scroll down the screen like the cast of some musty frontier melodrama: T. B. Catron, William Blackmore, Kit Carson, Julian Maxwell, "Manuel Martínez and all those who should care to accompany him . . ."

Somehow the unlikely tale had sprung back to life and into the 20th century with an archaic roar of six-guns, and the journalists and their readers sensed that the source of the drama's renewed energy lay in the personality of Reies Tijerina. What kind of a man was it who could rouse forgotten men to memorable acts, could unabashedly liken himself to Moses, could take such obvious relish from the prospect of his own martyrdom and who could reply, when asked why he had taken a young and uneducated woman for his second wife, "I married her to raise her above all women"?

"Charismatic" was the word most frequently used to describe the land grant leader's personality, with the cagey "mercurial" and the more honest "elusive" running close behind. But the mystery remained and few reports succeeded in answering the questions, often unspoken, but insistently there behind most public curiosity about the man. Was he a charlatan, a lunatic, a Communist, a racist, a violent man? Was he sincere, and if so, in whose cause? Was he dangerous, and if so, to whom?

Millions had by now heard of the raid, and many thousands knew the name of the man and something of his cause. Not all, by far, were entirely pleased with what had happened nor with what they had heard.

The reaction had, of course, been taking shape since before Tijerina's arrest. On the morning of his capture, Reies had taken care to assure reporters that, while he knew Professor Knowlton, he had not seen him while he had been a fugitive. But it had been too late for such a gentlemanly attempt to guard a personal trust.

On the Thursday before Tijerina's capture, reporter Peter Nabokov had been questioned for several hours by the district attorney and State Police. His description of his five-hour blindfolded journey was accepted as reasonable evidence that he had no clear idea where he had been taken and did not know where the fugitive Tijerina was. However, that same day State Representative Thomas Holland, a Democrat, had called for Governor Cargo's impeachment, hinting at dark doings between the governor, the OEO and Reies Tijerina. The following day, Alfonso Sánchez had phoned Robert García at his OEO office and had demanded that the priest name his contact with Tijerina. García protested later that when he had refused, the district attorney had threatened him. Sánchez denies the charge, explaining ruefully, "All I did was read him the statute making it a felony to harbor or aid a fleeing felon."

Pressed about the matter that afternoon, Governor Cargo dismissed Holland's charges with the comment: "He doesn't know what he's talking about. He's got wealth in misinformation and poverty in experience."

Asked about the airplane that had brought Professor Knowlton to New Mexico, the governor denied any knowledge that his office had authorized its use. He further protested the district attorney's threat to charge García as a felon, commenting that the priest "didn't really know anything anyway."

But then, the next morning, Tijerina was captured not only in the company of, but actually being chauffered by Ubaldo Martínez, an anti-poverty worker in Coyote and a paid employee of the Home Education Livelihood Program, division of the Office of Economic Opportunity. It was reported that Martínez was also an *Alianza* member. While his involvement in previous attempts to contact Tijerina was never established and charges against him of harboring and aiding a fugitive were eventually dropped, his presence in the company of the land grant leader was the first hard public fact connecting the OEO with Tijerina, and the reaction was swift.

Word came from Washington, D.C., scarcely 10 hours after Reies' capture, that members of New Mexico's Congressional delegation, headed by Democratic Senators Clinton P. Anderson and Joseph M. Montoya, were calling for an immediate federal investigation of the OEO's involvement with Reies Tijerina.

"We do not believe," declared the Senators, "That the financing of riot experts or the financing of people to aid and abet fugitives from justice is in keeping with the objectives of the poverty program."

The heat was on, and, while the Senators made no charge of similar involvement by the governor's office, there could be little doubt that such an attack was in the wind. Whatever his social sentiments, David Cargo was above all an astute and ambitious politician. Asked for his reaction to the charges, he replied without hesitation: "The poverty program is a federal program, and the state has no authority or control over the OEO."

And then, proving that he could be as adept as his Democratic opponents at the art of seizing advantage, he pointed out that it was the Congressional delegation which had originally gone along with Federal control of the War on Poverty programs. He added that he would welcome the Senators' aid in getting state control of poverty funds, should they now feel so inclined.

Clearly the time had come for passing the buck and mending political fences, for extraction of advantage from civil distress, for the selection of scapegoats, for the settlement of vendetti. The *grito* of Tierra Amarilla had been heard well enough, but there were many in Washington and many more in New Mexico eager to agree that it had been too loud, too much, too soon; and there was no lack of people willing to hitch a ride on a rising ground-swell of public indignation, most prevalent among the ruling majority, but also strong among the *Hispano* middle class.

On June 13, Reies and three others charged in connection with the Echo Amphitheatre trespass were brought in handcuffs before Federal Judge Howard Bratton in United State District Court in Albuquerque. There were scattered shouts of *¡Viva Tijerina!*, but inside the packed courtroom two dozen armed federal officers mingled with the crowd, while Judge Bratton entertained a motion to strengthen bonds on the defendants and ordered a federal warrant issued for the fifth defendant, Cristóbal Tijerina, who was still at large.

That same day, Moisés Morales, one of the last four suspected raiders at large, surrendered in Canjilón, telling State Police that he "just got tired of hiding and wanted to get it over." That afternoon, Governor Cargo posted a $500 reward for information leading to the capture of Baltazar Martínez.

The same week, the Department of the Interior reiterated its opinion that there was no legal basis for *Hispano* land claims in the Southwest. A press officer of the State Department denied that the Treaty of Guadalupe Hidalgo was invalid because it had been signed by an unauthorized individual. The government continued to maintain its stance of amused incredulity, as reflected in the by now well-known statement that *Alianza* claims were too fantastic to be refuted in reasonable words.

However, the troubles in New Mexico continued to produce problems for a variety of federal agencies, on other matters as well as the question of the land. On June 7, two days after the raid, the New Mexico affiliate of the American Civil Liberties Union had wired the Justice Department, urging an investigation of possible civil rights violations following the raid. The ACLU had also suggested that Governor Cargo appoint a Board of Inquiry into the matter, and Cargo had expressed enthusiastic interest, urging that his endorsement be included in the press release.

By the 15th, nothing further had been heard from the governor, nor had anything definite come from Washington. The delay on the part of the Justice Department could be explained by the fact that their civil rights investigators had their hands full elsewhere that month. On the 15th, 500 National Guard troops were called out of Tampa after three days of rioting following the shooting in the back of a 19-year-old black boy by a white policeman. The same day, 900 National Guard troops were called into Cincinnati to control rioting in a black ghetto. And Detroit was yet to come.

At noon, also on the 15th, Reies Tijerina and 17 other accused raiders were taken under guard to District Court in Santa Fe for a hearing to consider bond. Heavily armed State Police patrolled the streets outside the courthouse. Four days before, there had been a demonstration by some 40 *Alianza* sympathizers, among them Corky González and several of his Crusade for Justice followers from Denver. The demonstrators were on hand for the hearing. Sheriff's deputies and plainclothesmen guarded the halls and stood along the walls of the courtroom. Spectators were searched one by one, women, children and old men alike. Before the doors closed on the 50 or more left outside, shouts of *¡Viva Tijerina!* rang out.

Judge Scarborough had been disqualified; Judge Joe Angel was presiding. State patrolman Nick Sais was still too ill to be present. Dan Rivera was the first witness, then Eulogio Salazar.

Eulogio moved carefully and his body seemed wasted; the left side of his face was swollen out of shape and deeply incised with two stitched lines fanning out from the corner of his mouth. He spoke with noticeable difficulty, answering through the official Spanish interpreter.

Q. Who caused your injury to your face?

A. Reies Tijerina.

Q. Would you point that man out to the court?

A. This one right here.

Q. What did he do to you?

A. He shot me.

Bond was not to be granted that day, but would be taken under consideration by the court. Judge Angel pointed out that bail could not be granted to defendants charged with a capital offense. His decision on individual defendants would not only determine whether or not they would be released on bond, but would also indicate whether or not they would be charged with first- or second-degree kidnapping, the first of which was punishable by death.

That same day, Congressman Joseph Resnick, Democrat of New York and chairman of a Congressional subcommittee on rural poverty, was holding hearings to look into the causes of "the recent insurrection in New Mexico."

Among those to testify was Robert García, who said that the raid on the Tierra Amarilla courthouse had been essentially symbolic. "If they have not been treated as full citizens thus far by the United States, symbolically they are seeking to attain equality by creating their own community, with its own government." As evidence of symbolic intention, he said that empty boxes found around the courthouse had indicated that many of the shots fired during the raid had been blanks.

Governor Cargo, also among those to testify, agreed that his *coyotes* had for a long time been treated as "second-class citizens" and were the victims of social neglect and political deceit. "If you could pave roads with broken promises," he said, "we could have blacktopped all of northern New Mexico years ago."

However, the governor had an additional purpose in appearing before the subcommittee, and he wasted little time getting to it. The OEO, he charged, had spent too much money in New Mexico creating new agencies such as CAP and HELP and making sociological and statistical studies. "Instead of counting outhouses," he said, "they should have been teaching people to fill out applications so they could participate in the programs of already existing agencies such as the state Department of Health, Education and Welfare."

He urged that Congress turn control of poverty funds over to state and local governments at once. The War on Poverty, he said, had been a failure in New Mexico. He repeated his remarks at the western governors' conference in Montana the next day, to the general approval of the gathered governors. Poverty funds should be taken out of the hands of the federal agencies, he said. "Give us the money, and we'll show you how to spend it."

In vain would Robert García warn that this would mean a return to the pork barrel tradition and that the handout philosophy of the old-line agencies had never worked, while the self-help program of the War on Poverty had not been given sufficient time. "Because we haven't eliminated poverty in three years, we are condemned," he complained. "Yet they haven't done it in a hundred."

While national political conditions did not as yet allow Democratic members of the New Mexico Congressional delegation to openly welcome Cargo's move, they were already privately at work in the same direction.

Senator Montoya hastened to reinforce his original encouragement of State Attorney General Boston Witt's confidential investigation of Reies Tijerina, with the suggestion that investigators now add to their preoccupation with Tijerina's "Communist affiliations," the OEO's "involvement with the violence at Tierra Amarilla."

That same week, the very elderly Clinton Anderson wrote to Ralph Guzmán at the Mexican-American Studies Project at UCLA, demanding to know who Burgos and Aragon were and what they had been doing in his state.

Back in New Mexico, Robert García's description of the raid as "symbolic" brought swift reaction, typified by the protest of Chief Black that blank bullets could not have injured two officers, shot up three police cars and caused $5,000 damage. Apparently forgetful that he had been the original source of the report that many of the hundreds of shots fired had been blanks, he reported indignantly that State Police had dug 30 bullets out of the cars and seven out of the courthouse.

Upon his return from Montana, Governor Cargo continued to deftly redirect criticism of his handling of events before the raid. Accused by State Representative Bobby Mayfield, a Democrat, of coddling the insurgents, the governor suggested that it had all been the OEO's fault. They had "promised things they couldn't deliver," he said. "These promises did nothing but stir the people up."

He then announced his intention to visit the northern villages and "sit down with the people and see if we can't work out some answers," thereby giving himself the jump on other bureaucratic and political performers soon to join him on the northern tour.

June 15 had also been a special day for Alfonso Sánchez. That morning, the district attorney had received a letter which had been postmarked the day before in the Santa Fe post office, just three blocks from his office. Opening with the salutation, "Dear Rat," the letter promised: "If Tijerina is to die, so must you and the others. If we are not able to get you through sniper fire, we will sacrifice one of our members to do so. You are dealing with the underworld now . . ."

The letter was signed, "The Black Hand Gang." It was the fault of Governor Cargo, the district attorney said. "He gave these people status and he's still doing it."

As for the governor's previous suggestions that civil rights might have been violated during the National Guard occupation of Río Arriba, the district attorney replied hotly: "He doesn't even know what civil rights are. He should see a psychiatrist."

Ignoring the reference to civil rights, the governor chose to reiterate his opinion that the district attorney's radio broadcasts before the Coyote meeting had been "idiotic" and to repeat his criticism of the shotgun nature of the arrests of that weekend. He also pointed out that a number of the district attorney's indictments had been woefully defective in the past, that many of his warrants during the manhunt had been questionable and that the 26 charges against the raid defendants had already had to be amended twice.

A second scapegoat appeared to be in the making. But Alfonso Sánchez could not take time to worry about himself, he had the law to uphold. Hastily arranging for police protection to supplement the .38-caliber revolver he had been toting in the waistband of his trousers since Coyote, he set to work on yet a third revision of his charges against the raid defendants.

Nick Sais would not be present for the indictments, nor was he telling reporters who had shot him. He remained under 24-hour guard in his hospital room in Albuquerque. "It gives Nick peace of mind," Captain John Bradford explained. "He's apprehensive. Who wouldn't be?"

The tension had abated in the north, but only on the surface. State Police moved about more casually on lonely roads; the courthouse had been cleaned up. But residents of Canjilón and Coyote and Tierra Amarilla remained reluctant to discuss the raid with strangers. Some Anglo ranchers continued to ride armed, and the merchants of Chama kept their shotguns loaded and close to hand.

"They'll let them all off," one rancher muttered over his coffee in the Elk Horn Lodge Restaurant south of Chama.

"Why not?" said his companion. "They're nonviolent, aren't they? They only burn barns to keep warm."

"They'll let that Commie off with a $10 fine," Bill Mundy assured a visiting *New York Times* correspondent. "He's an outside troublemaker. I've got informants among his own people. Oh, he's been to Cuba all right. He's a Castro man all right." (Later he would fume: "I wouldn't mind gettin' close enough to that reporter fella for a good handhold. He made us sound like hicks.")

"On the news today we heard that Alfonso Sánchez is going to ask for the death penalty for us," wrote José Madril, who had been arrested on June 9 in connection with the raid. "*Y que viva Tijerina and his people, if it's God's will.*"

On June 23, the raid defendants were again brought before Judge Joe Angel in Santa Fe. Again there were the restless knots of country people waiting beneath the *portales* of the courthouse. Motorcycle police circled the block and State Police in Prussian blue and black stood at regular intervals along the street, shotguns propped on their hips. Again men, women and children were searched before being allowed to enter the courtroom; pointed combs were removed from purses, pen knives from the pockets of small boys. Again the cry of *¡Viva Tijerina!* went up as the doors were eased closed on those left outside.

As the defendants filed in, a little girl called out from her mother's lap, "Daddy," and Tobías Leyba gave her a guarded wave. The 16 men and a girl stood in a straggling line before the bench to hear the clerk read the 26 counts against them. Rose wore a pink blouse and faded wine-colored dungarees, and her black hair hung straight down on her shoulders. Reies and Reies, Jr., wore loose prison khakis. Alfonso Chávez and Esequiel Domínguez wore wrinkled suits; the rest were in faded work clothes. The 17 at the bar might have been exchanged for 17 selected from those behind them; there was the same predominance of dark eyes and homely clothing, the same weathered swarthiness of the older men, the same easy, unrecalcitrant pose of each.

It was sweltering in the high-ceilinged room. Toward the end of the 20-minute reading, Rose swayed. Mary Escobar rushed forward from a front seat, but was waved back. Rose was given water. Judge Angel asked for ventilation.

"The eyes of the world are on us today," he said and began the proceedings. A baby became fretful, women fanned themselves with sheets of paper. Twice the district attorney faltered on a legal point, laughter rippled through the crowd and plainclothesmen along the walls straightened watchfully. There were 150 people crowding the benches inside and another 100 outside the halls and down on the street.

Again the highlight of the afternoon came when Eulogio Salazar pointed his finger at Reies Tijerina and said, "That man there."

After four-and-a-half hours of legal wrangling, Judge Angel announced that all but four of the defendants would be granted bond. Juan Valdez, Tobías Leyba, Baltazar Apodaca and Reies Tijerina were to be held without bail. The question of a first-degree kidnapping charge was thus left open for those released, but the capital charge was upheld for the four who had been refused bond.

"For the property and culture of my people, I will not only go to prison," Reies wrote from his prison cell, "but I will with pleasure and pride sacrifice my life."

That day the second of several meetings was held in *Alianza* headquarters in Albuquerque to plan a campaign to raise funds for legal defense. Although there were already several lawyers for the defense, tentative offers of legal council had also been received from the New Mexico Civil Liberties Union and from the law firm of Leonard Boudin and Louis Rabinowitz of New York.

On June 30, the FBI announced that it had entered the hunt for Baltazar Martínez and Cristóbal Tijerina. Cris was wanted in connection with the Echo Amphitheatre trespass. A federal warrant had been issued for Baltazar on the assumption that he had escaped north into Colorado. Actually, he was still on *Mesa de Las Viejas*, dropping down into Canjilón now and then for food and to visit his mother. FBI agents visited the village but failed to make productive friendships. There was no mention of El Indio. However, Alfonso Sánchez was preparing an extradition warrant to be sent to Denver, charging Danny Tijerina, 14, with assault, assault to commit murder and kidnapping.

Reies says that that week he caught his only glimpse of Margarito across the prison yard and waved, but that Margarito did not appear to see him.

On the Fourth of July, an Albuquerque police detective named Fred Gallegos was fishing his favorite stream in Río Arriba, when he was approached by a tiny, bird-like lady wearing eyeglasses who said her son was ready to surrender, but that she was afraid he might be harmed. Gallegos contacted State Police and that afternoon, while Chief Black and another officer waited outside the little house in Canjilón, Gallegos went in with Mrs. Martínez to talk to Baltazar. An hour later, they emerged, Baltazar with them, unarmed but wearing his red beret and with a silk ascot tucked into the open front of his shirt. He told Black about some arms and dynamite hidden up on *Mesa de Las Viejas*, then he was taken south to Santa Fe and booked on the same counts. In due time, Auerilla Martínez received a state check for $500, the reward that had been offered for her son, some said, "dead or alive."

The New Mexico Civil Liberties Union had been pursuing its investigations and had collected dozens of complaints of false arrest, search and seizure. However, no Justice Department investigator had yet appeared. And after several written and telephoned reminders, Governor Cargo had called back on July 5 to say that he was "just too busy" to do anything about forming a civil rights committee.

Back on June 10, the day of Tijerina's capture, the Albuquerque *Tribune* had protested, "Two policemen have been shot . . . is this the proper time for the OEO to start forming an organization to 'protect the civil rights of those arrested?' " By the middle of July, the *Tribune* had not yet and was never subsequently to announce just when the time was right for such consideration. The Albuquerque *Journal*, a newspaper with a particularly heavy-handed style of manipulating the news, was giving strong front-page play to all charges against the OEO and would soon go so far as to quote Robert García as having advised the poor, in a speech in Los Alamos, to "circumvent the law," when in fact he had said, "I do not advocate breaking the law."

The Spanish-American poor "live in abject misery," García had told the Resnick subcommittee on rural poverty, and the touching fact had been duly noted. But the voluble priest had said other things, then and elsewhere, before and after the raid. "The poor want change, not handouts. The poverty force is beginning to challenge the local governments, the school systems. It is challenging the status quo and the middle class . . ."

If these stated objectives of the War on Poverty had been largely ignored before, they were not now. And the indignation with which they would be quoted in the press, and the vigor with which the war on the War on Poverty would be carried to its conclusion would be the best proof that Governor Cargo had not been entirely correct when he had declared the poverty campaign a failure in New Mexico and elsewhere. It had, in fact, been rather too successful, at least in challenging the status quo.

Late in January of the year to come, after the national poverty programs had been effectively crippled by Congress and the remains delivered into the hands of state and local politicians, Sargent Shriver, national director of the OEO, would explain that his organization had "failed to make white, middle-class Americans believe they benefit directly from helping the poor."

Beyond noting that the white middle class was experiencing a sharp increase in its traditional fear of becoming poor itself, Shriver would not go into the causes of the failure. Perhaps because behind that failure, as behind the fears of the white middle class, was the increasingly pressing fact that the majority of the poor in the United States of 1967 were not considered to be white in the first place, had long ago developed a profound distrust of the promises and the values of the white middle class and were lately exhibiting an unprecedented disinterest in joining their ranks. They were, in fact, in the process of declaring a war of their own, not merely as the poor, and against nothing so conveniently impersonal and abstract as "poverty."

In the meantime, the blame-fixing and nay-saying would go on for months, the promises would be more prolific and mellifluous than ever. But the name of the game would be the same, and as always, all the pawns on the board would be the same common color, which in New Mexico is most often the color of adobe, of brown skin and earth.

The *Pobres* and the *Políticos* 14

WEATHERED faces and dull country clothing once again gathered under the *portales* of the courthouse in Santa Fe on July 13, watched over by State Police and Santa Fe County sheriff's deputies in tight white denims and tooled leather gunbelts. The occasion was a hearing called by Judge Angel to consider the granting of bond to the last five raid suspects still in jail. Once again, all were searched at the door; once again, the plainclothes detectives stationed themselves around the courtroom. Freddy Martínez stood at the end of the jury box, studying the crowd with implacable sunglasses. Chief Joe Black leaned against the door at the back, looking like a kindly, heavily armed train conductor.

Of the 15 now out on bond, Rose was in the audience in yellow polka dots with a lily of the valley in her hair. Reies, Jr., sat stiffly in a dark blue suit with Patsy Tijerina, his stepmother, visibly pregnant. Tiny Auerilla Martínez was in her best dress, which was green, with a red flower in her hair. She studied her son intently as the five filed in. Baltazar wore his red beret, but removed it as he sat down, revealing a bone-close prison haircut.

Although the afternoon was mostly devoted to legal wrangling, now and then an enduring issue showed through in sudden relief.

Defense attorneys, led by Charles Driscoll, now Reies' chief counsel, began by attacking the district attorney's contention that not only had Larry Calloway and Pete Jaramillo been abducted, but Nick Sais, Eulogio Salazar and Dan Rivera had been kidnapped as well.

Reading from Blackwood's definition of first-degree kidnapping, Driscoll, short, assertive, blue-eyed, asked Dan Rivera if he believed he had suffered "great bodily harm, high probability of death, serious disfigurement, loss or impairment of a member or organ of the body."

No, the undersheriff admitted grudgingly, but he had been hit pretty hard on the head.

Defense lawyers contended that since the capital charge remained unsubstantiated, the court had discretion to grant bond.

Judge Angel agreed.

Alfonso Sánchez asked that the record show his objection. "I think the court has that discretion, but I don't want the court to think that because he has that discretion, he should exercise that discretion . . ."

Young Rosina Valdez took the stand on behalf of her husband, testifying that he had not been in any trouble "except just for drinking, a long time ago." Juan, 26, lean, serious, a logging partner in Canjilón with his brother Tony and cousin Moisés Morales, said that what his wife said was true, and promised not to run away.

María Leyba testified that she was 50, that she had passed the third grade, that she had 16 children, and that she thought her husband to be trustworthy. Forty-eight-year-old Tobías sat with his legs apart and his elbows on the arms of the dock and said, "*Que no*," that he would not run away, looking down and shaking his head incredulously.

When a Tijerina character witness, 60-year-old Fedelina Durán of Española, testified with evident awe that Reies knew more about the land grants than most lawyers, Alfonso Sánchez inquired in tones of weary despair, "And does he also say he can get the land back for you?"

Judge Angel decided to hold Tijerina in prison while the court continued to consider allowing him bond. Baltazar Martínez was released on bond pending his arraignment. Also released on bond were Juan Valdez, Tobías Leyba and the white-haired old rebel, Baltazar Apodaca.

Asked for his criminal record, the old man had admitted once paying a seven-dollar fine for public drunkness; and then he had been asked if, were he freed on bond, would he run away.

"No," he had answered. "To where?"

By the end of July, a large amount of material had been published in the national press concerning Reies Tijerina and the *Hispanos* of northern New Mexico and the Southwest. Although the *Alianza's* land grant claims were always mentioned, the implacable stance taken by agencies of the federal government was invariably accepted as evidence of the futility of the land claims. Tijerina's charge of cultural rape was faithfully recorded and his examples cited, but often with a subtle, almost involuntary lack of conviction. It was, after all, difficult for a journalist writing in English to agree with Reies that the teaching of that language to *Hispano* children was "an insidious means of destroying us as a people."

The "miserable curse of poverty" of which Tijerina complained was, however, something else again. For one thing, its existence could be proven and its characteristics established with statistics gleaned from the wealth of studies which had already been made, many of them long neglected but now in sudden and widespread demand.

The average individual in the depressed northern counties of Mora, San Miguel, Taos and Río Arriba had an annual income of a little over a thousand dollars. In Taos he lived on $997, in Mora on even less. This compared with an average of more than twice that amount for New Mexico as a whole, nearly three times that amount for the United

States. These counties averaged an *Hispano* population of around 72 percent.

Median family income in Río Arriba was $2,500, with *Hispano* family income running $734 less than the overall county level. Thirty-five percent of families lived on less than $2,000 a year.

Unemployment was 20 percent. Nearly 14 percent were receiving public assistance. Housing was 56 percent substandard. Only 25 percent of the houses in the county had been built after 1951 or had full plumbing. The median educational level was 8.1 years.

Conditions in the rest of the state and the Southwest were not much better. A quarter of the families in New Mexico lived on annual incomes below the "poverty line" of $3,000. The median annual income of individual Mexican-Americans in the Southwest was $2,000. New Mexico had less doctors per capita than any other state. Of every thousand infants born in the state, 30 died in the first year of life, a rate 20 percent higher than the national average. At the blood bank in Albuquerque, the average donor received $7 a pint, compared to a national average of $35 dollars, making human blood cheaper in New Mexico than in any other state in the nation.

"The poverty is there," said the *New York Times*. "Río Arriba is Appalachia with a language problem." "Dirt poor," *Newsweek* said of the villagers. Even Alan Stang of the John Birch Society's *American Opinion* had to admit "there is poverty in the north," although he hastened to add that "even the poorest of the adobe homes often had television antennas on the roof."

All agreed that there was poverty, and all agreed that it should be eliminated, either through some combination of charity, governmental aid and self-help education, or, as Stang suggested, "by those willing to invest and reinvest capital, and eager to do the work."

In mid-July, the report of Burgos and Aragon had arrived on Governor Cargo's desk from the Socio-Economics Studies Foundation in California. Its conclusions were not new and its language was drearily familiar:

Northern New Mexico suffered from a depressed economy and an eroding agricultural base. Measured by any index, living conditions were far below standard for the majority of the residents and virtually all of the *Hispanos*. There was deep-seated hostility toward all outside authority and government agencies, the Forest Service in particular. The land grant question persisted, encouraged by favorable settlement of long-standing Indian claims. Failure to solve these socio-economic problems had been responsible for and would continue to contribute mightily to the success of Reies Tijerina and his brand of militancy.

On July 25, after six weeks in the penitentiary, Reies emerged, carrying his personal possessions in a brown paper bag. Property bonds totaling $5,000 had been posted for him by two *Hispano* businessmen.

Asked for a statement, he said only, "Well, I'm hungry, I want to eat, and I want to see my wife and baby." Although he refused to discuss his plans, other *Alianza* officials had already made it clear that he would set out immediately on a tour of the villages "to raise funds for legal defense and to reunite the people behind the cause of justice."

The next day, Governor Cargo headed north to do what one reporter with a vaudeville background would soon come to call, "playing the poverty circuit," or, "doing a four-a-day on Heartache Time."

In Truchas, a tiny land grant village clinging to a rocky ridge in the mountains northeast of Española, the governor was greeted as the first chief executive to visit the grant, was loaned a horse for the half-mile parade to the church and was honored with a special mass, after which he was presented with a bill of particulars outside the church. He promised to do what he could to provide the requested cement-lined irrigation ditches and a better school. And then he moved on.

In Chamisal, he was given a chili dinner, and he promised to provide a bulldozer to help villagers smooth out their road. At Las Trampas he was offered a lump of the curative mud from the miraculous spring inside the chapel, and he said that he would try to arrange for state upkeep of the church. In Peñasco, he promised to find state funds to help the community build a livestock corral. He learned that, although there had not been a recorded death by starvation in northern New Mexico in years, many village children counted on the free school lunch as their main meal of the day, and a number had difficulty eating lunch because of decayed teeth or enlarged tonsils. He was told that one resident of Petaca had seen 13 persons die during efforts to transport them to medical facilities.

He promised to do what he could about improving schools and roads, increasing water rights, clearing up land titles and reinstating village grazing allotments.

Back in Santa Fe, 10 villages and two days after his departure, he reminded reporters that, "For many years I've felt that the northern counties were the forgotten counties."

Agriculture Undersecretary John Schnittker had done the village tour earlier in the month accompanied by Forest Service officials, among them Regional Forester Hurst, the same man who had promised to invite an agriculture official to the abortive grazing hearings before the Echo Amphitheatre trespass.

"I am here," Schnittker announced, "because I must take part in solution of these problems."

In Ranchos de Taos, Delfín Quintana of Cebolla charged that it was an unwritten policy of the Forest Service "to try to get rid of the smaller man." Denying the charge, Schnittker cited as proof a recent statement to the contrary by Agriculture Secretary Orville Freeman.

Confronted by the opinion of Oleofes Vigil of San Cristóbal that the

Forest Service provided more land for wild game than for small ranchers, the undersecretary could say only that there was always room for difference of opinion.

When another rancher protested that the cost of maintaining fences, as required by the Forest Service, was more than the grazing permits were worth to the small grazer, Schnittker had nothing to say.

When he headed back for Washington two days after his departure, the undersecretary could say, however, that he had visited five villages and had heard the grievances of at least 300 grazers.

On August 2, Cristóbal Tijerina materialized in Santa Fe, where one of Alfonso Sánchez's warrants awaited him. Appearing before Judge Joe Angel on raid charges, he was released on bond, went to Albuquerque to be interviewed on television, then disappeared before FBI agents could arrest him on the Echo Amphitheatre charges. Two days after that, he surrendered to federal officers at a hospital where he had gone for treatment of influenza. Dark under the eyes and wearing a mustache, he was asked what he had been doing for the past two months. He smiled and said, "Hiding."

On August 8, Nick Sais' sick pay ceased, leaving him with a monthly income of $60 until he could return to limited duty. Wearing a heavy cast, he was no longer under 24-hour guard, but spent much of his time in the presence of fellow officers. In Tierra Amarilla, Dan Rivera was being careful to be home before dark every night. Eulogio Salazar, however, had taken to visiting his brother's bar in town and sometimes arrived home late at his house, which was some distance out of town.

After considerable advance billing in the newspapers, Senator Montoya, as acting chairman of the Senate Subcommittee on Economic Development, convened hearings on August 7 in Albuquerque. Warmed by the television lights, he listened through the day while two dozen state and federal officials one by one explained and defended their policies and expressed the need for more money. The next day the Senator headed north to tour the villages accompanied by a large cast, including two Democratic colleagues, Congressmen Johnny Walker and Thomas G. Morris.

There were demands and promises on the usual topics with the emphasis on vocational training schools, a pet project of the Senator. In Española, Al Rodríguez stood up to protest that "you politicians . . . come here year after year and promise the same things without getting anything done. You people keep talking about vocational schools, but where are they?"

The Senator responded with the announcement that there were over three million dollars in federal funds available for Río Arriba County alone "for vocational schools, for access roads, for a paper pulp mill and on-the-job training in that mill"!

There were cheers.

But the next day, as the tour moved south into Río Abajo and San

Miguel County, the fatal hitch appeared. County officials pointed out that their tax base could not support the matching 20 percent funds required to qualify for federal education grants. "Twenty percent of nothing is still nothing," a Las Vegas school superintendent noted sadly. "This formula puts too heavy a load on the poorer school districts."

It was an old and hopeless story, and Little Joe and the politicians with him knew it all too well. There was a plan for arranging for the wealthier counties to contribute to a state educational fund, out of which the poorer counties could draw aid in raising the required matching funds to get federal money for improving the schools. But the wealthier counties, most of them in Little Texas, all of them predominantly Anglo, had long ago made it clear that they did not intend to share their advantage even though their cooperation would immensely improve the overall educational condition of the state. Besides, the plan—called PIE—was the Republican governor's project, and Senator Montoya and his entourage were not likely to give it exposure during their turn on stage.

Nor were they prone to discuss the unusually low property taxes in the state. Property reappraisal had never been a popular cause, particularly among the larger landowners. Nor would there be discussion of the possibility of a graduated state income tax, long anathema in a state which had an income spread that was dumbbell heavy at both ends and which, along with neighboring Arizona, boasted more millionaires per capita than any other two states in the union.

And, as the peculiarly New Mexican political bedfellows that they were, they were certainly not interested in getting down to the bedrock, plug-ugly heart of the matter, lest fisticuffs break out among them and democracy suffer an embarrassing setback right there in Las Vegas, where over a hundred years before General Stephen Kearny had assured the populace through an interpreter: "We come among you for your benefit and not your harm."

Instead, they found it expedient to encourage and make their own contributions to the growing popular sport of flogging the OEO.

One educator did manage to get in a reminder that the vocational schools already in existence had turned out a number of beauty operators, day nurses and barbers who had been unable to find employment in their native environs. "The students," he warned, "must be prepared for social mobility, to go where the jobs are."

After two days on the road, Senator Montoya returned to Albuquerque to announce that his campaign to get an "overview" of the situation had been a success. Although he had not played as many villages and could not top the total audience of 1,500 claimed by Governor Cargo, he had used up 5,000 feet of stenographic paper that would be duly transcribed into a fat volume which would join all the other reports and studies so vehemently decried by himself and others.

The show was almost over, although the curtain would come down in

187

jerks and starts on scattered encores and entr'actes. Many of those for whom the extravaganza had been staged would be satisfied; but it had been billed as a benefit performance, and in the end very little of real value would come out of it for those supposed to have been benefited.

Chamisal would get the use of a state bulldozer to help smooth out the village road, but before Christmas the road would be a quagmire again. Peñasco would get $3,000 to build its community corral, but the loan would be due for repayment too soon. The grazing allotment of Placitas would not be increased, nor would the allotments of any other of the villages. The Forest Service policy of steadily decreasing grazing on public lands would continue. *Hispano* herdsmen would continue to be forbidden the use of horses while hunting lodge operators would continue to graze pack horses unmolested. Ranger Smith would remain in charge at Canjilón for some time. In fact, Baltazar Martínez would be arrested in late July by Benny Naranjo for "assault with words" on the tender sensibilities of Ranger Smith and would be shuffled about the county in handcuffs for several days without being allowed to contact an attorney or his mother.

An interim committee to study land titles created by the previous state legislature and given an appropriation of $15,000 would meet only once. Governor Cargo would continue to declare his intention to seek legislation to create a permanent title commission, but would have done nothing about it by the end of 1968. Promises by the Congressional delegation to move toward creation of a federal land claims court would also come to nothing.

Senator Montoya's proposed vocational training school at Española would receive a promise from the Economic Development Administration for 80 percent of the $1 million needed, but there would be no sign that the county could come up with the matching funds required. In January, the Senator's office would admit that the proposal for a similar school at Las Vegas was also "lagging."

Robert Garcia and his OEO staff had hastily drawn up a lavish plan for a comprehensive CAP program in Río Arriba, Mora and Taos Counties and had requested federal funding of $5.4 million, with Governor Cargo's approval. But the plan had been immediately attacked by the press and the Congressional delegation, with criticism centering on the proposed purchase of an airplane to fly medical missions into mountain areas. The proposal would eventually be put aside, thanks to the efforts of the Congressional delegation coupled with the rapidly increasing animosity of Congress itself toward the War on Poverty. Aside from their mistakes, the poverty programs in New Mexico, as elsewhere, had been too successful in their efforts to remain aloof from partisan state and local politics, producing the kind of frustration reflected in Senator Clinton Anderson's querulous comment concerning OEO officials in his home state: "Who are these people? I don't know any of them!"

There would be no new major federal programs for northern New

Mexico for some time to come, nor would state attempts to change the situation be particularly effective. The impending return to traditional pork barrel patronage and piecemeal welfare was comically typified, complete with the ironic twist so cherished by the northerners, when Governor Cargo announced in mid-August that Auerilla Martínez had endorsed her $500 reward check over to her son, and that Baltazar planned to use the money to get married.

Irony would remain the only recompense of the proud, poor and powerless. The lunch allocation at Ojo Caliente school would be increased to 366, but the lunches would remain the main meal of most of the children, and some would continue to have difficulty chewing the food because of rotting teeth. There would continue to be only one doctor in Tierra Amarilla, none in Cuba. The Petaca old-timer would soon see another neighbor die while being jolted along mountain roads to the clinic 50 miles away in Española. The price of human blood would remain below par in New Mexico.

But it had been this way for many years now. Aside from increasingly dazzling performances by the politicians, excited attention from the sociologists and an impending plethora of new academic and popular treatises on the Forgotten People, was it really ever likely to change for them?

Somewhere toward the bottom of the stack of reports on northern New Mexico in the library of the governor's office in Santa Fe was a slim treatise commonly known as the Burma Report. Compiled in 1960 for the Thiokol Corporation by Dr. John Burma and David E. Williams of Grinnell College, the report had raised the hackles of many *Hispanos* when it had first appeared, as much because of its air of icy impatience as for its chilling conclusions. But it is this very undertone of puritan righteousness, thinly disguised as a call for economic efficiency, which gives the report extra value as a social document. Not only does it present, on the one level, convincing proof of a grim future for the *Hispanos* of Río Arriba, and, indirectly, for many thousands of others, but on a less deliberate level, it reveals many of the basic attitudes and motivations of those who have furthered that painful future.

The Burma Report 15

"**Y**OU tell Reies Tijerina for me that I've picked more cotton than he ever looked at," says Bill Mundy, and one could believe it by the look of him. He has the hard weathered face, stringy muscles and thrusting Adam's apple of one of those who came away from the Dust Bowl disaster of 30 years before with a lasting thirst and deathless determination. In faded blue jeans, workshirt and low-heeled boots, he sits on his wife's modern couch as he might a bale of hay, slapping worn leather gloves together, itching to get back to it.

"Nobody wants to work, country's going to hell. I've been up on the mountain since six this morning, chasing cows down, just Berto and me. I'm getting set to market and there's plenty of work, but will these people around here work? Hell, no."

"Why should they work, they don't have to," his wife says. Large-eyed, intelligent, watchful, Ethel Mundy does the books for her husband's various enterprises. Her house is new, modern, not large, with wall-to-wall carpeting, a pink telephone on the kitchen bar, a glass-topped coffee table bearing copies of *Field and Stream*. On one wall hangs a painting by a daughter, copied from a favorite photograph by a friend: the aspens atop her husband's mountain. Out one aluminum-framed window there is a clear view of the chimney of the old house, thrusting up from bare foundations and surrounded by a well-maintained rail fence, like a war monument. "We were at a funeral this morning," she says. "These people take these things seriously, you know. They had 16 people at that table, and I swear, there was food for 60. Why, they have more money in their mattresses than we have in the bank. They've been selling off their land for years, of course."

Mundy snorts. "And now they want it back for nothing."

Between 1930 and 1960, according to the Burma Report, the number of people living on farms in Río Arriba had dropped from around 90 percent to less than nine percent. In the same 30 years, just about half a man's lifetime, the total number of farms had fallen nearly 60 percent, while the size of the average farm had increased more than 366 percent.

"They're all looking for a seat near the stove at the courthouse." Bill

Mundy says. "Every time some *politico*'s nephew drops out of high school, the county budget goes up a couple of thousand."

In 1964, government—county, state and federal—accounted for 37 percent of employment in Río Arriba, but used mostly highly trained specialists and administrators and skilled clerical workers. Only 14 percent of the county's population had finished all four years of high school. Forty-nine percent over 25 years of age had less than an eighth grade education.

"Damn few of them are any good to me anyway," says Bill Mundy. "Half of them couldn't pitch hay over a hatrack, and the other half are liable to disappear after one good day's work. And they all want banker's wages."

In 1964, farm hands were paid an average of $5 a day in Río Arriba; laborers, $1 an hour; sawmill workers, clerk-typists and non-union truck drivers, up to $1.75; waitresses and chambermaids from 65 to 80 cents an hour.

"Back around '60, the year they burned my house, I had to fly in some wets," Bill Mundy says. "*Contrabando*, you know, but they'll work. They're doing a sight better up here than back in Old Mexico, and they know it."

In 1960, 32 percent of Río Arriba's resident working force went out of the county to find employment, returning when they could. And still, on any given day of the year, 20 percent of the work force could find no cash employment.

"It's the welfare that really does it, of course," says Ethel Mundy. "The state pays them not to work."

In 1964, 10 percent of the population were receiving welfare at an average of $75 per head per month. By 1967, nearly 14 percent were receiving the same amount, not counting medical and special assistance.

"Large numbers of people in Río Arriba and Taos," the Burma Report said, "are only too pleased to accept what others look upon as charity. Letting someone else be responsible for your food, clothing and shelter comes to be thought of as 'smart,' not something of which to be ashamed."

"They'd all get on welfare if they could," says Ethel Mundy. "That's just the way they are, and I suppose you can't blame them for it. It's really the politicians who keep it going."

"When receiving welfare assistance becomes a way of life," the Burma Report said, "then this is socially, economically and morally a decidedly unhealthy situation and one which should not be permitted to exist, no matter how convenient a source of power it may be to unscrupulous, grasping politicians."

"It's the old *patronismo* business, of course," says Ethel Mundy, rising to make sandwiches. "They have to have someone to lead them by the nose." From the freezer she produces a haunch of roast meat. "Goat," she says. "From the Gonzáles family down by the highway. The old man comes up and guards the house for us sometimes when we're out and watches the TV. He loves it. And sometimes they bring us up a present, like this meat, sort of an offering. Now there's an example. They're down there, five or seven in that little old house, no electricity, no inside plumbing, but they're happy. They're nice people, they just don't care about such things."

"Strong attachments to a given local community, to the larger family, and even to a particular piece of land is common among Spanish Americans," the Burma Report noted. "By receiving public assistance they are able to remain on the unproductive little farm, with no possible hope of ever making a living for themselves. Love of family is good, attachment to the family plot of ground is good, but when they are used as emotional excuses for failure to stand on one's own feet and be responsible for oneself, resulting in generation after generation of welfare clients, then they are not good."

"Of course, there's them that will work for others, but not for me," Bill Mundy avers, squinting out the window at the houseless chimney.

"People from outside the area," the Burma Report said, "have come in with sufficient capital and initiative to utilize some of this land and have met with 'bad luck' in the form of arson of their houses and barns and shooting of their cattle and horses."

"They ought to take them all off welfare," says Ethel Mundy. "Then they'd *have* to work."

"Here's Berto," says Bill Mundy, rising and reaching for his hat. A large four-wheel-drive pickup has pulled up out front with a horse trailer behind. "Come on, if you're comin'." He heads for the out-of-doors with evident relief.

To correct the welfare problem in Río Arriba, the Burma Report suggested "it would be necessary to cut off two of every three persons now on the public assistance rolls. This would bring the county's welfare percentage in line with that of the rest of the state."

However, "desirable and long overdue though such a pruning is," the report had to concede that it would do nothing toward solving the problems of unemployment and poverty-level incomes. "No economy can be healthy when its people receive so little income."

What to do about it? "Basically," observed the report, "there are only two ways in which to raise per capita income: (1) increase the total income to be divided, or (2) decrease the population to divide the income."

It is a long, rough and beautiful journey up the mountain, with Mundy working the gears with relish and shouting over the roar of the engine. "Berto here, his grandfather was one of the biggest ranchers in Guadalajara back before the Civil War. His father taught me my Spanish and the old man still rides for my father down in Hatch. The Teraces have been with the Mundys for two generations now."

Alberto Teraces rides on the outside, straw Stetson down tight over dark glasses that have side panels like a welder's goggles. He says little beyond a fragment of Spanish now and then to call Mundy's attention to a steer down a gully or off through the trees. Mundy's replies are in fluent Spanish with a near perfect border accent. At each gate, Alberto climbs down, opens the gate, waits for truck and trailer to pass through, closes the gate and climbs back in.

"Berto fixed up that little 'dobe we got down by the highway," Mundy says. "He's got his family in there, and they get along fine." A faint smile curls beneath Alberto's mustache and he bobs his head twice, but somehow it is as though Mundy is speaking and Alberto is hearing him on the radio.

The truck pulls up in the center of a meadow, and Alberto takes a box from the back and shakes a trail of white along a groove in a log. "Salt," Mundy explains, "and cotton seed, to draw them. They can smell it a long way. I had purebred stock before, but now I get my cattle from Old Mexico, they do better in this high country."

In order to improve the total income of the county, the Burma Report suggested a schedule of improvements in overall land management and more enlightened management of the large agricultural enterprises in the area, with a continued decrease in the number of small, inefficient farms.

"Hundred and twenty-five acres right in the center of me," Mundy says, fixing blue eyes on a stretch of rich pasture enclosed by new barbed-wire fencing. "Finally got him to put up his share to fence it last year," he says, naming the land's *Hispano* owner. "This year was the first his cows didn't get mixed up with mine, and he'd leave it to me to come tell him. That's the way they are." The blue eyes narrow speculatively; if a squint could squint, this is it. "Won't sell, says he doesn't need the money. But I'm neighborin' him," and he jams hard into a new gear.

The way is steeply upward now, the engine laboring, the two ponies fighting to keep their feet in the trailer behind. The road is a crumbling chute of broken rock and raw clay, with tall fir and ponderosa close on either side, interspersed with fresh-cut stumps.

Logging was already a big business in Río Arriba, with "vast potential for future growth," the Burma Report noted. The industry would continue to thrive as more areas of the national forest were opened to limited yield logging.

"Back in the beginning when I was having trouble meeting those $20,000 payments," Mundy shouts, "I tried a little sawmill operation of my own, but didn't do so well, it's not my line. Then, after I had to get that abeyance and was really up against it, I made a timber deal and sold five-year rights at $10 a thousand. Not bad, when you consider I only paid $11 an acre for most of this, and sure enough, it saved me and then some."

Recreation, the Burma Report noted, was already a significant industry in northern New Mexico and likely to increase. Nearly 250,000 campers, fishermen, hunters and winter sports enthusiasts had visited the national forests of Taos and Río Arriba in 1959.

Truck and trailer roll briefly on the level, lurching across a stretch of broad, bouldered alpine meadow, and Mundy points off over the trees to a distant slope. "Best potential ski run in New Mexico. I don't own the top part, just where the run will come out. But I happen to know that the people who own the top need money and need it bad, and I'm in a position to buy. Not on my own, hell no, but with these associates of mine, down south. Outdoor recreation, that's the future of New Mexico."

Elk herds introduced by the federal government into the area 20 years before had done remarkably well and attracted some 14,000 big game hunters a year, noted the Burma Report.

Truck and horse trailer clank to a stop amongst the lean white trunks of aspen, and the quiet of the top of the mountain is deep and clear. There is a hunting lodge of rustic mode perched on the rocky rim of the cliff.

"I only charge them $200 a week," Bill Mundy says, "and they always get their elk. We've got regulars coming out every year from the East. Also, friends, associates. Friend of mine from the State Patrol, fella I know on the Game Commission, another fella has oil down in Lea County . . ."

In the spacious main room there is a bar, a big stone fireplace and two large round tables, and it is not hard to visualize the roaring fire, the two circles of hunters at the end of the day, the poker hands, the limpid gold of Scotch in water glasses, the warm and hearty companionship of comfortable cabal.

"The economic benefit to the general population of an increased recreation industry should not be over-rated," the Burma Report warned. "Hunting and fishing license fees are large, but do not go to the local villages. Lodges, motels and cafes will probably be constructed by outside capital, but this type of enterprise, while very desirable, at best will solve only partially the economic problems of the mountain villages."

The conclusion of the report was, in fact, that all possible means of increasing the county's overall income would not succeed in raising the per capita income sufficiently to reduce the welfare ratio to "a respectable level."

That left the second alternative.

"The excess population should be encouraged to leave their little homes and tiny parcels of ground and go out into the areas where employment is available. Such out-migration is presently underway, but before it can reach sufficiently sizeable proportions, it will be necessary to overcome emotional attachment to the land and to the larger family and to the community."

A quarter of the way back down the mountain, a rocky ledge thrusts out above the tips of 60-foot fir trees, and all the broad, long valley of the upper Chama can be seen from there, from the Colorado Rockies in the north to the low ridge to the south, hiding the dying town of Tierra Amarilla. This is where Bill Mundy first stood with bear hunter Bill Dogget back in the winter of '51, and even now he can seldom pass the spot without stopping to take a look. "One hundred and twenty-five thousand acres so far," he says, squinting out over his domain. "A little more, and I think I'll have about what I want. But hell, I'm not the only big landowner around here. There's the Chama Land and Cattle Company, they have 36,000 acres over there, and that's just a tax dodge, and there's others, but I'm the only one's had his house burned down. See that little stretch of the Brazos down there, I let them fish that free, and anyhow, it's right by the highway. I'm the only one around here that lets them take deadwood off my land. There's no pulp industry anyway . . ."

He falls silent, absorbed in the magnificent view.

"Throughout Río Arriba and Taos Counties," the Burma Report noted, "the population is largely Spanish American. This means that myriad problems related to acculturation and assimilation are present, that there are two languages spoken, usually neither very well, that there are two sets of cultural norms. Inhabitants of the area are quick to point out, somewhat defensively, the 'good' qualities of the indigenous culture and the desirability of their retention. What they fail to take into consideration is that the problem is not so much one of quality as of difference."

"In my rodeoing days, my specialty was bull roping," Bill Mundy shouts over the roar of the engine, heading truck and trailer back down the mountain. "Not these itty-bitty steers, but a full-grown bull. They've outlawed it in all but five states now: New Mexico, Texas, Oklahoma, Arizona and, I think, Nebraska. You ride in close, drop your loop over the shoulder on the outside to catch a front foot, then cut off on the opposite tangent, and if you bust him, you bust him good, but if you don't bust him, he busts you, and better. That's the kind of odds I like."

"There can be no hope for northern New Mexico," the Burma Report said, "until ability and effort are rewarded and lack of effort and ability are punished. To increase out-migration, it will be necessary to overcome native inertia and laziness, the lack of marketable skills or education, the lack of knowledge of how to use resources to meet goals, the unwillingness to gamble a secure pittance as a welfare client for the risk of going elsewhere and becoming a self-supporting, contributing member of society. . . ."

The truck pulls up at the last gate, and Alberto climbs down from the cab. "Now there's a good man," Bill Mundy muses, watching Alberto open the gates and stand back. "A rare one, one of the good ones."

In what way is Alberto different from the others?

The blue eyes are fully aware but unflinching, the answer sure and unashamed. "He does his work and and he doesn't complain. And he's respectful."

Bill Mundy's cow ponies are well cared for and have gently trained mouths, but they obey. The initials of generations of sheepherders are carved into the trunks of the aspens at the top of the mountain, but none of them are new. Bill Mundy rides his mountain before dawn and affects a sweat-stained cowboy hat, but he is another man at the Elkhorn Lodge in Chama and yet another at the Cattleman's Association in Albuquerque. Bill Mundy hasn't chopped cotton to feed himself in a long time, and he does not intend to again. Bill Mundy is a businessman and doing well. Bill Mundy is a winner.

"Out-migration will be of no benefit to the local area if the remaining residents insist on having large numbers of children," said the Burma Report. "English must be their first and family language, unless they prefer to go to school in Mexico. Customs of eating, of religion, of wearing apparel, of language and etiquette; methods of recreation and use of leisure time; attitudes and beliefs relating to health, the *Penitentes*; reliance on personal force rather than law; all these and many other aspects of the old culture are both changing and disappearing."

"If they stay, the only alternative to starvation is public assistance," concluded the Burma Report. "The future is clear."

And, just as Bill Mundy was undeniably a winner, the Burma Report was undeniably correct in its conclusion. Not only regarding the future of the natives of Río Arriba, but the future of those of Río Abajo as well, and many thousands of other rural *Hispanos* living throughout the Southwest, in California and elsewhere.

Northern New Mexico had always been an isolated anachronism and could be expected to lag behind the general social trend. The "out-migration" predicted and recommended by the Burma Report had been taking place for several decades from the small farms and villages of most of the Southwest and California, but had become particularly precipitous in more recent years. Out-migration from the villages and farms meant, of course, "in-migration" to urban-industrial areas. It is estimated that between the coming of the Yankees in 1846 and the Great Depression of the '30s, the percentage of the Southwest's *Hispanos* living in cities had risen from less than 10 to only about 20 percent. But between 1930 and 1950, the figure had risen to 65 percent, and between 1950 and 1960 it had soared to 80 percent.

Not that there wasn't resistance. Testifying before the Resnick subcommittee back in June, Alex Mercure had cited statistical proof that by far the majority of the Mexican-American migrant families of the Southwest had home base villages and that, although they might sometimes be following work across the country for up to 10 months of the year, they always returned home when they could, albeit often for only a few months or even only weeks at a time, and usually to nothing more than a crumbling village adobe or a tin-roofed highway shack. Clark

Knowlton had stated that in 1951 a thousand migrant workers and their families had left San Miguel County to join the migrant stream and that 95 percent of them had stubbornly returned to their villages with their hard-won wages. Certainly the success of Reies Tijerina's *Alianza* among the rural people of northern New Mexico was a prime example of resistance, and there could be no more emphatic example of protest than the courthouse raid.

Nonetheless, between 1950 and 1960, the same period during which Reies had been building his organization, the percentage of the state's *Hispano* population living in urban areas had jumped from 41 percent to 58 percent, and the process appeared to be accelerating.

For the majority of those forced to leave their villages and farms, moving to the city meant living in shanty towns sprawled along the railroad tracks or in tumbledown tenements close to the industrial core: the *barrios*. And it was here, particularly in the *barrios* of the Texas and California cities, that they began to meet others with whom they had always before felt less than affinity, but whose lives, they now began to note, were really not so much different from their own when reduced to raw essentials by the unrelenting pressures of the city.

The movement from the country to the cities had, of course, been taking place in the United States for half a century, but the latest wave of migrations had a particular significance. The cities had originally been built and populated by predominantly white populations, who had in general enjoyed increased affluence beginning with the Second World War and who had set in motion a reversal of the in-migration movement, moving out of the rapidly congesting and increasingly uninhabitable centers into those motorized simulacri of the country village: the suburbs.

Beginning about the same time, the blacks of America had begun to leave the deep South and emigrate to the northern and midwestern cities. Arriving as still a predominantly rural population, they occupied the urban residential areas abandoned by the whites. In 1910, 70 percent of southern Negroes had been rural and only eight percent of the country's blacks had lived in the 25 largest American cities. By 1960, 72 percent lived in the larger cities. At the same time, the white exodus from the urban centers was continuing, so that by 1967, the blacks were in the majority in Washington, D.C., and Newark, and it was predicted that by 1984, the whites would be outnumbered in 11 major cities, including Cleveland, Detroit, Philadelphia, Oakland and Chicago.

By the same token, it could be predicted that the *Hispanos*, latest of the rural populations to migrate to urban areas, would one day find themselves in the majority in several cities in the Southwest and California, probably including San Antonio, El Paso, San Diego, Los Angeles and perhaps even Albuquerque. In addition, there was the steadily growing Puerto Rican population of New York City, which had increased over three-fold in the 10 years since 1950 to some 613,000 persons. (There was also an increasing number of Spanish-speakers in the cities of Michigan, Indiana and Illinois; although they still constituted a minuscule minority, they did cling together in clearly delineated communities.)

These two rapidly growing groups of in-migrants (both blacks and Spanish-speakers have a higher birth rate than whites) had a number of things in common. They were still predominantly rural in upbringing and outlook and poorly educated; they were forced to live in the most neglected areas of the urban core, called ghettos in the one case, *barrios* in the other; they were finding it increasingly difficult to find employment due to mechanization; and they were generally not considered to be "white." (Taken together, blacks and *Hispanos* represented a potential coalition in 1960 of 12 percent of the population of Colorado, 17 percent in California, 25 percent in Arizona, 27 percent in Texas, and over 36 percent in New Mexico.)

In 1967, they were already drawing together to share their common grievances, and among them there would develop the conclusion that all of the above mentioned disadvantages followed from the last.

On Saturday, July 29, while Governor Cargo had been wooing his *coyotes* in the north, Reies Tijerina had made his first public appearance since his release from the penitentiary. A capacity crowd of 250 packed the low-ceilinged, sweltering *Alianza* headquarters in Albuquerque. Defense lawyers spoke first, young Lorenzo Tapia declaring that Tijerina had "rights as an American citizen in every court in the land," blind Albert Gonzáles promising that, "Tijerina will be free and a martyr to his cause with only a slap on the wrist."

Then Reies. Within minutes the sweat was streaming down his face, the wooden rail of the little platform jumping beneath his fist. "We want our land back. The story here is a new breed of Spanish. We are writing a new history of New Mexico. Nothing can squash justice. Justice will win."

Twenty thousand dollars was needed before December to cover the cost of legal defense for himself and the other 20 accused raiders, he told them.

And then: *"Vienen,"* arms upraised in combined benediction and command, *"Vienen por frente,"* calling them forward to the defense of justice, those with $20 bills first, then the tens, the fives, the ones, the children with 50-cent pieces.

Seven hundred dollars was collected that night.

The next day at Tecolote, 150 crowded into a small schoolhouse to hear him. When he asked how many were *Alianza* members, no more than 40 held up their hands. But there were plainclothes sheriff's deputies circulating through the crowd.

With Anselmo standing behind him, a pistol apparent in his belt, Reies said all the things about the land and the creation of free citystates and the restoration of Spanish culture, and then suddenly he was talking about Detroit, which was still smoking, and where, according to a news story of that morning, two witnesses claimed to have seen

Chicago policemen murder two black youths in a motel called Algiers. His listeners had little trouble visualizing the National Guard troops, which he told them were still occupying Detroit, withdrawing from Toledo and preparing to move into Milwaukee. He talked about the riots that had already taken place in Wichita, Palm Beach, Newark, Portland, Harlem, and about the riots yet to come. "The black people are fighting for their rights just as we are."

A new dimension was being imposed on an old and basic theme. Some could not fully assimilate the association as yet, some would never find it acceptable. But all cheered as he finished with: "The time is right for us to get rid of fear!"

It had not been racism, only a statement of the facts, he told reporters afterward. He was aware that he had been commanded by the court not to advocate violence. All he had meant to do, he assured them, was to urge his people to stand up for their rights. Asked if he planned to carry his fund-raising campaign into the bailiwick of Alfonso Sánchez, he said, "Let him arrest me, if he wants to," and said that he planned to hold at least one meeting in Santa Fe and certainly one somewhere in Río Arriba. He would not be deterred, he said, from his determinations to carry the word of justice from Tecolote to Tierra Amarilla, and beyond. Eddie Chávez told reporters that $222 had been collected that afternoon.

"Read this," Cristóbal Tijerina invited the visitor sometime late in August, handing over a paper. It was dated January 24, a few months after the Echo Amphitheatre trespass, and was a speech in which Senator Joseph Montoya had deplored the plight of those he was wont to call his "silent people."

"They have labored silently in a million fields, stood silently at a hundred thousand counters, have waited silently at a million back doors. Now this is at an end! I say this once more! This is at an end! They are astir. Their hats are no longer in their hands. Their faces no longer contemplate the ground. They want. They need. They must have!"

Very eloquent.

"No, no," Cris shook his head, tapping the bottom of the page. "Read here."

The visitor read: "How shameful that while I speak, they ask politely for a minimum wage of $1.25 an hour and are treated as though they have asked to use the family toothbrush. The American Dream dances before their eyes, enticing them on. It is their dream too, no? They have fought for it, worked for it, died for it. They have believed in it. Are they to be denied it?"

"Hypocrisy!" Cris says, snatching back the paper. "He knows better than that. Unless he has sold out his blood along with his soul. Maybe they gave him a transfusion, maybe he is the *supervendido*, I don't know. But he should know better. It's not just about the toothbrush and the lousy starvation wage, but that about the American Dream." He leans forward, his handsome face wreathed in an expression of earnest intensity, almost of pain, reminding one of another Tijerina.

"Listen. Let's say you have a house and you are doing okay. You have your furniture, your things around you, your way of living. Then, somebody comes into your house, and maybe he has a paper from the court and maybe he has a gun or maybe he is just too smart for you, I don't know, but pretty soon he starts moving things around and telling you what to do and your wife what to do, and before you know it, you're out on the porch looking in. You can see him in there, pushing things around, putting up his pictures, making it all his way.

"It's bad, But you can still make it. You can go on living your way out there on the porch, even if it isn't as comfortable as it was before inside. You don't have to look in at him, you can look out at the mountains, maybe, or the trees. You can always go fishing if it gets too bad. If you can keep your wife from looking in all the time, you've got it made. But then he comes out on the porch and starts telling you how you are supposed to live out there too, that you have to do it all his way, that you have to speak his language and let your wife act like his does. You can't go fishing any more, he tells you, and now you have to go off and work somewhere else.

"Finally, he tells you that you have to move, he needs the porch, maybe he's going to make a national park out of it or make hydrogen bombs on it. You have to move into a little hole in the city, and there it is all his way, everything, there's not enough work and never enough money and you can't even go fishing any more, can't even see the mountains or a tree.

"We don't want the American Dream, not the way it is working for us. We had our own race, a life, a future, but they came along and tried to make us run like a rabbit. They are trying to make us go too fast. Our families are breaking up, our wives want too much. It has been too much, it has stunned us. We have been at a standstill for a hundred years. We have been, how do you say, in a state of enchantment. We want to slow down and get off this merry-go-round and do it our way. We don't have a shirt, a pants or a shoe that belongs to our culture, nothing in our houses that tells us who we are, and yet we know we are different and we know we had a dream of our own. It's still there inside us somewhere. How can we give it up?"

Hispanos tend to cling "somewhat defensively" to the "good" qualities of their indigenous culture and to try to retain them, the Burma Report had noted with impatience. "What they fail to take into consideration is that the problem is not so much one of quality as difference."

Could it not be that, on the contrary, the problem *is* essentially one of quality? Could it not be that the *Hispanos* of the Southwest are acutely aware that the difference between *Los Costumbres de Nuestra Gente,* as remembered by countless thousands, and the American Dream, as it is dealt out in the *barrios,* is coming more and more to approximate the difference between heaven and hell?

The same pure air and primal silence that Bill Mundy's elk hunters enjoy amongst the aspens of Río Arriba was once enjoyed by generations of *Hispano* sheepherders. The same magnificent view which Bill Mundy relishes from the rock ledge atop his mountain was once shared by those who viewed the land below as their common inheritance. The same streams now fished by thousands of visiting vacationers were once fished by those who can no longer afford to leave the airless alleys of the *barrios*.

It is generally agreed that virtually all of mankind enjoys fresh air and natural surroundings. The Burma Report acknowledges that "Love of family is good, attachment to the family plot of ground is good, strong predilection for a particular community is good. . . ." Few among us take pleasure from gasoline fumes and industrial gases, smut-darkened skies, concrete enclosures, rat-infested cells, enforced mobility and urban alienation.

It has to be conceded, then, that as Bill Mundy is a winner, so those he has displaced are losers, along with million of others like them. No man can remain a loser for long without asking himself how he has come to be such. In the case of most of the six to nine million *Hispanos* of the United States, as in the case of most of the 12 million blacks, there can be only one answer in the face of unrelenting disadvantage; only one reaction consistent with needs basic to every human soul.

The singular power and importance of these needs, so adroitly sidestepped by the Burma Report, are acknowledged with hearty honesty by Bill Mundy when he describes upending a 600-pound bull into the rodeo dust, when he gazes out across the rich green valley he has come to love and when he fixes the visitor with a cool blue eye and explains why Alberto Terraces is a "good one."

Despite the admirable ideals of the democratic Republic of the United States of America, here, as elsewhere and throughout history, poverty as disadvantage remains a tool of specific social purpose, primarily economic, but also emotional and, consequently, racial.

It so happens, however, that as a man becomes increasingly disadvantaged, he becomes increasingly dependent upon those things that are the least readily taken from him: the qualities of mind and spirit; the principles of personal integrity. It follows then that the more pressure society brings to bear upon him, the more sustenance he will be forced to take from those principles and the more fiercely he will tend to defend them. And personal integrity, in all men, is to a considerable degree determined by parentage and class and racial background, and is particularly so determined among those who have for six centuries thought of themselves as *la raza*, THE race.

Bill Mundy is a winner, and he is sure he knows why.

The *Hispanos* of the United States are losers. However, after a hundred years of what Cris Tijerina calls "enchantment," they are beginning to understand why, themselves.

The New Breed 16

"I feel I'm representing a new breed," Reies had told reporter Nabokov during their interview in the mountain hideout back in June. Late in August, the visitor went to *Alianza* headquarters in Albuquerque to ask him what he meant by the term.

Of the several presences of Reies Tijerina, the most impressive is that encountered upon first meeting him face to face. Of medium height, he is square-built, with strong features, thick crow-black hair and a complexion that can vary from ashen pallor to a deep mahogany flush. But it is his incredible nervous intensity which strikes one at first and which is particularly effective at close quarters. It seems to exude from him in electric excess, charging the air around him with insistence. His green eyes seem endowed with a special brightness; one half expects to see his hair stand on end. Muscular as he is, there is a subtle softness and fluidity, as though beneath his clothing he might be quivering with some painfully repressed ecstasy. He seems to be able to turn it off and on most of the time, but there are times when he seems more possessed than in possession of particular power, as though the banked fires have gotten out of control.

His handshake is eager, quick, asensual. He alternately labors at English with dogged determination and tumbles the words recklessly, driven from behind by impatient thought.

"The new breed was born ·October 19, 1514, by law to Title 1 of Book 6 of the Laws of the Indies by decree of Ferdinand V and reaffirmed by Philip the Second which legalized the matrimony between Spaniards and the native Pueblo Indians. Just like the Israelites, this new breed has served 400 years of servitude, of humiliation, injustice, being pushed by everybody, and all because our father, the Spaniard, was hated for the Spanish Holy Inquisition and was thrown out of the American continent, and our mother, the Indian, was held in a reservation. Leaving the new breed, a forgotten people and orphans without the heart of their parents."

It is true that the *Recopilación* contained numerous statutes encouraging and legitimizing marriage between Spaniards and native Indians, and that these laws were often honored, particularly in the isolated and underpopulated frontier settlements. The *Genizaros* who settled the valley of the upper Chama and much of Tierra Amarilla were Indian slaves ransomed from the Apaches and Comanches. Christianized and settled on the frontier buffer zone, they had the right to earn land and civil privilege by military service or through intermarriage.

It is also true that those born of Spanish parents in Spain were generally considered in the colonies to be of higher caste than those born of Spanish parents in the New World, called *criollos* or Creoles; and that those born of mixed ancestry, called *mestizos*, were considered a lower class. But it is also true that this caste system was generally flexible, varying from place to place, that it tended to disappear through 400 years, as more and more Spanish blood was infused with native Indian blood, and that ideas of strict racial exclusivity began to gain ground once again in New Mexico only with the coming of the first Anglos, many of whom came from slave states.

"We are not weak, this new breed, but like a four-year-old child that is just beginning to go to school. You cannot say we are inferior. You cannot say that about the child, you can only say that he is four years old, as we are four hundred years old. You will only know when the child gets to college. We have served the four hundred years that every new breed has served, such as the Jews, the Italians, the Anglos."

The concept of a new breed of mixed Spanish and Indian blood, with its implications of a potentially superior vigor, is, of course, not new at all to countries south of the border, where such artists as Diego Rivera had long been exalting the *mestizo* as the new man of the Americas.

"Now this new breed is ready to take its place. We have an obligation to identify ourselves, to prove our identity, to organize our rights to develop in knowledge, education, moral strength. We believe the virtues are not to be tampered with, but we also believe that it is our obligation for each home, each family to clean its backyard without pointing to the neighbor, preaching for everybody else to clean his house. First he has to do it himself. We are trying to clean ourselves, to become a model, if possible, an example. If they see fit to learn from the new breed, that is good."

Does the *Alianza* have agreement on these ideas with any of the Indian pueblos or tribes?

"The Hopis, the Hopi nation. Tomás Banyacya is their Speaker, and we agree on the overall plan, such as that the land belongs to the Great Spirit. It shouldn't be owned in the way it is now, to cause war and hatred and destruction. It should be used for the tenants, who should be entrusted with the land."

Does the new breed include blacks?

"In a way it does, but when I speak of the new breed, I don't include the Negro. It is those of Indian and Spanish extraction. There is a pueblo here, where two hundred years ago there were 200 people in that pueblo, and today there are still 200. The Indians will be absorbed by the Spanish-American people, because our mother was an Indian. I know many Indians who are married with Spanish-American women, the new breed women, and vice versa. By blood and by right."

Strict transcription of his remarks tends to give an impresion quite the opposite of that made by the passionate intensity and conviction with which they are delivered. An enormous quantity of generalized energy is being projected. The visitor asks him about the word justice in the *Alianza* motto. His jade eyes appear to darken and shine, and his hands grope at the air, struggling to encompass and convey some agonizing conviction and mystery.

"This justice, how can I tell you. Yes, it is in our motto: 'The Land is Our Inheritance, Justice is Our Creed." I don't know. The world is in agony. What is needed is an idea, a big idea. I can't explain it, but justice is the secret, the center of it. Not just for us, but for everybody. And not just the justice of the law, no, but something bigger, more powerful. It is more powerful than any nation, than the United States, than anything. How can I say it, except that it is a power, a great big power, and I feel it in me, growing. It is greater than anything, greater than me, greater than you, greater than all of us. It is so terrible, so very terrible, so huge, so powerful."

A week later, the visitor returned, to find Reies far too excited to continue the discussion. He was waiting for a call from Chicago, he said, pacing in shirt sleeves in the cluttered *Alianza* office and repeatedly running his hand through his thick hair. He was interested in attending, he said, but he did not think he could justify using *Alianza* funds for the trip. He added with nervous excitement that Martin Luther King was going to be there. When the call came through, he took it upstairs. A few minutes later, he reappeared in the office doorway, beaming, clapping his hands together and grinning. They had offered to pay the plane fare, he announced exultantly. "And they have reserved a seat for me right up there on the platform with Martin Luther King and the others!"

This was among the least impressive of his presences: the amateur publicist-activist and political social climber, as excited by his growing influence as a boy with a new bullhorn, as unabashedly concerned over his press notices as any second-rate night club comedian.

As such, however, he had good reason to celebrate, aside from the fact that he still faced federal and state charges, conviction of which could put him away for many years and possibly cost him his life. He had arrived, and his "coming out" in Chicago would firmly establish him as one of the fast rising stars of the New Left. But there had already been plenty of indication of his considerable and rather special impact on the radical end of the national political spectrum.

He had drawn the immediate admiration of the official Communist press and of most of that rapidly growing number of radical papers usually lumped under the heading of the underground press. Pat Blawis, otherwise known as Patricia Bell, successful defier of the Smith Act in 1940, elected in 1966 to the national committee of the Communist Party, described the raid and its aftermath in an article written in English for the *Sunday Worker* and published in Spanish on their *Trabajador* page. James A. Kennedy, young founder of the W.E.B. DuBois Club at the University of New Mexico, produced a four-page special supplement for *The Movement*, the paper of the Student Nonviolent Coordinating Committee, in which he celebrated the development of the *Alianza* "in the very heartland of Imperialism," described the arrests made after the raid as "a reign of terror" and called Reies Tijerina "a Mexican Malcolm X."

The *People's World* would soon describe Reies as a "man of action and vision." *The Militant,* organ of the Socialist Workers Party, would hail the Tierra Amarilla raid as another step toward industrial syndicalism. The *LA Free Press* would send reporters to New Mexico and print a number of articles celebrating the stirring of activist violence in the Southwest. The *Berkeley Barb* would print a photograph of Reies and would caption it with an innuendo aimed at Oakland landlords. New York's *National Guardian* would declare that "June 5, 1967, stands as a turning point in the history of the American Southwest. This land and its oppressed peoples have begun to awaken, to join their brothers to the South and to the North."

But it was upon the *Hispano* national community as a whole that events in New Mexico had their primary and most profound effect, and it was in the *Hispano* political arena that Reies first found himself a man of suddenly increased importance and influence.

Without question, no event since Pancho Villa's 1916 raid on Columbus, New Mexico, had so stirred the *Hispano* populace of the Southwest and elsewhere as had the raid on the courthouse. Regardless of opinion as to causes and ultimate value, few could remain indifferent to the event or to the land grant war which it had emphasized so dramatically. Not in 70 years had an organized group of *la raza* given vent to such an emphatic protest or raised questions of such impressive dimensions. It had been a *grito* to awaken the dead, and it awakened many a dead dream of a long-slumbering people. It was the first drama to come along in years worthy of recital along with the old tales of bold resistance and blood and thunder triumphs, and its hero quickly took his place among those who had gone before him. The blood had hardly dried on the courthouse floor before the first of many *corridos* commemorating the event had been written by Roberto Martínez and recorded against an accordion background by *Los Reyes de Albuquerque*, under the Hurricane label.

> *Año de sesenta y siete*
> *Cinco de Junio fué el día*
> *Hubo una revolución*
> *Allá por Tierra Amarilla.*

In the year of sixty-seven
The fifth of June was the day
They had a revolution
Up Tierra Amarilla way.

By the end of the year, Hurricane reported that sales had reached 10,000, a phenomenal figure in the tiny Southwest record industry; and, perhaps more significantly, orders had come from such distant and widely scattered places as San Francisco, Chicago, New York and Miami. At least a dozen other *corridos* were written without commercial motivation and were being sung throughout the northern villages and up and down the Río Grande grapevine. Several were disapproving of Tijerina, but all commemorated the raid and took melodic relish in describing its bloodier aspects.

A perhaps more convincing assessment of the general reaction among *Hispanos* of the Southwest in the months immediately following the raid might be made from the fact that, by the first of September, when Reies Tijerina left for Chicago, Senator Joseph Montoya had still not launched an all-out public attack on Tijerina, contenting himself with deploring the bloodshed of the raid and making only oblique references to its presumed instigator.

An even more apparent reluctance to condemn Tijerina or the raid outright was evidenced by the *Hispano* reform-moderates. Small in number and scattered throughout the Southwest and California, they were mostly professionals, scholars and dedicated social activists, some of whom could be considered radical, but none of whom could be considered revolutionary. Grouped generally to the left of center, they had for years managed to keep the *Hispano* far left in check, while attempting to inch reform measures forward within the accepted legal and political framework. But now they felt the ground shifting beneath them as the shock wave of the Tierra Amarilla incident began to move through the *barrios* and filter up among the students in the universities and colleges where many of them worked.

Not quite three weeks after the raid, Dr. Ralph Guzmán addressed the National Convention of LULAC, the League of United Latin-American Citizens, then in its 38th year as an influential organization of *Hispano* moderates. While neither Reies Tijerina nor the raid were mentioned directly, they were clearly the central subjects of the keynote address. Guzmán, the same who had helped provide Governor Cargo's office with troubleshooters Burgos and Aragón, described the troubles in New Mexico as "probably the closest thing to the outburst of anger and violence in Watts that has yet happened among our people."

In an obvious reference to Tijerina's *Alianza*, he said, "If we cannot condone their organization, we can plead the facts of poverty. If we cannot offer them congratulations on their methods, we can offer them our empathy—our understanding—and our support." While at pains to make it clear that LULAC did not condone violence ("All reasonable men reject violence"), he did not shrink from invoking the names of three who had made no such absolute rejection: Joaquín Murrieta, Padre Martínez and Juan Cortina.

Other veteran *Hispano* leaders were not so reticent to acknowledge the immediate source of the new pressure toward increased militancy. Bert Corona, president of MAPA, the Mexican-American Political Association, declared from his office in Oakland that "Reies Tijerina and his cause is the cause of all the Spanish-speaking people of the United States." César Chávez, the soft-spoken organizer of the Delano grape strike in California, would visit New Mexico in December and confer with Reies, who would announce, "We have agreed to find between him and me means to interrelate our problems and support each other's struggle." Chávez would, however, take pains to remind reporters that he was against violence, stating that he took his inspiration, not from the exploits of Pancho Villa, but from the words of the full-blooded Indian and one-time President of Mexico, Benito Juárez, who said, "Respect and the rights of all men are peace."

It was among the small but rapidly growing group of *Hispano* militants that Reies and the raid were given the most unqualified acclaim, not as unsettling pressure, but as welcome and valuable inspiration. Although they did not all qualify for Reies' blood ethic, they were certainly a new breed of *Hispano* leader. Militant, dedicated, angry and young, they eschewed association with any traditional political party, including, in most cases, the Communist Party. Their political thinking was more existential than programmatic. Their rhetoric revealed a predilection for the harsher traditions of a bloodier time, including such adamantly exclusive terms as *vendido, Tío Tomás* (taken directly from the blacks' Uncle Tom) and *Malinche* (the name of an Aztec woman said to have betrayed her people by prostituting herself to the invading Spaniards). They favored the older *gringo* and *gavacho* (outsider) to the more recent and more polite Anglo, and they preferred to call themselves *Chicanos* or Mexican-Americans rather than Spanish-Americans or *Hispanos*. They were for the most part urban, educated, disillusioned with conventional means of social reform, including the War on Poverty, and vigorously opposed to the Vietnam War.

Of all political *Hispanos*, they were the most encouraged by the *grito* of Tierra Amarilla. In July, Corky González of the Denver Crusade for Justice told an audience in Albuquerque that "instead of dying in Vietnam," *Hispanos* should "rather die in Tierra Amarilla." Editors of *La Raza* of Los Angeles termed the *Alianza* a "movement of liberation." Kelly Lovato, writing in González's *El Gallo*, compared the National Guard invasion of Río Arriba to the Yankee invasion of the Southwest in 1846, quoting Thoreau's description of the Mexican-American War as, "the work of comparatively a few individuals using the standing government as their tools," and further quoting Thoreau, with italics added:

"A wise man will only be useful *as a man* and not submit to be clay." Tom Cahill, editor and publisher of San Antonio's *Inferno*, likened Reies Tijerina to John Brown and the courthouse raid to the skirmish at Harper's Ferry. "Be moderate, be practical, be patient, and be damned!" he wrote. "Those who would sacrifice freedom for comfort deserve neither. Those who would speak for patience and moderation will one day curse themselves and hold their manhood cheap. ¡*Viva Justicia!* ¡*Viva Tijerina!*"

But it was Corky González who most succinctly expressed the admiration of the new *Hispano* left for the action at Tierra Amarilla and for its purported leader, and also provided a hint toward further explanation of the event's impact upon the *Hispano* community.

"Reies Tijerina," said González, "put everything he had on the line. You don't get people like that anymore. Everybody now wants to go home and watch TV."

Machismo is commonly defined as "manliness, strength, courage, virility." At its most specific, *macho* means he-mule, and in the Spanish context, and therefore to some degree in the *Hispano* also, the attributes of *machismo* are related to the English equivalents of *macho* and *hembra:* jack and jenny, stud and bitch, cock and hen, with their implications of bloody barnyard battle and strong undertones of sex. The term can be employed in mild or serious derision; the Spanish equivalent of the drugstore cowboy being mocked as *muy macho, mucho hombre,* strutting fool.

But as a compliment, the word virtually demands physical action. Strength, virility and courage must be proved by confrontation. No true challenge can be left unanswered, and it is the challenged individual who decides where the line is drawn. *Con él no se juegue:* with him you do not fool around; he is now ruled by rut and rage, righteous or not, and beyond the reach of that *coitus interruptus* known as reason or cowardice, depending on the point of view.

It is safe to say that Reies Tijerina and the raid on the Tierra Amarilla courthouse had appealed, to some degree, to the *machismo* of virtually all of the United States' *Hispanos*. The degree of approval among them would be consistent with their relative need for such a vicarious reinforcement of their sense of manhood. The poor are, of course, notorious brawlers, and the young have always been more prone to fight than their elders, as well as being more susceptible to ideals.

During his three days at the New Politics convention in Chicago, Reies met many of the leaders of the New Left, including James Forman, Julian Bond, Floyd McKissick and Dick Gregory. He contributed to a resolution calling for the United States to "uphold the Guadalupe treaty and its protocol," and he talked with several Puerto Rican leaders from New York. But it was the domination of the gathering by a minority of militant blacks which impressed him most, causing him to comment on his return that Martin Luther King was "sort of a philosopher. He is a slow-spoken man, who weighs his words very much before making his statement. He seems to be worried about these two factions among the Negro people, between the right and the left. He is being hard pressured from both sides."

On September 4 he headed home, stopping off in Austin to address Río Grande valley farm workers commemorating a 400-mile march to demand a $1.25-per-hour minimum wage law.

"I did it with shame, because so many people are making so much more than that."

While there, he took an advertisement in Tom Cahill's *Inferno* announcing the establishment of a San Antonio branch of the *Alianza* with his brother Ramón as representative, the offices to be in Ramón's home. The ad featured a photograph of Reies with his arms spread in the evangelical *"vienen por adelante"* gesture, with the acclamation *¡VIVA!* above, and below: *El Caudillo,* the Chief.

On September 10, making his first public appearance since his return from Chicago, Reies dropped a bombshell of yet another color into the uneasy racial waters of the Southwest. Speaking to a gathering of 200 *Alianza* members in the Albuquerque headquarters, he announced that he was preparing to sign a pact with the Black Muslims and other Negro groups. It was to be more a treaty of mutual respect than an alliance, he told his audience, "to prevent any friction between the peoples. The Anglos have too often played the Negro against the Spanish-American."

Announcing further that he had invited Martin Luther King to speak at the *Alianza* National Convention in October, he assured his listeners, "Of course we are only going to admit the Negroes when Martin Luther King speaks. After that they have to get out, because the convention belongs to our *raza.*" And he added, "I want, when he speaks, for there to be more *raza* than Negroes."

The fumbling ambivalence of his remarks partly reflected the beginnings of a change in policy. But his careful assurance to the membership that the impending visit of the blacks would not entail full racial embrace also reflected his awareness of an undetermined amount of anti-Negro sentiment among his followers. Many of the northern villagers had long regarded themselves as of *la raza pura,* with only the "pure" blood of the conquistadors in their veins, this despite the fact that at least 80 percent of them had Indian blood. In the urban wing of the membership, there were those who had been brought up in Southwest city *barrios,* where members of the larger minority had long taken solace from the presumption that skin tone was a measure of superiority, with black at the bottom of the scale. In certain circles, a woman who went out with a black man was called a *mayista* and scorned by the community.

However, the degree of such feelings among the *Alianza* membership was minuscule compared to that prevailing in the ruling majority, and news of the *Alianza's* new affiliation was regarded by its enemies as ominous indication of a new and threatening alliance in the making. In fact, their fears were neither entirely unjustified nor without precedent. During the Civil War, *Hispanos* had on several occasions plotted with Negro slaves to rise against the whites. In 1856, a committee of Colorado County citizens had reported: "We are satisfied that the lower class of the Mexican population are incendiaries in any country where slaves are held, and should be dealt with accordingly."

As recently as July, while avowing that he was opposed to violence, Reies had assured reporters: "We don't want to end up doing what the Negroes are doing."

But his public position on a number of questions was shifting rapidly, and while few of those on the right were surprised, many of those clinging to the center would be increasingly dismayed.

Ten days after his return from Chicago, Reies had his first hearing before the middle liberal establishment, at St. John's College in Santa Fe. The college is privately endowed, has a reputation for enlightened scholarship, a predominantly Anglo, upper-middle-class enrollment, and a faculty to match. The new auditorium had carpeted aisles, one soaring wall of tinted glass, and was filled to capacity. Reies stood at the lectern in his best dark suit. Cris sat on a folding chair behind him. Slim young women in tweed skirts tilted forward earnestly, professors polished their glasses, distinguished-looking ladies took pencils from their hair, the scrubbed, milk-fed boys and girls poised over their notebooks.

"This is the 430th anniversary of our new breed," he began. "I will lead you out of Egypt, God said to Moses, and after 430 years, the Hebrews came out of Egypt and into Canaan."

He was making an obvious attempt to give the necessary impression, but the English made it difficult, and as the phrases began to tumble and tangle, he began to revert to the rhythmic stridency and flashing ferocity of his accustomed style, shattering the careful atmosphere of muted concern and scholarly reason, causing the professors to frown, the handsome ladies to tug at the hems of their skirts, the boys and girls to fumble at their notebooks in confusion.

"The Hebrews had accumulated this pride to stand up and fight, and now it is happening to us, we fight for our lives, not only for our culture, for our survival, our land, all the money they spend investigating Reies López Tijerina and his wife they should spend investigating what the Santa Fe Ring did, the Spanish-American is only four-and-a-half years old, while the Anglo is 25 years old, and the Jew is 60 years old, Thomas B. Catron, I am told he was a Jew, it takes a well developed race to do what they did to us, but we will not have our rights tampered with, I told Robert F. Kennedy, you think you have trouble with the Negroes, wait until we get started, by the year 2000 we will have 600 million people who speak Spanish down across the Río Grande. . . ."

The Albuquerque *Journal* headlined it: TIJERINA PREACHES RACIST GOSPEL. "In a speech amply spiced with racist remarks aimed at Anglos and Jews in New Mexico, Tijerina said . . ."

Outraged letters-to-the-editor followed, one from a Santa Fe Jewish organization, but most from Anglo liberals. Those who were not indignant were disappointed. Many had found his fervor to be more distasteful than exciting and his dialectic not at all amusing. It was more convenient to condemn his eccentric conviction that the Missouri Confederate, Catron, had been of Hebrew extraction, than it was to examine their reaction to his far less respectful attitude toward their own progenitors. Racism wears many masks, not the least of which is charity.

Two days later, on September 15, Reies fulfilled his promise to carry his campaign into Alfonso Sánchez's bailiwick, appearing at a fund-raising *tamalada* dinner at El Toro Steakhouse, five blocks from the district attorney's office. Félix Martínez was there to greet the 150 guests, his Ché Guevara beard now trimmed down to mustache and goatee. One of his younger brothers, Danny, 17 and soon to enter the army, shook his head over a bottle of beer at the bar, telling of the legendary TA lawyer who had taken a million-dollar bribe. "A million bucks, that's hard to resist," he said, but added that he would never do it and Félix would never do it. But he shook his head and said it again. "A million bucks . . ."

A dozen reporters gathered at one table. At another were white-haired Patricia Bell of the CPUSA and friends: a bearded man in a Harris tweed jacket, a handsome woman with her hair pulled back and chunks of turquoise around her neck.

The King of the Indies was also present, teetotaling Jerry Noll, citing Nostradamus as authority for his assurance that in the year 1986, when his armies had completed the conquest of Europe, he would marry Anastasia Romanoff, uniting the Holy Roman and Holy Russian Empires at last. When asked how he planned to conceive an heir, since by that date he would be over 60 and all of the various Anastasias dead or in their eighties, he replied without hesitation that he had already chosen his successor. "He is in Israel and his name is Levi of the House of David. After the year 2005, he will succeed. His Holy Day is Thursday."

There were beans and tamales in a very hot sauce on paper plates, a round-faced man with an electric guitar who could make trumpet and bird sounds with his mouth and sang "Guadalajara," " Valencia," *"La Bamba,"* "Winchester Cathedral" and *"Malagueña."* Then Reies.

He spoke in half darkness under a low arbor of decorative vines, unfettered this time by alien language and sensibilities. The sweat stood out on his brow, the plastic grapes rattled against his upthrust finger, the flashbulbs popped and the TV cameras whirred.

"Those who say we are Communists are more Communist than we. What moves us is hunger and a thirst for justice, not desire for fame, for the cinema, for perfumed clothes. We want our land, our rights. They will not beat us with that stick, the dollar. We are 500,000 strong and getting stronger. In Chicago there were 2,000 delegates representing 80,000 people, and everybody asked, where is Tijerina. All the world asked for one person. On the front page of the *New York Times,* a newspaper that has one hundred pages, there was Tijerina, Tierra Amarilla, Canjilón. These idiots have to crucify somebody, but they will not succeed, we have our lawyers too. My *grito* is not for the politicians to hear, I do not cry out to the angels, not to hell, but to you. Communist or capitalist, give us help to pay the lawyers. *Pasa por adelante*, come forward, be a man, give!"

"There is white power and black power," a voice called out during the passing of the hat, "but we got chili power." And there was hearty laughter and applause.

And finally, on Sunday, the first day of October, the tiger went north. He lunched with his lieutenants in the big adobe house down the street from the Tierra Amarilla courthouse. Fernanda bustled back and forth with heavy platters. "Pass the macaroni please, Reies," said the King of the Indies. A conference was held in the kitchen out of the visitor's hearing. As the men finished one by one, the women and children took their places at the big round table.

Juan Martínez sat stern and upright in the shaded sitting room, in his best boots and broad-brimmed hat. "Not that I know of," he replied, when asked if he had Indian blood.

Asked about Reies' concept of the new breed, he shook his head a little and said, "I don't really understand that."

The rally was to be held in Chama. A hundred cars were waiting, lined up around a grassy space where two highways formed a Y just inside the city limits. There was a black truck with the Mexican eagle and writhing serpent painted on its door. A speaker's stand had been erected and draped in a white sheet lettered in black: *VIVA TIJERINA*.

More cars arrived, many of their occupants remaining inside to watch through opened windows. A half-dozen State Police cars were parked at regular intervals on the outer perimeter of the triangle, while plainclothesmen circulated through the crowd. A large truck with high sides had been positioned directly behind the speaker's stand, and from there several dark-faced men in battered straw hats watched the crowd and the police, while out on the edge Cris and Anselmo Tijerina, Félix and Juan Martínez took up watchful positions. A red-haired woman in frontier pants and boots inquired in a Texas accent what these so-called *Pueblos Libres* planned to do for money, and the King of the Indies replied cheerfully, "We'll print our own. Maybe we'll put your picture on it." And he giggled.

"Crazy," the woman muttered, edging back to stand beside her pink-cheeked husband.

"Another crazy Communist."

It was one of Río Arriba's beautiful fall days, with the air crisp and clear, the aspens gold on the mountain slopes and the cumulus high and blindingly white, rolling slowly down toward Río Abajo.

Reies held the huge, leather-bound book up against the sky and told them once again that they would defend the rights and lands of their fathers with their lives. Senator Montoya had introduced a bill in Congress, he said, to make it illegal to enter the White House with a weapon. "I say he should pass bills to protect the citizens from the police," he said, and there were cries of ¡Viva Tijerina!

"Say it in English."

The voice came from the center of the crowd. A man in his thirties, wearing a cowboy shirt with pearl buttons on the cuffs, blond hair close-cropped, face slightly flushed, starting toward the speaker's stand as he said distinctly again, "Speak in English, dammit."

Five men closed in on him before the crowd did, among them Cris Tijerina and a plainclothes policeman, and he was quickly hustled through the muttering crowd and away.

When Reies resumed, in Spanish, he had both clenched fists in the air and his lips were white.

A few days later, the visitor asked him again about his concept of justice. Did it apply to Jews?

"Of course, but the Jew does not need it as bad as we do. He is ahead of us, that is what I was trying to tell them at St. John's, about the ages of races and why this new breed must be allowed to grow. You see, the Jew was very old and wandering the world for a long time, wanting to own property, but never allowed to, so he learned all about it. He studied it for centuries. And when he immigrated to England, England accepted the Jewish idea of private enterprise, and that was what the English imported to the United States.

"Spain was ruling this continent at first, she was depriving all the other nations of it. Well, the Jew was bitter, he had been kicked out of Spain. The Englishman was bitter because he was called a pirate and had no rights on this continent. The Italian also, and the French, so they all got together against Spain, and the Jew steered the Anglo here. He was the oldest one, the more intelligent, he knew more about property, land, *ejidos* and that old system, so they all joined together, and Thomas Benton Catron was their leader in New Mexico."

What other Jews were there in New Mexico?

"I don't know, I don't think there were many, but I do think the steering wheel, the main pilot was some man with plenty of brain, with accumulated knowledge. A Negro, a Spanish person, just couldn't do what Catron did. He was a brilliant, well-developed man. You should go to the library and see his room, full of papers, boy, you'd be surprised, that man kept a record of everything, he would even make books out of the letters that he received and the letters that went out. He knew all about the land and the law. He had *sagaz*." (Sharing the same Latin root as the English "sagacity," it commonly implies, among the *Hispano* minority, shrewdness at survival and, often, the ability to make use of the foibles of the ruling majority.)

Would Jews be allowed to live in the *Pueblo Libres*?

"There won't be any Anglos of any kind. First we have to become a walking power, like a child. We are not just after land. It isn't just the land. We have to prove our identity, our strength, our knowledge. We are in the United States, but the record shows that we are discriminated against. The Anglo says, 'It's your complex.' But we know. We can detect it easier than the discriminator. He doesn't see it, because he doesn't feel it. It's like that man in Chama. It was an all Spanish-American meeting. He knew that. Why did he come there and try to command, ordering me to speak English? Why?"

Excitement lifts his voice without warning, as swift and smooth as the shift of an automatic transmission, and for a few moments he is the Reies Tijerina of pulpit and platform.

"Because of that same low-down rotten proudful spirit of conquering superiority! The same spirit of Uncle Sam was in that small Anglo right there. The people could have torn him to pieces, but he wasn't afraid. Because he had these feelings inside. Because he's so used to having his way, to the idea of the United States jumping on smaller nations, telling everybody what to do. Well, we are sick and tired of being forced to accept a culture we do not want. We object and we are angry against this so-called American way of life. It has gone so low that it is destroying the faith, the love of the home. Too many divorces, too many husbands changing wives, too many girls just playing and fooling around with their honor, their pride, their moral principles.

"We object against this, and we will change it, although there is nothing we can do about it at this time, such as to protest against these shows, these immoral movies that come from Hollywood and this sex education in the school system. Sex is like a bank. A bank is not for people to go in there and steal the money, a bank has its limits, its laws. . . ."

The frenzy subsides as swiftly and smoothly as it began, leaving him restive, his hands on the move.

"We are in a good position from the historical point of view, the global point of view. Most of the nations are against the United States, believing that the U.S. has made a habit to impose its views on other nations. Mankind is sick of these wars and the development of these nuclear weapons. There will be a great destructive war, and when it comes to that day, we will not be blamed."

Who is we?

"The Spanish-Americans, the Negroes, the darker-skinned people, the nonwhites."

Isn't that racism?

"Racism is one race thinking they are better than the other. There is nothing wrong with one child saying, 'I am Juan,' in school and the other child saying, 'My name is Billy,' but when somebody tries to force Juan to say his name is John, that is wrong, that is evil. If each race would limit itself to its own rights and keep to its own orbit, there would be no racism."

But isn't it true that such separatism only fosters the alienation and lack of understanding that leads to intolerance and eventually racial war?

"We must keep ourselves limited to the rights and boundaries of nature, and allegiance to race is natural. When a stray small chicken is put into the mother hen's brood, she kills it. You might agree now that we're friends, but when another Anglo comes and there is friction, a fight, you tend to defend your own race. It is nature. To ignore race, that is to try to live in a Kingdom of Justice. Many people have spoken about that kingdom, but it has not been accomplished. The Republic of Plato is a good one, but nobody has succeeded in doing it. The United States tried to build up a Republic of Plato here, but they ended up destroying Mexico and many others and crossing the oceans like never before, all because they thought their system was better than anybody else's. Trying to melt different races in one pot, like they call this the melting pot. Lies, that's a raw naked lie."

I am sitting here. Am I a lie?

"You are an Anglo."

"I am one-eighth Colombian Indian, one-eighth Spanish, one-quarter Scotch . . ."

"Why am I speaking to you in English?"

"Because your English is better than my Spanish."

"No! Because it is the language established by the powerful, put in by force. Okay, then immediately, right here, we come to the time when we say, 'No, I will no longer learn your language, no, you son of a so-and-so, now you learn my language before I'll learn yours, or you get the hell out of here before we turn the dogs loose!' "

Incited deliberately, it is there again, the flame of passion; his voice is under determined control this time, but he exudes the insistence of his mortal need.

"The time is coming, our time, I can feel it in me, like a natural force. The world is hungry, and the people are beginning to cry out. There is a change, a fever, and pretty soon they are going to start trampling on top of others and not caring a hook about regulations or methods, just hungry and crazy. I was surprised in Chicago, so many hundreds of thousands of people, and Martin Luther King used the words black power for the first time. He had to. He will be more and more surrounded by more radical forces, they are crowding him. And they had Negroes controlling the whole convention. Why? Because the whites, they know it, that the black man is right. The white nations and people have this guilt spirit in them because they have oppressed the black men. So, whatever he asked, they would accept it."

But the white liberals and radicals of the New Politics convention are not representative of the majority of the white population. There is a breaking point when they will fight, and there are more whites than blacks.

"Yes, but one Indian showed his child—in a funny book I saw this picture—a small bird in his nest with some babies, and here comes a hawk or eagle, and the small bird fought the eagle, and the Indian said, 'Look, the small one will win, even though the eagle has more claws and all that.' The Negro is the small bird, and all the torture and torment of the whites has given him an enormous spirit in himself, a victorious determined spirit, but the Anglo is weakened by guilt. How come Alexander with his few troops beat Darius with his million? Because Darius was an old king in an old kingdom, but Alexander and his soldiers were young and new, just like the bird in the nest. The spirit develops."

It is different when a bird is defending its own nest, but the blacks are taking the battle to the eagle, going to his nest and demanding his golden eggs. Sooner or later he will renounce moral pretense and rip the little bird open.

His green eyes glint through narrowed lids, then abruptly he leans back, breaking the charm and introducing an entirely new Tijerina, cold and watchful, subtly menacing. "You think so?"

Are there no basic values that transcend race? Can you conceive of a time when we will no longer be troubled with racial conflict?

"Do you believe in the Bible?"

I believe in it as an historical . . .

"I mean the prophecies, can you trust them?"

No.

"How about Nostradamus?"

I think the mind of man is capable of reaching out . . .

"I've never accepted the Bible as perfect, but I believe Isaiah was a man of vision. He was all the time trying to help his race, his people, and he said, even back then, that destruction would appear through flames and fire, and the last war would be a war of blood, of race. In other words, the time will come when the different races, especially the Negro and other minority groups, will build up a very strong spirit of nationalism, and they will build up that stigma or whatever you call it, that gap that separates races, and they will not ask you for your idea, what you think, they will look at your color, and if you're black and the white is the one that's opposing you, you're dead. If the black is the one that is opposing, the white is dead, regardless of his ideas."

Do you think that is good?

"No, of course not. But it's the best thing to whip and punish mankind. And after a purge like that, a war of races, people will behave and there will be strict law. No writer of one race will be allowed to write about another race, because that is just as bad as standing in your door and raising hell against your neighbor."

Aren't you raising hell against your neighbor?

"I'm contributing to this showdown."

Do you think it will happen in your lifetime?

"I think I will see it."

You have changed since you went to Chicago.

"It's not me, it's the times."

But your concept of justice, the land, the free city-states . . .

"That will come later, there is no time for that now. Things are moving too fast."

Poder Negro 17

THERE had been riots in two dozen cities that summer and trouble in as many more. Shots had been fired and buildings set aflame less than a mile from the White House; a dozen square blocks of Newark had been leveled; Detroit had been under virtual martial law for two weeks. Hundreds had been killed, thousands injured, tens of thousands arrested, millions of dollars in property destroyed.

"This is the beginning of revolution," H. Rap Brown declared in New York, flanked by glowering guards armed with machetes.

"Next time, shoot to kill arsonists and maim or cripple looters," ordered Mayor Daley of Chicago, flanked by police armed with guns, clubs, mace.

Already weakened by a creeping bankruptcy of moral purpose, white middle-class America trembled in its fragile cocoon of forced-consumption affluence, and the twin plagues of humorless fear and hatred reached out across the land to find the ground already well prepared in remote New Mexico.

In August, Jerry Noll announced to the fifth annual state convention of the *Alianza Federal de Mercedes* that he was prepared to call in foreign armies to help him oust the United States from those lands of which he was King Emperor, "including Disneyland."

At the back of the little hall in Albuquerque, a man stood up and cried out in an anguished voice, "We are not traitors, we are not traitors, we are not traitors to the United States!"

There were shouts of protest and a few of agreement. Folding chairs toppled. The King Emperor tittered. Reies Tijerina leaped to the platform and spread his arms to quiet the storm.

"I go along with the United States when it goes along with George Washington," he shouted. "But the United States is no longer like George Washington. I will not disown her, but I cannot support a whore and a prostitute."

He then announced that the *Alianza* would hold its national convention in October, the agenda to include a speech by Rap Brown and possible coronation of the King of the Indies.

A thread of quaint absurdity runs through the fabric of the story of the New Mexico land grant war, beginning at least as far back as the appearance of the robed and bearded Heralds of Peace in Lumberton. But alongside it runs the red thread of manic apprehension and fear.

Stone deaf to the merry mockery of the cosmic cap and bells, newsmen reported indignantly that Reies Tijerina had accused the United States of doing it for money, and solemnly alerted their readers to impending invasion by foreign legions:

ALLIANCE MAY CONSPIRE TO OUST US FROM N.M.

Fear excludes reason and its grace note, the blessed ease of humor. One more fright was added to the deepening unease of the majority, one more cue to prompt them to indignant approval of the campaign to silence the increasingly bothersome Tijerina and the nettlesome problems he represented.

On the legal front, action was slow but steady. Although Alfonso Sánchez had found it necessary to tidy up his indictments with some new amendments, the preliminary hearing for trial of the courthouse raiders had been tentatively set for early in the next year. On September 15, Tijerina and the other four Echo Amphitheatre defendants were indicted in U.S. District Court in Albuquerque and their trial arranged for December. Judge Howard C. Bratton issued an order forbidding defendants, lawyers or witnesses to make public statements about the case. The obvious intention of the district attorney's office to lock up as many of the Tijerina tribe as possible suffered a small setback on October 3, when a juvenile court judge in Denver refused to return 15-year-old Danny Tijerina to New Mexico to face the 28 raid counts waiting for him. However, Assistant District Attorney Chávez assured reporters, "We'll get him later."

The war on the War on Poverty was being vigorously pressed on all fronts, not only in New Mexico, but across the nation as well. Small-town politicians in the Deep South and big-city machine bosses in the industrial East and the Midwest had long been resentful of the invasion of their bailiwicks by idealistic and politically independent young poverty workers, and felt themselves to be particularly deprived by the OEO's policy of central control of funding. They had no need of a courthouse raid with which to incite public opinion; they had the riots, and it took little effort to focus majority resentment on the poverty programs, described by one critic as "the government subsidizing its own anarchic destruction."

Last-ditch defenders of the poverty program pointed out that in many instances Negro poverty workers had played a part, often at risk of life and limb, in quieting racial disturbances. That, out of 28,482 persons on the payroll of the War on Poverty, either directly or through subsidiary agencies, only six were among the thousands arrested in ghettos. They said that blanket exclusion of black militants from involvement in the poverty program only insured their return to the war in the streets, and that legislative punishment of the poor would not eliminate the problems of poverty.

But it seemed that such qualifications were appropriate for another, calmer time, and far too late now. The majority was running scared and had to have its scapegoats.

By late September, a move was underway in Congress to either eliminate the national anti-poverty program or turn administration and control of funds over to state and local agencies and officials. While New Mexico Congressman Johnny Walker did say that he thought "failures of the OEO have been over-publicized," the rest of the state's Congressional delegation had already agreed to join Republicans and Southern Democrats in the attack.

On the home front, the campaign was rapidly gaining momentum and spokesmen. Back in July, columnist Fred Buckles had suggested in a small truckers' magazine that the OEO had been involved with the *Alianza*. By early September, he was on the pages of the *New Mexican*, demanding that the poverty program be "junked and rebuilt from scratch or sharply revised."

In late August, Río Arriba County Commissioner Nick Salazar (the same who had defied raiders' guns to help carry wounded State Policeman Nick Sais to the ambulance) had called the War on Poverty a "complete failure in Río Arriba." By mid-September his impatient denunciations of the poverty bureaucracy had reached fever pitch. "The hell with it! We don't need it. We don't want it."

Meanwhile, underground forces were also at work. On September 13, State Department of Finance travel vouchers revealed that two men from Attorney General Boston Witt's office were roaming Old Mexico on a mission which Witt would describe only as "confidential." It was common knowledge that the same men had already covered most of the state.

By September 20, the newspapers were reporting that Witt's investigators were searching for links between Tijerina and International Communism, and were also on the lookout for "red influence" in the OEO. It was also reported that the investigation had been requested by Joe Montoya, but when the Senator was questioned in Washington, he denied knowing anything about it. He did, however, affirm that he was "always interested in leftist leanings of anyone working for the federal government," and that he had for a long time been "interested in ascertaining whether or not Mr. Tijerina has any rapport with any Communist, fellow travelers or their ilk."

That same month, John Birch Society writer Alan Stang ventured into Canjilón to question the natives. But his credentials had somehow gone before him, and he didn't get very far. A white-haired old man kept urging the others not to talk to him and shouting that, "somebody will kill

Alfonso Sánchez and those other s.o.b.s in Sante Fe," the implication being clear that Stang might at any moment find himself among the condemned.

Before beating a retreat, he had time to note that Leyba property had "a beautiful view;" that "the house was junky and needs some paint, but I saw no one preventing anyone from applying it;" and that Baltazar Martínez' arms were covered with scars, which a "high police official" later explained were the result of attempts to burn off tattoos in order to hinder police identification.

Repairing to the courthouse in Tierra Amarilla, Stang met with a warmer welcome from junior *honcho* Benny Naranjo, who assured him that "The War on Poverty stinks."

Stang's article, which appeared in the October issue of *American Opinion,* was titled "The Communist Plan to Grab the Southwest." Comparing the courthouse raid to Castro's raid on the Moncada Barracks in 1953, Stang charged, among other things, that Governor Cargo was "on immediate call to revolutionaries," and that Robert García and the OEO were "deliberately trying to create dissension between Americans." He also took alarmed note of connections between Reies Tijerina's *Alianza* and "the so-called black revolution, which, the Communists, as everyone by now should be fully aware, are running in an attempt to destroy the United States."

The issue had a strong sale in Albuquerque and throughout the Southwest, and the article was printed in excerpt and thousands of copies distributed free from Birch Society offices throughout the country.

On October 20, a committee of the U.S. House of Representatives approved the Green amendment, which turned primary control of poverty programs over to the state and local politicians, empowering them to initiate programs and contract with private or public agencies to carry them out. The amendment was firmly locked into the mechanics of the poverty bill and sent on to the Senate, where axes were being ground for further surgery.

That same Friday, delegates were arriving in Albuquerque for a gathering the likes of which hadn't been seen in the Southwest since the days of the discoverers, Cabeza de Vaca and the black slave Estevan; of the explorers, Coronado and his wily Comanche guide, the Turk; of the long-past *fiestas* and trade gatherings, where priest and medicine man, soldier and painted warior, mountain man and runaway slave had mingled and palavered on the crazy-quilt frontier.

The first National Convention of the *Alianza Federal de Pueblos Libres* convened Saturday morning in Albuquerque's civic auditorium, a huge inverted bowl of cantilevered concrete, steel and tarpaper located on the eastern edge of the city.

Convention coordinator Félix Martínez greeted delegates and newsmen at the lofty plate-glass doors, dapper in a dark blue suit, his Ché Guevara beard now shorn down to a glad-hander's tidy mustache. Assistants in broad-brimmed sombreros and *charro* costumes presided over tables heaped with free copies of militant *Hispano* newspapers. There were pocket-sized booklets with Rap Brown on the cover and, inside, a terse polemic promising black revolution in both English and Spanish. Prominent on the floor of the large lobby were two automobiles of unfamiliar shape, the larger one with its windshield cleft like a valentine heart and headlights shaped like human eyes.

Fernanda Martínez was there, her gray-streaked hair gleaming and freshly sculpted for the occasion. Juan stood tall in his best boots and hat, wearing a new simulated leather jacket. There were half a dozen pretty young usherettes in embroidered blouses and full, knee-length skirts, and a number of newsmen toting cameras.

All turned to watch as eight men and a woman moved across the lobby in tight formation, two of the young men in sweatshirts with black panthers stenciled front and back, the others in solid blue-and-red smocks, wearing sandals and sunglasses, their shaved heads burnished and gleaming. A reporter attempted to reach the rotund figure at the center of the moving group, but was neatly shouldered aside and found himself standing unsteadily in their wake, a blood-red calling card in his hand:

MAULANA KARENGA

Wherever we are US is

Convention proceedings began with Vice President Santiago Anaya's apologetic plea for the audience to bunch up in the center section of the vast auditorium. There were around 200 present; by noon there would be 300. A few outsiders and newsmen remained in the side sections. Alone in a back row, two federal officers in plainclothes nursed a tape recorder. Thirty officers were on standby at a nearby police station, and three patrol cars prowled a steady pattern around the building.

Santiago Anaya introduced the convention's chief interlocutor, pronouncing the name with reverent relish: *El Caballero* Reies López Tijerina.

Along the front of the stage were ranged cloth banners with hand-sewed inscriptions: Merced de San Pedro, Merced Real Antonio Martínez Lucero de Godoy, House of Hapsburg, Merced de Socorro.

After offering a few rousing promises of things to come, Reies began to read out the names of the land grant representatives seated behind him. They stood one by one as their names were called: among them, Jose María Martínez for the TA grant, gripping his battered hat in gnarled hands and ducking his head to applause.

The *Journal* reporter asked his young *Hispano* interpreter what was going on, and when he was told, shrugged and pocketed his pen. There were 27 in all, and finally the last: aged sheepherder José Salazar, one-time *alcalde* of the ill-fated Republic of San Joaquín de Chama, squinting rheumy eyes against the glaring lights, groping blindly for his chair as he turned to sit back down. The grants would be mentioned again only in passing; there were far more exciting things in store.

Reies introduced the guests. Ralph Featherstone of SNCC, wearing a loose tunic of red and gold, thrust up a clenched black fist in greeting. Initial surprise was followed by a roar of delight from the floor, and the *Journal* reporter made a note. Ethel Minor, also of the Student Non-Violent Coordinating Committee, told them in good college Spanish that she was delighted to be among such militant revolutionaries and that Rap Brown deeply regretted that a court order had prevented him from attending. Another black woman, handsome in a sculpted Afro hairdo, took the microphone to explain that Maulana Ron Karenga spoke 11 languages and would address them in their own tongue on the morrow; while behind her, the founder-director of US sat impassively between two bodyguards.

The speeches began. They would be interspersed with a variety of other activities. Petitions would be circulated, a painting would be auctioned off for $25, members were assured that an annual financial report would be given. Through Reies' tithing talents, a $300 travel fund would be raised, a total of $670 would be added to the legal defense fund and some 30 conventioneers would be induced to pledge purchase of $100 shares in an industrial cooperative which intended to manufacture automobiles with heart-shaped windshields and headlight eyes. Although there would be no wrestling match between *El Tigre de la Sierra* and *El Fantasma del Norte*, as promised in the program, Juan A. Roybel would sing all 17 verses of his corrido, *El Valiente Tijerina*, as scheduled.

The Reverend Clarence E. Duffy, a cleric who claimed to have once been threatened with excommunication by Cardinal Spellman, called for "repossession of the land in general by the people, for whose regulated use and benefit God created it." But he cautioned against violence. "Even were it morally right to use such methods, the forces against you would crush you inexorably."

Behind him on the stage, Ralph Featherstone slouched in his chair, eyes downcast, chewing gum.

Burt Corona, veteran labor organizer and head of the Mexican-American Political Association of California, spoke in shirt sleeves. "The cause of Tierra Amarilla is the cause of all our people," he told them. "You have no idea how great an impact Tierra Amarilla has had upon our young. We must take advantage of this inspiration and organize our young people."

He was applauded by an audience that contained practically no teenagers.

Celso Moreno, *Hispano* troubleshooter for the the Republican Party, summed up *Hispano* grievances and called for unity, but cautioned, "We don't want violence, we want attention. The solution is through political action."

Behind him, Maulana Ron Karenga sat impassively toying with the ebony talisman hanging from his neck. Half the 40 people on the stage were black, but there were virtually no Negroes in the audience.

Reies Tijerina launched one of his podium-pounding entr'actes with mention of the land grants, but quickly lapsed into fiery denunciation of Anglo racial bias against the blacks. "They despise and insult them," he cried. "They call them mulattoes, *sambos!*"

José A. Gutiérrez of San Antonio, representing MAYO, the Mexican American Youth Organization, was the first to invoke the picture of their common nemesis. "Our black brothers call him honky, but he is the same Anglo we know. Our devil has pale skin and blue eyes!"

On the sidelines, tow-headed, blue-eyed Rich Jamison, free-lance photographer, looked distinctly uneasy, but Fernanda Martínez threw him a wave and smile of reassurance before returning to hearty applause of the speaker. The already light-complexioned *Journal* reporter slowly turned more livid as the remark was translated to him.

Wearing loafers and a two-tone sport shirt, Corky González bore down on his favorite themes. "Robin Hood was a hood, but he was an Anglo, so he is a hero. Better to die in Tierra Amarilla than in Vietnam. If they want to call it social revolution, okay, industrial revolution, okay, rural revolution, okay, armed revolution—let it be that."

"At this moment there are 100,000 people protesting the war at the Pentagon," Reies told them. "We too are protesting harassment by the United States government. Judge Bratton has forbidden me to talk about our case, but Judge Bratton cannot tell us what to do. We know that the judge is using the law to drink blood and humiliate our race. No bomb in the world is as powerful as a human being full of the desire for justice. Our enemies respect only force. Ask the State Police if we are valiant. How many here want to go to Vietnam and fight for Uncle Sam? *No debemos luchar para el honky.*"

The *Journal* reporter wanted to know what Tijerina had said about Judge Bratton. When he could get no answer from those around him, he hurried over to the two federal officers and got them to play it back for him on their tape recorder.

Sunday found Tijerina in frilled *hidalgo* shirt, gold sash and gold striped trousers, introducing Tomás Banyacya, Speaker of the Hopi nation. The Speaker, wearing a red headband, flowered shirt and silver and turquoise jewelry, introduced David Banyacya, Hopi elder, and asked the assembly for silence.

Dwarfed by the podium, the small, wrinkled elder removed his steel-rimmed glasses, slowly threw pinches of corn meal in the six cardinal directions, replaced his glasses and sat back down.

"This elder has great knowledge of the ancient instruction," the

Speaker began in perfect English, but softly, in a slow, mesmeric cadence. "I would not fight in the last war, and I was six years in the Federal government's jail. Our very name, Hopi, means peace . . .

"There is a sacred stone tablet in Hopiland," the Speaker continued, holding up a piece of illustration board with a few crude lines and figures. "Carriages will run on the roads, the prophecies said. There will be roads in the sky, and we will be looking through cobwebs . . ."

Ralph Featherstone contemplated the floor, chewing gum.

"A hoard of ashes will fall, and there will be drought and great sickness. Then a man with the sun symbol will come, and our true white brother will be here for breakfast . . ."

Featherstone stopped chewing and looked up, then down again.

"Last September we met with the six nations of the Iroquois, who have suffered greatly," the Speaker said. "We have visited others, and they have visited us in Hopiland, and now the great circle of Indian people is closed. The Great Spirit gave us all of this land freely. We are the first inhabitants of this land, and we want all good people, all humble people to come to us . . .

"The Great Spirit is with us," the Speaker finished mildly, and sat down.

The applause was long, respectful, restrained.

"Thanks Brother Tijerina," said Maulana Ron Karenga in a startlingly shrill voice. "*Señores y señoras, con su permiso . . .*"

The reading was mechanical and the accent bad, but no words were mispronounced.

"*Somos juntos, somos hombres de color.* Our problems are not different from those of the Chinese, the Cubans. *Tenemos una misión nueva.* There is a new movement in the cities, and all people of color will fight. *Somos hombres, tenemos machismo.* Our enemy will not destroy us, we will destroy him. *La tierra es nuestra herencia y la justicia es nuestro credo.* We are of curious mystery and will build a new world. *¡Viva Tijerina! ¡Vivan los indios! ¡Vivan los hombres de color!*"

They cheered him heartily, appreciative of his effort, honored by inclusion in the new brotherhood of color, impressed by the menacing picture he made.

Ralph Featherstone sprang to the podium holding a red-and-yellow bumper sticker on high.

CHÉ IS ALIVE

And Hiding in Tierra Amarilla

The cheers were deafening. "All together now," he shouted, bringing them off their chairs with an upraised fist, punching it rhythmically ceilingward with each ringing shout. "*¡Po-der Negro! ¡Po-der Negro!*"

By the second enunciation they were chanting with him, all their weathered faces alight with the excitement of communal defiance; by the third, they too were punching the air with clenched fists. *"¡Po-der Negro!"*

As verb, *poder* means "to be able"; as noun, it means "power."

"Once again," Featherstone shouted. "Poh . . ." He faltered, turned hastily. The black girl leaned forward to refresh his memory; he nodded, turned back. *"¡Poder Negro! ¡Poder Negro! . . ."*

Six times. And then he told them: "We have a comon enemy. He is pale-skinned and blue-eyed and blonde, and he is a thief. He stole my ancestors from Africa and killed 100 million in the Middle Passage. He stole your ancestors' land and killed them with starvation wages. He took our music and put it in his wicked form. He raped your culture and robbed you of your language. We cannot allow this man to exist. We must take back what is owed us and what is ours by any means necessary. We can no longer promise nonviolence. I repeat, by any means necessary!"

They cheered, and heartily joined him, six times again, with clenched fists: *¡Poder Negro!*

From there on, it was all downhill to the King of the Indies. And yet, weary as they were, they greeted him with fond indulgence and a standing ovation. "Oh boy," cried a child. "Jerry's going to talk."

He beamed, receiving their acclamation with easy grace, rotund but regal in double-breasted gabardine, eyes blue, hair sparse but decidedly blonde. Ralph Featherstone folded his arms and looked away. The *Journal* reporter sent his photographer across the hall to get a picture of two self-invited convention observers, Patricia Bell and James Kennedy of the Communist party. Down in the second row Jerry's mother touched a hankie to glistening eyes.

"I would like to thank those who have respected my desire to remain incognito in the past," Jerry began. "However, I believe that these troubled times require that I declare myself. I am the King Emperor of the Indies, my dynastic name is Don Barne Quinto César, and I am ready to die for my people. It is part of being king. All in a day's work . . ."

As the last stragglers walked up the aisles at convention's end, a black girl in a vividly colored African robe paused to rest an arm gently across the shoulders of the youngest Martínez son, and a black man in dark glasses murmured, "I don't envy that boy, he's the one that's going to have to fight the Man."

Fernanda beamed proudly. "He's a good boy. It's his birthday next week."

"Yes, ma'am," murmured the black man. "It's a great fight, and we all in it together."

"Yes," said Fernanda with cheerful gusto. "We will get those honkies, Benny Naranjo and Alfonso Sánchez."

Violence 18

O
N November 7, court was convened in the Tierra Amarilla courthouse, with 15 armed officers stationed at strategic points throughout the building, half a dozen squad cars parked out front and as
many cruising the area. Eulogio Salazar was there, wearing his jailer's
badge, his jaw scarred with deep red welts. Benny Naranjo roamed
the halls in white denims and flopping holster. Upstairs in the courtroom,
Judge Scarborough, who had taken to wearing a Frontier Colt since
the raid, presided without robes. All who entered the building were
required to produce identification, and a number were thoroughly
searched. Of those searched, most joined the long line of welfare recipients waiting to receive their monthly allotment of food stamps. The
two cases on the court docket were minor, one a rape case, the other
a land suit. But it was the first time court had been convened since the
raid, five months before.

"No use taking any chances this time," said State Police Sergeant
A. S. Vega, keeping an eye out the repaired window of Benny Naranjo's
office. "But I don't think anything's going to happen."

"Oh, nothing's going to happen like that again," said pretty Dolores
Romero, indicating the State Policeman at the door of the assessor's
office. "They'll see to that."

The telephone was back on the wall inside the old wooden phone
booth; it was difficult to locate the neatly patched bullet holes in the
walls; the line of food stamp applicants crossed the exact spot where
Nick Sais had fallen, but there was no sign of blood on the scrubbed
floorboards.

Nonetheless, there was something more than the smell of sour ink,
mouldering paper and old woodwork in the steam-heated air. "Stay
where you are!" shouted Judge Scarborough as several spectators
casually rose to leave his courtroom. Calming himself with visible
effort, he murmured, "These precautions seem to be necessary," called
a recess and stomped to his chambers. The State Policeman guarding
the door wiped the perspiration from his brow and felt for the butt
of his gun.

Four hundred miles to the south in Las Cruces, 40 armed officers stood guard in and around another courthouse, where Reies and Cris Tijerina, Jerry Noll, Alfonso Chávez and Esequiel Domínguez were on trial on federal charges stemming from the Echo Amphitheatre trespass. Among the officers were seven deputy U.S. Marshals under the command of Emilio Naranjo, 20 Dona Ana County sheriff's deputies, an undetermined number of FBI agents, seven Las Cruces city detectives and at least two State Policemen, with more due to arrive when court closed in Tierra Amarilla.

Patsy Tijerina was there, wearing a bright green dress and alternately tugging at her long hair and chewing her fingernails. Félix Martínez was present, relishing his new role as *Alianza* public relations officer. But there was little of the usual earthy leavening of homely clothing and seasoned country faces. It was a long overnight drive and an even longer bus ride from Río Arriba.

Judge Howard C. Bratton questioned and selected the jurors, unchallenged by either prosecution or defense. Of the 12 finally chosen, four had Spanish surnames. Noting that four of the defendants also had Spanish surnames, Bratton asked each of the jurors if the fact would affect his verdict. They all said no. The judge then forbade smoking, photographing and gum chewing in the courtroom and ordered the jury kept under lock and key day and night, the first time a federal jury had been so sequestered in New Mexico in 30 years.

U.S. Attorney John Quinn, stout, sanguine and unruffled throughout, promised the jury that the prosecution would prove each of the defendants guilty on five counts of forcibly assaulting, resisting, opposing, impeding, intimidating and interfering with Forest Rangers Walter Taylor and Philip Smith, converting two government pickups to their own use and conspiring to do same.

Charles Driscoll, speaking for the four other defense attorneys, reminded the jury that up to 300 men, women and children had taken possession of the Echo Amphitheatre campground that day, but only five had been brought to the bar by the government. He promised to prove that one of the rangers had run for his truck, in which there had been a loaded pistol, and that prudent and timely intervention by the defendants had saved the ranger from serious damage at the hands of the crowd. Evidence would show, he said, that the trucks had not been touched by any of the defendants. He pointed out that federal agencies and their officers had been informed well in advance of the planned trespass, and he charged that those government agents had conspired to thwart *Alianza* plans to force a land case by allowing events to proceed just far enough to justify criminal charges.

He said that the background of events at Echo Amphitheatre went back a hundred years, that the *Hispanos* of Río Arriba felt that they had been deprived of their right to use ancestral lands and that Forest Service officials were responsible. "Right or wrong, that is the way they feel."

The first prosecution witness, Charles C. Doak, a government surveyor, was shown aerial and geological maps and the Echo Amphitheatre area was pointed out to him. He then identified documents, signed by Presidents Theodore Roosevelt, Woodrow Wilson and Warren G. Harding, proclaiming the area a national forest reserve.

"These documents do not prove that the forest is the property of the United States," objected defense attorney Driscoll.

The question was ruled immaterial to the criminal charges under consideration.

Reies Tijerina swiveled and reached across the bar to lift the heavy, leather-bound old book from Patsy's lap.

"Can you tell the jury of your personal knowledge how Carson National Forest became the property of the United States?" defense attorney Lorenzo Tapia demanded of the witness.

"No," Doak replied.

Reies thumbed furiously through the dusty pages, tugged at an attorney's sleeve, and stabbed a finger at the ancient print.

The question of ownership was immaterial, the court repeated.

Regional Forester William D. Hurst, a worried looking man upon whom public exposure appeared to weigh heavily, recalled refusing the *Alianza* letter proclaiming the Republic of San Joaquín de Chama and acknowledged that he had replied that "full resources" would be used to protect the campground.

Under relentless cross-examination by Driscoll, he denied that Secretary of Agriculture Orville Freeman had publicly chastized him in El Paso 10 days before. He also denied that during a confrontation with Reies Tijerina he had said that he didn't give a damn about the Treaty of Guadalupe Hidalgo. He said that all complaints about the Forestry Service had been refuted by the record and declared in a voice trembling with rueful indignation, "The relationship of our office with the Spanish-speaking people has been pleasant, productive and delightful."

"Why was Ranger Clinton Coe transferred to Arizona?" defense attorney Robert Poole demanded.

"We needed his talents over there on another forest . . ."

"Was it not true that he was found guilty of assaulting and battering José Martín in his office?"

"It's my understanding that, yes, he was."

"Was there a plan for handling the upcoming situation at Echo Amphitheatre, Mr. Hurst?"

"There was a consultation, yes. It was agreed not to force them to pay the entrance fee, but that if they impeded or molested the rangers, action would be taken."

Ranger Walter Taylor took the stand, tall in his heather-green uniform, and under the guidance of Assistant U.S. Attorney Jack Love, described running to his pickup "to lock my personal belongings inside." Cris Tijerina had then grabbed him, he said, they had exchanged words, and the crowd had closed in. "At that time, I thought I was a dead man."

"Were you aware that your superiors had ordered that no fire-arms were to be taken into the campground?" Driscoll asked.

"Yes, but I always carried my gun in the truck."

"When you used the word *primo* in your reply to Cris, what was your tone?"

"It wasn't condescending . . ."

"What do you mean by that?"

"I could have said *amigo*."

Forest Service Cris Zamora confirmed that he had been released after someone had shouted, "He's one of us," and that from across the highway he had clearly heard Reies Tijerina tell the crowd that Fidel Castro had guts.

There was a sudden piercing squeal of brakes outside the courthouse, and three officers shot to their feet. A city traffic crew was refreshing the white line down the center of the street.

For the defense, Professor Clark Knowlton spoke effusively of land grants, grazing permits, the decay of the villages and the forced migration to the cities while Reies teetered in his chair and cracked his knuckles one by one.

"Are you aware that some land claimants have gone through the courts?" Jack Love asked in cross-examination.

"Yes."

"Do you know how much money Tijerina has collected from these people he claims to represent?"

"No, I don't."

"Do you know what Reies Tijerina was doing before he came to New Mexico?"

"Objection."

"Overruled."

"Do you know," demanded Love, pointing to Jerry Noll, "that these people believe this defendant here to be Don Barne Quinto César, King of the Indies and all that?"

Knowlton grinned. Jerry tittered. U.S. District Court Judge Howard C. Bratton guffawed.

"Objection."

"Overruled."

A sudden influx of white-helmeted State Police signaled the arrival of a special defense witness. The governor took the stand, well-tailored, well-tonsured, smiling.

The land grant issue was symbolic of many grievances, he said. Although the Forest Service had been working hard in recent months to correct inequities, they had been negligent of the northern natives in the past. The people of the north tended to view all government with hostility, he said. "They are not violent by nature, they are very patient. But when they lose their water rights and grazing rights, they become bitter. They feel that no one cares, and they take it out on whoever is closest."

"I have a case study right at home," he took care to mention. "My wife is Spanish-American."

But the highlight of the trial was the prosecution's showing of two short films taken at the scene by television news cameramen. A screen was set up, Judge Bratton settled back, the jury strained forward, the lights went out and there it was in flickering black and white.

State Policemen leaned against patrol cars parked along the highway, while a white-haired old man in a VFW cap shook his fist at them from across the road. A caravan of cars and pickups swept into the Amphitheatre parking lot and their occupants spilled out: men, women and children. Reies Tijerina, wearing black-rimmed eyeglasses, gesticulated from the center of the crowd. Ranger Taylor lunged for the door of his truck, was clutched from behind by Cris Tijerina, was turned and was pushed hard enough to make him stagger back several steps. The crowd swirled, closing in, their faces excited. Teen-agers were laughing. Women shook their fists. The two rangers were half led, half pushed toward the camera. Esequiel Domínguez, recognizable by his rumpled salt-and-pepper hair, held Ranger Smith's arm on one side. On the other side, hawk-faced Alfonso Chávez, wearing a star-shaped dime store badge, hurried the ranger along. Baltazar Martínez grinned, wearing his beret. Reies Tijerina harangued the crowd from atop a truck, holding a big book overhead. A crude hand-painted sign read, "Republic of San Joaquín de Chama." A hand-sewed flag bearing the same legend flew from the trimmed shaft of a young pine. An old man sat watching a coffee pot over a smoking fire.

In his closing remarks, U.S. Attorney Quinn denied the defense charge of entrapment. "There was no attempt to break up the meeting. The defendants wouldn't be in court today if the officers hadn't been seized." And he added: "This is not a social problem we are trying today. This is a criminal problem."

In his final instructions, Judge Bratton reminded the jury, "We are not trying any land titles, like whether the Treaty of Guadalupe Hidalgo applies to the Echo Amphitheatre campground area. These are criminal charges."

Five days after the trial had begun, the jury retired. While they deliberated, U.S. Attorney Quinn filed a complaint of criminal contempt of court against Reies Tijerina for calling Judge Bratton a racial vampire and making other remarks in defiance of the court's gag order, and against Jerry Noll for similar statements also made during the *Alianza* convention in October.

The jury sent word that they could not reach a decision on the count of conspiracy, and Judge Bratton declared a mistrial on the charge. After more than eight hours of deliberation, the jury emerged to announce its verdict. Reies Tijerina was held to be guilty on two counts of assaulting Rangers Smith and Taylor, Cris Tijerina on one count of assaulting Taylor, Esequiel Domínguez on one count of assaulting

Smith, and Jerry Noll and Alfonso Chávez on four counts each, two of assault and two of converting government pickup trucks to private use. Each count carried a maximum penalty of three years in prison and a $5,000 fine.

(Sentencing would not take place until mid-December. Reies would be given a two-year prison sentence, with the provision that he be eligible for parole at any time. Judge Bratton would mete the heaviest sentence out to Jerry Noll, because of previous convictions in Seattle: three years in the penitentiary. Cristóbal would receive six months in custody on a two-year term. Esequiel Domínguez and Alfonso Chávez would each receive two-year sentences with all but 60 days suspended.)

With defense immediately announced its intention to appeal the convictions. The mistrial on the conspiracy count was "a major victory, just like getting an acquittal," Félix Martínez announced, claiming to speak for defense attorneys.

But Reies was clearly disgruntled by the outcome.

"The defense was bad," he grumbled, and then announced to incredulous reporters: "If it's tried again, I'm going to direct it."

The government appeared to be satisfied with the outcome. "I consider this a victory," said U.S. Attorney Quinn. And, although there were many who might have wished for an even more emphatic victory, an almost audible sigh of relief swept through certain segments to the population. At last the land grant rebels and their noisy leader had been legally chastized and would be duly punished. Many who had felt constrained to withhold judgment now felt free to pass it.

An old political equation was at work: the further from the center, the thinner the ice. Reies had already lost most of the Anglo liberals with his clumsy but forthright assault at St. Johns. ("Self-proclaimed angels," he would later call them, drawing his curious metaphor from inaccurate interpretation of the Latin "Angles" with which Julius Caesar had described the blond barbarians on his northern borders.)

By far the majority of the *Hispano* middle class had long been suspicious of him as a threat to their hard-won status. This intraracial hostility had been given typical expression in a speech made by state legislator Ed Delgado to the Santa Fe Lions Club in September. Entitled, "How to Get Real Estate Without Really Trying," the speech had scoffed at *Alianza* land claims and implied strongly that they were fraudulent in intent.

The *Hispano* moderate elite of the Southwest had also become increasingly uneasy with the unrestrained nature of Reies' relationship with, first, the new *Hispano* militants, then with the militant blacks. He had further alienated them by joining the new *Hispano* left in its denunciation and boycott of the President's Mexican-American Affairs Conference, held in El Paso at the end of October.

Many high-ranking *Hispano* professionals had gone to El Paso as delegates and speakers, hoping to persuade the government to help in various ways, hopeful that events in New Mexico had appreciably improved their chances. They had seen their expectations given encouragement in Vice President Hubert Humphrey's unprecedented and effusive acknowledgement that, "The Mexican-American suffers historic injustices because his forefathers were driven from their Spanish and Mexican land grants. Yet most of these same people have been American citizens for generations—many of them since well before the Humphreys arrived from Scotland"; only to have the promising moment soured by the presence outside the conference hall of Reies Tijerina and 20 pickets from Burt Corona's MAPA and the Political Association of Spanish Organizations (PASO) bearing signs with such nonnegotiable declarations as: "Today We Demonstrate, Tomorrow We Revolt."

Reies was even losing appreciable numbers of adherents from among the hard-core *Hispano* poor. At no time during the convention in October had there been more than 500 people in the auditorium; total attendance had been around 800, including out-of-staters. More than three times that number had attended the last *Alianza* convention the previous fall, before the raid.

Although there were a variety of causes for such defection and disaffection, there was one central point upon which most opinion turned against Tijerina. It was not so much that he had disturbed the civil peace as it was that in doing so he had resorted to physical violence. The citation of violence alone of course often concealed other, more essential objections, based on fear for vested power and property interests, impatience with unconventional ideas and behavior and resentment over the *Alianza*'s racial audacity and virtual rejection of patriotism.

But the fear and fascination of violence was at the center of both emotional and rational condemnation. "Nine-tenths of mankind are more afraid of violence than anything else," someone once said, but that was a hundred years ago. Violence, in New Mexico and in the United States at large, was clearly on the increase, and with it, a general malaise of reaction which reflected a normal fear, but also a kind of perverse and fatal love.

Ten months before, the Secret Service had informed President Johnson that they could not guarantee his safety anywhere outside the White House, and since then, the President had confined his public appearances to heavily guarded press conferences and visits to military installations. Gun sales had increased as much as ten-fold in cities, large and small. Police departments across the country were instituting riot control training programs and purchasing large quantities of the new weaponry, including armored cars. Several metropolitan police departments had already created elite forces of the sort formerly found in more totalitarian countries. Beginning in September, less than three months after the raid, the New Mexico National Guard had begun special training in riot control. Across-the-counter gun sales in New Mexico had nearly doubled in the months following the raid. It almost seemed as though the country was preparing to wage war upon itself.

Accompanying such elaborate "precautionary measures" against civil overthrow was a continuation of direct action against selected scapegoats, in the country at large as well as in New Mexico.

On December 11, the U.S. Congress approved a drastically cut extension of the poverty bill, with the Green amendment firmly attached. During the same session, the Senate saw to it that open housing legislation and a bill to protect black ghetto businessmen were severely weakened. Sargent Shriver, national head of the OEO, indicated his impending resignation, telling the press that the emasculated poverty program would be "a delusion of the poor—a deception of the general public—a fraud." Shortly thereafter, Secretary of Health, Education and Welfare John W. Gardner, resigned his cabinet post with the grim observation: "We are in deep trouble as a people."

The next day in New Mexico, State Attorney General Boston Witt's long-awaited report appeared, charging the OEO in general and Robert García in particular with aiding and abetting Tijerina and his *Alianza* and approving and fostering civil violence. The report, submitted to the state Legislative Finance Committee and immediately released to the press, was some 15 inches thick, its first part a plethora of innuendo and sweeping allegation, the remainder a bulgy collection of newspaper clippings, letters, travel vouchers and other papers supposed to document and prove the charges.

Meticulously outlining events involving the OEO, the Socio-Economic Studies Foundation and Burgos and Aragon in the attempt to contact Tijerina following the raid, the report then charged that OEO officials had acted "at exact cross-purposes with law enforcement officials. Not by inadvertence, but by purpose."

But the charge was not substantiated. No proof was offered of effect or intention on the part of the accused parties to interfere with law enforcement efforts.

Going after García, the report questioned "his dedication, ability and competence . . . to serve as director of the state Office of Economic Opportunity, or, for that matter, any other position of public trust in New Mexico." This broad and slanderous statement was supported by no proof beyond the fact that García had been involved in the attempts to reach and mollify Tijerina.

The report further charged that "García's whole posture in the matter of the violence of the *Alianza Federal de Mercedes* has been one of excuse and justification. Far from advocating obedience to law and order he seems to advocate accomplishments of goals, even by violation of law, if necessary." García's suggestion before the Resnick Committee that the raid had been symptomatic of deep-seated social ills and therefore symbolic was taken as evidence of his alleged approval of *Alianza* violence. The only other documentation for the charge was a photostat of the entirely erroneous Albuquerque *Journal* news item which had incorrectly quoted García as having advocated "circumventing the law" during a speech at Los Alamos, when he had actually said just the opposite.

Inept as the report was, it nonetheless had its effect, both on the general public, thanks to the press, and within the structure of state government. The day after its release, the *Journal* called for García's immediate resignation or dismissal. Asked to comment on the report, Governor Cargo sidestepped questions regarding his own office's involvement in the affair by calling for a U.S. Justice Department investigation. "If Witt's charges are true, then they had better get on it."

Cargo had already transferred the state OEO office, placing it under the State Planning Office, headed by Arthur Ortiz. The move had been made in anticipation of Congressional transfer of control of poverty funds to the state, but it had also placed García in subordination to Ortiz. Asked by newsmen if he would ask for García's resignation, Cargo replied impatiently that "It's Ortiz' department now."

That afternoon, García appeared before the Legislative Finance Committee and testified that Larry Prentice of the governor's office had approved the hiring of Burgos and Aragon, and that Lieutenant Governor E. Lee Francis had approved the use of the state airplane to bring Dr. Clark Knowlton to New Mexico. Francis flatly denied having approved use of the plane, although there were, and are, witnesses to the fact that he told OEO officials to go ahead.

The next day, Arthur Ortiz declined to say whether or not he planned to fire García, pointing out that most of the material in the Witt Report was not pertinent to the state OEO operation. He did say that he thought Witt was incorrect in charging that the use of state funds to bring Knowlton in had been illegal, since one of the functions of the state OEO was "to further lines of communication in every way possible." He would, he said, wait for the results of an audit of OEO finances before making a decision.

On January 12, Ortiz announced that following consultation with the governor, it had been decided to demote Robert García to a regional position with the state OEO office. On January 29, the audit of OEO finances was released to the press. While generally critical of the handling of OEO finances under García, the audit questioned only a few expenditures, totaling around $3,000 and including the cost of Knowlton's controversial flight: $157.50. The Witt Report had cost the state a minimum of $8,400. The audit had cost an additional $1,000. As the state legislature prepared to go into session January 24, a number of legislators together with the Legislative Finance Committee were prepared to reduce the state OEO budget to $1. On January 27, however, Robert García failed to show up for work at the OEO office, giving Arthur Ortiz the opportunity to fire him for being absent without leave.

Two days later, the legislature appropriated $15,000 for an emasculated state OEO program, with which the state hoped to join others in cannibalizing what was left of Federal War on Poverty funds.

Two weeks later, Robert García announced that he had married a 27-year-old California divorcee. Church spokesmen made it clear that the marriage meant that García would be automatically excommunicated and would no longer be a priest. "I still consider myself a priest," García told newsmen. "I personally do not believe that one can be excommunicated from the Christian community for an honorable thing like marriage."

Although he declined to talk about the OEO, he did say that he would remain in New Mexico. His plans were still indefinite, but he would continue to work in the "social action field."

One could not help wondering if this "controversial priest" did not feel a certain secret bitterness of his own over the fact that, unlike his predecessor, Padre Martínez of Taos, he had not had any actual part in insurrection, but only stood accused by implication, to suffer the consequences without having had the pleasure of full commitment. On the other hand, he made it clear to reporters that he was not through yet. He would not "go into hiding," he said. He would, he promised, "stand and fight."

The day after the release of the Witt Report, quite as if by pre-arrangement, Senator "Little Joe" Montoya broke his long silence with an all-out attack on Reies Tijerina, calling him "a damned liar, an enemy of the United States, an exploiter, discredited charlatan, imposter, racist and creature of darkness."

"When he claims an alliance with the Black Muslims, that's probably where he belongs," the Senator said, "but he's not going to take the Spanish people of New Mexico with him. . . . We do not lie down in the gutter with Ron Karengas, Stokely Carmichaels and Rap Browns who seek to put another wound in America's body."

Tijerina had met the year before with a Communist in Mexico City, Montoya charged. He had asked a man named Toledano to support his proposed poor people's march to Mexico City. What was more, the Senator added, as proof of Tijerina's allegiance to International Communism, "The Justice Department has a file on him."

(Boston Witt's preliminary report had made little reference to Communist influence on either the OEO or Tijerina, beyond noting that one Craig Vincent, known for strong leftist leanings, was associated with the CAP program in Taos and was "controversial." Witt had indicated that a follow-up report would have much more to say on the subject, but that it was being held back pending trial of the raiders. However, informed sources indicated that the attorney general's investigators had been able to come up with no more concrete evidence of Tijerina's alleged Communist affiliations than they had of illegal activities within the OEO.)

Tijerina was through, Senator Montoya announced. "I would stake my reputation that 99 percent of the Spanish people in New Mexico hate Tijerina and what he stands for—self-interest, words without action, violence."

The careful timing and unstinting vehemence of the Senator's attack belied his pretended confidence and indicated that he was acutely aware that he was doing just what he said he was, staking his political career on the efficacy, if not the absolute truth, of his charges. For Little Joe would be up for reelection in 1970, and he was staking his future against odds which were, perhaps, not nearly so good as he hoped them to be.

The Albuquerque *Journal*, however, hailed the Senator's strong language as "belated but welcome." "It is hoped Montoya's statements will help defuse Tijerina's efforts to set race against race," the newspaper said.

Reies Tijerina replied with equal vehemence, calling the Senator a "Judas to his people," and took particular care to refute Montoya's charge that he had been bilking *Alianza* members of their money. Outlining *Alianza* assets and expenses in detail, he concluded with the reminder that a few months before, the U.S. Internal Revenue Service had received a thorough accounting of *Alianza* finances and had found nothing whatsoever amiss.

That same day, 25-year-old Gerónimo Borunda, *El Indio*, was arraigned in Española on raid charges, including first-degree kidnapping. Asked if any more arrests were expected, Detective Freddy Martínez replied from behind his dark glasses, "No, that's the last one."

In the meantime, the reaction continued to accelerate, at times rising to unprecedented heights of absurdity. The October issue of the University of New Mexico's humor magazine, *The Juggler*, had carried this facetious news item:

> "TIERRA AMARILLA, N.M.—A $2 billion dollar electrical detection fence is currently under construction in New Mexico in a Defense Department attempt to curb the infiltration of NLF (National Landgrant Followers) members from the grazing lands of northern New Mexico across the DMZ (Damn Mexican Zone) to U.S. Forest Land in the central part of the state."

A week after the magazine's appearance, university authorities responded to a noisy storm of protest by suspending publication of the magazine and reprimanding its editors.

The same state legislature which had contemplated reducing the OEO budget to $1, had failed to enact any effective property reappraisal, income tax or education legislation and had made drastic cuts in the state's welfare budget, while at the same time spending a good four days of its short session debating a motion to bar Stokely Carmichael from appearing on the University of New Mexico campus, his fee to be paid from student funds.

It was another black militant, H. Rap Brown, who had made perhaps the most astute comment of all on the ruling majority's concern for "law and order." "Violence," he had said, "is as American as cherry pie."

In the Southwest and New Mexico, an appropriate substitute for the cherry pie of the aphorism would be hot chile, which was neither originally, nor is exclusively, an *Hispano* delicacy.

"Well now, no, I never killed a man that I know of," Bill Mundy allows with a touch of modest regret. "But I remember once down in Hatch we had this old fella was a little crazy and had terrorized a few people with a shotgun, and he had said he was going to shoot my cows, one sets foot on his land. Well, I'm going along one day, I happened to be on foot myself, but had some of my boys on horseback, and we come down along this fella's land, and there he is, waving that shotgun and cussin' and saying he's gonna shoot my cows. 'Well,' I says, 'I'm going to see about that.' I'm riled, mad as hell, and so I just start walking straight toward him, and he starts to cuss and jump around and wave that gun, and I point to my ear and say, 'Can't hear you, George, got a stick in my ear here,' and pretty soon I'm close enough and I go for that gun. Kicked him in the belly and grabbed it, all in one motion, and then, of course, it was all my way. Whaled the hell out of him pretty good and with the barrel, and pretty soon he got to worrying, thinking it was all over for him, and begging, and said his wife sent him out there with the shotgun. So I got him up and turned him around and said, 'If your wife wants her shotgun, you tell her to come and get it,' and I reached out as he was a-goin' away and gave him about three hoists with the barrel right back there, and my God almighty, it wasn't until just then I realized that the damn thing was cocked and had been all the time. . . ."

"Emilio Naranjo's father, he was the first one of the family to be sheriff, when I was a little girl," says Fernanda Martínez. "He had arrest this boy's father, I don't remember what for, and sent him to the penitentiary. So one night some time later the boy, who was 12 years old, wait for the sheriff to come out of the bar, and from the bushes he shoot him, this 12-year-old boy, and nearly kill him too. . . ."

On January 3, just a month before the scheduled preliminary hearing for the raid defendants, jailer Eulogio Salazar, the principal state witness against Reies Tijerina, was found dead in his car on the snow-covered slope below a back road a few miles west of Tierra Amarilla. He had been beaten to death. Within hours after the discovery of the body, Félix Martínez and Cristóbal Tijerina had been arrested and charged as accessories to the murder. Governor Cargo charged that the murder was "terrorism," and demanded that the district attorney revoke the bonds of all *Alianza* members charged in connection with the raid.

"This is the worst goddamn beating I've seen in 30 years as a police officer," bellowed Chief Joe Black. "Even if he was only a jailer, he was a fellow officer and a friend. We'll get the sons of bitches if it's the last thing we do!"

Sigmund Freud, among others, pointed out that whether violence is the result of the action of an individual or minority, as in criminal assault, rebellion or murder, or of the will of the community, as in the whipping post, public prison or capital punishment, it is still violence.

And violence is as American as cherry pie and as New Mexican as hot chile and cholla whips, *Penitentes* and *corridas de gallina*—as American, in fact, as the long-lost frontier, as New Mexican as the forgotten wilds of Río Arriba.

Omerta 19

Back in 1926, about the time that Emilio González was field *honcho* for the *Mano Negra* in Río Arriba, Santa Fe detective Bill Martin heard that the body of a boy named Valdez had been found near Canjilón several weeks before. According to Martin's informant, village elders had held an inquest without sending word to the courthouse at Tierra Amarilla, had announced that the boy had frozen to death and had hastily buried him. It so happened, however, that the weather had been quite balmy that week. Detective Martin rode north and had the body dug up. It was riddled with bullets; seven of them.

Ballistics evidence led the detective to a man named Vargas, who was eventually tried in Santa Fe and did some time in the penitentiary. The motive was assumed to have been robbery, although only a small amount of money had been taken from the boy's pockets. Martin preferred not to speculate as to why the villagers had attempted to conceal the affair. Perhaps his years of poking around Río Arriba with his fingerprint kit had given him sufficient wit not to attempt to apply the principles of scientific investigation to the social psychology of the northerners.

Forty years later, things had changed in Río Arriba, but not nearly so much as might have been expected. There was a strong suggestion of dark and archaic mystery behind the murder of Eulogio Salazar, despite the fact that in the beginning there seemed to be no doubt in the minds of the authorities, the press and most of the public as to who had murdered Eulogio and why.

Shortly after the body was found, Detective Lieutenant Freddy Martínez told reporters, "We would be the most surprised people in the world if *Alianza* people were not involved in Salazar's murder."

When asked by reporters whether *Alianza* members were responsible for Salazar's death, Alfonso Sánchez replied, "Of course, who else?"

While briefing his officers shortly after discovery of the body, Chief Black said, "Your prime target is Reies Tijerina. Salazar was the key witness against him. Tijerina is bound to be tied into it somewhere."

Headlines revealed an equal willingness on the part of the press to tie the murder directly to the raid defendants: "KEY FIGURE IN JUNE 5 RAID IS FOUND MURDERED: KEY TIERRA AMARILLA RAID WITNESS FOUND DEAD: SLAIN JAILER WOULD HAVE HAD LARGE PART IN THE TRIAL OF REIES TIJERINA . . ."

Governor Cargo, visibly shocked and angry, said, "This is nothing more or less than brutal murder, terrorism. We're not going to tolerate this sort of thing." A lawyer, he was careful to say of *Alianza* members, "I'm not sure if they had anything to do with this." However, he left little doubt that he felt that "a large group of men" rather than one or two individuals had done the deed. "The people that killed him are most certainly going to pay for it."

Police action was swift. Félix Martínez and Cristóbal Tijerina had been served breakfast by Fernanda at the Martínez house that morning, then had driven in the *Alianza* pickup up Tierra Amarilla's main street to the courthouse, arriving there about 15 minutes after discovery of the body. Félix asked in the sheriff's office about his unemployment check, and was told to pick it up in Chama.

"They were acting fishy," he said later, "but they didn't say anything about Eulogio."

He and Cris then drove to Chama, where Félix was told he would have to get his check in Dulce, near Tierra Amarilla. Heading back about noon, they were intercepted outside Tierra Amarilla by State Policemen Carlos Jaramillo and Tom Holder and held in a squad car for several hours while the officers waited for arrest warrants to arrive from the district attorney's office.

Félix says that Jaramillo's first question was, "Why did you kill Eulogio?"

"Then he said that they were going to do the same thing to us that happened to Salazar. They were going to pistol-whip us and then shoot us down like dogs. They just kept driving around. They didn't want the people up there to see that they had us. I guess they were afraid there might be another raid on the courthouse if they took us there."

They were taken to the courthouse late in the afternoon, and while a half dozen officers armed with shotguns stood guard inside and outside the building, they were arraigned before the justice of the peace and charged as material witnesses to murder, their bonds set at $10,000.

Already that morning, the governor had requested the district attorney's office to secure revocation of the bonds of all the courthouse defendants. Alfonso Sánchez had headed north immediately and was there in time to climb the 10 yards down the snow-covered slope to Eulogio Salazar's car and look in on the battered body of the jailer.

Eulogio Salazar had planned to attend a wake for a dead friend the night before. After eating dinner at home, he had stopped by the courthouse, where county employes were working late on year-end business. Night jailer Ernesto Samora helped him start his car and watched him drive off alone. There were no other cars moving, and the bars were closed. A few minutes later, around 8:15, Casilda Salazar stood at the window of the small Salazar home and saw her husband's car drive up to the front gate, only 120 feet away across the frozen yard. Eulogio got out of the car and stood in the headlights to open the gate; she recognized him. She went into the bedroom to get ready to attend the rosary services for the deceased friend. But her daughter called to her from the front window that the car was backing away from the gate.

Thinking that her husband was probably going to check the cattle or was turning the car around to face the highway, Mrs. Salazar returned to the window in time to see the car back all the way down the road and around a neighbor's house, then move off down the highway toward the village. She presumed that her husband had gone back to the courthouse. When he had still not returned after several hours, she decided that he was spending the night with his brother Tito, whose bar in Tierra Amarilla had been burglarized the night before. She went to bed. The next morning around 7:30, she started down the road to her babysitting job at a nearby trailer park and, at the front gate, discovered a large bloodstain in the snow and her husband's white cowboy hat lying nearby. She ran to the house and called Deputy Sheriff Dan Rivera and told him, "I'm afraid something has happened to Eulogio, there is blood all over."

Three hours later, cattle inspector Larry Turner, traveling the paved road to El Vado lake just west of Tierra Amarilla, spotted a car off the road and stopped to investigate. A few minutes later he flagged down State Patrolman Tom Holder, the same who would shortly pick up Félix Martínez and Cris Tijerina, and told him what he had found.

The car had apparently been stopped at the top of a gently sloping curve. There was a bloodstain at the edge of the blacktop. The car had then rolled down the slope and gone off the road, to come to rest upright and with only minor damage some 20 yards down off the highway. The body was lying on the floorboard of the front seat with the head up against the steering column. There were signs of a terrible struggle. Ceiling fabric had been clawed away over the back seat and the dome light was broken; the upholstery was saturated with blood; the face of the body was literally unrecognizable.

"I told them," District Attorney Alfonso Sánchez was heard to softly lament. "I told Judge Angel this would happen if he let them out on bond. I predicted this. . . ."

He was sped in a State Police patrol car the long way south again to Las Vegas to secure revocation of bonds from Judge Joe Angel, while a police wrecker dragged the car back up onto the highway and the body was removed.

On the basis of the expected warrants, State Police and sheriff's deputies began in midafternoon to round up the raid defendants, a number of whom had to be trundled around in squad cars until word came through that the arrests could officially begin. Tony and Juan Valdez, Moisés Morales and Salomon Velásquez were picked up in Canjilón.

José Madril, Gerónimo Borunda and Tobías Leyba were arrested in Española. Esequiel and Víctor Domínguez and Cirilio García were picked up in Bernalillo. Abelicio Moya and old Baltazar Apodaca were located near Canjilón.

Interviewed at *Alianza* headquarters in Albuquerque shortly before 4 P.M., Reies Tijerina said that he was "shocked and deeply disturbed."

"This is serious business, this is bad," he said. "I can't believe in my heart that members of the *Alianza* were involved. We don't have that kind of people. They might go for popular action, but not lowdown cold-blooded murder, which is the way this looks. I am praying that this is a well-financed and organized move by some people who are against my cause, because it jeopardizes my cause and my image . . ."

The interview was cut short by the arrival of State Police and Bernalillo County sheriff's officers. Reies, his daughter Rose and Jerry Noll were arrested and taken to the city jail to be booked, then driven to Santa Fe. By 6:10, when word came through that Judge Angel had signed the warrants revoking the bonds, nearly all the raid defendants were in police custody. By 9 P.M., when District Attorney Alfonso Sánchez arrived back in Santa Fe with the warrants, most had been transferred to the Santa Fe jail. By 10:30, eighteen of the twenty-one had been booked, leaving only Reies Tijerina, Jr., Ramón Tijerina and Baltazar Martínez, all three of whom would be located shortly.

The governor's office, the district attorney, the State Police and the sheriff's office had acted in concert and with dispatch, prompting *Journal* reporter Wayne Scott to note with satisfaction that a "rare unity" had been inspired by the murder. "No one raised a hullabaloo about 'civil rights.' No one sent out of the state for an 'expert on Spanish-American affairs' to 'try to prevent more violence.' No one said a word about how Spanish-Americans have been downtrodden. . . ."

What he said was true. It so happened, however, that not one of those taken into custody would be indicted for the crime which had prompted the arrests. Even as the jail door was closing on the last of the 18, political reporter Carrol Cagle of the *New Mexican* was writing that he and fellow reporter Jim Neal had seen Cristóbal Tijerina and Féliz Martínez at separate places and different times on the night of the murder. Neil had seen the two leave a Santa Fe restaurant shortly before 8 P.M. Cagle had seen and talked with them at a Democrats for McCarthy rally in Santa Fe shortly after 9 P.M. Eulogio Salazar had last been seen by his wife around 8:15. The autopsy would establish that he died between 8:15 and 8:30. It is at least an hour and a half's drive at top speed from Santa Fe to Tierra Amarilla. A disappointed Alfonso Sánchez accepted sworn affidavits from the two reporters and, on January 5, dropped the murder charges against Félix Martínez and Cris Tijerina.

The rest of those arrested would eventually prove to have equally convincing alibis, as would Ramón Tijerina, Reies, Jr., and Baltazar Martínez, the last of whom had been topping beets in Arizona at the time of the murder. Anselmo Tijerina, who had been in the Taos area for several months following an apparent falling out with Reies, would also be able to account for himself the night of the murder. Others, such as Corky González, picked up in Taos five days after the murder on a charge of driving without a valid license, would prove to have equally effective alibis.

In the north the day after the arrests, Chief Black warned his force of some 17 State Police officers and sheriff's deputies that many of the weapons confiscated during the raid had not yet been recovered. Investigating officers were to move always in pairs, he told them. "Check every bar, check every home. Put all your efforts into this. We'll get the people that did this if it's the last thing we do."

Once again, the mountain villages were searched one by one, the officers approaching certain doors, as always, cautiously, often with guns at the ready.

"They didn't bother to come here," says Fernanda Martínez. "But they went to my daughter's house. Her husband was working at the penitentiary, and they scared her, she's so skinny and nervous and doesn't have milk to feed that baby. They came again when she wasn't there, and her husband found the dog dead. I guess those cops they shot the dog to get into the house, or maybe because they were just so mad about what had happened to Eulogio. . . ."

There were others certainly as angry as the police. Eulogio Salazar's three brothers had been living outside the community for years, two in Denver, one in Los Alamos. It was rumored that one brother was already on the scene in Tierra Amarilla and another expected. There was the smell of vendetta on the winter wind. Whether it was new or the revival of an old blood feud, nobody who knew was likely to say. For another archaic social mechanism was imposing its dark discipline upon the inhabitants of Río Arriba: *omerta*. It means "code of silence," and it is identical to the Sicilian word of the same usage.

By the second day of the investigation it was clear that things were not going well for the police, although they were as yet reluctant to admit it. Their only hard clues were a fragment of broken pistol-grip found near the Salazar front gate and, possibly, fingerprints lifted from the death car. Search of certain houses had failed to turn up anything else. But it was the quiet recalcitrance of the natives that first alerted investigating officers to the likelihood that the case was not going to be so easy to solve as they had hoped.

The pall of communal silence had descended upon Tierra Amarilla immediately after the discovery of the body and had thickened with every passing day. "I heard about the murder on the radio," said Arthur Esquibel, principal of Tierra Amarilla's high school. "I went out and told the girls in the office. There was no talk, none at all, it was so quiet you couldn't hear a thing. Then I walked out into the hall. Some of the janitors were there. They shook their heads, and there was no conversation among them."

"Guess people aren't saying much at all," a store owner told the visitor, thereafter refusing to say anything at all.

Asked how villagers were reacting to the murder, a man replied, "Something like this is not taken lightly," and walked away.

"Your best friend might be your worst enemy," explained a young woman. "You never know who is listening, who is on which side, who might be next."

A man who had driven over the El Vado road shortly after the time of the murder but had seen nothing refused to give his name, because, he said, "Whoever did it might not believe that I didn't see anything."

There were at least eight uniformed officers and four plainclothesmen equipped with a portable lie detector engaged in finding and questioning possible suspects and witnesses. After four days, they had interviewed close to a hundred persons and had discovered nothing of positive value. By that time, Chief Black was ready to admit that there were as yet no substantial clues to the identity of the killers. The next day, more than a hundred persons crowded in and around Tierra Amarilla's tiny Roman Catholic church for the burial services with Governor Cargo among them. "Beware, vengeance is God's!" thundered the Reverend Father Pacien Mayers, while honorary pallbearers Emilio and Benny Naranjo, Undersheriff Dan Rivera, Deputy Pete Jaramillo and gathered members of the dead man's family looked grimly on and Casilda wept over the casket. After the mass, the body of Eulogio Salazar, World War II veteran and father of four, was taken to the snow-covered cemetery north of Tierra Amarilla and lowered into the frozen ground by, among others, Lee Woods, an old friend with a wooden leg. Then, three rifle volleys were fired into the leaden sky.

After the funeral, Benny Naranjo echoed Chief Black's statement of the day before, admitting to reporters that the investigation was bogged down. The following day, District Judge Joe Angel issued a gag order prohibiting all parties "from the governor on down to the sheriff's office and the state police" from making public statements regarding the murder and investigation. *Omerta* was thus made official and the circle of silence was closed. Which was convenient for the police, since there was a variety of curious facts which Chief Black and Sheriff Naranjo were not telling the press anyway.

Among them was the fact that possibly on January 3, the day of the discovery of the body, but more likely two days later on the 5th, a mysterious stranger had arrived in Río Arriba and begun to ask questions. Six-foot-three, weighing 215 pounds, round-faced and black-haired, he had been armed with a .357 Magnum pistol and accompanied by a large Alsatian police dog. Passing himself off as an FBI agent, he had spent over an hour talking with the widow Salazar before she had become suspicious of him and phoned the sheriff's office. Benny Naranjo had arrived in a hurry and closeted himself with the stranger for an hour, following which the two men had left the Salazar home accompanied by Detective Lieutenant Freddy Martínez, of the ever-present sunglasses.

The stranger was not seen again in Río Arriba. It was rumored variously that his dog had been shot, that he had been beaten up, that he was in jail somewhere in the state. Actually, by midnight on the 5th, he was in Providence Memorial Hospital in El Paso. Although he had checked in ostensibly for treatment of bleeding ulcers, he seemed inordinately anxious not to be seen and referred all phone calls to his lawyer, who would say only that his client was Charles Howard Ward, private investigator.

El Paso police were more informative. Charlie Ward had once been one of them, but had been discharged for "medical reasons." He had recently been convicted on a concealed weapons charge, was awaiting trial on a bad check charge, was rumored to have long been involved in activities of doubtful legality along the border and was considered by some to be "plenty tough and just a little nutty."

While word of Charlie Ward and other unpublished curiosities hummed along the *Hispano* grapevine behind the stubborn veil of *omerta*, the 21 raid defendants waited in the penitentiary for the State Supreme Court to consider their show cause order protesting revocation of their bonds. The court took the matter up on January 9 and seven days later agreed that bonds should be restored to 16 of the defendants, who were then released, after contributing yet another two weeks of their lives to profitless confinement at the hands of nervous justice.

Revocation of bond was upheld against four of the defendants on the grounds that "proof was evident and presumption great" that they had committed capital offenses, namely, the kidnapping and assaults charged in Alfonso Sánchez's raid indictments. Reies Tijerina, Tobías Leyba, Juan Valdez and Baltazar Apodaca remained in the penitentiary to await the preliminary hearing on the raid charges, less than two weeks away.

In the north, meanwhile, the police team had dwindled to a dozen uniformed officers, assigned to cruise the area 24 hours a day. Actual investigative work was now limited to three plainclothesmen, including Freddy Martínez.

Questioned by reporters, the detectives would say only that they had come across nothing new. It was not entirely true. A plaster cast had been made of a footprint. Certain suspects, including one of the victim's pallbearers, had been questioned at length, and one appeared to have fled the state. There had been an intensive search for a second automobile reported to have been driven by the killers. And there were other indications of various and sometimes peculiar action on the part of both the police and certain residents. But when they were pressed for investigative details, the officers found it convenient to cite Judge Angel's gag order banning discussion of the case.

Residents remained equally reluctant to discuss the murder with strangers or reporters and were painstakingly selective in discussing it with other members of the community. For there were many reasons for people to fear for their safety. Contentions and jealousies, old and new, seethed both within the police structure and within the *Alianza*, as well as within communities and even families. And yet the overall effect was unanimous and virtually absolute: *omerta*, communal silence.

By January 26, the gag order had been in effect two weeks; it had been 24 days since Eulogio Salazar's death and no arrests had been made. State Police broke their silence briefly to announce a plan for guaranteeing the anonymity and safety of informants. "Somewhere, someone knows who committed this murder," said Major Hoover Wimberly. "They can give us the key to its solution."

"We expect people to start contacting us soon," said Captain T. J. Chávez.

"This is our best friend right here," said another officer, patting the telephone at his elbow.

But apparently nobody called and no letters came with numbered corners torn off as suggested, for there were no arrests. "People are still somewhat afraid," said the priest, Father Mayers. And he added that he understood from his parishioners that many residents still felt that the *Alianza* had one way or another been responsible for Eulogio Salazar's death.

That opinion was still virtually unanimous in law enforcement circles and was shared by a majority of *Hispanos* and most Anglos. The fact that the entire *Alianza* leadership and hardcore membership were singularly well equipped with alibis only inspired speculation that the organization had hired outside professional killers to do the job for them. Invariably, arguments in support of the contention were based on the fact that Eulogio Salazar had been the only witness able to testify that he had not only seen Reies Tijerina in the courthouse during the raid and had seen him armed, but had actually been shot by him. It was pointed out that Salazar's only official testimony to that effect had been made at a bond hearing and was not thought likely to be admitted as evidence for the actual trial. Clearly, the argument ran, Tijerina had reasoned that by eliminating Salazar he could eliminate the most damning evidence against him. What was more, Salazar, together with Nick Sais, had filed a $1.5-million damage suit against the raiders and Reies Tijerina in particular. Dead men do not tell tales, nor do they sue.

On Monday, January 29, in Santa Fe, Judge Joe Angel began a preliminary hearing to determine whether there was sufficient cause to bring the raid defendants to trial. Once again, country clothing mingled with the Prussian blue and black of State Police uniforms under the arched portals of the county courthouse, while police motorcycles steadily circled the block. Inside, sheriff's deputies in tight pants and gunbelts enviously examined the M-16 rifle carried by a State Policeman, who told them regretfully that it was not the super M-16 in use in Vietnam; its clip held only 20 rounds.

All who entered were asked for identification, required to sign a register and searched thoroughly. Of the 150 or so spectators that daily crowded the high-ceilinged courtroom, most were dark of face and weathered, many in work clothes and boots, all watched warily by plainclothesmen positioned along the walls.

The defendants occupied the jury box and were for the most part relaxed, frequently amused and openly uncontrite. Of the 20 (Colorado juvenile authorities still refused to send Danny Tijerina), six wore ties, the rest were in casual or work clothes. The three Tijerina brothers wore matching dark suits and sat side by side in the front row, Reies in the middle. Chin up among the spectators, Patsy Tijerina chewed gum, while at a significant distance, Rose sat with her mother, the first Mrs. Tijerina, Mary Escobar.

First to testify was Nick Sais, who had been under round-the-clock police protection since the sudden death of Eulogio Salazar. Asked who had shot him on June 5th, he stood and pointed. Young Juan Valdez of Canjilon did not look away, but of all the defendants, he seemed the most troubled thereafter. Sais also testified that he had seen Reies Tijerina in the courthouse, armed. He identified Rose Tijerina, Baltazar Apodaca and Reies, Jr., as having been among the raiders. Then he described how Baltazar Martínez had put a rifle to his head and said, "Let me kill this unfortunate."

Leaning on the rail of the jury box, Martínez shook his head in boyish and utterly unguarded amusement. ("These guys can't seem to get it through their heads that they're on trial for their lives," defense attorney Driscoll said in dismay during a recess.) Lorenzo Tapia, one of the battery of eight defense attorneys, asked Sais if he had gone for his gun when the four raiders had first surrounded him.

"No," said Sais. "He told me to hand it over, and I was reaching to unsnap my holster when he shot me, wham."

"Was your movement fast?"

"I guess so."

Under cross-examination by Driscoll, Sais acknowledged that Juan Valdez had intervened when Baltazar Martínez had proposed to finish him off, and that Valdez had supervised the carrying of him to the ambulance.

The next day, County Assessor Estanislado Vigil described coming up from the courthouse basement to find Reies Tijerina, Jr., waiting for him with a gun "pointed at me, or I should say, in the direction where I was." He testified that he had also seen Reies Tijerina, Sr., with a gun in his hand. He identified José Madril and Tobías Leyba as having been armed and among the raiders. And he said that Baltazar Martínez and Baltazar

Apodaca had guarded those in the county commissioner's room and had later left them there.

"Why didn't you go out?" he was asked.

"Because I was scared," he murmured. There was great relish in the grins of a number of the defendants, and another outburst of laughter from the spectators.

On the fourth day of the hearing, County Clerk Cipriano Padilla identified Reies Tijerina, Rose Tijerina, José Madril, Juan Valdez, Tobías Leyba and Baltazar Martínez as having participated in the raid. He said that at one point the old man, Baltazar Apodaca, had told the captives in the assessor's office: "You are a bunch of *vendidos* who have sold yourselves down the river for a dollar."

"*Vendidos*, what's that?" asked Assistant District Attorney Chávez, who knew full well.

"I don't know what that means," Padilla replied solemnly, and, again, mocking laughter swept the courtroom, silenced patiently by Judge Angel.

The next day, Deputy Sheriff Pete Jaramillo told of his bizarre abduction by the two Baltazars. In the jury box, Baltazar Martínez grinned his delight as the deputy described his harrowing journey at gunpoint and final collapse among the trees. Jaramillo also identified Reies Tijerina as having been present in the courthouse and armed; and then he added a new name to the list: Cirillo García, who, he said, had been handed a rifle by Baltazar Martínez in front of the courthouse.

State Policeman Juan Santistevan described hearing shots and heading his squad car toward the courthouse, only to come under heavy fire from five men, two of whom he identified as Jerry Noll and Juan Valdez.

E. R. Gleasner identified Rose and Reies Tijerina as having been among the raiders, and pointed out Salomón Velásquez as the armed guard he had seen in the commission room. But during cross-examination by Driscoll, he abruptly announced that he had been mistaken, the guard had not been the 38-year-old, heavy-set Velásquez, but 26-year-old, slender Baltazar Martínez. Asked by Driscoll what Reies Tijerina had been wearing, the witness inquired of Judge Angel if he could make a comparison, and was told to go ahead.

"He was dressed like Castro."

"And you're dressed like a John Bircher!" shouted Driscoll.

UPI reporter Larry Calloway testified that from his hiding place in the phone booth he had seen Reies Tijerina stride toward him carrying an automatic rifle, then turn and go into the sheriff's office, where Eulogio Salazar was shot a short time later. He identified the two Baltazars as the ones who had abducted him and deputy Jaramillo. He pointed out José Madril as the man in green shirt and trousers who had been running around waving a pistol and shouting in Spanish, "Now they're not so brave!"

Undersheriff Dan Rivera described being discovered in the upstairs jury room and identified Juan Valdez as the one who had hit him the first time.

Gloria Sifuentes, typist, added young Moisés Morales of Canjilón, to the list, and said that she and Dolores Romero had been discovered hiding in the little room off the assessor's office by a man whom she pointed out in the jury box: Esequiel Domínguez. But when she was asked by Driscoll to repeat the last identification, she pointed to Victor, Esequiel's older brother.

"Could you be mistaken?" Driscoll inquired dryly.

"Yes," Gloria admitted and gave a petulant toss of her head.

Sheriff Benny Naranjo then took the stand to identify Juan Valdez's younger brother, Tony, and Danny Tijerina as having been present at the raid. And he described how, just as he was getting ready to go out into the hall to investigate, Reies Tijerina had rushed into his office and "knocked the gun out of my hand and knocked me to the floor."

Justice of the Peace Tomás Córdova testified that he had seen Salomón Velásquez across the street from the courthouse with a rifle, and that when Reies, Jr., had accosted him, Velásquez had said, "Let him go; I know him."

And finally, on February 6, the ninth and final day of testimony, the words of Eulogio Salazar, spoken at the bond hearing over eight months before, were read into the record as evidence by decision of Judge Angel, over strong objection by the defense.

Q. Who caused the injury to your face?

A. Reies Tijerina.

Q. What did he do to you?

A. He shot me here.

Q. Let the record show that the witness indicated the left side of his face.

The next day, Judge Angel announced dismissal of all charges against nine of the 20 defendants. Nine others were bound over for trial, but kidnapping charges against them were reduced by the court to charges of false imprisonment. Those bound over were Reies Tijerina, Baltazar Martínez, Juan Valdez, Tobías Leyba, Reies, Jr., José Madril, Salomón Velásquez, Moisés Morales, Jerry Noll and Esequiel Domínguez. (Attorneys for the 20th defendant, old Baltazar Apodaca, had requested a separate hearing in Tierra Amarilla.)

Many were surprised and not a few outraged by the "leniency" of the judgment, and Judge Angel would soon be disqualified from the case by the State Supreme Court. But the fact remained that the prosecution had failed to offer proof that six of the released nine, among them Ramón and Cris Tijerina, had been anywhere near the courthouse at the time of the raid. The three others released, including Rose Tijerina, had all been seen by witnesses in or near the courthouse, but had been unarmed and could not have been successfully prosecuted under the district attorney's charges of kidnapping and assault. In light of the testimony, the first-degree kidnapping charges now seemed to be clearly excessive and needful of reduction, if the state was to secure any convictions at all. Judge Angel had done the best he could under the law to vindicate an outstandingly inept prosecution. And he had seen to it that the testimony of jailer Salazar had been admitted, setting a precedent for trials yet to come. Death had not silenced Eulogio Salazar after all.

In the north, the investigation continued under the stubborn pall of *omerta*, communal and official. By the beginning of February, rewards from public and private sources totaling some $2,000 had been offered for information leading to the arrest of Salazar's killers, and the police continued to guarantee anonymity and protection for informants; but still there was no letter, no phone call. Chief Black ignored Judge Angel's gag order long enough to report that certain physical evidence had been sent to the FBI for analysis, that four criminal investigators were still on the scene and that they were "running those rumors down." However, he refused to disclose the nature of the physical evidence, to reveal what his investigators had been doing or to quote the rumors they were pursuing.

Speculation and hearsay were rife indeed behind the veil of silence, and at least some of the rumors were based on fact.

"A stranger came here after the murder," reported Fernanda Martínez from beside her new green enameled woodstove. "He was big and black-haired and an Anglo. He talked to Eulogio's widow, then Benny and Freddy Martínez ran him out. He had a big police dog and it bit Freddy. They say somebody find his gun. It was a pistol, .357 Magnum, I think."

Private investigator Charlie Ward was reportedly an old friend of Chief Black. He had called Black shortly after the murder and had asked permission to come up to New Mexico and do a little nosing around on his own. Upon receiving Casilda Salazar's nervous phone call, Sheriff Naranjo had phoned Black to verify Ward's story and had objected, demanding that Ward leave immediately. He and Ward had left the Salazar house in the company of Freddy Martínez early in the afternoon, and by midnight, Charlie Ward had checked into the hospital in El Paso for an ulcer cure which had apparently required that he neither see nor be seen by any visitors whatsoever. Reliable sources reported that his dog had attacked Freddy Martínez, but there was no sure confirmation of the equally persistent rumors that the dog had been shot, that Ward's pistol had been found empty in an arroyo near the Salazar house and that he had been thoroughly beaten before fleeing back to El Paso.

Nonetheless, it remains a fact that within hours after the stranger's departure, literally hundreds of Río Arriba residents had known of his visit and were able to describe him down to the color of his hair, the breed of his dog and the caliber of his pistol. Behind their barricade of silence, the northerners missed very little of what went on in their yellow land. And, just as much of the rumor among them was based upon accurate observation, so a good deal of their speculation had the ring of authoritative deduction. After all, who knew them better than they themselves?

"It had to be someone that Eulogio trusted," said Fernanda Martínez. "Someone who was right in the car with him, because they didn't find anything but rabbit tracks."

According to the police reconstruction of the crime, the attack had come sometime after Casilda had seen her husband in the lights of his car, opening the front gate. The pool of blood and the hat found near the gate indicated that the first blows had been struck as Eulogio had started to climb back into his car. He had apparently revived during the six-mile drive to the El Vado road and had put up a fight, which explained the bloody condition of the back seat and, to some degree at least, the ferocity of the final attack upon him. Police theorized that there had to have been at least two attackers, one driving the car. The pool of blood at the top of the turn indicated that the body had been switched from the back seat to the front before the car had been rolled down the bank.

Police investigators reported that they had found no footprints in the snow near the Salazar front gate. The investigators therefore concluded that they had driven up the road behind Salazar's car, their headlights out, their presence unnoticed through Salazar's frosted rear window. In which case, the killers would not necessarily have had to be persons the victim knew or trusted. In fact, the furtiveness of their approach would indicate that they had been someone he either did not know at all or, more likely, someone he knew and did not trust. Such as the Tijerinas or other *Alianza* members.

However, Mrs. Salazar and her daughter had watched Eulogio's car back down the road and had seen no second automobile. The police had experimented and reported that they were unable to spot an unlighted car backing down the road behind a car with its lights on. This seemed to verify their ghost car theory.

On the other hand, Mrs. Salazar had reported that after backing around the neighboring house, her husband's car had emerged, no longer with headlights pointed into her eyes, and had moved off toward town. She had seen no other car following. She had been looking over a distance of a hundred yards, but even with headlights out, a second car of almost any color except white would probably have shown up against the snow. Eulogio Salazar could, after all, have been murdered by someone riding with him, someone he knew and trusted. Someone not a member of the *Alianza*.

There were other rumors, other theories and an abundance of unanswered questions.

It was said that a cast had been made of the footprint of a crippled or one-legged man found on a side road near the Salazar home, and that a similar footprint had been found years before in the snow near Bill Mundy's burned house. Others said that the cast showed a print made by a boot of the kind worn by workers on the Chama road, several of whom were known *Alianza* members. Two Anglos from Chama were said to have been together in Española the afternoon of the murder, driving a white car and telling friends they intended to go "coyote hunting" that night. It was said that the owner of the Chama pawnshop (the same who had once demanded that Reies Tijerina "speak English, dammit") had been questioned at length by police. It was said that Lee Woods, one of Eulogio Salazar's pallbearers and a long-time member of the Río Arriba sheriff's posse, had also been picked up and questioned for two hours. It was reported that he had left the state, then that he had returned, then that he had never left at all. It was widely rumored that a second car, white, had been found abandoned near Cumbres Pass with bloody clothes in it, and that its Anglo owner claimed to have sold it to "some Mexican" the day before the murder.

"I think they did find a car up there," Chief Black told reporters on February 26. "I don't know what they did with it, and I haven't got a report."

A week later, the second car had apparently disappeared, like the ghost car it was said to be. Asked about it at the courthouse in Tierra Amarilla, Freddy Martínez said, "By George, that's news to me. Well, there are so many rumors, and most of them are false."

The questions were equally numerous and equally elusive of answer, further compounding the mystery.

Why had Chief Black failed to notify either Sheriff Naranjo and, apparently, even his own man in the north, Freddy Martínez, of the fact that he had invited an independent investigator into the case? Why had State Police Major Hoover Wimberly said with some bitterness, according to one informant, "We used to investigate and then arrest, now we arrest and to hell with the investigation"? Why was it that a full day after the removal of the body and car, the snow-covered slope showed no sign of a search for a weapon or other evidence more than a few feet away from where the car had come to rest? If the murder had been a professional job, why had the killers taken the unnecessary risk of attacking Salazar within a hundred feet of his lighted home? If the deed had been done by local people, why had they chosen the one night when they could be sure that Eulogio's wife would be up waiting and watching for him to take her to the wake?

There were nearly as many theories as there were rumors and questions. Of those that did not implicate Tijerina and the *Alianza*, the most frequently heard was the speculation that some former inmate or inmates of the Tierra Amarilla lockup had murdered the jailer for revenge.

"Eulogio Salazar was the kindest man I ever knew," Sheriff Naranjo said. "He always treated the prisoners well, made sure they were warm and fed well. I don't see how they could have held a grudge against him." And in the shock and regret following the ugly crime, many residents had echoed the sentiment. Reies Tijerina himself had said, "I considered

Eulogio Salazar a friend and a kind man. In 1960 he helped me with clothes for my children."

But the verdict was not unanimous. Eulogio Salazar was from a family which, in his youth, had been known in Tierra Amarilla as notably forbidding, even for that quarrelsome community.

"I don't like to say anything about a dead man," says one Tierra Amarilla resident, "but I was down in Española at the clinic about two years ago, and I saw this woman there. Her husband had been found hung up in the jail by pieces torn from the mattress, and they said he killed himself, but his face was all beaten, and they said one of the convicts in there with him had done it. But this woman, she said that Eulogio had helped the convict do it."

Only a few months before Eulogio Salazar's death, four young men in his charge had escaped from the TA jail. Two of them had been captured after a chase, and it was said that they had been badly beaten before being returned to their cells by their captors, one of whom had been jailer Eulogio Salazar.

On February 8, Reies Tijerina once again emerged from the state penitentiary, his bond reset by Judge Angel at $5,000. "We're going to organize harder, work harder and sacrifice more," he told reporters. "We are planning a West Coast fund raising tour. We have invitations from New York City, San Antonio and Washington, D.C."

So saying, off he went to explore the possibilities of his fast growing, if somewhat enigmatic national image. Behind him, he left an *Alianza* at its lowest ebb in terms of public acceptance and membership, and a Río Arriba still locked in the hardening embrace of *omerta*.

"Before the murder, the pro-Tijerina people were getting stronger, less afraid to speak out," said one long-time TA resident. "But now it's worse. They'll be backing water to get away from being associated with this thing. The stragglers and hangers-on aren't going to hang on any longer. Those that aren't disgusted are scared to death."

By early March, two months after the murder, there had still been no arrests, and Freddy Martínez would only describe the progress of the investigation as "very slow." As many months later, neither he nor Chief Black nor U.S. Marshal Emilio Naranjo nor his son the sheriff would have anything further to offer. On March 30, a contribution from an Albuquerque radio station increased the reward for the killers to $2,700. But nobody called to collect it.

Tiger Tiger Burning Bright 20

REIES TIJERINA had come a long way in the six years since Alfonso Sánchez had attempted to dismiss him as a Communist-inspired religious nut. But he was to go even further, and there was one particular triumph yet to come which would leave the district attorney himself in a state resembling mental collapse.

"I am a symbol," Reies had explained to the visitor in October. "I can't help it, I didn't mean it this way, but it's true. It is bigger than me, this demand for justice. An Anglo woman called long-distance and told me, 'You are the symbol to all, white, black and brown.' " And he added in typical exuberance, "We talked for an hour and a half, long-distance, and *she paid!*"

In the months following the preliminary hearing, he would become quite casual with the long-distance telephone, as well as with the jet airplane, radio microphones and the peering lenses of television and newsreel cameras. He would traverse the country several times and would find that his name had gone before him. He would consult with and be consulted by people of position and power, and there would be a variety of invitations to compromise. But through it all he would retain a certain inner purity of purpose which some would deride as naive, some would dismiss as megalomaniacal, others would denounce as spurious and not a few would consider evidence of secret allegiance to an alien ideology.

In February, he left for California to address himself to that state's two million *Chicanos,* nearly half a million of whom were said to be *manitos*—"little brothers"—from Mexico. On the 18th, he delivered a fiery harangue at a rally in the Los Angeles Sports Arena, with Stokely Carmichael and Maulana Karenga in attendance. The *LA Free Press* celebrated the event with a photograph of him seated at a table flanked by Anselmo and Cris, the three looking like a troika of grim-faced commissars. Behind them stood two young men with berets and menacing scowls. They were members of the Brown Berets, the recently formed *Chicano* version of Oakland's Black Panthers.

Two days later, Reies spoke at length of land theft, cultural rape and the New Breed on a Los Angeles television show. Two days after that, he was at UCLA to confer with Ralph Guzmán. Then he traveled north to visit Bert Corona's MAPA headquarters in Oakland and to learn his way around the underground complex of radical left organizations centered in the San Francisco Bay Area. The Berkeley *Barb* featured a photograph of him in action at a microphone, again guarded by a scowling Brown Beret. He traveled south again to Delano to speak to the grape strikers and confer with César Chávez.

Early in March, Reies conferred with Martin Luther King concerning *Alianza* participation in the poor people's campaign which King was organizing to march on Washington, D.C. By mid-March, he was back in northern California, where an unsteady liberal-radical coalition calling itself the Peace and Freedom Party briefly named him as its Vice-Presidential candidate, with black comedian-activist Dick Gregory to be his running mate. At the end of March, he was back in Albuquerque, playing host to Gregory, who said in a speech at the University of New Mexico that if something was not done quickly, "Negroes are going to burn this country down house by house, brick by brick."

"We don't condone violence," Reies reassured reporters once again. "There has been too much talk of revolution. We hope to change the mind of the state with moral and legal pressure."

Two weeks later, on April 4, less than a month before the scheduled poor people's campaign, Martin Luther King was assassinated in Memphis, Tennessee, and many were sure that nonviolent protest had died with him.

A few weeks later, the author intercepted Reies at the Oakland International Airport. He was on his way to Los Angeles for a series of meetings which he would not discuss. After that, he was bound for New Mexico to begin organizing the Southwestern *Hispano* delegation to the poor people's campaign, which was now headed by King's successor, the Reverend Ralph Abernathy. How did Reies feel about King's death?

He ran a hand through his thick hair, quicker and more intense in that alien atmosphere, green eyes glinting disapproval of passing miniskirts. "I think it will be better for me. I get along pretty good with Abernathy so far."

"Charismatic," many journalists were calling him, and more than one reader took the word to mean "elusive" or "enigmatic," since he often seemed to be just that. He was nationally known by now, but did anybody really know him? What kind of man was it who could so casually extract advantage from the making of a martyr, could hobnob with gun-toting Panthers and still disavow violence, could unabashedly compare himself to Moses and still claim to be the humble servant of a cause above himself?

Reies dealt in ideals, yet he could be chillingly pragmatic. In 1961 he had rejoined the Catholic Church, "Because my people expect it.

They are like children about such matters." He was not a land grant claimant himself, but his marriage to young Patsy had made him one, for she was from a land grant family. "That might seem sort of low-down to you," he explained. "But to my people it means they can trust me more when they know I have a concrete interest in the land grant cause."

He honored peace, yet delighted in danger. "After the trouble in Arizona, those years when I was a fugitive, I escaped from the FBI 17 times. Once I was in the bathroom when they came. I could hear them talking to my wife just on the other side of the door, and I went out the window. I carried a gun all the time. But that was the closest they ever came."

He sought humility, yet he could be suffocatingly righteous. "On one of my first trips to Mexico I went to Jalisco to ask a very famous holy man what I should do with my life. When I got there, he was still in bed, and his retainers said it was forbidden to wake him up. I told them that I had come 400 miles to seek this man's counsel, and I said, 'What kind of a holy man is this that won't talk to a pilgrim seeking help. Saint Paul wouldn't do that, Jesus wouldn't turn away someone in need.' And I left and went to Mexico City and gave my car away to the poor."

He was no prima donna, but he could be vain. "That picture in the *Journal*, pretty good of me, no?" He was strong, but he could be deeply hurt. "After my wife left me, I lived for two months in that big freezer in the basement and didn't see anybody." He was emotional, but he could be forbiddingly rational. "I don't go to see Mario in jail, what good would it do?" He was loyal, but he could draw the line. "I can't help Baltazar with the police this time; the people's money is not for that." He was a reformer, but he was conservative. " Modern wisdom is foolishness." He was a political man, but he disdained theory. "Industrial syndicalism, what is that?" He advocated communal property and derided capital, yet was indifferent to Marx. "I started to read it once, but I put it away, all those economic games." He was pragmatic, yet he was a compulsive dreamer. "We will build our pyramid there and it will scrape the clouds!" He was a dreamer, yet he could be impatient with ideals. "Not to have race, that is to dream of the Kingdom of Heaven." He condemned others as racists, yet was obsessed with race himself. "We are Indo-Spanish, a new blood, a new greatness!" He was impatient with the world, but gentle with those close to him. "*Tuti, dame un beso*, kiss your papa goodnight." He could love, but he could hate as well. "Those Texas Rangers in El Paso, pigs!" He had control, but some pressures must out. "My throat is killing me, the doctor says it's nerves." He was attentive to women, but wary. "Sex is like a bank, you can't just go in and take what you want. . . ."

He was a man of contradictions, with myriad flaws and failings and a number of hidden conflicts. But he was no mere collection of errant hungers reacting randomly; he was not a passive man. Beneath the tangle of contradictions there was a pattern; behind the moments of awkwardness, the tactical errors and the emotional pyrotechnics there was a sense of direction. Inner conflicts had somehow been brought into balance to form a central core of compulsive determination. Inside, he was something like a psychotic, something like a machine, and like both, he was essentially incorruptible.

This stubborn single-mindedness of purpose was evident during his stormy participation in the poor people's campaign, which took place in Washington from late May through June. Upon arrival at Resurrection City as head of the New Mexico delegation, he discovered that the Reverend Ralph Abernathy and his staff were not living with the majority of the delegates in plywood shanties, but in a well-appointed motel nearby. In the camp, the roofs of the shacks leaked, half the campsite was without electricity and the promised showers and sewers would never be installed. Organization was poor and getting worse; communication was breaking down.

"It was the worst confusion ever seen," Reies said later. "The SCLC [Southern Christian Leadership Conference] was in full control and failed to share the leadership with all ethnic groups. We felt that we were being used in the name of the poor to raise money for an organization that was not sharing that money. Justice was being corrupted."

To the press and to delegates he charged that Abernathy and his followers were neglecting the interests of the Indians, Appalachian whites and Spanish-Americans. He threatened to withdraw the entire *Hispano* contingent. SCLC officials hastily agreed to give nonblacks representation and promised other concessions. But the SCLC continued to dominate, and the campaign continued to falter. By now it was clear that Abernathy, who was no Martin Luther King, seemed reluctant to exercise even the modest talents he possessed. There was a curious air of mummery about the whole thing, almost as though it had been designed to fail from the beginning.

Abernathy did join Reies and Corky González in leading 300 demonstrators to the steps of the Justice Department to protest the jailing in Los Angeles of seven *Chicano* student protesters, but somehow the planned all-night vigil ended in a spiritless songfest and broke up shortly after nightfall.

"Nothing was really happening," Reies said later. "We were like beggars asking for crumbs. We did our little dance, then went away. It was an insult to the poor people. Somebody had to do something."

The cry was ¡*Viva, viva!* as he and Gonzáles led a crowd composed mostly of *Hispanos* and Indians up the steps of the Supreme Court to protest a ruling upholding revocation of Indian fishing rights on the Columbia River. A few windows were broken before security police closed the big steel doors. There were no arrests, but there were pictures in the papers. It was the most effective protest of the campaign, and among the last.

The militant young blacks had long since left in disgust; now the moderates were drifting away. By the end of the fourth week, the population of the camp had dropped from 2,500 to around 500. The government refused to renew the camp's permit and prepared to move 1,500 police in to evict its occupants. Last-minute talk of active resistance began to spread through the camp. But on June 24, the Reverend Abernathy climbed up on his wagon, clucked to his mules and, like the Pied Piper, led the last campers off to Capitol Hill, leaving the way clear for government bulldozers to move in and bury Resurrection City.

"It was a farce," Reies said later. "The poor were being used, not helped. Their demands were not being represented by their leaders. There was a vacuum, something missing, something needed."

The implication was, of course, that he was the one to fill the vacuum. In fact, he had stayed on in Washington for two weeks in an attempt to organize 700 diehard delegates into a Poor People's Coalition, with himself as head of its Supreme Council.

The poor jerkoff thinks he's Moses come again.

In a sense and to a degree it was true. But if all the truth be told, aren't ego, ambition and enjoyment of power to be expected, even required, in a leader? Can the presence of any such character traits be compared in importance to the question of a leader's allegiance to his followers?

"Those tall pines, they were in New Mexico. The three angels were the angels of the law coming to tell me what I should do. And the frozen horses, they were the land grants that belonged to the pueblos, to my people. I tell you that when I realized that, it was the biggest moment of my life. I had found my calling, like a mission. My razón."

Dictionaries say *razón* means reason, right, justice. *Razón* can refer simply to the process of mental reasoning, as in, *perder razón*, to lose one's mind. It can also mean reason and right as justification. *Tener razón*, literally, "to have reason," means to be justified, in either the practical or the moral sense, or both. The patrician *hacendados* of Spanish America called themselves *gentes de razón*, "gentry of reason," considering themselves to be not only intellectually and socially superior, but divinely appointed and therefore correct and just in their leadership. The attribute bore a stronger moral implication among those of the lower classes, where education and social position mattered less in the measure of a man. Andalusian *bandoleros* of the 1850s were long referred to by their peasant admirers as *hombres con razón*, troublemakers with good reason.

Because it can mean to be morally justified, to have *razón* can have an even more profound meaning to the man of Spanish heritage, basically Catholic and passionately self-involved as he usually is. It can mean, literally, to have a reason for living. And simultaneously (as with the *Penitente* on the cross), to have a reason for dying.

Ay, cómo estoy deshonrado, nail me, nail me!

"I used to be afraid of dying," Reies once said, following a phone call threatening his life. "But I'm not afraid anymore. Sometimes I almost want it. Whatever happens, I'm ready now. I have been ever since I first came to New Mexico and found out what I had to do for my people. Somehow, all at once, everything was settled, and I didn't doubt any more, so I wasn't afraid."

The psychological roots of his dedication, along with the main source of its intensity, can be found in the details of his early life. Herlinda, the strong and pious mother who had died, left him with an uncompromising moral mandate.

Which is not to say that he sought death. Nor, on the other hand, that his apprehensions of a violent end were without foundation.

He returned to Albuquerque in June to discover that the plate-glass windows of *Alianza* headquarters had for the second time been smashed in the night by unknown foes. A week earlier, an off-duty sheriff's deputy had attempted to throw a bomb into the building from a car, but the mechanism had gone off prematurely. State Police had intercepted the deputy racing toward Santa Fe at 85 miles-an-hour with his arm in shreds. The heat of vendetta had not diminished in New Mexico, nor had the fears of the ruling majority.

Several months before, at a camp meeting in Río Arriba, Baltazar Martínez had been converted. "He came forward and felt the presence of God," blond-haired evangelist Sally Quinn told reporters. "He told about how mean he had been and how sorry he was, and I'm sure he meant it. He has seen the light."

Ethel Mundy thought differently. "That religious business is a coverup," she assured the visitor a few days later. "That's a Communist training camp they're running up there."

She may have had her rumors mixed up. On June 5, the anniversary of the raid (and the day Robert Kennedy was fatally shot in Los Angeles), Alfonso Sánchez had announced to the press that the *Alianza* was about to declare war on New Mexico again. *Alianza* members were being trained in guerrilla tactics in Cuba, he assured reporters. Known Communists were infiltrating from Mexico and conducting war games on a ranch near Taos.

From Resurrection City, Reies had issued a flat denial. "I have no knowledge of such things."

"Ridiculous," State Representative Severino Martínez said in Santa Fe. "It defies intelligence."

State Policeman Joe Black appeared to be somewhat embarrassed by the panoramic nature of the district attorney's charges, but he admitted that his men had looked into a rumor that 60 guerrillas had been imported to New Mexico from Cuba. The investigation had revealed that a dozen or so young men had indeed been meeting on a ranch near Taos.

They were sometimes in the company of Corky González of Denver and had been seen wearing brown berets and jackets with the legend *Comancheros del Norte* stenciled on them, and they appeared to be addicted to target practice. But they were all citizens and were breaking no laws.

These details were not, however, reported to the public, and Alfonso Sánchez stuck to his guns. He was up for reelection, and the primary was only two months away. "I don't have the budget to hire my own investigators, so I can't check this thing out myself," he explained ruefully. "But it looks to me like the good people of Taos are in danger, and I don't want them to get hurt."

His opponent for the Democratic nomination, James Thompson, took the opportunity to charge that the district attorney's statements were a serious breach of Judge Angel's gag order and could lead to a mistrial. "The job of the district attorney is to try cases in the courts of law and not in the newspapers," he said. He declined, however, to either confirm or deny Sánchez's war scare.

There were others equally prone to turn the previous year's events to political advantage. In May, Benny Naranjo had pledged to run again for sheriff if the killers of Eulogio Salazar hand not been caught by the filing deadline. "And I will remain in the sheriff's office until the brutal murder is solved."

It seemed, however, that Emilio Naranjo had other plans for his son. Less than a month after Benny's grandstand play, Marshal Naranjo announced that he had spent his annual leave helping Benny investigate the murder and that they had uncovered "strong and positive evidence." The murder thus presumably all but solved in the public's mind, Benny was free to go ahead and file to run for county magistrate instead of sheriff. The "strong and positive evidence" never came to light. Police had been questioning a former mental patient, but his statements had proved to be worthless. Silence reigned over the grave of Eulogio Salazar.

In mid-September, final preparations for trial of the raiders began with a hearing to consider change of venu. Ten of the 11 defendants were present. Jerry Noll had been shipped back to Seattle to face trial for shoplifting and assault with a dinner fork. The battery of defense attorneys included Morton Stavis, a member of the Center for Constitutional Rights, located in New Jersey. At one point, prosecution witness Robert Gilliland of the State Police balked at a question from Stavis and indignantly asked the court if he had to answer questions from "someone who has represented extremists like Rap Brown."

District Judge Paul Larrazolo, whose easy drawl was in contrast with an almost obsessive preoccupation with time, allowed as how the witness probably should answer the defense attorney's questions, then urged the participants to get on with it. The defense had asked for dismissal on the grounds that pretrial publicity, including Alfonso Sánchez's cry of wolf, had made it impossible for the defendants to get a fair trial in New Mexico. Failing dismissal, the defense asked that the trial be held in the Tierra Amarilla courthouse.

Alfonso Sánchez was not about to submit his case to a Río Arriba jury, and so was obliged to argue that the defense could get a fair trial anywhere in New Mexico except in the county where the alleged offenses had been committed. Larrazolo cut off proceedings after two days, and on September 13, denied all defense motions and set the trial for January 12 in Albuquerque.

Politics dominated the remainder of the year. Early in August, Tijerina had announced *Alianza* endorsement of David Cargo's candidacy for reelection as governor. But Eulogio Salazar's killers had still not been found, and the onus of bloody murder still clung to the *Alianza* in the minds of many. Reies several times protested that the State Police were withholding a report absolving the *Alianza*, but there was no response from official quarters. In addition, Cris Tijerina and Félix Martínez had been arrested back in April for receiving stolen goods following a jewel theft.

Cargo publicly repudiated the *Alianza* endorsement. Which is not to say that he threw it away. It was clear that he was going to have a tough race against Democrat Fabián Chávez. Small as the *Alianza* vote was, it had provided him with the winning margin in Río Arriba once before and could again. On August 15, alleged jewel thieves Cris Tijerina and Félix Martínez announced that they would work for Cargo's reelection in the north, and there was no objection forthcoming from the governor.

Following Cargo's repudiation, Reies had announced his own candidacy for governor at the head of a new party, the People's Constitutional Party. The decision was undoubtedly influenced by the small coterie of advisers that had gravitated to him since the raid. Among them were California attorney Beverly Axelrod, former friend and associate of Black Panther Eldridge Cleaver, and attorney William Higgs, also from out of state, also of radical-reformist reputation. It was obviously the intent of these new advisers to turn Reies' erratic efforts to more efficient and immediate political and legal effect, but it remained to be seen whether they would succeed in adapting what had always been a conservative, nativistic, essentially emotional crusade to their own progressive, cosmopolitan and directly political aims. It is one thing to attack a courthouse out of pure indignation and rage; it is quite another to calculatedly chip away at social inequity with votes, the Constitution, common law and other blunt instruments.

The People's Constitutional Party barely made the ballot, and the qualifications of its candidates were immediately challenged, first by Secretary of State Ernestine Evans, then by Attorney General Boston Witt, who ruled that Reies Tijerina was disqualified from running for governor because of his federal conviction as a felon in connection with the Echo Amphitheatre trespass. Assisted by Civil Liberties Union attorneys, Reies objected that his appeal of the Las Cruces jury verdict was yet to be heard in court, and therefore he was not yet legally convicted. Nonetheless, at the end of October, the State Supreme Court disqualified him and eight other PCP candidates, leaving five on the ballot.

On November 7, Richard Nixon was elected President of the United States and his fellow Republican David Cargo was reelected governor of New Mexico. Out of over 300,000 votes cast in the state, People's Constitutional Party candidates received a grand total of less than 2,000 votes. Derisive laughter mingled with sighs of relief in congregations of the ruling majority. The electorate had delivered a resounding rejection of Tijerina and his gang, they said, and within the week, the law would proceed to deliver the final blow.

The celebration was excessive on both counts.

The election figures were misleading. The PCP campaign had suffered from a late start, lack of funds and legal troubles. It had been excluded from absentee ballots. Voting machines in several populous counties had not been equipped to list a straight ticket for a third party.

More pertinent, on October 20, at an *Alianza* meeting in Canjilón, Reies had announced that if he was disqualified as a candidate for governor (which he by then fully expected to be) he would support Cargo. The governor had again avoided public acceptance of the endorsement, but Cris Tijerina and Félix Martínez had been electioneering for him without interference since August. Cargo won the election by less than 3,000 votes, a margin smaller than that which had first put him into office; and this time as last time, most of the margin had come from counties where the *Alianza* had always been strongest. The PCP, it appeared, had received no more than half of the potential *Alianza* vote, probably considerably less. The rest had gone to Cargo.

After its abysmal low of a year before, Reies' popularity appeared to be slowly rising again. A year had passed since the Salazar slaying, and no *Alianza* leader or member had yet been charged with the crime. The raid was rapidly passing into the bloodless unreality of legend. Reies had joined Albuquerque's new contingent of militant young Brown Berets in protesting police brutality before city commissioners, but he had not been present in October when 20 of them had angrily invaded a University of New Mexico "leadership conference" near Taos. Possibly under advice of his new associates, he assiduously deplored violence at every public opportunity. In answer to an old but still common criticism, he had asked Denver attorney Eugene Diekman to draft a suit against the government consolidating all old land grants on public or forest lands. He had retained Washington attorney David Rein to submit *Alianza* land claims to the United Nations. He had unsuccessfully sought a meeting with UN Secretary General U Thant in June, and would soon petition the Spanish government for aid in charging the United States with violation of the Treaty of Guadalupe Hidalgo. He had been out of the state a good deal in the past year, but had said and done much to please his old followers while abroad.

On the other hand, at his best, he had never commanded anything like a majority, and unless he or New Mexico changed drastically, he never would. He was a minority leader, by his own nature as well as by the nature of his place and time. Attempts to secure the approval of the ruling majority would only lead to alienation from the roots of his ambition. Even to eschew violence was to symbolically disclaim the outrage, dismiss the grievances and betray the trust of those who had given vent to the *grito* of Tierra Amarilla. A politician could view the *grito* as no more than a stepping-stone. His brother Cris, brooding and oblique though he was, was showing signs of the required flexibility, and former revolutionary and Electrolux Salesman of the Year Félix Martínez didn't appear to be embarrassed by his counterrevolutionary activities on behalf of Governor Cargo.

But Reies was neither a doctrinaire revolutionary nor a true politician. He was a social evangelist helplessly beholden to a minority flock. By force of blood and virtue of conviction, he was a rebel whether he liked it or not, and by definition, at odds with the majority. He was the self-conscripted champion of the few, the deliverer of their dreams, the stuff of their legends.

Even as the election results were being announced, they were saying in the tin-roofed shacks of Río Arriba and the crumbling adobes of Río Abajo that it didn't matter, Reies had shown them before and he would show them again. And, incredibly, they—perhaps 4,000 of them, mostly the unlettered and the unenlightened, the poor and the unemployed, the old and the angry, the broken and the abandoned—were right.

On November 6, the state solved the problem of prosecuting a 73-year-old man on capital charges. Baltazar Apodaca was declared mentally incompetent to stand trial and was put away in the state hospital.

The remaining 10 defendants appeared for trial six days later in U.S. District Court in Albuquerque, each charged with three of the 10 charges (broken down into 54 separate counts) pending against him. Remaining charges would be considered later in what could become a 10- to 15-year legal marathon. There were no less than 15 defense attorneys, most of them court appointed. Confusion reigned and jury selection dragged on, punctuated by Judge Larrazolo's frequent pleas to "move along." After a week of it, Larrazolo abruptly announced a severance ruling. Proceedings were taking too long and costing the state too much, he said. Reies Tijerina would stand trial alone, with the rest to be tried at a later date. Attorneys for Tijerina objected, as did the prosecution. Judge Angel had previously dismissed all charges of conspiracy, but the prosecution was apparently hoping that a mass trial would give jurors an impression of "conspiratorial doctrine." But Larrazolo stood firm. The other nine defendants were dismissed, and selection of a new jury began.

And then, as court convened on Wednesday morning, November 21, the defendant suddenly stood up and began to talk. "I find myself being surrounded by jeopardy, being forced to represent myself so Your Honor will not be bringing up repeatedly that the cost and time of this trial is more important than my rights. My lawyers have become obsolete, as I see it, when we were cut off from the other defendants. My lawyers are not representing me. They did not put up the fight I would have. . . ."

Judge Larrazolo waited, hunched forward in his robes, a lean man with a bony geniality of expression, his gray hair sheared straight up from the ears. The spectators were beginning to buzz, but neither prosecution, defense attorneys nor the judge appeared to be particularly surprised.

Reies finished, and Larrazolo contemplated him. "All right then, do you want to represent yourself?" He raised a hand, palm outward. "I don't want to hear any speeches from you, just an answer."

"I would like to talk to my attorneys. I will give you my answer in a few days."

Larrazolo shook his head. "No, you will go to trial today. I'm going to give you 30 minutes to decide if you want to represent yourself or retain counsel."

Reies hesitated, chin up, but clearly taken aback. He and his lawyers had decided on the tactic the night before at *Alianza* headquarters, but apparently both court and prosecution had somehow found out and prepared themselves. At the prosecution's table, Alfonso Sánchez wore his usual courtroom expression of fixed, faintly saddened solemnity, but there was a hint of the expectant fox in his eye.

Defense attorney John Throne arose hastily. "Your honor, the defendant needs time to consult with his counsel."

"This is a tactic to delay this trial," Jack L. Love objected for the prosecution. "The state can't wait until these men can teach Mr. Tijerina how to try a law case."

"We request one more day to prepare," said defense attorney Gene Franchini.

Judge Larrazolo repeated his concern for the state's time, its money.

"A half a day, Your Honor?"

The court ordered a recess.

Three hours later, Reies stood at the lectern, which was constructed very much like a pulpit, and said loudly and rapidly, "Your Honor, I am going to defend myself."

At the prosecution's table, Alfonso Sánchez smiled a slight, wry smile, but in his eyes as he studied the man at the lectern, there was a furtive gleam of helpless dazzlement.

The Trial 21

PERHAPS because Albuquerque was that much further away from the northern mountains than Santa Fe, security was not nearly so tight as it had been on previous occasions. There were uniformed and plainclothes officers present, inside and outside the courtroom, but never more than a dozen at a time, and spectators were not searched.

Each day about a hundred people crammed the pews of the low-ceilinged, windowless courtroom. There were old men with battered hats in their laps, men in work clothes with dung on their boots, a trio of young men with *Comancheros del Norte* stenciled across the backs of their jackets. Patsy Tijerina was down front in a simulated leopard-skin coat, her chestnut-colored eyes anxious, her pretty face working a wad of chewing gum. Nearby, a mother rocked a fretful baby. Behind her, a handsome middle-aged woman read from her copy of a new militant newspaper *El Grito del Norte* whenever proceedings got dull. But she did not often have cause to do so.

For one thing, Judge Larrazolo ran his court in a style that left plenty of room for surprises. Given to long periods of leniency interrupted by sudden bursts of impatience, the judge more than once suggested dryly to a procrastinating lawyer or verbose witness that if they didn't hurry along they might find themselves "upstairs," meaning in the Bernalillo County jail; and at one point he became irritated enough with the defendant's courtroom conduct to remind him dryly, "Mr. Tijerina, a trial can be run in the absence of the defendant."

But for the most part he maintained the paternal bemusement of a good bartender, tolerant of the shenanigans of his customers and ready to mediate their differences, but obliged to now and then remind them of closing time. He seemed at pains to allow the defense, particularly its untrained director, as much technical latitude as possible, and was consequently obliged to allow the prosecution the same. The result was a distinct flexibility of procedure that loosened the orthodox limits of questioning and testimony.

The unquestioned star of the proceedings both in terms of legal performance and pure entertainment, was the chief defense counsel, the defendant himself, Reies Tijerina. He remained silent the first day, leaving matters to attorneys Beverly Axelrod, John Thorne, Gene Franchini and William Higgs, who had been directed by the court to act as defense advisers. But by the second day he had begun to question prospective jurors, and by the third he was exhibiting the first signs of an eccentric but decidedly effective courtroom style.

He was compulsively direct. During his questioning of a retired air force colonel, the court had to caution him not to insult the prospective juror. He had asked the colonel if he was honest.

He seemed either disarmingly innocent or stubbornly blind to the compulsions of human nature as he asked again and again, "Deep down in your heart, do you feel you could be an impartial juror as to my guilt or innocence?" (Not a single prospective juror answered in the negative.)

On the other hand, he was clearly neither frightened by the task he had undertaken nor awed by the court, and he early showed that he had a bold, swift sense of humor. "This is a rare case," he declared at one point during the jury selection.

"Mr. Tijerina, to me this is not a rare case," the judge corrected.

"To me it is," came the immediate reply.

Nor did he shrink from mentioning matters which he might better have avoided. He asked one prospective juror if he knew about the murder of Eulogio Salazar, "a witness against me," and began to elaborate with mounting enthusiasm: "I was accused of the murder, and the governor of New Mexico, believing I was involved, revoked my bond. The newspapers are crucifying a man in this land of the free and I'm concerned. . . ."

At which point Judge Larrazolo interrupted with the plea, "Don't keep making speeches," and urged, "Let's move along, move along."

And he showed early in the game that he could salt his questions with the best of them. Although the unabashed excess of his efforts seemed only additionally naive, his insertions were usually shrewd and telling.

"The newspapers say I'm a bad man, a rabble-rouser," he said to one prospective juror. "They probably will bring in the governor and generals of the army to testify. You will not give more weight to an officer than to other persons, will you?"

Again, the answer was foregone, but he had made his impression, and his point.

By the seventh day, 11 jurors had been selected. The prosecution accepted the twelfth, Mrs. Andrew Johnson, a hospital employee, and, although the defense had already used up its 12 preemptory challenges, Tijerina stood up to declare loudly, "We accept her."

There was amused laughter, but Mrs. Johnson, a handsome middle-aged black woman wearing glasses, remained thoughtful. Her fellow jurors included a fireman, a company supervisor, a machinist, an auto mechanic, a retired State Highway Department employee, a finance company employee, a grandmother, three housewives and a medical technologist. Six were men, six women. Five had Spanish names.

The next day they were sworn in and told they would be kept in seclusion for the duration of the trial.

On the following day, November 12, the trial proper began with opening remarks by Jack Love, the same who had helped U.S. Attorney Quinn secure criminal convictions against Tijerina and the four other Echo Amphitheatre defendants the previous year. Apparently impressed by that success, Alfonso Sánchez had hired Love as special prosecutor for this case. The three charges against the defendant were: assault on a jail, false imprisonment and kidnapping. Although the last was a capital offense, the prosecution apparently did not intend to ask for the death penalty; it had been mentioned only once during jury selection, and then by the defense. Most observers still agreed, however, that a verdict of guilty was inevitable. If anything, Tijerina's decision to conduct his own defense only strengthened the consensus, although there were many who felt that clumsy pretrial handling of the case by both the district attorney and the courts could lead to endless appeals.

Tall and assured, with carrot-colored hair and a Texas drawl, Jack Love promised that the prosecution would prove that Reies Tijerina had been armed and a leader of the raid, that he had participated in the false imprisonment and kidnapping of Undersheriff Dan Rivera and that he had been among those to "assault" the jail and order the release of two prisoners. Tijerina, for the defense, reserved his right to opening remarks for a later time.

Which is not to say that he remained silent. He had been gaining confidence daily, standing at the end of the defense's table in the beginning, with his advisers seated behind, whispering advice, tugging at his shirttail in alarm at his more unorthodox sallies. Soon he had moved to the lectern, closer to the jury, affording them a clear view of every glint of his eyes, every expressive gesture of his flailing arms.

He began to introduce the first of a number of themes which he would hammer away at with the impassioned tenacity with which he had first hammered home the gospels, and later his dialectic of royal inheritance and cultural rape. Calling for a mistrial, he charged that the news media were part of a conspiracy against himself and the *Alianza*. "The newspapers have only showed one side of the story, through the FBI and the police," he charged. "I want to bring out evidence that they have threatened my life, and that the news media have been helping them paint me as 'King Tiger.'"

He offered stacks of material in evidence, including a copy of Allan Stang's *American Opinion* article warning of a new Cuba in the Southwest, another article entitled, "King Tiger—Wanted Dead or Alive," and Hurricane's recording of the *Corrido de Río Arriba*, which named him as leader of a "revolution" in Río Arriba, and which he proposed to play for the court.

The court demurred. "No, I don't want to hear it," Judge Larrazolo said with evident distaste, and denied the motion for mistrial.

But another was immediately forthcoming. The defense was fatally hampered, Tijerina charged, by the use of listening devices by the state. His own telephone and those of other defense attorneys were tapped, he said, and he charged that the prosecution had known of his proposal to conduct his own defense before he had announced it in court. As offer of proof, he proposed to subpoena witnesses. Judge Larrazolo quashed the subpoenas and advised the defense to take its complaint to "the proper agency."

But there was more. The conspiracy included threats and attempts on the defendant's life, Tijerina charged. Earlier, the defense had offered in evidence a copy of a Salt Lake City newspaper which it said Tijerina had received in the mail and which had included, next to an account of a murder, an inked notation promising, "You're next . . . ," the third word being Anglo-Saxon and obscene. Beverly Axelrod had also reported a threatening phone call. Judge Larrazolo had ruled the threats immaterial to the charges under consideration, had turned the newspaper over to the FBI and had suggested that Mrs. Axelrod do the same with her telephone complaint. He now repeated his dismissal of the conspiracy question as immaterial and urged defense attorneys to "Move along, move along."

As testimony began, new themes were introduced to enrich the defendant's thesis that he had been and was still being treated with less than due consideration by both the press and the state. "Haven't you heard that I am known as the terrible 'King Tiger'?" he asked several witnesses. "You must have, it was in all the newspapers and on television. It was even in *Time* magazine."

He insisted that the term "raid," as used by the news media to describe the troubles at the courthouse, was prejudicial, and again and again he objected to its use by the court and the prosecution. For his own part, he demonstrated considerable inventiveness in providing substitutes for the term, referring to the event as "The Explosion," "The Attempted Citizen's Arrest" and "The Famous Historical Event at Tierra Amarilla." On several occasions he slipped in the heat of the contest and used the term himself, but the point was so doggedly made that both court and prosecution began to avoid the term in favor of "assault," which echoed one of the charges anyway.

He seldom allowed one of Judge Larrazolo's injunctions to "move along" to pass without objecting that "The court seems to be more interested in saving time than in administering justice." And he several times pointed out to the jury that while he, as a certified pauper, could offer his attorneys no more than the minimum fees provided by the state, Alfonso Sánchez had been given a special appropriation of $40,000 by the State Finance Committee and had hired Jack Love for an undisclosed portion of that amount. "Is this justice, is this every man's equal right before the law?"

It was to be expected that he should be accomplished at exhortation and polemic, but as the testimony progressed, it soon became apparent that he had an equal talent for cross-examination. State Policeman Nick Sais took the stand to once again tell of turning from the courthouse bulletin board to find himself surrounded, then reaching for his gun and being shot. While on the floor and bleeding, he stated he had seen the defendant, and the defendant had been armed.

"Did you see me fire any shots?"

"No."

"I didn't shoot you, did I?"

"No."

"Did you hear me tell any of the other people there what to do, give them orders?"

"No."

Former Sheriff Benny Naranjo told of starting out of his office, gun in hand, encountering the defendant, having the gun knocked from his hand, then finding himself on the floor.

"Just kocked the gun out of your hand, just like that. I did that?"

"It was you."

"But I didn't shoot you, did I?"

"No."

"You didn't see me fire any shots."

"No."

"Did you hear me order anybody else to shoot?"

"No."

"Did you hear me order anybody else to do anything?"

"No."

He had spent no more than 500 hours of his life in court, but it had always been to helplessly listen while other men, usually Anglos, deliberated his fate or that of a friend or brother, and that kind of impotency had long been a goad to fierce ambition and hard study. Naturally quick, he knew the value of rapid-fire questions and unrelenting pressure. But he had also learned more subtle tricks of timing and misdirection. Probably from his former chief counsel, Charles Driscoll, he had mastered the art of setting a witness up with a series of mundane inquiries, usually delivered absently, while he fiddled with his notes.

"What is your business, Mr. Santisteven?"

"I'm a State Police officer."

"Where do you work, Mr. Santisteven?"

"Right now I'm assigned to Las Cruces."

"Where were you before that?"

"Río Arriba County."

"How long were you there?"

"Six years."

Then came the sudden pause, deliberately extended, while the witness shifted in his chair or gazed vacantly off. Then the attack.

"Mr. Santisteven, isn't it true that you were a part of a campaign by the district attorney and the police to keep the *Alianza* people from peacefully assembling at Coyote on June 2, three days before the explosion at Tierra Amarilla?"

"I don't know about that, but I believe we did go over there on that date."

"Didn't you go over there to harass and arrest those people and keep them from having their meeting?"

"I didn't make any arrests."

"Did you search their cars?"

"No."

"I'll bring four witnesses who will say you did, Mr. Santisteven."

He could be expected to shift his line of questioning at any time, only to return with equal suddenness to one of his central arguments, not always in faultless English, but with relentless persistence.

"Have you ever been told that I am a Communist, Mr. Santisteven?"

"No."

"When you drove up to the courthouse and got shot at, did you saw me there shooting at you?"

"Nossir."

"Did you saw me giving orders to shoot?"

"Nossir."

And, although he was careful not to do it often, he was not above holding a witness up to derision when the opportunity presented itself.

"After you ran away from your police car, what did you do?"

"I went behind the school house. I could hear them saying, 'He's behind the house,' in Spanish."

"Exactly what did they say in Spanish, Mr. Santisteven?"

"*Está detrás de la casa, el chingao.*" (Spectator laughter at the derogatory *chingao*.)

"What did you do then, Mr. Santisteven?"

"I got out of there."

"Did you jump the fence, Mr. Santisteven?"

"Yes." (More mocking laughter, silenced by the court.)

Finally, he had a showman's hearty enthusiasm for staging and the use of props. The four-foot wooden pointer provided by the court became a supple extension of his continually gesturing hands. He moved about the courtroom at every opportunity, carrying his tattered Esso roadmap to a witness for consultation, inviting the witness to step down and locate an action on the state's elaborate model of the courthouse.

He staged several dramatic tableaux, one of which featured former deputy, now sheriff-elect of Río Arriba County, Pete Jaramillo, who found himself standing with his hands in the air, while Reies Tijerina probed his ample midsection from behind with the pointer, impersonating the man who had allegedly come up behind the deputy in the hall of the courthouse, poked a gun in his back and said, "Where is Alfonso Sánchez? Tell me, you son of a bitch, or I'll kill you."

Assistant District Attorney Chávez arose to ask dryly just what it was the defendant thought he was proving, and found himself looking up the length of the pointer into Tijerina's green eyes.

"I am showing that it would have been difficult for him to see me if I had come up behind him like this, Mr. . . ." The tip of the pointer trembled as he drew a bead. "Mr. *State.*"

Laughter rocked the courtroom, and Judge Larrazolo had to pound for order and threaten to clear the court of spectators. "You may think this is a show, but it is not, "he admonished them. "Any of you who think it is, don't come back tomorrow."

But it was in fact a show, and one of the most satisfying many of them had enjoyed since the raid itself. However, Tijerina's conduct of the defense did not consist merely of melodramatic maneuver and forensic trickery. Among the serious legal contentions making up his argument was one of particular importance, with a potential effect far beyond the limits of the immediate trial. Among the first to be taken aback by it was State Policeman Juan Santisteven.

"Mr. Santisteven, are you acquainted with Amendment No. 1 to the Constitution of the United States?"

"No."

"Do you know what a citizen's arrest is?"

"No."

"Are you acquainted with the provisions of the Constitution of the State of New Mexico that pertain to citizen's arrest?"

"No."

"Did you know that citizens of the United States could arrest an officer if they believed they had a grievance against him?"

"No."

"Mr. Santisteven, isn't it your job to protect the rights of all citizens?"

"Yes."

"Mr. Santisteven, how can you protect the citizens if you do not know their rights?"

The same questions were put to Pete Jaramillo and other testifying officers, and in each case the results were the same.

"Did you know that civil codes provide for arrest by citizens of law enforcement officers who are a threat to citizens or violate civil rights of citizens?"

"No."

"Are you aware that an armed officer who does not know, has not been briefed on citizen's rights, that that officer might be considered a threat to those citizens?"

"No."

"Isn't it possible that sooner or later these people, pushed to the brink of desperation, might assert their rights? That they had to teach you a lesson, a lesson your superiors did not teach you?"

"I don't know."

It was bold and inventive argument, worthy of Clarence Darrow. However, there was no assurance that the concept of citizen's arrest would be admitted by the court as law applicable to this case.

In the meantime, the charges remained. By the end of the second week, the prosecution had produced considerable testimony to prove that the defendant had been present in the courthouse and that he had been armed, and they had attempted to prove that he had led the raiders. Pete Jaramillo had testified that Tijerina had ordered court-house employes held in the commission room with the words, "Put them back there," but there was no evidence that the defendant had taken actual part in holding them. Pretty Gloria Sifuentes had testified that she had heard the defendant say in Spanish, "Do away with all of these." "I thought that meant to kill everyone," she said.

But during cross-examination, Tijerina suggested that he had said instead, "Stop all this," and had pointed out the similarity between the two phrases in Spanish:

Acaben con todos éstos.

Acaben con todo esto.

He made a point of reminding the jury that shortly after the first shots, Pete Jaramillo had heard an unidentified voice yelling, "Stop it! Stop it!" And in conclusion, he inquired of the witness with gentle irony, 'Weren't you surprised when you went into the commission room and found everybody alive?"

"Yes," Miss Sifuentes replied, but faintly, looking away.

The charges were: false imprisonment, kidnapping and assault on a jail (not assault on a courthouse, for which there was no statute). Substantiation of the imprisonment and kidnapping charges did not require that a victim be taken from one place to another, but only that he be held against his will. But there was no evidence that the defendant had participated in the holding of employes in the commission room, none that he had taken part in the abduction of Jaramillo and reporter Calloway and little substantial evidence to prove that he had ordered either action. Therefore, the prosecution's case hinged on the testimony of Undersheriff Dan Rivera, who had testified on other occasions that he had been taken under guard in the jury room (false imprisonment), had then been taken downstairs at the point of a gun (kidnapping) and had been forced to go down to the basement and release the two prisoners from their cells (assault on a jail).

Rivera testified on December 3, the third week of Tijerina's trial. He said that he had been discovered hiding in the jury room on the second floor of the courthouse and had been beaten by two other raiders while the defendant had looked on. He said that he was then disarmed, taken downstairs and directed to go down to the basement and release the prisoners. But he was uncertain as to who had given the order, and he faltered badly when the prosecution sought to establish that he had been forced to release the prisoners. At one point, he said that he had let them out because there was "a gun on top of my head." But he could not be induced to state that he had actually seen anyone accompany him downstairs to the jail. "I know someone was behind me when I was going down the stairs, but I never looked back."

Under cross-examination by Tijerina, certainty on the matter abandoned him entirely.

"If you didn't look back, how do you know there was somebody there?"

"I had a feeling."

"But you didn't see anyone?"

"No."

"You didn't hear anyone?"

"No."

"Nobody touched you?"

"No."

"Mr. Rivera, did you hear me giving orders or commanding anyone at any time?"

"No."

"Then you didn't hear me order anyone to beat you?"

"No."

"Then as far as you know, I am not to blame for your injuries?"

"I'm not blaming you for anything, sir."

It was incredible. But he had said it. The state's key witness had personally exonerated the defendant. The defense immediately moved for dismissal of the charges, and this time the motion was not denied but was taken under advisement by Judge Larrazolo.

But if the prosecution was shaken by the mutilation of Rivera's testimony, they showed little sign of it. That afternoon they quietly rested their case.

The following day, the defense asked permission to call the district attorney to the stand. Alfonso Sánchez had remained curiously dormant through the past two weeks, leaving the questioning of witnesses to Jack Love, rising to make an objection now and then, but spending much of his time in brooding contemplation of Tijerina's courtroom performance. Now he revived long enough to consult with his special prosecutor, whereupon Jack Love rose to oppose the request, charging that the defense only wanted to harass the district attorney and "bring side issues into this case."

The defense argued that Sánchez had played a direct part in events which had led up to the raid, and that therefore his testimony was vital to consideration of whether or not the raiders had been justified in going to the courthouse to make a citizen's arrest.

But the court was still doubtful that the citizen's arrest principle was admissible in the first place. While noting that state law did give a citizen the right to arrest another citizen seen committing a felony, Judge Larrazolo said that he did not think that "in this case, there is any legitimacy of a citizen's arrest, from what I've heard so far."

However, he did add, as he announced delay of the motion to call Sánchez, "I may be wrong, I'm open to argument; I've changed my mind before."

The defense met with another setback during the testimony of one of its own witnesses. Albuquerque real estate man E. R. Gleasner was describing the first chaotic moments after Nick Sais had been shot, when he abruptly asserted that Reies Tijerina was the one who had come up behind him, told him not to look, then clubbed him on the head with a rifle. "My nose swelled up and my ear."

How did he know it had been Tijerina? "By his inclination, voice and speech, by the way he uses his arms. By process of elimination. He is the only one who could have done it."

Why had he neglected to identify his attacker on the two previous occasions when he had testified? "This is the first time we have had a direct confrontation. This is the first time I've heard him speak."

During the two hours of intense cross-examination, Tijerina managed to get Gleasner to admit that he had not actually seen the man who had hit him, but the witness remained firm in his opinion. "The man who hit me is the same man who spoke to me, and even though I did not see him hit me, he was the only one who could have. In my mind, I am convinced you did it."

However, the impartiality of his testimony had been brought into serious question when he mentioned earlier that Tijerina had once been pointed out to him as his attacker "by Eulogio Salazar, the man who was killed so he could not testify."

Despite the fact that the court had not yet ruled on the citizen's arrest question, the defense continued its efforts to establish that the initial purpose of the raiders had been to take Alfonso Sánchez into popular custody.

Cruz Aguilar, of Río Arriba, testified that he had been arrested for unlawful assembly in connection with a peaceable May 14, 1967, meeting of the *Alianza*. He had been present for his scheduled arraignment on June 5, when the raid occurred, and had been allowed to leave unharmed because he was an *Alianza* member. Alfonso Sánchez had never called him back to judgment for unlawfully assembling.

The next witness, Ubaldo Valásque, was no longer an *Alianza* member. He testified that the June 3 meeting at Coyote had been called to draft a petition to the President for help with the land grants, but that the meeting had been stopped by the police.

The next day, sociologist Clark Knowlton, now of the University of

Utah, outlined the long history of frustration and loss suffered by the northern villagers, and described the complex of fears and resentments which had contributed to the success of the *Alianza*. He testified that he had several times heard the possibility of a citizen's arrest discussed at *Alianza* meetings.

However, the jury was removed during his testimony on a motion from the prosecution, and Judge Larrazolo reserved a decision on the admissibility of his statements.

At one point, the prosecution attempted to introduce in evidence four placards bearing hand-lettered challenges to Alfonso Sánchez, which it said had been carried by the pickets who had been marching daily outside the courthouse. During the brief debate over the admissibility of the signs, a young man approached the bench and said that he had made the placards. "I think if Sánchez had nothing to fear he would take the witness stand," he said, looking toward the prosecution's table. "I made them because maybe that way he'll have the guts."

Alfonso Sánchez raised his head from his notes and peered through his reading glasses at the young man with *Comancheros del Norte* stenciled across his jacket, then gave a small, melancholy shrug and looked down again.

That afternoon the jury was allowed to hear the testimony of a second sociologist, Mrs. Frances Swadesh, who said that she thought the raid could have been unpremeditated, pointing out that "many things up there happen spontaneously." She also talked of the frustrations of the northerners and described the *Alianza* as their means of expressing a need for social change.

"Do you think a raid of the Tierra Amarilla courthouse would be a proper way of expressing change?" Assistant District Attorney Chávez inquired caustically.

Through the laughter that followed, Dr. Swadesh answered tartly, "I don't know what really happened up there. I don't know who fired the first shot."

The next day, Albuquerque truck driver Fabián Durán testified that he had seen Nick Sais go for his gun with intent to use it. Durán had entered the courthouse with Rose Tijerina, he said, and had seen four men facing the officer. "I heard one of the men say in Spanish, 'We came to arrest Alfonso Sánchez,' and then I saw the policeman go for his gun, I grabbed Rose and we ran out."

Under cross-examination by Prosecutor Love, Durán maintained that he had seen no guns in the hands of the four and that he had recognized none of them, but he readily admitted that he had been an *Alianza* member at the time.

Rose Tijerina confirmed Durán's story during testimony so enthusiastically attended by her father that Judge Larrazolo felt obliged to reprimand Tijerina for "putting words in your daughter's mouth." Rose said that she had run into the courthouse with her father for fear police would kill him. She said he was not armed at that time, but took a rifle from one of the raiders, and later took a gun from another man. She quoted him as shouting in Spanish, "Stop all this. (*Acaben con todo esto.*) Don't hurt anybody. Now you're giving the policeman a chance to kill us all."

A half-dozen other friendly witnesses confirmed the defense's contention that the arrests and abortion of the Coyote meeting had brought *Alianza* resentment to the point of desperation and that there had been talk before the raid of making a citizen's arrest of Alfonso Sánchez.

Finally, Reies himself took the stand.

He had been in action for nearly four weeks, some 17 full days of court, sometimes with only one or two of his advisers present, responsible for much of the defense's strategy, improvising most of its courtroom tactics, handling virtually all of the questioning, ignorant of the intricacies of courtroom decorum, repeatedly reprimanded for his mistakes and audacity, continually frustrated by the limitations of his English, regarded with open contempt by the prosecution, handled with veiled condescension by the court, yet utterly uncowed and unashamed, sometimes dressed only in ironed work pants and shirt, the tip of a woman's comb sticking out of his back pocket, his voice strident with determination.

He was on the stand for four hours, testifying for two, cross-examined for two. He said that on the morning of the raid, his daughter Rose had arrived at the Juan Martínez house in Tierra Amarilla and told him, "There will be a citizen's arrest." Shortly afterward, a boy came to say that there was shooting. "I felt cold and numb immediately," he testified, and confessed that he could not remember all that he had said and done from that point on.

He remembered being driven a few hundred yards up the street to the courthouse. "There were people all over and there was yelling. Some were panicked, some frightened, some excited. Some were calling it an ambush. A bursting headache developed in my head."

He started into the courthouse, while voices shouted behind him, "Don't go in, you'll get shot." Inside he grabbed a rifle from someone and shouted in Spanish, "Stop all this," and, "Now you have given them an excuse to kill all of us." He told someone to get an ambulance for Nick Sais. By this time he had lost the rifle and grabbed a gun from another man. Others were now shouting, "Reies doesn't want anybody hurt." He said that he did not go into the sheriff's office, nor upstairs. A few minutes later he left, still holding a handkerchief to his face in the hope that he wouldn't be recognized.

Some time afterward, he said, a man named José Salazar had come to him and said he was "absolutely responsible" for what had happened at the courthouse. He had not seen the man since, nor had other defense witnesses.

"And you never reported that Salazar said he was responsible, did you?" asked Jack Love in cross-examination.

"Well, I had only his word. I didn't see if he did any shooting or who started it."

Love produced a number of newspaper reports, one of which quoted Tijerina as having said the Coyote meeting had been called to force "a possible showdown with the Federal government." Another quoted him as saying of the raid: "I gave orders no one was to be hurt, but things got out of hand. . . . Soldiers don't always obey orders." The defendant denied having made both statements. Love produced Peter Nabokov's report quoting Tijerina as having said that during a meeting at Canjilón on June 3, "We decided we should make a citizen's arrest of the man who violated our constitutional rights—Alfonso Sánchez."

The defendant said that he had been told of the circumstances by other *Alianza* members and had been "speaking in the third person for the *Alianza*." (He appeared to mean "first person plural.")

He said that he had not attended any meeting where a citizen's arrest had actually been planned. He admitted that on the morning of the raid he had been hiding in the Martínez home to avoid arrest on Alfonso Sánchez's conspiracy warrant. He admitted that he had once been deported from Mexico for making an inflammatory speech. He admitted that he had fled Arizona as he had been about to go on trial on charges concerning the theft of two truck wheels and other hardware and possession of five Forest Service axes.

Three days later, on December 13, he stood at the podium for the last time to offer his closing argument. He outlined the defense's contention that official harassment had precipitated the raid, that the raiders had intended to make a citizen's arrest of Alfonso Sánchez, that Nick Sais had triggered the violence by trying to draw his gun. He reminded the jury that the prosecution had failed to establish that he had either shot anybody or ordered anybody to shoot, and had produced scant evidence that he had been in charge. He went over the tattered remains of Dan Rivera's testimony and did not neglect to remind the jury that the witness had said he did not blame the defendant, sir.

"How can the state blame me for something the victim is not blaming me for?"

Writing large on the air with his hands, he likened himself and the *Alianza* to David, and the state and Federal governments to Goliath. "Yes, we are guilty of claiming our lands, guilty of unifying northern New Mexico, guilty of believing in the Treaty of Guadalupe Hidalgo."

True guilt lay elsewhere he exclaimed passionately, turning to point a finger toward the prosecution's table. "The state is guilty. The district attorney should be behind bars."

And finally, without lowering the accusing hand, he turned a mask of savage anguish to the jury and revealed himself as clearly as he would ever be able. "Do not allow these prosecutors to fill your hearts forever that you convicted me on the basis of a bunch of lies and frauds. Do not allow these gentlemen to allow you to crucify me and then wash their hands of it."

Alfonso Sánchez arose and moved to the podium, small, neat and diffident, brown suit, brown tie, brown eyes. Judge Larrazolo had denied the request to call him to the stand. This was the district attorney's answer to the challenge of *Los Comancheros del Norte* and others. He spoke for 35 minutes, quietly, with muted passion; his fires were banked with reason and law, tended with deliberation and dignity. The defendant was a troublemaker and an opportunist, he told the jury. (He did not say Communist, he did not say lunatic.) Tijerina had come to New Mexico uninvited and for 10 years had been "misleading his followers into believing they could take over the land grants they claim without due process of law."

Tijerina had never filed a civil suit to test *Alianza* land claims in the state courts, the district attorney pointed out. As for all this talk about a citizen's arrest, it was an attempt to confuse the issue. Tijerina had many times demonstrated a lust for publicity. He had organized and led the raid solely for purposes of making trouble and headlines.

Witness after witness had testified that Tijerina had been in the courthouse during the raid and had been armed, he continued. One had testified that Tijerina had brutally struck him from behind, another that Tijerina had stood by while he was beaten. As an aider and abettor, the defendant was guilty of a wide range of illegal acts.

If Tijerina was so interested in human rights, what about the rights of the employees who had been terrorized, of Dan Rivera, who had been beaten, of Nick Sais, who was lucky to be alive, of Eulogio Salazar, who had not been so lucky?

The law was clear, and the jury's duty was to see that it was applied. The prosecution asked for conviction on all three counts, including first-degree kidnapping. The district attorney would not mind, he said, if the jury recommended life imprisonment.

Now it was his turn to point a finger. "This court must have jurisdiction over this man's life." And if Reies had revealed himself at the end, so did Alfonso Sánchez now, his muted passion equally righteous, a telltale trace of longing in the rueful glance he bent upon the defendant. "He could have been such a great man, if he'd just understood and carried out what he believed in, if he had done it within the framework of the American system instead of inventing his own."

Judge Larrazolo read his instructions to the jury in a slow and deliberate voice which changed in neither tone nor pace but droned smoothly on through the startling surprise he had prepared for the occasion:

"The court instructs the jury that anyone, including a State Police officer, who intentionally interferes with a lawful attempt to make a citizen's arrest does so at his own peril, since the arresting citizens are entitled under the law to use whatever force is reasonably necessary to effect said citizen's arrest and to use whatever force is reasonably necessary to defend themselves in the process of making a said citizen's arrest."

It was a precedent to shiver the timbers of traditional law enforcement. Some would welcome it as a much needed check on half a century of broadening police powers and a reaffirmation of the essential equality of interest in the law of all citizens, wearing badges or not. Others would resent it as a potential encroachment upon their professional prerogatives and an obstacle to pursuit of their duties. Still others would fear it as an invitation to anarchy, envisioning a nationwide epidemic of citizen's arrests, particularly of police and public officials.

Judge Larrazolo finished. The defense still looked anxious, the prosecution still confident. The jury filed out. Four hours later, they returned. The defendant stood, his fists on the table, his head lowered. Foreman Charles Burand arose to read the verdict: not guilty on all three charges.

A hundred throats gasped in concert. The defendant slumped to the table, his head in his arms. "He's free!" cried Patsy. And Alfonso Sánchez sat as if stricken to stone. Women, children and lawyers were weeping all around. The defendant embraced his wife and some of his children, his eyes glistening. "I feel great," he told reporters as he worked his way out of the crowded courtroom, embracing, shaking hands. "I want to get rid of King Tiger and get my name back," he said as he reached the hall. A trio of State Policemen stood against the wall with drawn faces, their eyes tracing his progress to the elevator. Outside, he started down the courthouse steps with Patsy. A half dozen *Comancheros* surged up to surround them; one gave a rebel yell and shouted, "Let's go again!" As the group moved off down the sidewalk, a car passed and a blond-haired woman yelled out, "We'll get you yet, Tijerina!"

In the courtroom, Alfonso Sánchez's brooding eyes were beginning to show signs of a sorrowing acceptance. Back in August, he had told reporters that he was not all that sorry to have lost the election. "This is a thankless job. It will be a relief to get back to a nice peaceful law practice."

Now he told reporters that he couldn't yet say what would be done about the remaining charges against Tijerina and the nine other defendants. Of the verdict, he would say only that it had been a surprise. Jack Love echoed his reaction. "It came as a complete shock. Never can I remember so completely misreading what the mood of a jury seemed to be."

Benny Naranjo's reaction was less restrained. "If it wasn't so close to the first of the year, I'd probably resign as sheriff right now. Let them do their own arresting from now on!"

However, the assumption behind this rueful outburst, shared by many others, was not precisely correct. All of the jurors afterward said that the citizen's arrest question had not been a crucial factor in the final verdict. When deliberations had begun, the jury had been split, with eight for acquittal and four favoring a guilty verdict. Only one juror had insisted nearly to the end that the defendant had been proven guilty of all three charges. Three jurors, all *Hispanos*, had insisted from the beginning that the defendant had not led the raiders and had tried to stop the violence after it had started. All the jurors had eventually agreed that there was not enough evidence and that too much of it was in conflict for guilt to be established beyond the shadow of a doubt. The prosecution had simply failed to prove its case. Most jurors agreed with defense attorney Gene Franchini, who had said that the state had tried Tijerina on the wrong charges.

But there was more to be learned from the jurors than the process of reduction by which they had failed to convict. The majority of them had believed throughout deliberations that Reies Tijerina had probably led the raid, had certainly been in sympathy with its purpose and had definitely been present at the courthouse. And yet the same majority expressed distinct admiration for the man.

"We thought that he was behind it," Mrs. Andrew Johnson said afterward. "But there was nothing we could do about it. We tried awfully hard but couldn't come up with a thing as far as the charges were concerned."

And yet, she chuckled when asked what she thought of Tijerina as an attorney. "He was a pretty good one. He had a way of getting what he wanted out of the witnesses."

"He did an unbelievable job for not being an attorney," said juror Mary Hochstatter, who also felt the defendant had probably been involved in the raid. "The man has a fantastic mind."

"I believe the man is what he says he is, just as sure as I believe he helped shoot up that courthouse," said another juror who declined to be identified. "He is all for his people, and that's okay with me, I just don't happen to be one of them. But he has something all right, I'll give him that."

The night after the acquittal, Tijerina played host to a hearty fund-raising and victory celebration at *Alianza* headquarters. Chili and hot tamales were served on paper plates, a mariachi band played without pause and dancing couples dipped and whirled before the bricked-up front windows of the hall (A week before, while Reies and his wife and child had slept in the living quarters at the rear, the plate glass had been shattered for the third time.) By 10 P.M., some 250 celebrants had arrived, and they kept coming. Reies circulated, shaking hands, slapping backs, his energy clearly renewed by triumph. To reporters, he announced that he had that afternoon fired off a telegram to the Civil Rights Commission demanding assistance in filing land grant suits. He planned, he said, to institute an *Alianza* suit against the New Mexico

Board of Education, charging discrimination against Spanish language and culture and demanding special studies programs for *Hispano* students. (Two months before, Santa Fe High School had had its first demonstration, led by sophomore Ricky Narvaiz. Within the month, *Chicano* student leaders, like Roger Alvarado, 22, of San Francisco State College, would be demanding "brown studies" programs in the universities, state colleges and high schools of California.) Reies assured reporters that he had modified his militant outlook and broadened his racial objectives as a result of his experiences at Resurrection City. "I intend to reorganize the *Alianza*," he explained. "It means Alliance, not for peace or politics, but for justice and understanding."

As he spoke, the mariachis were enthusiastically playing the tune he had introduced in court as evidence of the campaign to slander him:

> *Año de sesenta y siete*
> *Cinco de Junio fué el día . . .*

On the sidelines, dapper Eddie Chávez beamed. "He's something else, Reies is. Sharp and fast. He thinks fast, talks fast, he even drives fast. That guy can park a car on a dime. He has *sagaz*, you know; he knows just how to get things done. And he has *razón*, that fire inside that you can't put out with money or jail or guns. It brought the people to him in the beginning, and now it's bringing them again. Yessir, we won quite a victory yesterday." And then, to indicate that he was fully aware that he had changed person, and that he did not mean merely the *Alianza* leadership, he swept his hand in a gesture which reached out beyond the gathering to *Hispanos* in the city, the state and beyond. "By we, I mean us."

The people danced and chattered. There were perhaps 300 now, and more arriving every minute, stepping in past the Brown Berets and *Comancheros* on guard at the door. (It had been gunfire that had shattered the windows the third time.)

The leathery welfare *vaqueros* of the north stood in muddy boots with broad-brimmed hats in their battered hands; and rheumy-eyed old men muttered in Spanish over their canes, waiting to shake hands with Reies. The women watched him, wherever he was, from wherever they were. Young people stood stiffly, shyly against the wall, taking it all in with shining eyes. ("Schools are for Dreamers, not for Schemers," one of the placards had read at the Santa Fe High demonstration.)

"I am writing a new science," Reies fervently informed newsmen. "I now believe that the gulf between the black and whites can be bridged by the browns." (Before the year was over, Roger Alvarado would be arrested six times, and San Francisco's club-swinging Tactical Squad would double in size three times. There would be violence in New York during an attempted table grape boycott in support of César Chávez's once peaceful Delano strike. Informed sources predicted that a minimum of 20 cities would be torn by serious riots during the coming summer. Both black and white leaders throughout the United States began to talk up "black capitalism" and the "separate but equal incorporated minority enclave," or legislated ghetto.)

The visitor abruptly gave up the effort to separate Reies from his cause. It wasn't that the cause sometimes fluctuated in character and size, nor was it that Reies himself was given to mercurial shifts. Neither changed that much; it was simply that by reason of upbringing, temperament and force of circumstances, Reies was his cause.

That decided, the question for the future was, could that cause survive the wave of reaction building upon its successes and that of related movements; and in the broader sense, could meaningful and relatively lasting social change be effected through manipulation of racial emotions by leaders of heavily outnumbered and underpowered minorities?

The only answer the visitor had at hand was that such change had always been initiated by minorities, racial or otherwise; and that the odds had by now narrowed to such a point that only time would tell if the change would come before or after bloody rebellion and bloody repression.

In the meantime, right or wrong, wanted or unwanted, the United States' first Indo-Spanish tiger burned bright upon the pinnacle of his latest triumph, declaring that the time had come and he was the one. "We will bridge the gulf, for justice and understanding, that is my real hope, my real dream," Reies declared.

And the band played on:

> *Año de sesenta y siete*
> *Cinco de Junio fué el día,*
> *Hubo una revolución*
> *Allá por Tierra Amarilla.*

Epilogue

THROUGH late 1968 and early 1969, yellow and black posters began to appear in Río Arriba, tacked to trees and Forest Service signs in Carson National Forest. The posters featured a mustached *bandido*, complete with rifle, sombrero and crossed ammunition bandaliers, and above him, the words, *Tierra o Muerte*, Land or Death.

As June 5, the second anniversary of the raid approached, the rumors began to fly again in Río Arriba, the Law prepared for trouble, and Reies Tijerina promised that the anniversary would be celebrated. Exactly how, he would not say, but there were many who would have preferred to see him behind bars for the occasion.

In mid-February, the 10th Circuit Court of Appeals upheld the Echo Amphitheatre convictions, but Tijerina's lawyers announced that they would appeal the case to the United States Supreme Court. Reies remained free on a $2,000 appeal bond.

In May, the Presbyterian Church moved to implement its recently announced policy of responsible social action. At a meeting of the church's General Assembly in San Antonio, liberal elements moved that some of the church's Ghost Ranch land be turned back to the *Hispanos* of Río Arriba, and that $50,000 be allocated for the administration and improvement of the land. Members of the New Mexico delegation, among them the Reverend James Hall, director of the Ghost Ranch complex, objected strongly, protesting that the wording of the motion "seemed tailored to the *Alianza*." After a brisk floor fight, the wording was changed, directing only that "a group of Spanish-American leaders" be convened to take charge of the land and money.

News of the church's directive caused considerable consternation back in New Mexico. Most prominent among those objecting was Governor David Cargo, who protested that the directive would only cause dissension and was likely to lead to more violence.

On the first of June, 100 Presbyterians, among them a few *Hispanos*, met at Ghost Ranch to discuss the proposed release of the land. Reies Tijerina showed up, accompanied by 150 *Hispanos*, but was met with a policy statement signed by the Reverend Hall, which began: "Mr.

Tijerina has seized upon the actions of the general assembly as being directed to the *Alianza*. At no time was this the intention of the assembly. The church will move to exercise its own deep concern for the progress of the Spanish-speaking people, but it will do so on its own terms and in ways it considers appropriate."

Ghost Ranch sits on the edge of the San Joaquín de Chama Land Grant—the same upon which Tijerina and his followers had camped during the Echo Amphitheatre incident in hopes of getting national publicity for *Hispano* land claims. It would be difficult to deny that the Presbyterian Assembly's decision to turn some of the land back to *Hispano* hands had been to some extent prompted by Tijerina's Echo Amphitheatre camp-in. A new irony was added to Río Arriba's fund of bitter folklore. And there would be still more.

On June 2, U.S. District Court was convened in Albuquerque to consider a suit filed by 13 *Alianza* members against the National Guard, the New Mexico State Police, and Alfonso Sánchez. The suit, drawn up with the help of the Civil Liberties Union, charged that the defendants had conspired to deprive the plaintiffs of their civil rights in aborting the Coyote meeting and had violated those rights in holding the plaintiffs in Tobías Leyba's cow pasture and in the process of making certain arrests after the raid.

Alfonso Sánchez testified that he had thought the arrest of 11 *Alianza* members before the Coyote meeting on charges of unlawful assembly had been justified. He did not mention that none of the 11 had ever been brought to trial on the charges.

State Police officers testified that after the raid they had arrested Sevedeo Martínez for disorderly conduct and assault with words. He had slipped into "bad language" when they had attempted to search his house without showing a warrant.

The former employer of two *Alianza* members denied that he had fired the two men after the raid because they had turned up amongst those held in the cattle pen at Canjilón. He had fired them, he said, because "they condoned the activities of a group which used violent action."

Alfonso Sánchez testified that he had suggested that the people be held under guard in Tobías Leyba's cow pasture because "We knew some of the raiders were there intermingled with the others." But State Police Chief Joe Black said that armed National Guardsmen had been placed around the people "so if the raiders came back there, these people would not get hurt."

The civil rights trial was to drag on for three weeks.

Meanwhile, on June 3, Reies Tijerina flew to Washington D.C. to make a citizens' arrest of Warren E. Burger, President Nixon's new appointee to the Supreme Court, charging Burger with "previous judicial decisions detrimental to the civil rights of minority groups." He was prevented from confronting Burger, and was forced to leave his warrant with the Clerk of the Court, who received it without comment. Burger was duly sworn in as Chief Justice, under heavy guard. Tijerina headed for home, pursued by Senator Everett Dirksen's comment on his visit: "I thought it was perfectly stupid."

On June 4, Reies arrived at the Albuquerque airport to announce that the anniversary of the raid would be celebrated with a gathering of *Alianza* members near Coyote. The meeting would be no more violent than the original Coyote meeting, he promised, nor did he intend to violate any court orders. However, he did announce *Alianza* plans to release a small herd of "hippie cattle" inside Carson National Forest. "They (the cattle) are going to roam in the roads only to prove they've been forced into a hippie kind of life because they have no food," he said.

On June 5, the *Alianza* pitched camp on a small plot of land near Coyote, virtually surrounded by Carson National Forest. The land and the mobile home headquarters located on it had been purchased with *Alianza* funds. An unusual number of State Police units cruised the nearby roads and Forest Service employees patrolled the trees. The Forest Service had made it clear that any unauthorized cattle found on government land would be rounded up and held against the payment of fines.

Tijerina told reporters that the police were there "making sure nobody kills me." But they could leave, he said, the Pueblo of San Joaquín would provide its own security forces. A dozen rifle-toting Brown Berets and *Comancheros del Norte* did take up positions around the perimeter of the camp, but otherwise the day passed uneventfully. No cattle appeared in the federal forest. The small crowd of 75 began to dwindle toward nightfall, and most of the reporters went home disappointed.

The following day was equally un-newsworthy. Then, on June 7, a caravan of 15 *Alianza* vehicles entered the atomic city of Los Alamos, south of Coyote. They were there, Tijerina told reporters, to arrest Los Alamos Laboratory Director, Norris Bradbury, for his part in constructing weapons of mass destruction. But Los Alamos officials had been alerted to *Alianza* intentions, and when Tijerina arrived at Bradbury's front door, the scientist, like Chief Justice Burger before him, declined to answer the doorbell. The arrest warrant was left in his mailbox.

Governor Cargo was next, Tijerina announced. "Cargo objected to the Presbyterians handing over the land," he said. "He's in cahoots with Jim Hall and those people. They don't want that land to go to the Spanish-Americans. We are going to arrest Cargo for conspiring to deprive us of our land and our rights."

But the State Police reached the governor first, in Santa Rosa, where he was attending a rodeo parade and barbecue. He was whisked away to the airport, and his plane took off immediately for an unannounced destination.

The next day, Sunday, June 7, a group of *Alianza* members left the Coyote camp, accompanied by reporters, trailed by Forest Service employees, and under close surveillance by State Police. At Gallina, about 12 miles west Coyote, Tijerina's young wife Patsy, now the plump mother of two, put a match to a bottle of gasoline and threw it at a large redwood Forest Service sign. The sign burned for a short time, while a small pistol was discharged into it, to the great rejoicing of the crowd. Asked why she had thrown the bottle, Patsy said, "If Reies is going to jail, I want to go with him. And I feel the federal government is trespassing on private land, the land belongs to the people. The signs have to go down. If I don't do it, someone else will."

A dozen or more State Police officers and Forest Service personnel observed the event, several of the officers from the perimeter of the crowd, but there was momentary confusion as to what to do about it.

"I was for arresting the whole bunch of them," officer Robert Gilliland later testified, "but the chief didn't agree with me."

U.S. Attorney Victor Ortega was advising the police. There were a hundred men, women and children in the crowd, all of them vociferously approving Patsy's action.

The crowd moved on, trailed by reporters and police. At the Ranger Station, a half mile west of Coyote, Patsy lobbed another flaming bottle at another Forest Service sign. This time the police were ready. Officers converged on the milling crowd, heading toward the center, where Reies Tijerina stood with his brother Ramon, his son Reies Jr., and others. The first to reach Tijerina was Forest Service investigator James Evans, who carried a loaded .30 caliber carbine automatic.

Announcing himself as an officer of the Forest Service, Evans told Tijerina that he was under arrest. Tijerina objected that he had done nothing illegal, but was only observing his wife's actions along with the others present. He demanded to know what he was charged with. Evans repeated that he was an officer of the Forest Service and said that he was placing Tijerina under arrest for destroying government property. Tijerina replied that he was a citizen and was placing Evans under arrest for conspiracy, breach of the peace and false arrest. Evans grabbed Tijerina by the belt. The angry crowd moved closer and several members intervened to separate Tijerina from Evans' grasp. Tijerina started for his car, and Evans took cover behind a nearby patrol car. Tijerina reached into his car, then looked up to see Forest Service employee Jack Johnson aiming a gun at him from the other side.

"It looked like a cannon to me," Tijerina later testified. "I thought I was going to die and I could see in my mind Senator Kennedy and Martin Luther King and I was saying, 'On my God I hope I'm right'."

He came up out of the car waving a 30-30 carbine, shouting at Evans, "Get your gun-slingers out of here!"

"Drop it, Reies, or I'll kill you," Evans replied, leveling his carbine over the hood of the patrol car.

Tijerina hesitated. "I saw him raise his gun to his shoulder pointing at Evans," Jack Johnson later testified. For his part, Johnson drew a bead on Tijerina's head with his Colt revolver. A few feet away, officer Gilliland aimed his shotgun at Tijerina's head.

"Drop it, or you're a dead man," Evans repeated.

"Surrender, Reies, you haven't got a chance," advised his bodyguard, Juan Roybal.

Tijerina dropped the gun.

"Why they didn't shoot me will always be a question in my mind," he would later muse.

"I wanted to shoot the son of a bitch," Evans said shortly afterwards, according to the testimony of Rees Lloyd, an Albuquerque *Journal* reporter.

"No, I didn't have any deep desire to shoot Tijerina," officer Gilliland would testify. "That is just what he would like—the glory of being a martyr."

Tijerina was taken into custody along with seven others, including Ramon, Reies, Jr., and Patsy Tijerina. They were arraigned Sunday night at U.S. District Court in Albuquerque. Patsy Tijerina was charged with destroying government property, which crime carried a maximum penalty of $10,000 fine and ten years in jail. Two others were charged with "participating" in her actions and were subject to the same penalty. Ramon Tijerina, Reies, Jr., Jose Aragon, and Rudy Trujillo were charged with interfering with the arrest of Reies Tijerina. Tijerina himself was charged with assault on a federal officer—pointing a carbine at Evans "in a threatening manner"—with a maximum penalty of $10,000 fine and ten years in prison. He was not charged with destroying government property. Pending a preliminary hearing, he was released on his own recognizance, since he had already posted $42,000 in bonds on other charges.

Early the next day, Monday, Tijerina announced the formation of a "posse comitatus" for the purpose of making a citizen's arest of Evans, who was charged with conspiracy to deprive *Alianza* members of their rights, including that of free assembly; with assault and battery on Reies Tijerina; and with attempted murder, false arrest, and kidnapping. Evans had 24 hours to get out of the state, Tijerina said, "and this time we are not going unarmed. If he resists with a gun, he will be shot resisting arrest."

Reading from a legal reference work by Clarence Alexander, Tijerina cited a number of sections relating to the citizen's arrest concept, including: "A non-officer may arrest an officer committing a crime—perhaps against himself—as an officer is not above the law."

Upon hearing of the arrest intention, Evans gave orders for Forest Service officials at the Coyote Ranger Station to arm themselves and move their families out of the area, then went into hiding himself, remaining with his family under police guard in a motel near Albuquerque.

Governor Cargo, back in his office in Santa Fe, told reporters that he had spent the weekend with his family at their cabin site near Las Vegas "as usual," and added, "We had a wonderful weekend." He didn't mention that two heavily armed State Police officers had shared the wonders of the weekend with him.

That Monday morning, a car containing six *Alianza* members approached Forest Service officer Evans' home, where four State Police patrol units and the Valencia County sheriff and two deputies stood guard. The car was stopped and its occupants searched. They were unarmed. The *Alianza* group proceeded to Evans' front door, where *Alianza* vice president Wilfred Sedillo knocked twice without result, then attached the arrest warrant to Evans' house and left.

The next day, Tuesday, Evans filed an affadavit with U.S. Attorney Ortega, charging that Reies Tijerina had made "public threats that he intends to arrest me and shoot me if I resist arrest." He also protested that, "My family and I have been placed in fear and apprehension." U.S. Attorney Ortega immediately filed a petition for revocation of Reies Tijerina's $2,000 bond, granted four months before, pending appeal of the Echo Amphitheatre conviction.

The next day, Wednesday, June 11, Governor Cargo told reporters that Tijerina and his followers were welcome to try to arrest him, but that if they did, they might find themselves in "lots and lots of trouble." That afternoon, Judge Howard C. Bratton temporarily revoked Tijerina's federal bond, and within the hour Reies was once again in custody in the Albuquerque jail. The Santa Fe *New Mexican* headlined the story with relish, CITIZENS ARREST TIJERINA.

That same day, it was announced that six attorneys, several of them widely known for successful legal defense of civil liberties, had filed a petition with the U.S. Supreme Court for review of the Echo Amphitheatre convictions. The petition criticized Judge Bratton for calling Tijerina and Jerry Noll "ringleaders of the mob" and for failing to inform the jury that specific intent of criminal action was required to be shown. It pointed out that at no time had any of the defendants touched or attempted to control the two Forest Service pickups, and that the Rangers had been given back the keys. It argued that in taking the rangers into custody for a mock trial the defendants had attempted to save them from worse damage at the hands of the angry crowd. It pointed out that the government had failed to prove that Reies Tijerina had participated directly either in briefly impounding the trucks or taking the Rangers into custody. It argued that political leaders cannot be held responsible for the acts of participants in a demonstration and charged political persecution in violation of the free speech amendment. The convictions, it said, "smack of harassment and vindictiveness unbefitting the majesty of the U.S. government in its dealings with a group of justly aggrieved citizens."

Federal attorneys had 30 days in which to answer the petition, at which time the Supreme Court would rule on whether to hear the appeal. The Court, however, was due to recess in two weeks. It would not be able to rule on the appeal until the Fall term. It would do so, of course, under its new Chief Justice, Warren E. Burger.

On June 12, in Judge Bratton's U.S. District Court, the jury returned its verdicts in the *Alianza* civil rights suit. Exonerating the National Guard, State Police and Alfonso Sánchez of all charges of conspiracy to deprive the plaintiffs of their civil rights, the jury granted one verdict in favor of a plaintiff. Sevedeo Martínez was awarded $3,000 as compensation for being arrested while protesting the unwarranted search of his home. Judge Bratton had instructed the jury for over an hour, the longest instructions he had given, he said, in all his years as a judge.

On June 15, Judge Bratton convened court again, this time to hear cause why the federal bond of Reies Tijerina should not be revoked permanently. Forest Service officer James Evans testified that Reies Tijerina had resisted arrest and aimed a rifle at him in a threatening manner.

"Would you consider it a good thing if they put Tijerina away so he wouldn't cause any more trouble?" asked William Kunstler, Civil Liberties Union attorney.

"I certainly would, sir," Evans replied.

State Police officer Robert Gilliland confirmed Evans' testimony regarding the incident. No, he had no deep desire to make Tijerina a martyr, he told Kunstler, but he did hate him.

"He claims to be the leader of the Spanish people," he said, pointing at the Brown Berets and weathered northerners crowding the courtroom. "For everyone he's got in this room, I'll put ten against him."

A 19-year-old-free-lance photographer testified that while he was riding in Tijerina's car, Tijerina stopped at a gas station and filled a bottle with gasoline, and that the gasoline was later poured into smaller bottles which Patsy Tijerina threw at the Forest Service signs.

"There has not been one shred of evidence that Tijerina burned any signs, ever employed any violence, laid a hand on anyone or ever even succeeded in arresting anyone," Kunstler reminded the court in his closing argument.

"No bond can reasonably assure that Tijerina will not pose a danger or threat to any persons or the community," U.S. Attorney Ortega countered. "The community is quite concerned about Tijerina going around threatening citizen's arrest, which I think is a bunch of legal nonsense."

Judge Bratton concurred with Ortega's opinion of Tijerina's attempts to arrest governors, scientists, Forest Service investigators, and judges. "Legal nonsense is a moderate characterization. The concept of citizen's arrest does exist, but misuse and abuse can be tragic," he said, and ordered Tijerina's bond permanently revoked.

Two days later, U.S. Marshall Emilio Naranjo removed Tijerina from the Albuquerque City jail to the federal prison at La Tuna, Texas, "for his own safety."

Two weeks later in Albuquerque, a District Court jury found Juan Valdez guilty of assaulting State Policeman Nick Sais in the Río Arriba County Courthouse on June 5, 1967, with intent to kill or maim him; and of false imprisonment of Pete Jaramillo, sheriff of Río Arriba County.

During the trial, Geronimo Borunda, "El Indio," had surprised the prosecution by confessing on the witness stand that he, not Valdez, had shot Sais. However, Sais had clung to his identification of Valdez as his assailant, although he had previously testified that the man who had shot him had had a beard, and some witnesses testified that Valdez had not had a beard, while some testified that Borunda had been bearded at the time. State's witness Pete Jaramillo neglected to appear for trial testimony; he went fishing in Utah instead. Valdez was sentenced to from 2 to 10 years in prison.

On October 10, 1969, Reies Tijerina was convicted in U.S. District Court in Albuquerque on two counts of aiding and abetting in the destruction of Forest Service signs and of assaulting and threatening a Forest Service agent, James Evans. Tijerina was sentenced to three years in prison. Three days later, the United States Supreme Court, under Chief Justice Warren Burger, refused to review the Echo Amphitheatre convictions, and Tijerina began serving his first federal prison term of two years.

Two months previously, in August, Baltazar Martínez had been brought to trial on charges of falsely imprisoning Pete Jaramillo and Larry Calloway. Martínez was acquitted on the grounds that he, like his elderly uncle, Baltazar Apodaca, had been insane at the time of the raid and had been unable to tell right from wrong.

Ranchos de Taos, June 15, 1967
Larkspur, California, October 30, 1969

Bibliography

A complete list of sources would run to many pages, including government and scholarly studies and reports, newspaper accounts and personal interviews. The author's files, including taped interviews, will be given to the Zimmerman Library of the University of New Mexico. For further reading the general reader is referred to the publications listed below.

Alianza Federal de Mercedes. The Spanish Land Grant Question Examined. Albuquerque, N.M. *Alianza Federal de Mercedes,* 1010 Third Street NW, 1966.

Dobie, J. Frank. *A Vaquero of the Brush Country.* Dallas, Texas: The Southwest Press, 1929.

Gonzalez, Nancie L. *The Spanish Americans of New Mexico.* University of California at Los Angeles. Mexican-American Study Project, Advance Report 9, 1967.

Haring, C. H. *The Spanish Empire in America.* New York: Oxford University Press, 1947.

Hobsbawm, E. J. *Primitive Rebels, Studies in Archaic Forms of Social Movement in the 15th and 20th Centuries.* New York: W. W. Norton & Co., Inc., 1959.

Holmes, Jack E. *Politics in New Mexico.* Albuquerque: University of New Mexico Press, 1967.

Jenkinson, Michael. *Tijerina.* Albuquerque: Piasano Press, 1968.

Keleher, Wm. A. *The Maxwell Land Grant.* New York: Argosy-Antiquarian Ltd., 1964. Limited edition: 750 copies. Library of Congress No. 63-21490.

Le Farge, Oliver. *Santa Fe, the Autobiography of a Southwestern Town.* Norman, Okla.: University of Oklahoma Press, 1959.

Manuel, Herschel T. *Spanish Speaking Children of the Southwest.* Austin, Texas: University of Texas Press, 1965.

Martin, Molly Bradford. *Bill Martin, American.* Caldwell, Idaho: The Caxton Printers Ltd., 1959.

Nabokov, Peter. *Tijerina and the Courthouse Raid*. Albuquerque: University of New Mexico Press, 1969.

New Mexico Bureau of Business Research, *The Economy of Río Arriba* (other publications available). Albuquerque: University of New Mexico Press, 1967.

Otero-Warren, Nima. *Old Spain in Our Southwest*. Chicago: The Río Grande Press Inc., 1962. (Harcourt-Brace & Co., N.Y., 1936.)

Paz, Octabia. *The Labyrinth of Solitude; Life and Thought in Mexico*. New York, London: Grove Press Inc., 1961.

Rosenfeld, E. D., and Associates. *Survey of Regional Health Services Needs of North Central New Mexico*. New York: E. D. Rosenfeld Associates Inc., Consultants, 545 Fifth Avenue, 1967.

Swadesh, Francis Leon. *Hispanic Americans of the Ute Frontier from the Chama Valley to the San Juan Basin, 1694-1960*. Boulder, Colo.: University of Colorado. Research Report #50, Tri-ethnic Research Project, 1966.

WPA Writer's Project. *New Mexico*. New York: Hastings House, American Guide Series, 1940.

71 72 73 74   12 11 10 9 8 7 6 5 4 3 2 1

COLOPHON BOOKS ON SOCIOLOGY